UPTOWN

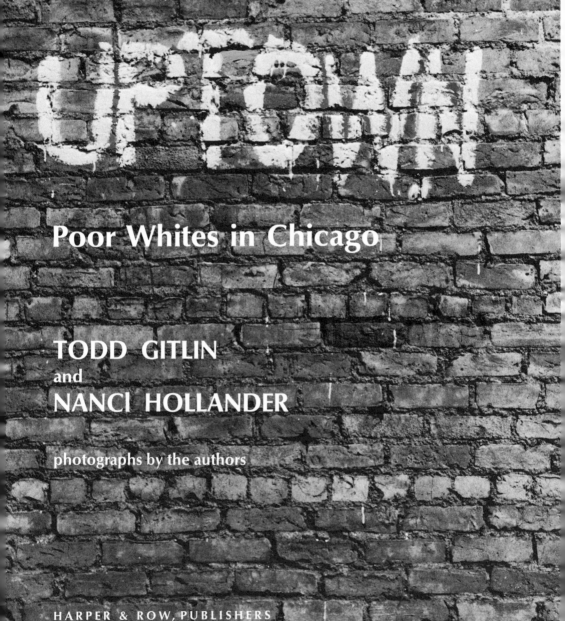

UPTOWN

Poor Whites in Chicago

TODD GITLIN
and
NANCI HOLLANDER

photographs by the authors

HARPER & ROW, PUBLISHERS
New York, Evanston, and London

The names given all persons in this book are fictitious, except for public officials, celebrities, and organizers identified by name. Moreover, the statements attributed to individuals are given in order to convey a sense of the attitudes of the Uptown community, and do not necessarily reflect the opinions or conclusions of the authors.

The lines on page vii are from Walt Whitman's "Song of the Broad-Axe," from Leaves of Grass, published by Doubleday & Company, Inc.

The lines on pages 237 and 256–57 are from The Trial by Franz Kafka translated by Willa and Edwin Muir. Copyright 1937, © 1956 by Alfred A. Knopf, Inc. Copyright renewed 1965 by Alfred A. Knopf, Inc. Reprinted by permission of the publisher.

The lyrics on pages 420–21 are from "The Sounds of Silence," by Paul Simon. Copyright © 1964 by Charing Cross Music. Used with permission of the publisher.

Excerpts from articles from Uptown News are reprinted with permission of Lerner Home Newspapers; excerpts from articles by Burnell Neinecke and John Reddy are reprinted with permission of the Chicago Sun-Times.

FIRST EDITION

LIBRARY OF CONGRESS CATALOG CARD NUMBER: 69-15309

Designed by Lydia Link

To the men and women, uncommon common human beings, who speak through this book;

and to the organizers in Uptown and a million other Uptowns of this globe, who dare a commitment that these men and women and millions like and unlike them will triumph—"with the masses, not from them," as Debs said—in their own names and for all our sakes;

with love and fraternity this book is dedicated.

The great city is that which has the greatest man or woman;
If it be a few ragged huts, it is still the greatest city in the whole world.

The place where the great city stands is not the place of stretch'd wharves, docks, manufactures, deposits of produce,
Nor the place of ceaseless salutes of new comers, or the anchor-lifters of the departing,
Nor the place of the tallest and costliest buildings, or shops selling goods from the rest of the earth,
Nor the place of the best libraries and schools—nor the place where money is plentiest,
Nor the place of the most numerous population.

Where the city stands with the brawniest breed of orators and bards;
Where the city stands that is beloved by these, and loves them in return, and understands them;
Where no monuments exist to heroes, but in the common words and deeds;
Where thrift is in its place, and prudence is in its place;
Where the men and women think lightly of the laws;
Where the slave ceases, and the master of slaves ceases;
Where the populace rise at once against the never-ending audacity of elected persons.
Where fierce men and women pour forth, as the sea to the whistle of death pours its sweeping and unript waves;
Where outside authority enters always after the precedence of inside authority;
Where the citizen is always the head and ideal—and President, Mayor Governor, and what not, are agents for pay;
Where children are taught to be laws to themselves, and to depend on themselves;
Where equanimity is illustrated in affairs;
Where speculations on the Soul are encouraged;
Where women walk in public processions in the streets, the same as the men;
Where they enter the public assembly and take places the same as the men;
Where the city of the faithfulest friends stands;
Where the city of the cleanliness of the sexes stands;
Where the city of the healthiest fathers stands;
Where the city of the best-bodied mothers stands.
There the great city stands.

—Walt Whitman, 1856

Two characteristics . . . are common to all great cities. They all have an exciting downtown filled with a great variety of shops, theatres, museums, and other attractions, and laid out as a place of great beauty—designed, in the words of architect Louis Kahn, to be "the cathedral of the city." Equally important, they have a large middle class population residing near downtown, possessing the purchasing power and the tastes to help sustain its activities.

—Edmund K. Faltermayer,
"What It Takes to Make Great Cities,"
Fortune, January, 1967

Contents

Acknowledgments

Dozens of people made this book possible; if it has value, they gave it that value. The people of Uptown stand first, especially those who spread out their lives on tape for us, but they cannot be named, since we guaranteed them anonymity. Some of the JOIN organizers are mentioned by name in the text; to them, and to the others, and to our friends in the radical movement who helped maintain our resolve and sharpen our ideas and move us from ideas to book, our gratitude is beyond rhetorical flourish, including this one.

Parts of the manuscript were typed by Judy Statts, Jean Tepperman, and Nancy Bradburd Moss.

The Louis M. Rabinowitz Foundation supported us, as they have supported many dissidents who stand beyond the pale of the big foundations.

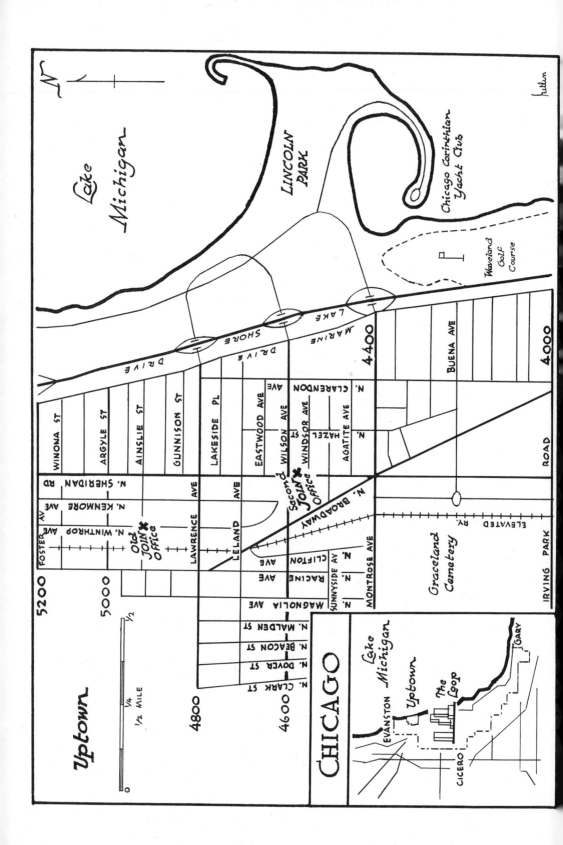

Into Uptown

Drive up Lake Shore Drive from the Loop. In the skyline of Chicago, the Second City, office buildings advertise their corporate wares in neon at night; in Chicago majesty is privately owned. No longer Hog Butcher for the world, but another kind of butcher, the stockyards having moved to more profitable sites. Now remember Algren—this is the city on the make. You lose sight of Lake Michigan as you pass convenient Lake Shore East Apartments, high glass with a garish dome-enclosed swimming pool for the executives. The lake is not fit for swimming but the harbor is crammed with boats. Slowly take the 90-degree curves, which every morning the Chicago *Tribune* asks to have straightened: one of the few items its owners want straightened to perfect the city. Drive over the drawbridge Franklin Roosevelt dedicated with his quarantine speech in 1937; there is the steel scaffolding of another terrace beside the lake, but then the lake spreads before you again, and somewhere over the horizon is another shore: Chicago does not go on forever. Drive on past the Chicago campus of Northwestern University, more office buildings, the Drake Hotel, whose owners have bought a one-third share in the *Queen Elizabeth*. Watch for the construction work: the Drive is being enlarged for your convenience, repaved—the paving doesn't last very long—and the signs are up:

THIS IS ANOTHER IMPROVEMENT FOR CHICAGO.
RICHARD J. DALEY, MAYOR.

On your left, the Gold Coast, one apartment tower after another, some browned, almost yellowed with age, some hermetically sealed in new glass. The Gold Coast goes on to the end of the Drive, past Loyola University, past the hotel-motel strip, seven miles of gilded skin for the North Side of the city. Pass Lincoln Park, the zoo, pond, grass, tennis courts, and on your right, beaches, some private, some public. The boat docks, the yachts, the Gun Club, the golf course. Look to your left: an unbroken wall of affluence, fabrication of glass and steel, and before it the moat of Marine Drive. If you were on your way home to the North Shore of Evanston, Winnetka, Wilmette, you would take the Drive to its end and keep heading north. The intermediate exit signs are dim landmarks to measure your progress home. Montrose . . . Wilson . . . Lawrence.

Maybe you have heard of Uptown, but it sounds like a limbo, not a place: a vague name conjuring up only faint images of gray-brown places, somewhere on the farthest reaches of the el where no one would live by choice. Uptown stands for the empty space which is not downtown, where neon lights are few and crowds mean riots, where people mask their faces with newspapers back and forth to work every day, where "life goes on" means "death is just around the corner." "Come on Uptown," says a jingle on the radio: Uptown Federal Savings and Loan invites your dollars. They pay good interest.

Risk it, penetrate the skin, turn onto one of these streets, five miles north of the Loop. Pass the park; on summer days it will be choked. You might hear a country-western or a rock band. At night, the roar of motorcycles and drag races; unless the police have just passed through. Something is wrong: but up ahead, the reassuring sight of Marine Drive, the modern Weiss Memorial Hospital. Your Chicago is still recognizable. Drive one block west on one of those main streets. They are real streets, this Montrose, this Wilson, this Lawrence.

Something is badly wrong. If you are literal-minded you may suddenly appreciate the language of the radicals: this police state looks like one. Only one block from the prosperous sea wall, you are already noticing a police car every minute. Check your watch: *every minute*. The paddy wagons cruise like tanks. It looks like a permanent occupation. You may remember that this is the Summerdale police district, renamed Foster Avenue after the 1959 "burglars in blue" scandal, when Mayor Daley brought in O. W. Wilson, Dean of the School of Criminology at the University of California, to clean up the mess. You can see the blue and white of the squad cars and paddy wagons a long way off: that was one of Wilson's first acts, intended, in his words, "to create an impression of police omnipresence." At night you can see the ice-blue light of the flasher from an even greater distance. The words on the side of the car: "We serve and protect." Every minute. You feel safe. The "burglars in blue" who had been storing their booty in the basement of the police station are in jail. Law and order.

The old pillared mansions, subdivided after World War II, each into a dozen apartments, are smudged, decaying. There is the old Aragon Ballroom, where Paul Whiteman and Benny Goodman were comforts during the hard years—now the Cheetah discotheque. This was once Chicago's Bohemia; prostitution is said to have been legal on Wilson Avenue until 1922. Across the street from the go-go joints, the high Sheridan Plaza Hotel, once a showplace, a very proper place to pass the week, now a piece of property sold back and forth for tax loss and who knows what purposes. If you have a whore now that is where you take her, and there is some heavy gambling on an upper floor. Dotted here and there an old one- or two-family house, gardens fresh, likely as not the home of a Japanese or Chinese or Eastern European family holding tight to property values. For the rest, three- and six-flat tenements, the red brick shining in the light, but the gray is never anything but gray, and the faces are white. Between Wilson and Lawrence you might find the two black blocks, with their own pool hall and their own history: one of these blocks has been black over forty years, the servants' quarters for Marine Drive. Puerto Ricans, Filipinos, Mexicans, Cubans have moved into other blocks, and the kosher signs still occupy the butchers' windows on Argyle Street. One block north on Winthrop, old Temple Agudas Chabad looks not too busy on a Friday night: you read in the paper that it was just burglarized.

Must have been those hillbillies, crackers, stump-jumpers, ridge-runners, white trash: a few blocks away, appropriately, stands Mr. Charlie's Restaurant. Look at them in the southern neck of the neighborhood, four-block-long Kenmore Street, four thousand people (two anthropologists made a survey), 20 percent on welfare, on a summer night some playing guitars, twanging songs of Hank Williams and Johnny Cash. Bisecting that super-block, Buena Circle, called "The Jungle" a few summers ago after all the gunfights. Remember Danny Escobedo of the Supreme Court's Escobedo decision, the one that said a lawyer must be present at a police interrogation of an arrested man? He lived on Buena. The el tracks, another route to the Loop, and underneath, the stripped-down, burned-out shells of the American dream, and their dusty license plates of origin: West Virginia, Virginia, Kentucky, Tennessee, Alabama. Make sure to drive in the center of the street, avoid the fragments of glass, watch for kids: the street is both playground and garbage dump.

On the western fringe there are quieter streets, shaded, the lawns being watered, the school freshly built, a new church, the men at work paying off the cars but choosing to live here rather than more respectable places, to stay near kin and, yes, community: Magnolia, Malden, Beacon, Dover. Good names: but what of this Sunnyside? Sounds like Scarsdale or Glencoe or Beverly Hills, but you wonder what these people would name their street if it were theirs to name: Darkside?

But be reassured. The wreckers are at work; the bulldozers smoothing the desolate lots, a new fire station is coming up, high-rises for the elderly:

ANOTHER IMPROVEMENT FOR CHICAGO

Whole blocks are gone. Valuable real estate, ten minutes from the Loop, a view of the lake if you build high enough. Sheridan Road, built during the wave of great strikes and the Haymarket riot at the end of the nineteenth century, as quick access to the city for the troops at suburban Fort Sheridan, and east of it this sign:

ENTERING
OPERATION
PAINT
REPAIR
IMPROVE
DECORATE
EVERYONE
AREA

but the paint is already beginning to peel. On Sheridan itself, only the front columns of an old mansion are standing at the last, a lingering façade. Indian kids, looking for a reason, fight each other with the stone rubble, one of them yelling in a mock-august tone, perhaps copied from a TV newscaster: "Once this was a magnificent wall." He has not read "Ozymandias," does not know he will have to move soon. Some rents have gone up $25 a month overnight.

And, after all, Uptown has been designated a Conservation Area under the Urban Renewal Act. Federally subsidized "moderate income" houses will expand the city's tax base by holding the solid citizens, those making $8,500 (the two-bedroom standard) to $10,500 (three-bedroom), cushioning Marine Drive against the blight at its back. "The area," says Alderman Robert O'Rourke, "once the outstanding shopping area outside the Loop, is in serious trouble." But it has two strengths: it is "well organized" (voters passed the urban-renewal bond issue, he explains; in a light vote, he doesn't explain) and it is "well located." Perhaps you have read about the JOIN troublemakers, who defy progress, who carry the peculiar idea that the strength of the neighborhood is its people, who have been arrested at the City Council for insisting that housing must be decent *for the people who live in the neighborhood now.* "People of Uptown must approve any urban renewal setup in Uptown," says JOIN. "I don't think ideology matters any more," says Frank McAllister, prominent civic-minded (read: well connected) resident of the Uptown skin, Director of the Roosevelt University Institute of Labor Relations, President Johnson's special representative to independence celebrations in AFL-CIO-CIA-financed Guyana. "I think we have manageable problems that can be solved by men of good will."

Manageable problems. Men of good will. The neighborhood Conservation Council was appointed by Mayor Daley. "Parts of the area," says the city's official Plan, "have become ports of entry for newcomers to the city. Many of these persons are low-income, rural Appalachian whites for whom adjustment to an urban environment is difficult. . . . Poor property maintenance standards of large numbers of families in the overcrowded and densely developed Uptown neighborhood often lead to rapid deterioration of housing." (No matter that the "low-income whites" have been made "low-income" precisely in order that others might be high-income. This is no manageable problem.) Of course there are complications: "Serving to compound this problem of inadequate maintenance," says the Plan, "is the unwillingness of many landlords to improve properties that have begun to deteriorate." But there is light at the end of the tunnel. In 1965, Mayor Daley said all slums in Chicago would be gone by the end of 1967. It was a good year for predictions: Secretary of Defense McNamara said the troops would be home that Christmas.

Uptown. One square mile, fifty or sixty thousand residents at any one time, including the Lake Shore skin. Perhaps half were born in the South, mostly in the states of the Appalachian ridge. In 1960, 21 percent of all residents were over sixty years old, and over half the housing units were one or two rooms. Thirty-eight percent of all units were deteriorated in some respect; 27 percent lacked what the census called "adequate plumbing facilities." Despite a 13 percent vacancy rate, Uptown ranked second (to black Lawndale) in population density in the city of Chicago. In 1966, 8,608 X rays showed 125 suspected cases of tuberculosis, second highest rate to the Skid Row of Madison Street. In 1961, 11 percent of store spaces were vacant, 21 percent in "marginal uses" (pawn and secondhand shops, missionary churches, fly-by-night businesses), 17 percent in taverns, but the city has since closed many of the bars to polish the neighborhood's image. This is important real estate, think Kemper Insurance and Combined Insurance, which have their national headquarters here. W. Clement Stone, president of Combined, his family and foundation worth $327 million, is author of The Success System That Never Fails, coauthor of Success Through a Positive Mental Attitude. The home offices rise like occupying sentries over the paper-blown streets, fortresses of dotted-line security over the gutters of sodden hopes, over the men breaking like wine bottles, the hard stares at the squad cars and the mufflers cracking and tires screeching around unending corners and "love" blaring from a thousand radios in a thousand apartments that these hillbillies, greasers, spics, winos, niggers live in but no one calls home.

Explanations

What could the Peruvian poet have meant? Probably this: the illiterates could not read, so he would sing; and he would write in their name; he would write for their future.

This book is about hillbillies, about their flight to Chicago, about their uneasy settlement and their efforts to organize and their efforts to live in an American city. There are many voices here, not least those of the authors, who take the responsibility of offering you traces of a reality we do not purport to "understand" and the most private and public words of people who are not our "field." We had better explain ourselves.

We call ourselves radicals, by which we mean people committed to equality, the ennoblement of men and the interminable struggle to replace utterly a system that values money first. Activists, we had worked for peace and civil rights and student rights in Students for a Democratic Society (SDS); provincials, we felt ourselves incomplete as long as we took refuge in playground universities; believers in the capacity of ordinary men to govern themselves, we decided to align ourselves with the struggles of just such ordinary—that is, extraordinary—men. In 1964 SDS founded a number of projects—experiments, though with an intention of permanence—political engagements with the poor of the cities of the North. The reasoning was that the black movement, having secured legal rights in the South, needed to turn to the harder matters of economic justice and substantive control over life conditions; that poor whites might be their natural allies if a common approach could be worked out to counter the centrifugal force of racism. Unspoken too was the democratic principle: any political change, the structures of any radical reconstruction, would be hollow unless filled by the real people those structures aimed to serve, the best energies of the voiceless people, organized for their own defense and due.*

*The full political reasons for these projects may be found and judged in other writings, and it is not our purpose to cloud the present work with the orthodox radical calculations. In fact, we believe this entire book enters another realm

That summer, 1964, one of us worked on the Near West Side of Cleveland, an area divided among Appalachian whites and Eastern Europeans. The other worked with JOIN, then standing for Jobs or Income Now, which wanted and failed to be an organization of the unemployed scattered over the white North Side of Chicago. The Chicago staff decided the jobs-or-income goal was too remote, and the unemployed too diffused, to keep an organization together, and an alternative emerged: to bring poor whites together to fight for seemingly more accessible rights—changes in welfare policy, recreation, schools, decent housing, *whatever needs were felt* by a definite community of hitherto powerless people. By winning some victories, organizers could show that "a whole lot of people is strong," could break the cycle of private hopelessness and plant the seeds for a political movement, for the self-determination of the poor. If organized self-interest could bring tangible results, JOIN would stand as a model for other movements. So, in the winter, organizers moved JOIN to the neighborhood of most concentrated white poverty, Uptown, "hillbilly heaven," and declared themselves JOIN Community Union.

We decided in the spring of 1965 to locate near JOIN as midwives for a sort of literary and political support, true to the bottom-up spirit of the organizing. We settled in Chicago, where the project seemed more enduring and the neighborhood more distinctively Southern poor-white in tone than in Cleveland. Besides, Chicago loomed as a larger challenge, this unjustifiable city fallen from a dubious glory, the rotten center of America and its Undemocratic Party.

When we got to Uptown we knew very little about poor whites except that their migration from the Appalachian mountains was epic; even now we proclaim no expertise. We knew the militant unions that once fought for the miners had succumbed to the calculation of capital, accepted the mechanization of the mines and the casting-off of most of the miners in

---

of political analysis, a different medium though not less rational or engaged or polemical than the standard format. Readers seeking handier, more explicit political rationale may consult Tom Hayden and Carl Wittman, "An Interracial Movement of the Poor," in Mitchell Cohen and Dennis Hale, eds., *The New Student Left* (Boston, 1966); Norm Fruchter and Robert Kramer, "An Approach to Community Organizing Projects," *Studies on the Left*, March–April, 1966; Hamish Sinclair, "Hazard, Kentucky: Document of the Struggle," *Radical America* vol. 2, no. 1 (January–February, 1968); Richard Rothstein, "The Evolution of Community Organizers," *Radical America* vol. 2, no. 2 (March–April, 1968); Todd Gitlin, "The Radical Potential of the Poor," *International Socialist Journal* no. 25 (December, 1967), or write to Todd Gitlin in care of the publishers. All interesting and useful analysis, but it does not take you as far as we want to take you, namely, to the fiber of reality within (and often, necessarily, concealed by) the shell of political claims, bravado, and hunch doubling as analysis.

return for the benefit of a few.* The consequences are well documented, need no repetition here. The grim history of the plunder of the Appalachian colony is in Harry Caudill's *Night Comes to the Cumberlands* (Atlantic–Little, Brown, 1963), and the statistics of the flight crawl over the big pages of an academic book edited by Thomas R. Ford, *The Southern Appalachian Region* (University of Kentucky, 1962). But a few numbers will sketch the magnitude of the calamity. Between 1945 and 1965, the number of coal miners in the United States fell by three-quarters, while productivity tripled. The total population of Southern Appalachia (West Virginia, eastern Kentucky, eastern Tennessee, the western ridge of Virginia and North Carolina, some counties in north Georgia and northwestern Alabama) fell 3.4 percent from 1950 to 1960, and the birth rate started falling in 1945: the young were leaving. Logan County, West Virginia, the home of several people in this book, lost more than 40 percent of its population between 1950 and 1960, and it was by no means the only such county.

Before we moved to Chicago we had already tested ourselves as organizers, door-to-door, may-we-help-you, and felt ourselves disqualified—by the same temperament that drove us into radicalism—for the quite unromantic, plodding tedium of the organizer's life. Rather than sulk in the wash of our guilt we decided to declare ourselves another way. We would offer ourselves to the people around JOIN, offer them a medium for their free expression—a book, an amplification system, a chance to cast their light up from the bottom of this society with the special illumination that comes only from victims. JOIN would emerge, shining or blurry, through the composite prism of the biographies of the people engaged in it, or detached

---

*Early in 1967, W. A. Boyle, President of the United Mine Workers of America, was elected chairman of the National Coal Policy Conference, succeeding the President of Consolidated Coal Company. "We in NCPC," Boyle said, "represent divergent interests—interests which have often been in conflict. But, in a more basic sense we share a common goal—a goal which binds us together in mutual effort. That goal is the preservation of coal as a strong industry, an industry growing to meet the energy demands of a modern America.

"In finding this unity amid the diversity of our interests, we have fashioned a weapon of great strength for the struggles in which we are engaged. As we go forward we move not as coal operators, or coal miners, or manufacturers, or transporters of coal, or utilities, but only as industries and organizations who depend upon coal, and who serve to bring it to the public in one form or another.

"Within this functional context all of our differences disappear. . . ." And so on. The UMW under John L. Lewis had always taken a modest view of itself, as a counterweight to the companies under the sign of profit; but profit powers technology and explodes even such modest intentions, and most of the miners paid the price.

from it, but in any case fixing its substance and its possibilities more exactly and—we hoped—compellingly than we could with a more orthodox description. Poverty would emerge as more than the sum of separate afflictions and oppressions, more than "problems" of income and jobs and welfare and police, rather as an indivisible machinery which is in turn a component of the larger political-economic machinery, but finding its full weight in the individual life.

We moved to Uptown in August of 1965 and began to search out the people whose book we would assemble. We do not pretend to know if they are typical of anyone but themselves. Probably they are a fair sampling of JOIN's community, but not typical of Uptown as a whole, even of the migrants. They are less settled, less centered on family and work than is the norm. The two years we lived in Uptown were a curious interlude in the postwar years: unemployment was comparatively low and the war was booming—not unrelated facts—and therefore white skin and an able body were rather good guarantees of a job (though how lasting and well-paying and useful a job is one subject of this book). The people who speak through these pages are probably more articulate than their neighbors, which is not to say better educated. But articulateness is no ironbound characteristic of personality: articulate to whom, and to what point? People who seemed vague or laconic on the street suddenly opened up before a tape recorder and a listener who seemed to value their thoughts. Most were in that minority inclined to take action against their conditions, the 2 or 5 percent of the population who found in a radical movement, some briefly and others perhaps for their lives, a form of effective or necessary opposition. The easy summary would be that these were people more estranged and better insulated than their friends from the established routine of stoicism and complaint and reliance on the hard lonely climb up that muddy ladder of mobility. But "explanations" based on individual quirk breed and multiply, explaining discontent and commitment *away*: so many ways of diverting your gaze from the undissectible fact that here are people with something to say to you, raw offerings of neglected experience, weights in the teetering balance of the American future.

There is something else about the gossamer concept of typicality. The statistical mean often cancels out the most interesting deviations, the signs of strain and shift in what would statistically be taken as "reality." Statistics and surveys do not by themselves make a useful social science, though of course they frame the reality as intercepted at a fixed point of time. What they cannot touch is the *potential* of a neighborhood, a community, a people. If the future is embedded in the present, then there is more to be learned from the volatile and extraordinary people, the first to feel and reshuffle the prevailing tensions, than from the ordinary. The people whom conditions jiggle loose to stand up and fight may differ from the others only enough to break loose. Just so when the guerrilla finds support among the people it is not simply because the people admire his political program, it is because the people *recognize* the guerrilla as their own, consider him brother. "I could be like him" is the other side of "he is like me but with more guts, or crazier." He is the man pushed perhaps one inch too far.

In any case, the question of method was moot. The residents of Uptown had been subjected to so many questionnaires, so many earnest surveys from Ph.D. candidates and anthropologists, Labor Department and war-on-poverty agents, we could not bear to inflict still another battery of tests for what would be, with the best of intentions, another round of exploitation, another display of people boiled down into a statistical population to be digested as tasty or fashionable objects. A deep and passionate engagement with one life matters more, teaches more than a nodding acquaintance with ten or a door-to-door survey of a thousand, if the passion does not obscure one's faithfulness to what one sees. Better to let some people stick in your throat.

Our interviews were literally that—exchanges of views: irresistibly we became friends, usually before we even broached the subject of the book. Sometimes we helped these people weave their ways through bureaucratic mazes: it was hard to fight back pity but we were trying to feel our way toward another mode of being *with* these people. We were organized, in a sense, into becoming organizers again. Mostly we grew close to a few people, let them call on us for help in *their* organizing. Because we looked and talked like the other ex-students, we were probably seen less as oddities than had we been the only middle-class refugees around, but because we were usually not entangled in JOIN's day-to-day decisions and pursuits (at the beginning, at least), we could serve as sounding boards for disputes and grumbles. But this is to put too fine a finish on our ambivalence. In fact our responsibility was divided, compiling a book and organizing, listening, and promulgating.

Over the months we edged farther away from the precipice of neutrality. At that time in the New Left there was much anguish about "manipulation of community people," an anguish that concealed the grave and unalterable fact that to act is to engage yourself with others, and more, that to propound radical change is to risk disturbing the delicate balance people work out to keep life tolerable. When the structures of equilibrium topple, in times we call crisis, people are cornered, have no choice, fight back, clamber for a new equilibrium: a new society. The Southern migrants, like most of the American poor, still find many corners for hiding, and the

sensitive organizer fears the damage he may bring to quiet lives, but the lives turn out to be not so quiet either.

The reader is entitled to know how the plainspokenness of our own commitments affected the words that came from people's mouths, for certainly it did. The "subject" is always prone to suit the interviewer's sense of him, to please him; the "student" then learnedly measures a peculiar feedback *through* but not *of* his "material." Speaking across a cultural chasm, some of our friends no doubt told us what they thought we wanted to hear. When we thought we heard the tinkle of falsity, we probed underneath. As the people came to understand our interests better, perhaps—who can say?—to trust us, they plunged into their purer experiences, their firmest political attitudes, told us what they would withhold—out of impatience or embarrassment or fear of betrayal—from strangers. In a few cases, when we failed to dig under to the reservoirs of mystery and deep feeling in the course of a series of interviews, we chose not to use the material at all, or only in the margins. When someone insisted on concealing himself—even from himself—we relented, before that most precious prerogative of a human being. So finally these people appear as they want to be seen, as they ought to be seen, and as we have selected and framed their appearance. Let the complexities stand: they speak clearly enough themselves.

A word about dialect and syntax. These are no mere technical problems. There is first the matter of standing true to the people who recorded. Ideally we would offer you a phonograph record or a tape or a film, but they are beyond our means. Therefore, second best, with the feeble medium of the printed page we have maintained enough dialect to ensure that you do not forget these are foreigners who are speaking to you, and who would speak to your face as foreigners if they had the chance: foreigners in many senses, at least in that they have codes and meanings and experience, condensed into language, which are not yours. So must the language of this book, a translation, be true to those differences, thus to its own roots. But so that the translation may be read we have made it more regular, imposed a rough sentence structure where there had been the irreproducible rhythm of speech, eliminated word contractions that would be hard to understand. "You know" as a punctuation is common, and we have eliminated many of them as distractions. Those that remain should, of course, be read "y'know." "I" has usually been left as "I" though, depending on the person, it stands somewhere between the Northern "I" and the Deep Southern "A." "Ah" would have caricatured it too badly. Final g's in -*ing* endings have usually been omitted, though in this as elsewhere we have refrained from lending the pronunciation any more consistency than the speech itself contains. Transcriptions of our own speech would betray more slurring and uneven contraction than writers and others of the literate class like to take credit for. Before you become enamored, or scornful, of the simplicity of the language, please consider your own language and *its* platitudes, how it might sound to foreigners, how their enthusiasm for *it* would conceal their disrespect for *you*.

That these people do not speak the official language, that they speak smudges of an Elizabethan English, does not make them quaint. The quaintness is in the ear of the listener, or, as in the case of *Beverly Hillbillies*, the sales-managing producer who can only depict a quite drastically different way of life by converting it to farce. To a generation reared to appreciate camp, even dialect intended to honor and not degrade—Finley Peter Dunne's, for example—seems to have the opposite effect. On the Left and among some hippies, romanticism and snobbery fuse in an easy American blend: "Hey, did you *hear* that guy? I mean, did you really *hear* him? Dig it!" Though it has more decent political credentials, this attitude smells of Geronimo movies and the African art exhibitions at the Whitney Museum lovingly gathered—such respect for tradition!—by mining magnates. The official American style is so bland, we are quick to elevate any difference into a uniform "coolness," regardless of its quality or intention. Thus we ride roughshod over the specific meanings of specific phrases, and their roots in history and culture. It is an imperial mentality we are worried about here, which converts a culture into cherishable commodities in order to collect and finally destroy it.

When you read this book, please strain to throw off the easy attitudes, the quick appreciations, and bear in mind that you have inherited your leisure to read this at the cost of the labor of the disinherited. Realize that our relative privilege, the standard of living we may disdain but still accept with the utmost aplomb, are products of the bent and thwarted lifetimes of men and women like Ras Bryant and John Dawson. Let us speak plainly, authors to readers, since we share a certain station: precisely, in hard economic fact, one of us* was enabled to attend the University of Michigan Graduate School because of a scholarship donated by a corporation, or rather by its owners, who paid the minimum wage to an old Alabamian we interviewed in Uptown; and therefore in some small but definite sense, this book and our authorship were made possible by him.

Consider that exploitation is more than a word. Don't cherish but learn; permit yourself to be disconcerted; learn in order to act.

*T. G.

Chronology

Since JOIN is at the heart of the book, the reader may want to have handy a simplified chronology in which the individual life-chronicles can be located:

1964

SPRING JOIN (Jobs or Income Now) office opens next door to unemployment compensation office on North Kedzie Avenue.

1965

JANUARY Office moved to Winthrop and Ainslie in Uptown; renamed JOIN Community Union.

FEBRUARY Montrose Urban Progress Center, Uptown branch of the Chicago Committee on Urban Opportunity (war on poverty), opens; JOIN pickets, demanding that funds be controlled by the community.

JUNE The 4800 block of Winthrop votes its desire for a playground on a parking lot, in an election conducted by JOIN.

Four JOIN organizers are arrested at the welfare office, demanding that a recipient have the right to examine the rules.

JULY JOIN staff apartment raided, staff arrested on narcotics and other harassment charges. (Charges subsequently dropped for lack of evidence.)

OCTOBER New JOIN structure: decisions will be made by an Organizing Committee composed of staff and the most active members at open weekly meetings; there are also weekly discussion meetings for the entire membership. (This structure remains basically unchanged throughout the subsequent history of JOIN.)

DECEMBER JOIN pickets war on poverty head Sargent Shriver at a downtown hotel.

Welfare and housing committees organized.

At Christmas JOIN pickets central welfare office demanding increased budgets.

1966

JANUARY   JOIN pickets Marsha Apartments, demanding landlord make repairs; landlord accedes.

FEBRUARY   JOIN office gutted by fire of undetermined origin.

MARCH   New JOIN office opens on Sheridan Road near Wilson Avenue.

JOIN attends PTA meetings at Brennemann Elementary School, where lakeshore parents want the district boundaries drawn so that Southern children will be sent to other, older, more decrepit schools.

APRIL   JOIN pickets Price-Rite radio store when member is cheated; wins fair-treatment pledge.

First JOIN rent strike; after days of picketing and handing out leaflets in the landlord's own home neighborhood, JOIN and tenants win contract with landlord, the first such contract in Chicago.

A JOIN committee submits proposal for a nonprofit day-labor agency to Advisory Council of Urban Progress Center; proposal pigeonholed.

MAY   JOIN Welfare Committee organizes march from JOIN office to downtown welfare headquarters, coordinated with nationwide demonstrations; three organizers arrested in sit-in.

JULY   Formation of Uptown Goodfellows, a movement for young neighborhood guys allied to JOIN.

Urban Progress Center fires Gerald Akers, a well-known young Southerner, for booing Sargent Shriver at a Washington meeting.

AUGUST   Second and third rent strikes; both result in landlord-tenant contracts, both of which are quickly violated by the landlord; in one building, an arbitration committee votes that the tenants should take over the building, collect rents, and make the agreed-upon repairs.

Goodfellows gather affidavits on police brutality and organize a patrol of Uptown.

Over two hundred Goodfellows and other Uptown residents march on police station, demanding civilian review, end to police brutality, and the firing of one particular policeman.

SEPTEMBER   Local and state narcotics agents raid JOIN and another antipoverty office, find planted narcotics, arrest two JOIN organizers, a minister, and two bystanders; they demolish JOIN office. (Months later charges are dropped except for those on one defendant, who is acquitted.)

The next night, police shoot and kill Ronnie Williams, brother of an active Goodfellow.

Landlord (see August) sues for injunction against tenant control of "his" building; judge grants injunction on grounds of a typographical error in the contract, refusing to rule on the legality of the substance.

NOVEMBER JOIN theater formed, performing political skits at meetings and in the neighborhood.

FALL AND WINTER JOIN organizes block meetings on urban renewal; participates in meetings with middle-class liberals to develop a way of fighting city's plans; decides not to run a candidate for alderman on grounds the organization is not strong enough to keep a campaign from degenerating into votemongering.

1967

MARCH JOIN organizes food-buying cooperative on Leland Avenue.

SPRING JOIN organizes block club on Clifton Avenue.

Goodfellows open a Ping-pong, jukebox, band-practice hall on Wilson Avenue.

MAY JOIN Welfare Committee becomes the independent Welfare Recipients Demand Action (WRDA, pronounced War Day).

JOIN Newsletter replaced by *The Firing Line*, a newspaper edited by a welfare mother, Peggy Terry.

JUNE Clifton block club organizes ballot over construction of a playground on a vacant lot; over five hundred residents vote unanimously in favor.

JOIN, with black groups from other endangered neighborhoods, demonstrates in City Council chamber when Council refuses to consider poor people's guidelines for neighborhood reconstruction; three JOIN organizers arrested, including one of the authors.*

JULY Uptown Conservation Council, the policy committee on urban renewal appointed by the Mayor, holds first meeting.

SUMMER AND FALL Clifton block club holds meeting with recreation and local officials.

DECEMBER Former Goodfellows and other young guys and organizers form National Community Union, to train new organizers and seed new poor-white projects in other cities.

1968

WINTER Several ex-student organizers leave Uptown.

*N. H.

FEBRUARY JOIN office closes.

AUGUST Many old JOIN members participate in demonstrations during Democratic Convention.

AUGUST-NOVEMBER JOIN activist Peggy Terry nominated for vice-president by Peace and Freedom parties in California and other states. She campaigns counterposing radical politics to the false messianism of Wallace and the law-and-orderism of Nixon and Humphrey.

SEPTEMBER National Community Union becomes the National Organizing Committee (NOC), discarding the community-union model in favor of organizing networks of radical white working-class youth in neighborhoods, factories, and schools throughout the Midwest.

NOVEMBER Bobby Joe Wright and other Goodfellows form Young Patriots Organization to "serve the people." Later they start a free breakfast program and health clinic.

1969

JUNE First issue of *Rising Up Angry*, a newspaper put out by ex-JOIN organizers and others to build organizations among white working-class kids in Chicago and the Midwest.

SUMMER Poor People's Coalition defeats urban renewal plans for Uptown.

Roughly speaking, the history can be broken into four phases, overlapping but distinct:

(1) *January, 1965, through February, 1966:* JOIN builds support and skeletal organization by providing *minimal services* (assistance in getting welfare checks, forestalling evictions, etc.), with some direct action.

(2) *March, 1966, through December, 1966:* JOIN moves to steady *direct action* involving large numbers of residents, trains new organizers from the neighborhood by working with them in the heat of movement. Finally threatened, the powers-that-be in the city react with violence.

(3) *January, 1967, through October, 1968:* Not being able to win concrete changes in the neighborhood, or to sustain work momentum, the organizational forms break down. Radical organizers, most of them indigenous, *hunt for new approaches* to poor and working-class white youth, looking beyond the limits of the neighborhood.

(4) *November, 1968, through 1970:* Popular movement against urban renewal secures the neighborhood as an arena for organizing. *New organizational forms* make explicit alliance with revolutionary groups.

UPTOWN

When I die, the devil won't have me, cause I been too mean; and I ain't done nothing for the Lord. So just put me on a bus out to Shopper's World. They have everything and handle all kinds of people.

I don't know how to make nothin 'cept noise.
—Ras Bryant

Ras Bryant, 62

SEPTEMBER, 1965

The JOIN meeting was sputtering its way to an end. Slowly, but easily, people—mostly old—disengaged themselves from the overstuffed second-hand armchairs and sofas, rose to their feet, made whatever point came to mind, and sat down. Shreds of personal history, complaints about housing, welfare, day labor, and the Mayor, arched in the air like so many different colors of confetti. At this early stage of the organization, the weekly meetings had no order or principle other than that everyone had something to say worth listening to. The old hawk-nosed man everyone called Pop popped up and stayed up in unknowing disruption, agitated, repeating something which was deeply felt and utterly incoherent.

I* stepped outside into the warm autumn air, and Pop appeared a few seconds later, looking as though he might be on his way.

"Where are you going, Pop?" He was hard of hearing even when sober. Tonight he was weaving considerably. I repeated the question.

"Goin to take Ras home. He's awful sick."

Ras came out the door behind him. We had heard he was someone we should interview, but I had not met him before. As Pop walked away a few steps, I asked Ras what was wrong.

"Ain't nothin wrong with me."

"Oh, I thought Pop said you were sick."

He wore thin-rimmed glasses and his hair, incongruously black, was full. (At the time he was using Lady Clairol; later he gave it up.) His left cheek was tremoring, but now he smiled, and the whole right side of his face

*T. G.

lifted and stayed up for a moment, his lips tight together, the entire expression a summary of wryness. Then he winked at this inquisitive stranger. "I had to tell him somethin to get him home. Now you know who's the sick one." And he took Pop by the elbow and walked off down the street.

The next day I asked if we could interview him and he agreed without hesitation. He took an empty beer can with him and we walked straight to our apartment. I didn't understand its purpose until later: it was his receptacle for tobacco juice, which he let fall unerringly into the hole every few minutes. ("Spitting" conjures up images of hawking and random uncouthness: he was neither random nor uncouth, and the can was only functional.)

We had talked vaguely before about interviewing but suddenly, faced with the prospect itself, we were more nervous than Ras and wholly unprepared. All we knew about him was that he was from West Virginia, so when the recorder was set up not too obtrusively, all we could think to say, awkward and embarrassed, was, "Tell us what it was like in West Virginia."

The way he chose to answer this blurted and inane question was to set us at ease, his ease. We wondered at once whether we had forced him into parable as a protection against our prying, whether we were in that sense inventing a famous man. But as he continued talking, never shedding his initial aplomb, and as we came to know him well, we learned he was not choosing his words as if on ceremony, but that he had moved directly into his natural expression.

We begin his narrative with those unhalting first words, as he spoke them.

They was a man out there in West Virginia, you know, just walkin the road with four little kids. They had no place to stay and they was hungry. And they stopped at a man's house, you know, and asked him for somethin to eat. Well, he told em, all right, come on in and just in a few minutes he'd give em somethin to eat. And while they was settin there talkin and was eatin, this guy who's on the road, he asked the man if he knows of anywhere in the world he could live for a few days, till he could get a hold a somethin. Well, the man told him he didn't know of no place in the world but a barn out there, with the cows. The man who lived there, he was poor, you know. Had a bunch of cows, maybe one or two, somethin like that.

And he said, "If you want to clean that out, mister," he said, "I'll let you go in there and won't charge you no rent."

"Well," he said, "I'd be glad to do that."

This man he was talkin to had a little pickup truck, you know. He went and hunt im a stove to put in, hunt im some beds and things they could sleep in, and there they was living in that barn, right there on the dirt floor.

I came along just a few days later, after they moved in, and I only had two dollars, all I had in my pocket. And the man told me what kind of a shape he was in, bein out on the road. And he take me in this barn and show me what he was livin in, see. And I said, "Buddy, I got to have a little money to get home on, but I got one dollar I can give you."

He said, "Well, that'll be fine. That'll give me some taters and some beans to cook and a loaf a bread," he said. "That'll feed em, all right." And he never get through thankin me for that dollar. If I'd had more I'd of give him some more. But I had to have a dollar to go home.

My foreparents was from Kentucky, lived in Kentucky as far back as I know. Don't know where they was fore that, but my dad and mother was all born in West Virginia and raised there. Up until they died. Oh, my father he made good money all his life, practically. Farmin. Until he got old, you know. After he got old he lost everythin. Back in the depression he lost everythin. We had four hundred ninety-six acres of land, about as good a farm as there was in Lincoln County. Well, he went an got it all paid for, you see, and my daddy he wanted to build a new house, you know. I told him, I said, "Dad, I think you'd be better to live in that old house."

"Nah," he said, "let's build us a new one."

I said, "Well, go right down, build us a new one."

He borried a thousand dollars, see, and lost the whole farm with that thousand dollars.

Well, he got on relief then, and first one thing and another—just made out the best way he could. He couldn't get on relief hardly at all, you know. There was a little bit of relief but there wasn't no such thing hardly as gettin on it. An they had a DPA* there then that they was runnin. My brother, he worked on it and give him some money out of what he made, you know. I sold whiskey an help him, you know. I made whiskey and sold it, and I'd give him money all the time to buy some groceries with. He had a turrible time. He died back in '44. Last day of '44, December the thirty-first.

I started makin whiskey, I was only twelve years old. I just taken it in myself. I done drinkin it for quite a while. So I just went to a man and asked him how to put up a barrel, what he would put in one if he was goin to. He told me. I just got me one thirty-gallon barrel—was the biggest one I could carry then, you know. I went up to his house one day and got im to go with me to the barrel.

*Department of Public Aid.

He said, "Boy, that'll make five gallons right now."

"Well," I said, "you gonna help me make it?"

"Mmmm, I couldn do that. I don't know how." Said, "Go down and get Harold, he'll help you."

I said, "Noooo, I got sugar right over here to sweeten this, and he'd steal it all. After I sweeten it all he'd come back here and slip me a lug."

"Yeah," he said, "he'd do that. Well," he said, "I know where a hid still is and I'll show it to you."

It's his still, you know, but he wouldn tell me that it's his. I knowed it was his; I'd seen the still two or three times before that. I was rabbit huntin, you know, hid around the hills.

He went and showed me where the still was and told me how to make it an all, and I went on and made it that night by myself. He showed me where to put the door on the still, you know, and what to do. You just got to set up your barrels, let em sour. Takes em about, oh, three to seven days for sour to work off. Then you go back and run em. Maybe you get three or four gallons out a the first run. Then from there on you get more. When you sweeten em back, pour the sugar back around and work off, you goin a get more the next time. Did you ever drink any a this moonshine? It's a lot better 'n this whiskey they sell in these stores around here. Won't hurt your head as bad as this stuff they got here. That ole artificial colorin they put in that stuff, it'll nearly kill you.

I carried 't in the next mornin. Whiskey was twenty dollars a gallon then, see. I ate breakfast with im and he tempered that whiskey up for me. Had four gallons and three-quarters. We stood around there and talked for a while, and had us a few drinks, you know.

Here come the biggest bootlegger there was in Branchland, out there huntin for whiskey. He said, "Come on, Luke," he said, "let's go out here and look around your stock at your barn. Well, I sometimes buy hogs and cattle and stuff." He went out there—he was wantin whiskey, you know; wouldn tell me. He thought I'd tell it, you know.

He got out there, he said, "Luke, you got any whiskey?" He couldn talk plain, you know.

He said, "No, I ain't got any, that boy got some."

He said, "All right, just call him here. Just as soon buy off him as anybody."

Called me out there and asked me. I said, "Yeah, I got some here. How much you want?"

"I got the money on four gallons if it's good."

I said, "O.K."

Went up on the hill, and when he tasted it, said, "That's the best whiskey I've tasted yet."

Luke said, "Told you it was."

He said, "Son, I want four gallons of that," and I just sacked her up there. He done take it all. I thought I was the best bootlegger in the United States. Me just a boy, you know. Oh, it was a lot of money then.

I sold plenty of it, see. Branchland's just a wide place in the road, but it was wild back then. They used to tell this story bout a man who got on a train. The conductor came around, he said, "Where to, sir?" He said, "To Hell." He said, "All right, sir," he said, "I'll take you there." He wrote him out a ticket to Branchland. When he got to Branchland he put him out. He said, "This is just as near to hell as I know of," and boy, hit was. My, they were drunk, a-fightin, and havin one a the awfullest times you ever seed in your life. Hatfields and McCoys was all around, livin all up in there. My daddy used to tell me bout them settin in the courthouse with rifles 'cross their laps.*

I started workin back when I was twelve year old, in the mines. Oh, I don't remember just what year it was. I was born in 1903 and I went to work when I was twelve years old. You can kinda figger about what time it was. I told the boss a lie, see, to get a job—told him I's sixteen years old. See, I slipped off from home; they didn know where I was at. Bout four months I was gone. See, I was workin ever night, two shifts a night, almost all the time.

The first evenin when I got a job in the mine, I went up on the hill. I had two arms then, see. I didn get my arm shot off till I was sixteen. I learnt the boss' name fore I got up on the hill where the mines was, and I asked some guy up there whether if he knew where the boss was at. He said, "That's him with that white cap on, standin right out yonder." He was—I don't know, a Irishman or somethin like that, you know, a German I believe it was. Everything he said, he said, "The bloody hell! The bloody hell!"

I went out there. I said, "Hello, Mr. Davis."

He said, "Hello."

I said, "Mr. Davis, you hirin any men now?" I thought I was the biggest man in the world.

He said, "The bloody hell!" He said, "You're lookin mighty young. How old are you?"

*Just south of Branchland, on the other side of old "Devil Anse" Hatfield's big house, alongside the road, is Hatfield's General Store. A little farther down, McCoy's Red Dot Market.

I said, "I'm sixteen, past."

"The bloody hell!" he says. "Where did you come from?"

I said, "Branchland, West Virginia."

"Well," he says, "the bloody hell! You know I got plenty a men workin from Branchland, West Virginia," he says. "Do you know Harvey Bryant?"

I said, "Yes, sir, he's one a my cousins."

He says, "What's your name?"

I told him.

He says, "Well now." He said, "You know Jim Sizemore?"

I said, "Yes sir, he's my brother-in-law, he married my sister." And there's a lot of people there I knowed. He just kept askin me different ones by name. I said, "Yes sir, I know em all." Just about all them people from Branchland. Knowed ever one, you know, from Branchland.

"Well," he says, "the bloody hell!" He says, "I'll give you a *jobe*." He called it *jobe*, you know. He said, "I'll give you a *jobe*." He said, "Can you work tonight?"

"Oh," I said, "I'll be glad to."

He said, "O.K." Then he gave me some papers to fill out, to send to my parents for them to sign, you know; and then some to take to the office to get signed up for the job. I had to cross this swinging bridge over the river to go to the office, you know. And these papers he give me to send to my dad and my mother, I throwed them on the river. Didn want them to know where I was at, see.

I was pretty smart for a boy. I came back over to the office, back up on the hill, where there's a little doghouse. They call the office a doghouse. He said, "Did you send those papers down?"

I said, "Yes sir, they went right down."

Bout three, four days, he said, "The bloody hell! What you reckon's wrong with those papers we sent down?"

I said, "I don know, Mr. Davis. Mighta got lost in the mail or somethin."

"Yeah," he said. "The bloody hell!" he says. "We'll fill out some more." He seed I was a good worker and never did mention those papers no more.

Hit was a pretty good-size mine. Low coal. I saw five months I worked there. I got used to it just in a few days. I unloaded slate that night: I believe about seven cars of slate, right out on that trestle. Big trestle. What it was, a trestle went across a big deep holler down there. All you had to do was just clear the car with that shovel, you know, and that slate just went on through, see, and fell way down a big holler there, where the slate's suppose to go, you know. Well, I went to work at four o'clock and I was so small I couldn raise the endgates up in these cars, see. And this

6   UPTOWN

boss told the brakeman and the motorman, said, "You boys help this boy raise them endgates cause he can't raise em."

Just about dark I went out and said, "Hello, Mr. Davis."

He said, "Hello, Bryant," he said. "What's a matter now?"

I said, "Mr. Davis, I got that all unloaded." Bout two hours, I had it all unloaded.

He said, "Come on, let's go out there and look at that."

"Hell," he said. "Boy, them cars look like they been swept out." Says, "Come on in the doghouse. You done got your year's pay. Ain't a man on this job woulda made a shift outa that."

Oh, I said, I got somethin here now. That's what I thought to myself, you know; I got somethin here.

Next night I went brakin on a motor. That's as dangerous a job as there is in the mines too. You got a couple up these cars, and motor backin up, you know, and hittin em cars; and you gotta couple em, jump off from the end a these cars you're ridin ahead in, you know. You gotta jump off and throw switches. And some of em, you gotta kick em as you go through. Kick latches, you know. You gotta be fast too. Thousand and one guys got killed, you know. I worked four months at it, never got hurt. My dad and mother kept writin to me, as high as two and three letters a week, come back home, come back home, after they'd found out where I was at, you know.

Times was pretty hard then too, you know.

My arm? Shot 'toff with a shotgun. I set the gun down on the doorstep, laid my arm right across the muzzle, when it fired away four inches of bone. I don't know whatever knocked that gun off. Me and another boy killed twelve rabbits the day before that, with shotguns. You did have a time of gettin a doctor, had to go about five miles to get one. Ride a horse there and then him ride a horse back. Wasn't no such things as cars and trucks and such things like that, you know, when I was growin up. That's the reason I lost my arm.

I got shot at three-thirty in the evenin, got to the hospital eleven-thirty the next day. They had to haul me about ten miles on a sled that night, and then wait on the train to run. Train got in at eleven-twenty and they had the ambulance settin there. These doctors didn have mind enough to know what to do, you know. They just poured a bottle of iodine down that place where it was shot, and put a thong around it, loose, you know. You've seen people wearin them leather thongs, I guess. That's all they done with my arm. I lay there and bled all night long and the next day till I got to the hospital. It take two or three of em to hold the sled, the holler was so rough where I had to go down. Take three or four of em to keep it from turnin over with me. I tried to get one a these doctors to let me walk. He said, "No, you'll die before you could get there." When I found my arm was shot off I offered a ten-dollar bill to somebody to bring me a pint of whiskey. I wasn't drinkin a drop now, then. They had plenty of whiskey but nobody wouldn give me a drop. Fraid to, you know. Rush your blood up and make you higher, you know. Why, I'd of drunk enough to pass out, I tell you, if I'd gotten a hold of it—when I seen what happened. Done well to save my life then. They wasn't no such thing as blood transfusions then. They pumped salt water—see where these patches are sewed up? Nurse held my pulse all night long there, and about every two or three minutes she'd come call the doctor, and he'd come and put about two or three drops of salt water at a time, makin more blood. When I come to myself I didn't know what's the matter. They had that patch sewed on there. I got that patch and tore her, stitches and all, out. I wanted to see what they done to me, you know. Nurse came in—boy, she was very upset. I didn't care what they say, I was goin to find out what was the matter with me, what they'd done to me.

This hospital was in Huntington. Best bone specialist there was in West Virginia then. Probably the best there was in the world, best they knowed of, anyway. He was a Hatfield.

I've loaded coal with one hand, just like that. I loaded coal, shoveled it up in the cars, and banked it. I can dig a hillside, turn and plow with a good team, go out and plow all day just as good as a man with two hands.

I heard my dad talkin with my mother one night after I went to bed. "Well," he said, "I'm gonna have to hire my plowin done this spring." Said, "Ras can't plow."

I got up bright and early the next mornin. I went to try to see what I could do. I knowed I could do it. I was stout then, too. I went to the barn and fed my mules before breakfast. Had a big heavy span a mules, good ones too—young, stout. I went back on the hill and I started plowin. Had a big ten-acre field.

I was back there about three days and a half, and Dad said to my mother, said, "Let's go back on the hillside and see what Ras is doin." Well, they came back there, down the ridge. I was down there plowin, you know. I wasn't sayin a word. I didn know they was back there, see; I was busy plowin.

Dad said, "Well, he's tryin to do somethin so let's just slip off and not go down where he's at." They went on back to the house. See, I been doin all his plowin before that, me just a boy. They went on back to the house. And the next day, after I went in and eat dinner, fed my mules, you know, they asked me what I was doin. "Oh, I was just out foolin around, you know." He traveled up and down there—I don't know how many different times he *did* go up and down across that way. He come back to the house. He said, "I'll swear that's plowed just as good as any-body can plow it." I said, "I know it."

I done it all. My mother always wanted me to do the plowin when I hoe corn, cause I'd watch my plow and let the dirt roll right to this corn, and not cover it up, you know. And the rest of em just go down there and let that plow way down deep, you know; just cover that corn up, a lot of it. And if my dad hired anybody that had two good hands to work, she said, "Well, you let Ras do the plowin." And she didn want me to work for nobody else.

Went back to the mines after a while, after I got my arm shot off. I was workin for this same boss, now, what said, "The bloody hell!" He wanted me for a trapper, a course. That's openin doors for the motors to go through, you know. See, this ore's gotta be pushed back there. Well, they gotta put doors across there to put the ore into another section over here, you see. I had maybe three trap doors to watch back there, see, and maybe three, four switches too. And I had to know where these motors was at all the time, you see, so I can watch em, see. And I'd sit in there, in that mine, all day long for two dollars. Eight hours, you know, two dollars; just settin in the mine.

I worked for two dollars a day, and the boss he come up on the hill one mornin and he says, "The bloody hell!" He said, "You know you got a raise?"

I says, "Well, no, Mr. Davis, nobody told me about it."

"Oh, the bloody hell!" he said. "Yes, you got a raise," he said, "about six days ago."

I said, "What are we gettin now, Mr. Davis?"

"Oh," he said, "you make two-twenty a day now—two dollars and twenty cents."

"Well, that's pretty good." Oh, you could buy a sackload of groceries, about all you could carry, for a dollar maybe, at some stores. Course these commissaries, they charge you high for what you get there.

These operators, they're jest skinnin the miners out a what they make, that's all. Miner good and well, pretty well knows that he's got to trade at their commissary, you know, and they go in there and get stuff that they actually don't need. Course that's their bad luck, you know, but they'll go in there and get stuff actually they don't need. And when payday comes it's very little they draw. They make plenty of it but they don't draw none of it. Time their house rent comes out, and their union dues, and this and that and the other un, have to have insurance and everything has to come out of the pay, you know, and the time they count up, lots of em don't draw. I've knowed a people not drawin a nickel of money for as high as three years at a time. Never had a nickel in money but they'd go to the commissary and get anything they want, see. They'll go get a big lease. Maybe there'll be somethin or other else they'll want, they'll add somethin else on this lease, make it more and more and more and first thing you know, the company gets back all the money. It's just another day older and deeper in debt, just like the record. You've heared that one, ain't you? Yeah, that's all it is, just another day older and deeper in debt. I owe my soul to the company store. That's just about right too.

One man had been there at Spankham mine practically all of his life, I reckon, as fer as I know. He was raised right there, and when he got large enough, got old enough to go to work, you know, he went to work there. Now he's got kids around there. And he's been there all that time, and owed the company fourteen hundred dollars the last count I had of him, and that was a long time.

Back when I was just a boy, there used to be three old rich people come down to my house, sit down and talk with my daddy, drink with em—my dad would drink then, fore he joined the church. They'd buy whiskey twenty years old. They had a date right on the head of the barrel with a hot iron the day it was put in there, see. And it stayed in there twenty years. They'd order that whiskey and paid twenty dollars a gallon for it —you'd see it rope, thick and heavy you know—and drink it down, set around drink with my dad. That was back when they was a-payin about, oh, anywhere from two to not over three dollars a day. And old Colonel Branch, he owned this mine there at Branchland, he was there before the railroad ever went up through there, see. And when it come through there they just named it Branch-land. And he set there and told my dad one night, he said, "Mr. Bryant," he said, "You know what I could do?"

"No," Dad said, "I don't know, Colonel," he said, "what?"

He said, "I could pay them men ten dollars a day for diggin that coal out a that mine's up there, and still make money on it."

"Well," he said, "why don't you do it?"

"No," he said, "Mr. Bryant, I can't do that." He said, "If I did," he said, "in a little while they'd get to my place. There'd be nobody to do the work." He said, "I've got to keep em diggin that coal." That's the way the rich cramps the poor, you see. They've got to keep em down to work, they know they ain't gonna do the work but they've got to keep them down on the rocks so they're gonna *have* to work.

After they got this union in there, they cut me out of the mines. The examinations started, I didn't get to work a day after that. United Mine Workers. They came in about '38, I believe it was.

I was talkin to a man on a train one time. I was comin out a Huntington, see, and he was out a another state. And he was tellin me he was a United Mine Worker, but said, "Now, I don't want you to say nothin about it."

I had some moonshine whiskey with me. I take me couple, three pints to drink. I'm goin down to Huntington and back on the train—go down mornin, back every evenin. And he was settin there and I said, "Buddy, would you like to have a drink of whiskey?"

He said, "Yeah."

I said, "Walk back here and we'll drink a drink. It's moonshine, see?" Now he seed then I wouldn tell nothin. He said, "You know what I am?"

I said, "No."

He said, "I'm a United Mine Worker."

I said, "What are you doin in this section?"

"Well," he said, "just talkin around with people and stuff, you know." Said, "I can't let em know I'm a United Mine Worker. Why, they'd of killed me if I'd of let em know," he said. "Now, I know you won't tell."

I said, "Lord, no. I'd be glad if you could organize with em, see. Well," I said, "how you gonna manage to get em organized, now?"

Said, "We gonna starve em out." Said, "They're just about ready to break over now."

The union couldn let nobody know what they was, see. Finally at last, they had a big battle back on Blair Mountain. That is, they thought they was havin a battle. Now I'm gonna tell you somethin. There was a sheriff down there and so he said he'd give everybody that promised him to fight five dollars a day, car to ride in, rifles and everythin to fight with. Oh you could see cars just one right after another goin with rifles, see the rifles stickin up through the door glasses, windshields. And some of em went round this part of the knob, you know—it was just like a big knob, high up like a big knob—and some of em went around this side of the knob and some went around the other side of the knob, and they run together and thought they was runnin into the union, and commenced shootin each other and killed one of em back there. There was never a union man back there, see. They just thought they was comin in there; they got word they was comin in there. And Don Chafin—he was sheriff, see—he spread it all the way through, cause he was a gettin ten cents a ton on every ton of coal that run out of Logan County. God—why ever train that went out, why he was gettin five dollars a car on this coal, you see. Oh, he was a rich man when that all got through! Well the papers said, now, that his boys had seven mines up there, goin up Ridge Creek, the coal a-rangin from thirty-six inches to seven foot. I read the paper m'self. You take seven-foot vein a coal, that's a mighty good vein a coal.

That was part of the times when passenger trains had to lay over for the freight trains hauling that coal through, they was needin that coal so bad you know. And people'd get off'n that train there in Logan, a stranger, oh man, them deputy sheriffs'd gang him around, you know, find out what his business was there and everything, and a lot of em they'd put em on the next train back out. Lot of em they killed em and pitched em in that furnace over there, burnt em up.

Don knowed hell was a-waitin for im when he did die. Why sure I believe it. Not a doubt of it. See now he was a-cheatin the poor people out of a livin right there. That's before the union got in there, see.

They had a time of ever doin it, just to tell you the truth. They had a time of ever doin it. Finally they got over with it, see, by talkin to people, writin to em and stuff like that, and they got people to see what everythin's all about.

I tell you, why I quit the mines then, you see. They had somethin what was called a yaller dog, and you had a sign that or you had a leave the mines. If you worked in this mine, you had to sign this yaller dog too, that you would not coal-operate with this union in any way. You had to sign that. If you lived in that camp you couldn let your dad and your mother come in an stay all night with you, less they would give information and let them write your dad and mother. Oh, it'd take about a month fore you'd get your dad and mother to stay all night with you.

And so they throwed that paper out. I read it over, you know, looked it over. Went back, I said, "The hell with that yaller dog."

They said, "You won't work here no more."

I said, "Well, I'm glad of that. But," I said, "I won't sign no yaller dog." I said, "I got plenty of other places where I can work. But," I said, "I'll never sign agin the pore workin man." I told the man right in the office, you know, superintendent settin right in there.

Super said, "You mean to tell me you won't sign it?"

I said, "No sir, I ain't gonna sign it, I'll never sign it." I said, "I ain't got nobody to look after but myself and I ain't signin no yaller dog." I said, "I'll help the union out any day they come in here," which I did.

I said, "I'm goin down the road. Gimme my money right now."

He said, "I ain't a gonna do it."

I said, "Be damned if you don't, or somethin or other will happen." Now I'd a German Luger pistol on his belly. I said, "This'll be the bloodiest office you ever seed 'f you don't give me my money."

He said, "I can't do it."

I said, "You gonna give it to me or this'll be the bloodiest place you ever seed." I said, "I'm goin."

"Well," he said, "if that's the way you feel about it," he said, "I guess I'll have to give it to you."

I said, "It's me or you one, or you give me my money." And he throwed it out to me too. And I just caught the next train out.

I went back to home, back to Branchland, worked on the farm. Why, I wouldn't a signed that for nothin in the world. Agin the pore labor people. Course there were people who lived there who had families that

couldn't do no better, had to sign it, see. But not all of em did. Them that didn't got fired. They had to go hunt the best they could. They had to move out, you know, go back to the farms.

I stayed a good bit on the farm. I went back there and went to makin whiskey, you know, on the farm—raisin part of what I could eat, makin enough whiskey to buy the rest of it. Made it on up all the time I stayed in West Virginia, practically all the time, when I didn't have a job, you know. I'd go out and hoe corn all day, make whiskey up till two, three o'clock in the mornin. Go in and lay down to sleep, couple or three hours till daylight, have up and go to work, hoein corn. Any night I didn't make a batch, maybe I'd travel for five miles, and sell it and come back in. I was out pretty near day and night, tryin to raise my family. Back in Hoover's times—times of depression. That's what we had to do to make a livin back there, you know. Oh yeah, yeah, I was raided lots of times. If you got caught you just got time out of it. I got a year and a day, one time, for makin whiskey. Why I didn mind it. It was either that or let my family starve. And then, if they put me in the government had to send em a check to live on, see. Well, it was the only thing there was to do. Wasn't nothin else left.

Back in the depression times, they had a farm loan went around you know, and I borried thirty dollars offn the government to buy seeds and things with, to plant that spring. The bloomin check never come in till way up about July or August! Too late to plant anything, you know, except sow turnips, that's about all you could do. Well, you could get as many seeds for a dime as you'd want to sow, for fifteen, twenty cents anyhow. The same year that we borried this money my crop all burned up. Oh man, it burned up—the corn burned up plumb to the top; you could plant a big field of corn, you're just lucky to get a few nubbins out of it. It just dry, all burnt up, just dry that summer. Wasn't no rain at all. And so they extended the loan until another year, see.

So in the fall of the year, after I got my crop over, you see, I went to makin whiskey to pay this loan off. That's when this boy turned me in, see. It was my still but he turned me in for it.

Well, we went out to make the whiskey, you know, and told this feller Calvin not to come in there. Still he come in there and lay down in the pit, after he got him a few drinks, you know, and he got to cryin, fell off a the side a the pit we had the barr'ls set in, you know, cryin, hit the ground, lay down and went to sleep. As soon as we got the whiskey made, why I taken down eight gallon and a half of whiskey and carried it down to the woods myself, you know, and my buddy, he taken the whole still on his back. Whenever they waked Calvin up, you see, the law did, why he asked where Ras and Albert are at, see. Said, "Where's Ras and Albert at?" Albert was the other guy. Calvin went and told em where the still was hid to get out of it hisself. Went and got a federal warrant for us.

They give him sixty days in Logan County Jail. Give me a year and a day in Petersburg, Virginia. Give Albert four years in Atlanta, Georgia. Four years, cause it was his fourth time up, see. Calvin turned us in to get out hisself, and he just got sixty days.

Well, later on, they found him over in Wayne County over the hill, dead. His brother had to go identify him by a gold tooth he had, that's the only way he could identify him. Been there about thirty days fore they ever found him. Nobody knows how he died. I guess somebody does, I don't know, I guess somebody knows, I don't. Yeah, it was for a good reason, I guess.

The judge, when he called me up, he asked me how long I'd a been makin whiskey. I told im, "The last twenty years."

Said, "You got by a long time, didn't you?"

I said, "Well, I got by a while."

If they ketch you with that moonshine whiskey they charge you thirteen dollars for tax, on each gallon. That's what they charge you when they take you to court, they charge you thirteen dollars on each gallon, plus the jail sentence, the fine, and everything. That's the tax on it. Federal gets that, you know. They give me a year and a day in Petersburg, Virginia, the Federal Reformatory pen, and a six-hundred-dollar fine. You get good time off, you know.

Well, my time was just about four or five days of bein up they called me up to the administration building and said, "Well, Bryant, your term's just about up now." Said, "Are you in shape to pay your fine?"

I said, "Noop, I ain't gonna pay it."

"Then what are you gonna do, do thirty days for it?"

I said, "Whatever you put on me, I got to do it." Said, "I ain't gonna pay it." I could've got the money to paid it, fer as that's concerned, but I wouldn't of. No six hundred dollars. Just had to do thirty days for it, you know.

Said, "Well, Bryant, your time's just about up now."

I said, "Yeah, I understand this." They told me I'd have to do thirty days and then if I ever got a hold of any money, like earned a big lot of money or somethin or other, they could come in and take that, for the amount of money out of that, you know. I said, "Let me worry about that."

I was home about three days, somebody knocked on the door and I went to the door. They said, "Is your name Bryant? Erastis?"

I said, "Yes sir."

"Well," he said, "Mr. Bryant," he said, "I'm a collectin agent for the government."

I said, "Is that right?" I said, "What do you want me to do about it?"

"Well," he said, "I've got a note here agin you," he said, "for thirty dollars, and the interest." Said, "How are you in shape to pay any of it?"

I said, "Yes sir," I said, "I'm in shape to pay it all." I said, "Come on in, have a seat."

He came in the house, you know, and set down. My wife she was in there. He figured up the interest and everything, you know.

Now I said, "Mister, I want to explain to you how I'm gonna pay you." I said, "I have worked for the government for ten months and twenty-one days, and," I said, "I haven't received any check for my pay yet, for my work."

He said, "You mean you worked for the government and he wouldn't pay you?"

I said, "That's right."

"Well," he said, "where did you do the work at?"

And I just up and explained it to him, told him why I went there and everything. "Now," I said, "you go up there and get a check for my ten months and twenty-one days work, and you take out what I owe you and then you mail me a check for the balance. And I want to see the check come in here in a few days, too, for my work." I never did see that man no more.

My wife said, "How in the world do you have the heart to talk to people like that?"

I said, "How in the heck did I have the heart to work for nothin?"

Oh Lord! I worked different places. Lord, yeah, lot of places I've worked. I been in all kinds of different states, you know. I used to haul stuff out to Ohire, and down to North Ca'lina, different places, into Huntington market. Fruit market, big fruit market there. Had a ton-and-a-half truck, International. Maybe get a load a potatoes this time, maybe next time we'd get apples, maybe the next time we'd get somethin else.

I was just workin for nother guy, you know. He give me three dollars a day, board and tobacker. Well, it was purty good, you know, for so much as ridin—you wasn't doin nothin much but ridin, but Lord, it was long hours. Sometimes we'd ride out all night long and all the next day. Then when we sell in the market, see, you got up about four, started work at seven, and you didn't close till nine, ten o'clock that night; maybe stay out there till twelve o'clock that night. Then went to sleep till four, then back out the next mornin. Altogether I handled vegetables about seven years. Off and on, you know; different times.

Times was real hard, then, you know. My dad come to Huntington one time, to my house. I thought he had a good coat but he had on a raggedy old coat. Come in to get some medicine for my mother, you know. And he said, "Well," he said, "do you know where the drug stores is?"

I said, "Yep." I said, "Give me your paper, let me see, Dad." And he let me see his paper and I read it off, and I said, "Yeah, I know where to go get it. I'll go with you," I said. I said, "My wife's just about got done with it and we'll eat dinner. I'll go down and get your medicine," I said. "Ain't you gonna stay all night with me, Dad?"

He said, "No." Said, "I got to get back." He said, "Your mother's bad off, I got to get back, you know."

"Well," I said, "I'll take you to the bus terminal."

I taken im to the bus terminal and give im—I believe it was eighteen dollars I had in my pocket when I went to the bus terminal. I give im that eighteen dollars, help im along. I had plenty a money at the house, see, but never thought a goin back to the house. That was a lot a money right there, you know. You could buy all kinds a groceries with it, pay doctor bills and anythin else.

His coat was just as ragged as it could be. I had some brand new jackets there, good jackets, you know. I said, "Dad," I said, "wouldn this suit you better?" I got plenty a coats now but the coats was mostly too small for him, my coats was. He was a pretty good-sized man.

He said, "Yeah, that'd be nice." He put it on. "Well," he said, "that just fits me." He said, "That's a good un, too."

I said, "Yeah."

"What'd you have to pay for that?"

I said, "Five dollars."

"Well," he said, "hit's sure worth it."

I said, "Glad I had the money to buy it."

A few days after that I went out and taken him a big heavy sweater— slipover sweater, real heavy one. He put it on and wore it up to the barn and back and we walked around a while, me and him did, lookin around.

I said, "How you like that sweater, Dad?"

"I ain't given one thought to it," says. "Hit's too hot."

I said, "Wait a while. It won't be after a while."

I went back; it'd turned real cold. I said, "How's the sweater now, Dad?"
He said, "I'm tellin you, hit feels real good."

I been married twice. Back when I was twenty-two years old, the first
time I got married. I had four kids. One was born dead, another one died
when it was twenty-seven years old, of cancer; and I got two now livin in
Washington, D.C. They're married, and their men's workin. I don't even
know their names now, who they'd married. They won't write to me or
nothin. I said, "If that's the way y'all feels about it, why, suits me." Don't
know what's wrong with em. I can't imagine whether they think they's up
above me or what's wrong with em. I reckon they married pretty well off,
you know. They want to act like a big shot, I guess.

She had her a baby—while I was gone. I got in a little trouble and had
to go to the penitentiary. I was in there sixteen months, she had her a
baby. And I know I didn send this baby back in no letters, cause I didn
write her none. My people wrote and told me she was talkin to another
man. I came back, this baby was four years old. And they'd been a-tellin
him, "Daddy Ras is gonna kill you when he comes in."

I wanted to see my kids, you know. I was thinkin to telephone, call em
to meet me somewhere, when I run into one of em walkin up the street,
and she had this boy with her. He commenced runnin around and around
and around, screamin, a-cryin. I said, "What's the matter with you, boy?"

"Oh," she said, "Daddy," said, "they've been a-tellin him Daddy Ras
is gonna kill him."

I said, "Boy, I ain't gonna kill you thirty minutes yet."

And I said, "To come to tell you about it, I'm not your daddy either."
That made me hot, you know. So my daughter, she kept beggin me to go
to the house and see the other kids. She says, "Come on," she says, "you're
goin out and see Betsy and Janet too." Said, "You ain't saw them now in,
oh, five years."

I said, "I know it."

Well, I went out to the house. I was just as good to my wife as I could
be when I went in. Said, "Hello, honey."

She said, "Hello."

I said, "How you been gettin along since I been gone?"

"Oh," said, "just fine, how're you?"

I said, "Oh, just fine." I said, "I'd like to talk to the kids private for a
few minutes, you know, honey."

She said, "Go ahead." Said, "Take em in that room there and talk
with em." Said, "I want a see you in the kitchen soon's you get through
with the kids."

I said, "O.K., honey." I went in and talked to em a little while, you know, and asked em if they wanted to go with me or wanted to stay with their mother. Said no, they'd stay with their mother. I said, "Well, O.K." When I got to the kitchen door, she just throwed both arms around my neck. Said, "Honey, ain't you goin a come back and stay with me?"

I said, "Nope."

She said, "What's the matter?" Said, "I didn't do much wrong while you was gone." Said, "I just got drunk and had me a baby."

"Well," I says, "Honey, *still* you ain't done nothin wrong. Just stay drunk and *raise* your baby." Best answer I knowed how to give her right off the rim. I just take and run off. I was not goin a fool with that no more.

See, they locked me up for cuttin a guy with a knife. Two of em were on me, see, and I had a do what I done. Hit all started when they come in tryin a make me buy em a pint a whiskey. See, I'd been on out there in the bootleg joint two or three times, you know. Well, quite naturally I was always tryin a be goodhearted to ever-body. Said, "Ras, you want a buy us a drink?"

"Yes," I said, "give the boys a half a pint." See, that'll make em a good drink apiece. I paid for it, see, with a quarter. That all it cost then— bootleg, you know, moonshine.

Well, they come out and said, "By golly, today you goin a buy us a pint."

I said, "Well, boys, ain't that too bad."

"Well, by golly, we goin a make you buy us a pint."

"Uh uh," I said. "Wait a minute now. You start tryin a make me do somethin, that don't work very well."

What they was goin a do was take all my money, see. If I'd a got to my pistol I'd a killed em all, both of em; but I just couldn't get to it. This un just grabbed around me, right around my shoulders. So I eased my hand in my pocket and got my knife and he had his head layin there across my head, and I just reached up and I raked around his neck. I cut im right here, on down this a way and around to him under the throat here, as far as I could get. And this had been while he was holdin me, see; I couldn't bend down. About this time that other un throwed a big heavy milk bottle at me and I tried to get down as far as I could, you know— couldn get no further. That bottle hit me right in the top of the head, and glass fell all over the floor.

Well, when I cut this other man, he run back on the porch and got a hatchet, aimin to knock me in the head with this hatchet, see. I had it out there fixin up junk and stuff. I was peddlin junk. Any way to make a nickel, you know what I mean. Makin good money, though, at it.

Well, he run back there and hollered at this law, he said, "Run in there. Man cuttin a man all to pieces with a knife." Yeah, he busted right in that door, that law did.

He said, "What are you tryin a do, kill this man?"

"No, I'm just tryin to keep from gittin killed."

Went down to court, they give me two to ten years over that. I done five years, two months, seventeen days straight up.

The doctor's statement was harsh agin me. He said the one I cut never be well all his life, have a headache all his life, see. Well, I cut im down through here and across this way. He'll have im a headache all his life. Oh, I wished I'd a cut him everywhere else, you know, where I could. If I'd a had a good sharp knife, I'd a killed im.

And the other un, he got up and told a big tale about it. And then this doctor's statement. And this one that was cut all to pieces, too, he told a big tale, you know. So there was too many witnesses agin me. They stuck me.

State penitentiary, West Virginia. Moundsville State Penitentiary. 818 Jefferson Avenue. I never will forget the number, I don't reckon.

Hit was plenty rough. But I made out to get it over with. Plenty rough. I went out on road gangs, worked on state roads. Lacked twelve days of bein three years, I worked on state roads. Worked on new walls eleven months, and then worked on Huntingsville farm four months. While I was in the road gangs I got ten cents a day for my work. On new walls didn get nothin but outside good time, Huntingsville farm didn get nothin but good time.

But I made money loanin out stuff for interest. See, I had some money when I went up there, and I drawed scrip. They got a little commissary where you can spend this scrip. I didn order nothin out a the commissary, see, while I was there. They'd come round and sell me a two-dollar book a scrip for one dollar in cash money, see. Wanted to gamble on it. Well, I take this scrip down around the commissary. Just a little while, first one I see says, "Get me a cone of ice cream, I'll give you cash for it," see. Or, "Get me a bottle a pop, I'll give you cash for it." Had to watch when the guard come in, had to duck my scrip from em. One say, maybe, "Gimme a pack a cigarettes now, and I'll give you some money for em." That a way, you see, I could double my money there. Trade and trafficked about. Had about seven, eight hundred dollars when I came out a the penitentiary.

I got in May the fourteenth in '40, and I come out the last day of August in '45, just when the war were over. Five years, two months, seventeen days straight. Just when the war broke out, December the seventh, '41, when they bombed Pearl Harbor, well, I thought we was goin a get out then, you know, to go in the war. But you see, instead of us a-gettin out, goddamn, they wouldn parole nobody then. Cause men got scarce up there just like they did out here, you know, to do the work. And the judge wouldn't send nobody up there, see, unless some ratty old man who couldn't do nothin. They would either send you for a job or send you to a mine to work somewhere, if you was an able-bodied man to work. Or send you to a farm to work, or somethin or other, the judge would. Or either give you a choice: go in the army, if you was able to go the army, or go to the penitentiary. Well, you knew you'd take the army fore you'd take the penitentiary! So there wasn't nobody comin up, see, and we had a stay there to do the work. They wouldn let none of us out, neither.

They was seven hundred behind them walls when I went in there. Some of us was in the road camps, farms, and other places; also, some of em were in state police barracks; some this place and some the other place, you know; some around hospitals and places like at. I don't know how many was in the whole institution all together, but they was seven hundred behind the walls when I went in there. They had the colored on one side and the whites on the other. They had dormitories just like the army, you know, army camp. Just exactly the same difference. Nice place, all right—recreation, ball games, pitch horseshoes, and oh, a lot of stuff you could do for pleasure. Pass all the time.

They have certain times they'd let you out for this recreation. Other times you go to your dormitories, just like the army does. Guys bet cigarettes on them ball games. Whites played the coloreds all the time. You get three or four pack a cigarettes and give em to one a them colored guys and he'd throw the game our way, you know—miss a ball or somethin on purpose. Course it was accidentally the purpose, too, to throw the game our way. We knowed exactly what to do, me and another feller. We'd take around four packs a cigarettes apiece, you know, after the game was over. Course, if we lost, we wouldn have to pay em nothin, see. Three or four guys and I used to throw that game. You could do it. Say, "We'll give you three or four packs." Say, "O.K." Well, we'd bet maybe a hundred packs on that game. Why, I had forty-some cartons a cigarettes when I started to leave there. I just give em out to the boys, then—what I'd win on them games, you know. A lot a them a long way from home, didn have nothin to smoke. "But heck, here's you a pack of cigarettes. Didn cost me nothin."

We got books to read and stuff like that. Readin and writin, you know, I learnt that in there, after I got grown. See, I went to the third grade.

Didn't go through it, just went to it and quit. See, we had to work on the farm and raise ten acres a tobacker a year. Only had trustees there; didn have no—like they got now—truant officers. Three trustees they come round. "What the matter? Your kids ain't in school." "Oh they got to work." That's all they had to say, they'd be gone. So I didn get any education. I just taken it up myself. And I just went up and got me a lot of papers, sit down, and went to writin and learnin. You know, a boy brought me a book a these ABC's. Writin ABC's. And I just set down and went to makin them, and got so I could make em pretty good, so I just went to linkin em up. I was there about three weeks and I was writin my letters back home. I just mostly read anythin, you know, to learn what I could. But that didn make any difference. I just wanted to learn somethin better. It didn make much difference. I always could spell purty good, you know.

I didn't have a bit a trouble with them guards. Never had one to say a ill word to me while I was up there. They was just as nice to you as they could be. And boy, you talk about eatin. They piled everythin on that. . . . Well, you got a cafeteria style. You went through, get anything you wanted. They want to see you eat. It's cheaper to feed a man than to pay doctor bills.

Escape? There wasn't nowhere I could have went. They'd identify me too easy, you know. No, all I had to do was just stay there and do my time. Oh, a lot of em did try. None of em got away much. One colored guy, I don't know if they ever found him or not. We went out to—they called it Tom's Run, you know, to plant a guy one day. He died there, you know. We went out to bury him. This colored guy bet on ball games and tradin and traffickin around lucky: he had a pocketful a money. We taken him with us. We never brought him back, though. And I never did hear a them catchin that guy. Course, you know, them's people are hard to identify.

Lord, I couldn number the times I been in jail. I had a ole box in my house one time. Ever time I get in jail they give you a spoon to eat with, see. You carry this spoon around in your pocket. Well, when I get out I'd stick it down my pocket and carry it home, and then I'd throw all them spoons in that little box. I went to countin em one day. They were thirty-some of em.

It wasn just for makin whiskey. Hit was just for bein drunk, 'n fightin first one thing 'n another, like 'at. Everythin but stealin. I never did steal nothin in my life. That's one thing I wouldn do. I didn think it was right. My daddy always taught me, the first thing, don't steal, and don't lie; and

I didn think it was right to steal anythin. I'd rether be caught for makin whiskey or anythin else rether 'n stealin.

Fore the next time when I got married, I went to cuttin timber with a good friend o' mine, Ben Baxter. I used to talk to his daughter all the time, Lucy her name. We got a dollar an hour for cuttin timber, workin as many hours as we wanted to, just a dollar an hour straight time. We didn't get no overtime, no time-and-a-half, just straight time, that's all you got. Dollar an hour. Oh, me and him on the yard would saw four hundred timbers a day.

There was a man called Lorry, had the best timber contract in Logan County. I was stayin on my porch one mornin, and Lorry come out, he said, "Ras," he said, "Did you ever saw any?" I said "Yeah, a little bit, Lorry." And he was just about to lose his contract, see, couldn't keep the timbers on the hill, about to lose his contract. People wouldn't work with him, you know, on account he was so hateful, you know—holler at men, tellin em, "Join that log up! Join that log up! Join that log up!" Never said a word to me all the time I was workin fer him. He knowed better than to say anything to me, I'd a walked off down the holler. I'd a throwed a hand spike at him or somethin.

I dated Lucy all the time before I come out here. I went over takin Ben's check one day, you know, and Ben jest as soon as he got his check he taken right up the holler to a coal pile there was up there to pick up coal, you know. He knowed about what was gonna happen—I guess I was kinda flirtin around with Lucy a little bit.

He said, "Well, Ras, I've got to go up the holler and see about some coal." Said, "I'll see you later on."

I said, "O.K.," and he just walked off, you know, fast. He didn't care what she done, you know. I'd been good to get him whiskey to drink, you know, every evenin when we come out I'd always have whiskey up the holler. So Lucy, she said, "I been tryin to get me a permanent," she said, "for a long time," she said, "and I ain't got the money."

"Well now," I said, "if you want to be my girlfriend and give me a date," I said, "I'll buy you a permanent."

She said, "All right."

And so we just kept datin each other, you know, for—oh, I don't know—she was nineteen years old, she's about I guess twenty-seven or twenty-eight now.

I finally went there and went to boardin. My brother Bud just got to drinkin so bad I couldn't stay with him. He'd just quar'l all night long, pinchin, ridin. I couldn't stay with him no longer. So I just taken off. He was on a big drunk, you know, and I'd go in he'd have about two pints sittin up on the mantel, you know. He said, "I can bring my whiskey right in the house and set down here and drink it where I please."

"You can't do that," I said.

I said, "I would think more of my mother than to bring it in here around her like that." She belonged to the church and didn't want us to have no whiskey there. I said, "I think more of my mother'n that." Course she wouldn't say nothin to us at all, you know. But of course you knowed she didn't like it. I never brought none in the house, you know.

And he said, "I thought you said you'd get a place to stay."

I said, "I can't."

I waited till he sobered up, you know, first—I wouldn't leave him. I was afraid he'd hurt her, you know. But I said, "I'm gonna take care of my mother, till you come to get straightened up a little bit, till you're capable of takin care of yourself, and then I'll go.

Finally he kinda sobered up. And I taken Lorry's truck and loaded my stuff and moved in with Ben.

And I got cut off, you know. Lorry was wantin to cut me off, you see. He wanted to put his nephew on, wanted to cut me off cause of his nephew. I was boss, you know. So that tickled me to death, cause I didn't want to work no how. No work for a dollar an hour. I was just doin it more so to help him out than I was myself. I could make more money makin whiskey than I could doin that. So on Monday mornin I went out and met Lorry.

"Well, Ras," he said, "just have to cut you off this mornin."

I said, "That's the best thing I've heard since you hired me." I said, "I'm certainly glad of it, Lorry, and," I said, "I want a cutoff slip, too."

He said, "Never wrote one in my life."

I said, "You or somebody gonna write me one, or," I said, "there's gonna be one hell raised, the kind you never heard talked about before."

He said, "I'll tell you what to do." Said, "You go up and tell Maxwell to figure up your time and write you a check and I'll be up at one o'clock to sign the check." Maxwell's the man in the office, see.

I said, "O.K. You take and write you up a cutoff slip. O.K." I went over, told Maxwell what he said, and Maxwell said, "I'm not writin no cutoff slip," said, "you don't need one," said, "Lorry ain't payin no compensation."

I said, "You'll write me one or somebody'll write me one or this'll be the bloodiest office you've ever heard of in your life since you've ever been in it. When I come in here at one o'clock to take the cutoff slip and my check," I said, "well, won't be nobody left in here but me and I'll be goin out pretty soon."

I'd a nine-millimeter Luger pistol, shot nine times, I had a six-inch barr'l on it. I stuck that Luger out a my belt and went over and he throwed me out my check already signed and the cutoff slip. I stood right across there, I said, "Well, that's good enough, Maxwell, thank you," and just turned around and walked out. And I went down to Logan. Lorry, he didn't think I could get anything, you know, so I just went down, went in front of a doctor and got on this general relief, I just got on this general relief, you know, get me a check every month.

Lorry said, "How'd Ras make out down to Logan?"

"Ah," Ben jest said, "He just signed up on his unemployed compensation."

Lorry said, "How'd in the world'd he do that?" Said, "I'm not payin in none," Said, "How'd-he-do-it?" Nobody wouldn't tell him nothin, you know. Nobody knowed nothin but me. They didn't know it was a DPA check, none of em didn't.

I'd give Ben a check every month, you know. I was makin whiskey and sellin it. I was sellin ten dollars a gallon. I was makin it good. She got to likin me, Miz Baxter did, you know, cause I was stayin there and good to pay my board and everything, and watched Lucy. Miz Baxter'd just go off anywhere, stay all night, she said, "Ras, will you take care of Lucy till I come back?" I'd say, "Yeah, I'll take care of her." So I went and asked Lucy one day, I said, "Would you like to sleep with me a while every night?"

She said, "God," said, "Mommy'd kill me."

I said, "No she won't." I said, "I'll fix that."

"Oh," she said, "you'll have to fix it, I ain't gonna have nothin to do with it."

I said, "I'll go in and talk to her." I said, "I'm not a-scared of her a bit," I said, "I'll go in and talk to her."

She said, "Well, you go see what she says. If it's all right with her," says, "you know it is with me."

Said, "O.K." I just got up and went in. I said, "Miz Baxter," I said, "I got a question I want to ask you."

"Why," she said, "come right in, Ras." Said, "I'm ready to listen to you." She just got her a chair and set down, and said, "Set down there." She thought I was gonna ask for Lucy to get married, I believe.

I said, "Now listen," I said, "which would you reether see, Lucy out here on the road, a-runnin around every night, or layin here in the bed with me?"

"Why," she said, "I'd reether see her lyin in the bed with you."

"Well," I said, "O.K. Now that's all I wanted to know." I said, "You won't get mad."

She said, "No," she said, "If you can keep her in," said, "keep her in."

I taken her in there every night, you know, and sleep with her a while. I said, "Well, you better go get into bed with your mommy now, she's liable to get mad." And into bed she'd go! And her daddy sleepin in the bed right beside of me, by golly! I swear that's the truth!

I had to quit that though. She got to runnin around tellin we were livin together up at the house.

Oh man, she was goodlookin, before she got too fleshy. Now she's picked up, you know. She's too fleshy now to look good, but she looked good when she was right slim, you know. Oh, me and her'd just go anywhere in the world we wanted to go and stayed as long as we wanted to stay. Miz Baxter and them wouldn't say a word, or Ben neither.

Oh, I've had lots a women. I don't know, must be the way I treat em, I guess. Just be good to em, you know. I never had no trouble with nobody. If a woman stays in her place I ain't goin a say nothin to her.

You can always tell a woman wants a date with you. I can easy. . . . The way they act. Oh man, West Virgina is the awfullest place for women you ever seed in your life! If you had a place for em to go and somethin for em to drink, man, they'd be there all the time. They'd get up there and git jealous and fight all over the place. I had eleven different women the first month I moved into that house, not includin the different times I went with em. And they come runnin. I never seed em before. "Hello, Ras. How you gettin along?" They'd hear other women sittin around beer gardens talkin about me, you know. I tell em, "Come on in."

I stayed with a man and his wife one night and they were racketin all night. I nary slept much, they racketin all night. Got up the next mornin, they take em a drink or two and they got into it. The woman, she taken off. She said, "Come on, Ras."

And this man said, "Go on with her, Ras, if you want to."

And I said, "No, heck, I'm goin home." Well, she taken down the road to where I lived, you know. I didn know which way she went, but I got down there.

Here come Walt McCoy come up the road in his car, you know. He said, "Ras, you got nary a drink this mornin?" Said, "I'm sick, I'm about to die."

I said, "Yeah, up Ridge Creek, Walt. If you'll run me up Ridge Creek I'll give you a drink."

He said, "Yeah," said, "I'll be glad to."

And here come a woman up the railroad tracks, holler at me just as I was fixin to get in the car. Walt says, "Ras," says, "there's a woman down the end a the ridge a waitin on you."

"Well," I said, "go back there, tell her I'll be there in a few minutes." And she went down to the end a the ridge and waited. See, this woman down there waitin on me, she'd come across the ridge and met this other one right there at the bridge. And she told her to go up there and see if she could git me to come down there. See, her old man was up at the house, you know. And I just got in this car and went up the road and turned around and come back. And I told Walt, I said, "Walt, pick them both up. Let's take em on to Ridge Creek."

He said, "All right." He stopped and picked them up. We went up there, up the road a piece, and just got out and got a half a gallon a whiskey, and set it down to them. Walt, he taken two, three drinks, 'n taken off. He said, "Ras, I might be back after while."

I said, "O.K., Walt, come back any time you want to."

Well, I was about half drunk myself anyhow an didn't care for nothin. I went over to the house and I pulled all these women's clothes off, right out in the bushes. Pulled one's clothes off and hung em down the creek in the bushes, hung the other one's up the creek—so I'd know which clothes to put on each one. Didn't leave a rag on em. I just taken my time on em, you know. I'd get on one a while, over on the other un a while.

After a while Walt come back up and git him another drink. He said, "Ras," he said, "I knowed you was ornery, but I didn't know you was that damned ornery!"

I said, "Well, ain't nothin to it. Come on over, get what you want."

He said, "No, I'm goin back to the house in a little bit." Said, "All I want's a drink of whiskey." Then he walked off down the road and got him a drink of whiskey. He went on back to the house and after while he brought his boy back, and told his boy what there was there. And said, "If you want to see two naked women," he said, "just go there and look at em."

Why, his boy, he ain't nearly growed! He said, "Jesus Christ! If I'd seed that, I couldn't eat a bite a dinner. Mommy's fixin a good dinner over at the house." Said, "I don't want to see that!" I take an laugh to hear Walt tell about it.

So Walt, he come back about three o'clock that evenin. "Well," I said, "Walt, run me over to the store. Let me get somethin for these women to eat." I said, "They be starvin to death." And I went on and got purty near five dollars' worth a meats, canned meats, and I got pop, bread, crackers—

I don't know what-all I did get, just a whole bunch a stuff, you know, and got a half a gallon a sweet milk. Taken it back up there. Got more than they ever eat, you know. They carried some of it down to the holler the next mornin when they come out. And I got up the next mornin at nine o'clock, I put them women's clothes back on em and drove em out a the holler. I say it went all that day and all night till about nine o'clock the next day.

I've had as high as four a them up there at a time. The law livin a short ways from me, and he never said a word. Got away with everything, cause he was sorta kin to my wife—you know, that first wife I married—and he wouldn't bother me a-tall. He said, "Ras, why I know every night you gonna make whiskey. I see you goin up the track here with a poke in your arms." Says, "I know what you got in it." He said, "Now, be careful and don't run out here when the other law's out here." He said, "Some of em might arrest you." The other law come down and see him ever once in a while, you know.

Yeah, I had as high as four of em up there at a time. That's what made em jealous, you know. They'd git mad and fight all over the place. Turned the table over I don't know how many times, broke dishes. Oh boy, I had some of the awfullest times you ever seed.

Next time when I got married, I was about fifty-seven or fifty-eight, somethin like that. I married a girl, she was so young that I had to get her dad and mother to sign the papers fore I got married. She wasn't twenty-one years old.

Me and her great-aunt set down and talked for hours at a time, you know, before me and her got married. And I asked her what she was gettin married fer. Did she want her a home or was she marryin just to get away from there? And she said, No, she wanted her a home, see. And I told her that was all right, then. That's why I married her, see.

Stayed married less 'n a year. Was married August the third and she left on—next June, I believe the twenty-second. Less than a year she stayed with me, down at Big Creek.

Everybody down there, nobody knowed what made her go. I didn't either. Never had a word or nothin. We was gettin along just as good as two babies could, you know, as babies. And she went out and tole everybody, all the people round us—she said, "I've lived in the best home I've ever had in my life, I've had more to eat since I got with Ras." And her people come in here from Chicogger, see, out there on a visit. And they came along as they was going up the river, see. They come in, you know, and want some coffee. Well, she made em coffee and gave em all coffee and asked if they wanted somethin to eat. Said, "We got plenty to eat." They said, Nah, they wasn't hungry, just wanted a cup a coffee and they was goin on, see. Well, they all drank a cup a coffee and went on.

And it was about a week later me an her went up to the store. I just had got my check that mornin.

Well, we got back down purty near to the house, why she seed the car a-sittin there. "Oh," she says, "there's my people." She run ahead a me and run down to the car, see.

Well, I was takin my time. Walked on down, spoke to em, asked em how they was gettin along. They said, "Just fine." Said, "How're you?"

I said, "O.K."

One a thc women—there were two a them—they got out a the car and went in the house with Clara, talkin to her, you know. This man, I asked him, I said, "Come on in, buddy." He never said anything. I said, "Come on in, make yourself at home."

He said, "I'll just sit here, see."

I said, "Well, O.K.," and I walked on in. I said, "Clara," I said, "make em all a cup of coffee, maybe they want a cup a coffee."

She said, "Yeah." She went in, you know. She said, "Come to think about it, we didn't get no cream." And neither one of us didn't drink no cream in our coffee, you know.

I said, "Well, I'll step right down to the store"—wasn't what you'd call a half a block from here, you know—"I'll step down to the store and get some cream."

She said, "O.K."

Didn't think nothin about it, you know. I got down there and walked right around the corner of the store, you know, and knocked on the woman's door, aimin to pay my rent, see. Well, she was gone out somewhere. I just went back around, told the lady how many cans of cream I wanted. I throwed her down her money, an she gimme the change back, an I just got out and walked up the street, you know.

I got about halfway home, just a short ways, you know, an I looked up an the car was gone. I said, Well, them people must a been in a hurry. I went up there an Clara was gone too, see.

I didn know what the heck was the trouble. We had a eight-room house, four rooms downstairs an four upstairs; an I said, Now, she's tryin a play a joke on me. She's just a very small woman, she could hide in a rathole, as the ole sayin is. She wouldn a weighed over than eighty pounds, I don't guess. Maybe she's hid upstairs somewhere. And I looked in every room, behind every door, everyplace, went upstairs and looked all around. Nobody there. Ah, I said, they just went out for a drive somewhere. Maybe they'd be back in a few minutes. I sit there and waited and waited and waited all day; stayed there that night; and nobody come back.

We'd been there now about ever since March; and this was in June. We'd been there that long. I never drunk a bottle a beer nor another drink a whiskey. Workin in my garden, growin tobacco on the hill, didn't want nothin to drink, see. Every once in a while she'd say, "Honey, when you gonna get you somethin to drink? Whyn't you get you somethin to drink?" I said, "I don't want nothin to drink." And she wouldn't drink a drop, you know.

Well, I wait up till, oh, about nine o'clock the next mornin, and I said, I'll go let somebody know somethin about this. Cause somebody might a take that girl off an killed her, somethin or other; maybe heaved her in the river, and accused me of it. An I went down the street to a place where me and her'd been goin all the time.

This woman, Sylvie, she was awful friendly. She said, "Lordy mercy, Ras, where's Clara at?" That's the first thing she thought of. Says, "This is the first time I ever seed you out you haven't had Clara with you." She follered me everywhere I went, you know.

"Why," I said, "that's what I'd like to know." I said, "She's gone."

"Whaaat?" she said. "Are you kiddin?"

I said, "No, I'm not either." I said, "She left yesterday somewhere, Sylvie."

Said, "Where in the world'd she go to?"

I said, "Lord only knows, Sylvie. I don't know." I said, "Her people come along in the car." I said, "I come down the store right here to get a can a cream, and she left while I was gone."

"Ah," she said, "you're kiddin me." Said, "Way she was lovin on you? What she thought a you?" Said, "You mean to tell me she left?"

I said, "I ain't saw her since yesterday, about around eleven o'clock."

That girl had more clothes than all a us could carry when she left there. That's why hit worried me why she left, you know, for a while. It worried me now. I didn't know why she left or what happened, whether they just stole her in the car an made her go or what. That's what I had in my mind they done. Just grabbed her and throwed her in there and taken off. Cause she didn take no clothes but just two or three old uns. Just grabbed em up and throwed em in the car and taken off. And had on a new pair a slippers when she left.

I didn know where the heck she went to. Oh, I don't know how long it was before I knowed where she went to. She went out there to Chicogger, you know. She stayed with her people one night, part a one night, whatever time they got into Chicogger here. They wanted her to come out here and baby-sit for em, y'see, while they worked. Well, one of em was her aint see, and her aint had to work the next day and they got in here like to-night, you know, and her aint goes out to work the next day and her uncle by marriage he went out too, see, to work. Well, he gets in an hour earlier than his wife does, see. And he tried to go with Clara, soon as he got in you know. And so when her aint come in she told her aint about it and and she taken off. She wound up in Florida and stayed out there for I don't know how long, a long time fore she come back to West Virginia. She wrote me a letter one time, she's in Tampa, Florida, told me she was gonna have a baby. Well, I jest set down and give her a quick answer, you know, and told her when the baby was born, send it to me C.O.D. I'd pay the postage on it. Why no, no, she didn't have no baby, but she wrote and tole me that, you know, thought she'd scare me up or somethin or other. I'd write an tell her to come back, I guess, but I just wrote back and told her when the baby is born, send it to me C.O.D. and I'd pay the postage on it. That's about as good a one as I knowed to tell her.

Then she come back, then, about in October I believe it was. Yeah, October. I was diggin potaters. Oh, I had a big room, it's larger than this, you know. Potaters about piled up like that, you know. About six inches deep, all over the room, everywhere. She walked in, looked at em, and said, "Oh, them's big potaters." Said, "Lordy mercy," she said, "what you goin a do with them?"

"I don't know. Give em away, I guess." Bout all you could do with em out there, you know.

Well, I asked her, I said, "Now, I want a know why you left."

She said, "I don't know."

I said, "You have enough to eat while you stayed here?"

"Lord, yes!"

I said, "Was drinkin cause of it?"

She said, "Well, Lord knows," said, "you wouldn't drink a drop of it."

"Well," I said, "I want to know the cause for it."

She said, "I just take a notion to leave." That's all the explanation she give me. Said, "Just take a notion to leave."

"All right," I said, "would you like to come back?"

Said, "Yeah."

I said, "Uh-uh, nooo, you can go back stay with the people where you've been. You can't stay here." I said, "That's cut and dried already." I said,

"You left for nothin, now you can stay for nothin. You ain't stayin with me no more." I wouldn't *let* her come back. I told her, I said, "No, you can't come back to me no more."

She stayed with me one night and got two big suitcases full of clothes and taken off again. And I haven't saw her since. She lives right close to here now, but I didn't tell nobody about 't, see. I don't want her to know I'm out here, see. I didn know where she's at till I came here, but I found out where she's at. I know where she's at now for bout six months. I won't go out to see her or nothin.

"HE DESERVES MORE THAN THAT"

Charlotte Gibson* knew both Ras and Clara, and was willing to cast her angle of light on the matter:

"I don't know Ras all that good, but I feel sorry for him because he just has this one arm, and I don't want to see him or no one else done dirty. She's run off so many times with other men that I don't think she's the right woman for him, I think he's better off without her. I'm not sayin that because she's with Harold's brother, my husband's older brother, but he thinks a lot of her and he's been hurt by other women too. She just keeps runnin off with other men—other times.

"I was talking to her about Ras, the other day, and Jim and Harold were in here and me and her went in the kitchen and she said all he did when she were with him was drink. And I told her I got real acquainted with Ras; I liked him and I said he's real nice and I said he's friendly and she said, "You just don't know him" and she made all kinds a statements about him. She said he were mean to her and she got pregnant and he beat her up and caused her to lose her baby. But Ras says it wasn't true. I knew Ras drunk a lot but otherwise I like him. Ras doesn't seem like that kind of person to me.

"And the reason I think it wasn't true's because she goes around now wearing maternity clothes and making out like she's pregnant and she's going to have a baby and she's never that way. She like kids a lot. I think she's silly myself in a way because it takes somebody pretty silly to carry on like that. She's got a real good life if she'd just appreciate it; Harold's brother really likes her, I mean he buys her all kinds of things and he's really good to her. So I guess in one way she's a little bit cracked in the head, she don't really understand these things. But she would never be

*See p. 239.

nobody that Ras could trust anyway. *And I think he deserves more than that, I really do.*"

RAS BRYANT

When Clara was stayin with me I was farmin then. Oh yeah, I really love to farm. I like to go out in the garden and get me a mess a dry stuff, you know, like beans, potatoes, tomatoes, peppers, and stuff. And just cut it all up and have her make me a big pot of vegetable soup now. Go get some kind a meat to go with it. Now you talk about eatin, that's eatin when you get it like that.

I was drawin a check then to live on, see. I drawed a check ever since—from fifty-two up to about sixty-one. Till they cut me off. Run out a funds. See, 'twasn't a DPA check. It was general relief. It was made up for people like me that didn't have any children, you know, the people that couldn't make out without some help. And that's what they claimed, they run out a funds. But they didn't. They had plenty a funds. But they elected another sheriff there, you see, a man by the name of Okie Justice. And the county had to pay just a small percentage of this money—a very small percentage of it. Well then, because the sheriff he didn't want to pay it, see, wouldn't pay it, they cut all a us off who were on general relief. And he was in the hospital

sick and wrote a check from the taxpayers' money, for to get gas with for this car, that he was supposed to be drivin around, him in the hospital. They got him there, but they didn't do nothin with him, unless made him pay the money back. That's all they done. Well, if it'd been me or you, why the ink wouldn't a got dried on the check until they had us in jail.

It was about three months now, after I lost this check, you see, I went to sellin whiskey. Sold whiskey for about three months, and they caught me and put me in jail. And I stayed sixty days in jail. Had to leave my house, couldn't pay the rent. Didn't have no money to pay it on. When I come out, why, the woman wanted me to go back and stay at the house, and I wouldn't go back. She come up and talked to me three or four times, and wanted me to come back and stay there all the time. "If you ain't got the money to pay no rent," she said, "that's all right. You can stay there anyhow."

I said, "Nooo, ma'am. I don't wanna do that."

I still owed her forty dollars rent. I was only payin ten dollars a month for an eight-room house. That's how hard times was back there. Now, if you get one like that here, why, Jesus Christ, cost you five hundred dollars a month. It didn't look so good on the outside but on the inside it was sheet rock and everythin. Good on the inside. Only paid three dollars up in gas bills, in January. Had to pay my own gas and electric, you know. Wasn't no water in the house. Had to get the water out of a dug well, see.

Well, then I did first one and then another. Just went around to work for my board. First one and another, hoein corn, farmin, potaters—whatever they had to do, I had to help with it, see. Worked for my cousin Bill, the preacher, for a while. Just for my board. You got to get out in the summertime; you got to hoe corn; you got to plant the beans and pick beans. You work from daylight to dark, all two months, see. Just for your board. And I don't like to do that, see. Too hard on you. It don't make so much difference, you gettin somethin out of it, you know. Overworkin never killed nobody—well, there was only one man ever killed by too much work that was John Henry. But you don't wanna work for nothin.

Oh, times was mighty hard out there. You know, West Virginia was counted the most disaster area of any state yet. They called it that. And that wasn't even countin the floods. I had a lot of big stuff in the flood myself, lost it. That was back bout two or three years before I come out here. I don't remember just what year it happened in. Was the biggest flood they'd had out there in West Virginia, you know. So I went over to the Red Cross. I would go in, you know, and tell em that I needed so much stuff, you know. Well, they sent me over here to a furniture store and have me make off my list there at the furniture store see, what-all I needed, and then I'd never get a dime's worth. But they'd fill out these papers, and I had to sign em, see, and they'd fill out these papers and send em in and get this money. Then them and this furniture store would split it, see. Oh, some few people got a little bit of stuff, but they run around and told the people after they made up the big list, you know, they put people up and down the roads, you know, a-tellin people, "Don't get nothin on it, just about what your bound to have to have, just buy just as little bit as you can, because its a-comin another flood bigger than that one, just in a few days." Now how in the world did they know that? And they didn't come another one. No, they don't give you no money. They give out clothes for some people, some couldn't get none.

By golly, they're cheatin us. I don't know what they do with it but they keep it. The Salvation Army does the same thing. They don't give away no money. No nothin. What they do now, on Christmas, they make a big to-do over Christmas out there, they'll give away about maybe a hundred baskets of stuff, you know, bushel baskets, just different stuff in it. And they'll give you a chicken or a duck or somethin like 'at, you know, to each one a the baskets. 'Cordin to how many members you got in your family how much they put in that basket. They'll give you a few old potatoes about that big, and a few little apples, just small ones, you know, maybe three of four of em, and they'll give you one orange, and they give you, you know, a little bit of stuff, not much. But that is what people give them to give the poor people, see. They don't spend no money for em. The big firms give it to them to give to the people for Christmas, you know, whatever they get they give it out, you know. Never did get nothin. Go back in, all gone. Said they had to help the people had children you know. Well, some of em they did and some of em they didn't. There was some people didn't have a thing nor couldn't get nothin for Christmas. And what they'd give em, if it was a big family of em it wouldn't be enough for their dinner. They'd just give em one chicken. Why, you take it where there's a big family and them hard up, why you know they'd eat more'n one chicken. Maybe eight or ten of them in the family, they'd give em one chicken. That's all they got. And a little bit of other stuff, you know, little candy, and they give you a little hard candy, Christmas candy, you know, this real hard candy. Oh, you could buy it all for a couple or three dollars, what they give you. Then they go out and beg all kinds a canned stuff all year around, you know, and I've went there and tried to get some canned stuff off of em. "Oh, we ain't got nothin now, we ain't got nothin now." They'll have plenty of it stacked back there but they won't hardly give ye any of it at all unless it's Christmas time. Why I woundn't bury em in my back-yard. If I could I'd kick em out fore they kicked in.

Back then time of the flood, my cousin was takin care of the Red Cross at one place and I went up and told him, I said, "Well, I need some a them clothes."

He said, "Well," he said, "you're not livin in the house now, are you, Ras?"

I said, "No." I done lost my house, you see, but I had my furniture a-stored in there, and a lot of it had got destroyed in the flood, you know, and I told him all about that.

He said, "Well, you wasn't livin in the house, you can't get nothin." Him my first cousin. All he had to done was go in and give me some of that stuff. See, he was a-managin the thing over, see. All he had to done was go in there and tole em t'give me some clothes, that's all he had to done. He wouldn't do it, you know. It was my Uncle Ol's boy. He never was worth anything. It's my first cousin, see. He's a preacher, you know. Preaches for the money, of course. Gets about three hundred dollars and some a month, and his wife teaches school and he ain't got no kids, you see. They're just layin that money back.

My daddy and them belonged to the United Baptist Church. My dad and mother did. I never belonged to a church in my life. I just never did get started on it, I don't reckon. I had too much other stuff about. I had to raise my family, you know, makin moonshine whiskey. I didn't have time to go to church I was makin whiskey. Seven days and seven nights I didn' have my shoes on.

Some of them preachers is all right, I guess, and some of em ain't. Once there was this preacher come to town and he seed this woman and must a taken a likin to her, because he said, "Woman, you must leave your natural husband and your children and come with me. I have spoken to the Lord and he told me you and me must go together to bring the word of the Lord to the people." Well, she believed him and her husband found her packin to go, you know, and he asked her why and she said, "Preacher come today and said the Lord had spoken to him and told him I must leave you and the children and go with him to preach the word of God."

"Well, O.K.," he said, "I'll go say good-bye to him, maybe he'll give me a blessing." When he got to the preacher he said, "Preacher, I heard you spoke to the Lord and he told you to take my wife with you to preach the word of the Lord."

The preacher said, "Yes, that's right."

And the man said, "Well, I spoke to the Lord after you did and he told me to beat the shit out of you." And there wasn't no prayer meetin that night.

We don't need no preachers around JOIN. They'll charge you fifteen dollars a night.

They got a program out there now in West Virginia goin that the President started—Kennedy, he started this. I heard a him bein in West Virginia, but I never seen him. Put em out on the roads and work em for a dollar an hour, see. And how he got by with workin these men for a dollar an hour, he called it a pauper fund, you see. You go to work for a dollar an hour and then get called a pauper. That is not right. I don't think for a man to go out and work for his money and then call im a pauper over it. They get out there and work on em roads only so many hours a month accordin to the family you got. That ain't no good.

Set this up fore he got killed—Kennedy, you know. I was settin up on the mountain, you know. Little bit up, little mountain. You had to climb just a short ways, wasn't far up there. I didn't have my radio turned on. I got a good radio out there yet, see. I hadn't turned it on. This man comes up and says, "You hear about the President gettin shot?"

I said, "No," I said, "what's wrong with that?"

He said, "Well, I don't know." Said, "It looks pretty bad."

I said, "I ain't heard nothin about it." He just turned around and walked off. He didn't say nothin more about it much. And I didn't think too much of it myself, you know. I didn't give it no thought. . . .

I'll tell you, if I was a president of the United States, I'd rather help the pore people. I wouldn't send my money to these foreign countries and let people here starve to death. They ought a do somethin for the old people, the same way they's bringin them furrners over here. Every month they bring about seventy-five a month over here. And bring them cars over here and build them big mansions to live in, modern house, bathroom right in the house. They don't have to step out for nothin. Take em hunkies and put em in big hotels and feed em up until they can get these apartments ready for em, you know. Get these houses all ready for them, and then they turn around and give em the best jobs that they are in the United States, the biggest-paying jobs. There are a lot of pore people all over the world, but listen—let them take care of their poor people, we'll take care of ours. And there wouldn't be so damn many poor people if it weren't for them. Listen, can you find an American store in town? There are very few. You'll find American restaurants but you won't find an American worker in that restaurant. When you go to the head of it there's some big hunky owns it somewhere. You'll find maybe one American restaurant out of every dozen. There might be American people working in there but then when you come back to the head of it, it's all Jews and hunkies and things.

I'm not braggin on myself or nothin like that now, you don't get me wrong. But I've not been here these sixty-two years, and soon be sixty-three years, for nothin. I've learned a lot since I been here, boy. If I had my way about it, if I was president of the United States and had the authority to do it, you know what I would do? I would take every furrner man down to the edge of the water. I'd ask em, "Do you want to take a ship or do you want to swim over?" I believe in takin care a my own people. And then if I had any left, well, they might have some of it.

I have often said, ever since they started sendin that money over to furren countries, that it'd be shot back at them some day in time. Now you see it is too. They're getting part of it right now. What they did with this money when they sent it over there, instead of livin on it—they're not as hard up as they claim they are, see—they take that money and work it up in war materials. Exactly what they do with it. Now when the war breaks out, shore we get the bullets back. Where we sent the money over there from.

That's exactly what's goin on. President Roosevelt and the ole Kaiser met out on the water, you know. Had conference, about four hours at a time. One said, "Oh, well, if I win I'll make you corporal of the war"—that's what they called it over there, you know—"over my nation." The other one said, "If I win, I'll give you some kind of big shot over here." That's the way it went.

I don't believe in that damn junk. And look what it is a-costin the United States today to do this work, to put these bullets out and all these men they've got over there. You know they got to pay their men who fight in Vietnam. Now do you believe in that? I'm a hundred percent agin it. Like them people over there, they never done nothin to me. Do I want to go over there and fight em when they never done nothin to me? Jesus Christ almighty, let them people alone over there and keep your nose out of their business. Takin pictures of every holler—the government knows every holler over there now. Run all over these people, well that's what makes em so damn mad, see. Have they come over here and done the United States thataway? Oh by God if they did you know what would happen. Why they'd get shot down every day. Shooot! Why don't they take that money and instead of sendin it over there and puttin it out like that and kill them people which you never seen before and never heard tell of before, why don't they put it back out here and feed the pore people on that?

Oh, it's all a money racket, to tell you the truth about it. You ever seen a rich man in the army? Oh shore, once in a while they take one. But it's a rich man's war, and the pore people fight it. It's a pore man's fight and a big man's money. That's all there is to it.

And they are spendin millions of dollars, and look what they have done—send a rocket to the moon. If the Lord intended for us to play with that moon, he'd a put it down here close on earth where they could a got to it. Jesus Christ, oh God, I would hate to have to sit down and figure out how much money is bein spent to send that rocket to the moon. Millions of dollars. They say the President is crazier'n hell and the man is crazier'n hell that rides them up there a-tryin to get to the moon! I say no, the man that's tryin to get to the moon is not crazier'n hell. You let them give me what they are givin the rest of these guys, damn if I won't take a chance on tryin to get there. When I come back I won't have to worry. If I don't hit the ground I don't have nothin to worry about nohow. But if I hit the ground, by God I'll have enough to live on the rest of my life. Man there's billions of dollars for people who try to fly a rocket to the moon, you know. I don't mean millions, there are *billions*. Jesus Christ, I could get up that far if they would give me what they are givin these other guys that try to go there. The way it is, what have I got? Nothin.

RETURN TO WEST VIRGINIA, OCTOBER, 1965—I

Lundale, West Virginia, is the fifth or sixth mining camp alongside the narrow mountain road that winds out of the town called Man. Cramped between the road and the railroad tracks are two rows of old gray wooden houses, on either side of a dirt track running the length of the camp; perhaps thirty houses in all. A sign over the tracks names the camp Lundale.

Rising from the other side of the tracks is Lundale's mountain, blotched with smoldering heaps of slate; and high up on it Lundale mine. From the mine a great metal chute conducts the coal down to the black funnel at the bottom. Sixty or eighty tons are loaded into each car, and then, every few minutes, the train screeches forward until the next car is in position. There are three shifts a day. Thirty-one cars are loaded for each shift. On each car is painted: "C & O for Progress."

At this late hour, Carolina, Ras's younger sister, would ordinarily be in bed. But she hasn't seen Ras since Mommy died, two years ago, and she will stay up until Ras decides to turn in. She talks slowly, and in the same

tone, of her arthritis and doctors and social security and her dead husband and her other dead, and how Ras smuggled money out of the penitentiary in a picture frame. Her retarded forty-four-year-old son O. C. shows off his collection of gospel records—"Satan is Real," "I Shall Not Be Moved," all bought at the commissary. He has just been cut off from the mine and is drawing unemployment compensation. He curses John L. Lewis for his huge salary—"as rich as Vanderbilt"—and likens him to an operator. Mostly he talks of the quantity of his faith, God's cure for the pain of his polio. Ras sits at the other end of the well-worn couch, chewing, scratching his head, chatting about Chicago, about JOIN, and how much it helps the poor people, and reminiscing a little himself. The dialogue, like so many in West Virginia, is more often an alternation of monologues than a two-way conversation.

Carolina asks, "Things are better out there in Chicago, ain't they?"

Ras says, "Shore they is."

"Ain't nothin down in these hollers. Nothin for me and O. C.—hit's only that we done bought that house." She bought it from the company; the former home of the straw boss, it is the only one in the camp with indoor plumbing.

Now there is a lull, and the radio is switched on. The news is of President Johnson's recovery from his operation.

Carolina shifts her bulk. "All you hear about is Johnson. He takes a walk and you hear about it."

"Johnson?" Ras spits into the can at his feet. "Oughta cut his head off—"

"Cut his head off?" she asks, not surprised.

"Yep, cut his head off. Sendin boys out there to get killed. . . . He's no better 'n any of em, you know. Don't do nothin for em. . . ."

"Does it all for the coloreds. . . ."

"Does it for the hunks. Brings these hunks over. They come over here and he puts em in big fancy houses. . . ."

"Yep," Carolina affirms. "Coloreds and furrners."

Ras turns toward her, earnest. "You know, Carolina, we picketed the Vice-President Humphrey last summer. Up there in Madison, Indiana—no, Wisconsin, it was, Madison, Wisconsin. Why, they was at least a hundred of us went up there, signs an everythin. Carolina, let me tell you, we told him to stop this sendin them boys over. . . . Oh, hit was a sight. They was laws and plainclothes and FBI's everywhere, you couldn hardly see the man they was so many of em."

"Well."

"Yeah. Next January we'll be a-goin to Washington, D.C. And we'll picket that Johnson, too. If he needs it we'll picket him too."

RETURN TO WEST VIRGINIA, OCTOBER, 1965—II

We drive Carolina to visit her older sister Pearl. Living less than forty miles apart, they haven't seen each other in four years, neither having access to a car, neither within miles of a bus route. Pearl lives with her deaf-dumb son on twenty-six acres in a holler four dirt-road miles from Branchland. With $155 a month in social security between them they "get by," though not so well as they might have had she not signed away the subsurface rights to her land: three natural gas pumps bring her neither the unexpected royalties nor the promised free gas. She is proud to show her basement, lined floor to ceiling with food she has canned, enough to live on for more than a year: "I canned all these since Rob died," referring to her late husband, who had gone looking for work in Detroit not long before he died. She measures all her time by family death, not morbidly, only availing herself of the most convenient calendar: "Ras, was it when Mommy died that you were here, or when we buried Becky?"

At seventy-two she is all face and hands and wrinkles, but she stands straight, and when she has work to do she moves with the grace earned only by practice, and leaves images of frailty clambering behind. Those oversized hands form biscuits, milk the cow, plant turnips, and pump water with equal agility, as now they clasp the sister who weighs nearly twice as much. We leave the sisters to spend the night together.

They talk all night, of family, doctors, death, dependent sons, sharing a goose-feather bed. We return in the morning with Ras and his preacher cousin Bill to find breakfast of fried eggs, gravy, fried potatoes, fried apples, biscuits; fatback, pork ribs, vegetables—these canned, from the basement; coffee and milk; a long morning's temptation for foreigners unused to the custom of placing all the day's food on the breakfast table. But Pearl's eyes glow, her hospitality is relentless: "Help y'self, help y'self!"

At last she can no longer put off her chores, Ras perhaps tires of reminiscences, the visitors "have to go"; we prepare to drive Carolina back. Out on the porch, the last good-byes. But Pearl begins crying: "I might never see Ras alive again. Let's all go in and pray." All walk back into the living room, the two of us following Ras to the couch while the others kneel on the floor. Loudly and independently they chant in their singsongs, each gasping for breath and inspiration at the end of each phrase, rocking, waving their arms. At some unheard signal Bill says Amen, the sweet ca-

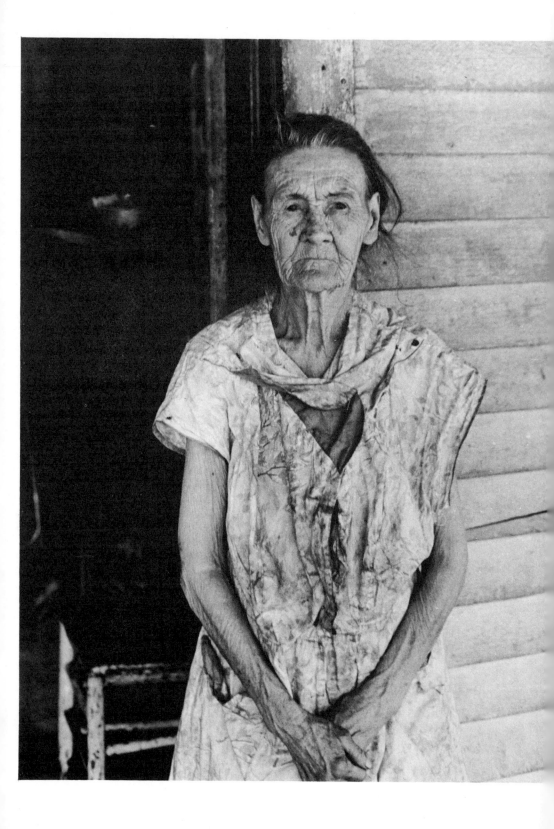

cophony subsides, and he walks around the room, shakes everyone's hand, blessing each of us, and the deaf mute rises from the Sears catalog he'd been skimming and prays in an unintelligible monotone, pointing to the ceiling, then the floor, then to the family around him, inspired in turn by his inspiration. When he finishes, Pearl stands up to weep her pleas to "Jesus' tender mercies," that He care for her son when she is gone, that she see Carolina again in the next world if not in this one. Then Bill jumps up—in what Pearl has called "one of his spells"—clapping his hands, whooping, "Help us, Jesus," "Help us, Jesus," "Lord we have worked for you" . . . storming around the room, shaking the house, until he sings "The Hand of the Lord," and now shaking, now grinning, nodding his head, he shakes each hand again. Again the room only sounds with the loud tick of an ancient clock. Pearl wipes her tears.

Through it all Ras sits, a twinkle-eyed spectator with a small but discernible smile, spitting tobacco juice into a can placed strategically by the couch; not scornful, even enjoying the revival, but certainly detached. Do the others find him an impossible cynic? A hardhearted prodigal sinner? Perhaps, after all, they mark it as a minor miracle that he sat through the ceremony at all. At the end, Pearl confides, "Used to be, he didn't care for anythin, but he's a whole lot better now than he used to be."

Now John tells anybody off, you know, when he gets pissed off. He'll tell the biggest and to the least'n, now, he doesn't care, John doesn't.
—Ras Bryant

Rennie asked me how I learned to speak like that—you know, me a man with no education. Well, I told him, it's from experience. Every time I walk down the street and see these streetlights they spent money on fixin, and these rundown traps of buildings, and the beer joints—I'm gonna tell it straight—and I think about where our tax money is goin, I get mad. . . . I will say —and I'll say it again when I'm sober—I will say that all the veterans, all that was GI's, enlisted men and those that was drafted, all of us that's been in wars should rebel. I been eleven years in the service, World War II and Korea, and where did it get me to fight for this fuckin country?
—John Dawson

John Dawson, 40

At first glance he folds neatly into your literary image of the poor white trash, vintage Erskine Caldwell: red neck, hard lines in his thin face, long calloused hands. He often preaches his politics, a younger John Carradine playing Preacher Casey in The Grapes of Wrath. When he makes a telling point, which is often, his brow furrows, he grins demoniacally and pierces you with his eyes. His opinions are fierce, he is easily insulted. When he is sullen he still dominates the room.

Then learn to know him better and the pattern of his ferocity seems to emerge. He is outraged but also pensive, pensive more than moody, though his moods seem blank until they are penetrated. He enjoys relaxing with 500 Rummy or Monopoly, where he is skillful yet not aggressive. His rage focuses on figures of authority, but in the face of such authority he is at first servile. Authority has a chance to respond to his humble petition. When authority puts him off, he shoots his questions and denunciations like weapons, his eyes burning. But it is still not plain "what makes him tick": he is not the packaged Populist for which the political organizer miscasts him. Perhaps he could have been a leader of his people in some other time. He has developed a keen sense of who They are who rule unjustly, but it is not constant, for he excepts certain big shots who in real and imagined ways stand between him and the worst excesses of authority, and whom he might use. His occasional exaggerations of his dialogues with power also serve another purpose, to reveal the seriousness of his commitment to drastic political change. For a year and a half that commitment could not be doubted. Despite his periodic departures, he did work with JOIN as consistently as anyone in the neighborhood, and more than most. If his limits are not as plain as his strengths in this account, we cannot pretend to document them any more clearly.

Over a year of friendship and coworking and more than twenty-five hours of formal interviewing, he opens some of the private storerooms of his past, though some stay locked; he says almost nothing about the sons by his first marriage. A hush comes into his voice, he admits to agony and indecision. It is that thick-tongued liquid hush, like the static from an imperfect hi-fi speaker, which we have come to associate with Lyndon Johnson in a mock-doleful mood ("Your President calls on you to pray . . ."). Yet when John Dawson says that combat is "somethin I don't do much talkin about," he is sincere. He is not "out of character" with his violence; violence is only one state of his character.

Perhaps it is his regular state, the ground being from which he moves, to which he returns. But the objects of his violence are not as sharply defined as his political targets. When one of the four kids bothers another one, he urges the loser to "smack im." One night we heard him scream at Clarence (three), "Go to bed! I'll kill you!" Clarence promptly tore up a toy. When Lila (five) defended him, John roared, "You're a damn liar," and called him and J.T. (two) "you bastards." But when Lila hit Clarence, Clarence became "baby." He is often sorry afterward: "That place tires me out."

Etta is John's wife, that is the first and the last thing about her. Her quietude is not tranquility, but boredom and submission. In the rhythm of their frequent quarrels, a bout of screaming is often settled in front of the TV. It was an old-fashioned radio-TV-phonograph console, carried from apartment to apartment until money ran out. Lila told us her mommy cried when it had to be sold. When John is feeling good he helps with the cooking, but the family is largely an abstraction—no refuge in a time of declining fortune. But this is too quick a judgment. His ambivalences speak for themselves.

John Dawson's inflated estimates of money are certainly idiosyncratic. As Ras says, "You know John. If he's got one of somethin he's got ten thousand of it." Like his wish-fulfilling tales of personal prowess this is more than a personal fetish. For someone who has never seen much money, a hundred dollars may seem the same as a thousand. While throughout the narrative he may be trying to underscore the injustice of his present plights by manufacturing a height from which he has fallen, his exaggerations also stand for a blind distance from the world of really big money, a distance shared by men whose guesses are less garish than John Dawson's. He inflates not only some of his own past income but, at times, the wealth of the wealthier. Perhaps he was trying to impress; in most cases we doubt his motives were so bald. Anyway, we have not edited his figures down to what we would imagine more reasonable. The reader may judge for himself when the figures, like certain incidents, are inflated, for which reasons and with which meanings.

My mother died when I was nine days old. And at that time we were livin at Rockwell, Alabama, and so we moved and went from there, we went to Tennessee. They carried me to Etowah, Tennessee, when I was thirteen days old, and all the kid sisters with me. And we lived there a year or so. Daddy, he worked there in the rock works there in Etowah for a long time. We lived with my granddaddy and them then. Well, then the rock works shut down, and so he went back down to Gadsden and went to work and we stayed with my granddaddy and grandmother. That was my mother's parents.

My granddaddy was a section foreman with the L&N railroad. Well, they transferred him to Cartersville in Georgia there, right out of Rome, and we moved over there between Rome and Cartersville, over to what's called Aragon, Georgia: a little small post office, a little small place of a town. Course back then, when I was comin up there, Rome was only about eleven thousand people. Well they kept buildin, buildin, buildin and people kept quittin the farm and comin to town. They kept buildin mills in there and more industry. People wants to work in town. I can remember when they was places there that you couldn't see a house.

And granddaddy bought the farm out there, and my grandfather and grandmother raised us children besides their six. My daddy, he came up and lived with us a couple of years. Course, my daddy always helped. Don't get me wrong, my daddy helped raise us kids, he didn't leave us out. But then he married this woman, and I don't know what was wrong with Fay, I never could understand anyway. She had the attitude that the stepchildren was just some dog or somethin or 'nother, and I never did have that attitude about nobody myself. And that's where me and my father had our fallin-out all along. I don't know what caused him to remarry. She was just selfish, and that was just it. He just didn't see it that way and he was supposed to be a minister, and I just couldn't see it his way. Yeah, he was a minister, Holiness, he was a Holiness minister.

While I was growin up he came around maybe oncet a year or twicet a year; that was all the time I ever saw him. He never done anything for us. And you never did know when he was comin or when he was goin to do nothin, or what. And so I didn't have no desire to go back and live with him. And in fact after my three sisters went back to live with him and Stepmother, my granddaddy and myself and some of my uncles, we had to support the kids. Well, I raised my sisters up till they married off. For hell, he wasn't makin money to do it, and then what he did, my stepmother was wantin big fine clothes and things. Well, he wasn't that type of person to have that kind of money and so he just couldn't afford what she wanted and have the children what they needed. They married off soon on account of it. They all married before they was eighteen.

Well, naturally I felt more for my grandmother and grandfather than I did my daddy, for they was the ones that had always bought my things, bought all my clothes and seen I had money and stuff like that, to go to shows and things like that. I was brought up on the farm, brought up the hard way. And I was just a poor boy, I always was, I always will be. And we lived on the farm, worked on the farm, and course back then the section foreman didn't make but ninety cents a day. Course ninety cents a day back then was a lot of money too, but it was still a hard way to bring up a bunch of kids, to have to feed em all. But he done very well for us, for a big family. He had six of his own and we were raised up with the kids. The grandchildren, in other words, were treated just like his children was. He kept me in paper, he kept me in pencils, he kept me in books, he kept me in colors or whatever I had to have. And we grew up the hard way, just a hard livin for us.

I was raised right, I'll guarantee you. I was raised up in a religious home. That's one thing my granddaddy and grandmother was. My granddaddy, he was from a religious home and they was no such a thing as drinkin around our house back then; they was no such a thing as doin wrong. For if I went to town of a night, I had a certain time at night to be in off the streets and I knew to come in, for if I didn't, he'd take my privileges away from me. He didn't whup me, didn't beat me, nothin like that, but he'd take my privileges away from me. Say I'd been a-goin to the show a couple of nights a week, he'd cut that off for a month. Well, you know, that hurt worse than if he'd a-taken a stick and whupped the devil out of me, actually. Oh, yes, he did whup me at times—when I disobeyed his orders, he'd whup me but he didn't believe in beatin me and that made a lot of difference. After I went in the service he passed away, but up until that time I had been takin care of him and my grandmother. Well, I see today where he was right. That's the way I'm tryin to raise my children today.

When I finished up the eighth grade I left school and I went to work in this textile plant. I would've been fifteen in March, and I went to work in January, sweepin this big textile plant. My granddaddy got disabled to work, and, well, all his children at this time had married off. Well, I felt this way about it myself: he has supported us, me and my sisters, and I felt like it was my obligation to return at least part of it to him and my grandmother. Which I did, and I'm not sorry, not one bit in the world. Back then they didn't make too much money. The first six months I worked there, we worked nine, ten hours a day in the mills, and I made twenty-seven dollars a week. But twenty-seven dollars then was worth a hundred dollars now in buyin stuff.

I wanted to go to work. I wanted to work. At this textile plant, at that time, there was a good opportunity for young boys to learn different parts in the mill—different machinery and stuff like that. I fixed linens in the weave shop, I also fixed spinnin machines in the spinnin room, I fixed cards in the card room. I even inspected the supply. There's very little in a textile plant that I haven't done. Which if I went in there right today, there's nothin to those machines that I couldn't do somethin, go and fix em right today. I can fix any kind of a machine in textile. I can go anywhere down South, anywhere out West, where they got textile plants. I can walk in and say I want a job. They say, "Where do you work?" I say I got a recommendation from the house where I was loomin fixer, spinnin-machine fixer. I can get a job. It's like the railroad: I can run any kind of a section, any kind of a steel gang, or I can run a freighthouse. And I think that a man, when he's comin up through life as a young guy, I think he should learn some several different things. For right now, you take this automation that knocks so many people out of work, where that if a guy would learn a lot of different things, he won't have no trouble actually gettin a job.

I went to Copper Hill, Tennessee, one time; that's where the copper mines is. I went there to get a job when I was fifteen years old. I was workin still in the mill, but I went up there to see about a job because it paid better wages. And the foreman had done told me to go on over to the office, and sign my papers; I could go to work the next mornin. He asked me if I'd like to look around, see over the copper mines there before I went to work. I told him I'd appreciate it. And at that time, they had this walkway built across from one of these furnaces to another place where they dumped this hot copper, where it was melted. They hauled it in iron pots, big iron pots, like the old kind a wash pots. They had this on these wheelbarrows. They had these men that pushed this wheelbarrow across this walkway. They went over and they dumped this copper in this hot place where it was poured in. And so I was standin there watchin these men roll this hot copper. Course I wouldn't a been rollin the hot copper, at that time; course I probably would've later on, for you know the dangerouser the jobs was in the copper mines is where you made the more money. And so while I was standin there watchin these men roll this hot copper on these wheelbarrows, one of these guys started to duck his wheelbarrow and he staggered, and he went head first in this hot copper.

That was it with me, and that was it with him too. I said, "I don't want no job." I walked over to the office foreman, I said, "Thank you for the job," I said, "I'll stay with textile."

I worked day and night. I worked in the textile plant and I worked on the farm. I'd come in every mornin from work, from workin the night shift, and I'd work till about two or three o'clock in the afternoon and I'd go to bed and go to work at night. I done that for about three years. And course, I don't know, I always enjoy workin, and I guess that's today the reason that I like to see a person make a decent livin today. Yeah, I know they's a lot of people down South, there's a lot of people up North that never have made a decent livin in their life. They don't know what a decent livin was.

One time I was sixteen years old and I had worked that year till it was pitiful. And I'd come in on that Saturday mornin from the mill and it was rainin and my daddy he was there when I come in; he'd come in Friday night while I was at the mill. And I always cleaned out the wells on Saturday mornin. It was rainin, I said I couldn't do that in that rain, so we had a big wood shed and I asked him about helpin me saw off some wood and so he said he would—for pay. And I just looked at him right there settin in the house and told him, "Pay, hell!" I said, "What do you think this is, vacation?" I said, "I work day and night and I see you about oncet a year." I said, "You never send me a Christmas card, you never send me nothin." And he was tryin to tell me what I had to do. And I just flatly told him I didn't have to do a damn thing he told me to do. I said, "Everything that I've got," I said, "I've helped work and pay for it. And," I said, "this farm belongs to us and," I said, "the car out there belongs to me and," I said, "I've got a little bit of money in the bank. Not much, but," I said, "you sure ain't puttin any there." So he jumped up right in the house—and this rain goin on—jumped up and grabbed his coat. Out the door he went.

I didn't see him no more for, I think, two years. He came back by and I didn't see him no more until the big fire in Gadsden, 1946; and then I hadn't saw him in about seven years when he passed away. Well, I didn't even see him then. Course I would a went to the funeral just for the respect but I didn't get called until about an hour before. My sister that lives over here at Hammond, she said they were down there about three months before he died and that he'd been a-talkin about comin to Chicago to see me. She said that he said that he would like to go and talk to me and apologize for the way he had treated me, but that's somethin I couldn't answer for myself, I couldn't answer it for a fact.

That textile is good work, it's a good place to work, but the only thing about it is that you work in that lint and stuff so long, it gets to where you just get disgusted workin inside, in one department all the time. Another thing, it's not healthy inside that plant year after year. The lint and filing, the doctors and science doctors and all these doctors claim that lint and filing will cause you to have cancer, and sech as that. And it'll ruin your health, which I believe it will, for I know the seven years that I worked in Pepperell Manufacturing Company, I got to where that I was just on the drag. I was runnin completely down. It was fer about fourteen months that I didn't work nowhere, I couldn't even work on the farm. I took malaria fever, chills and malaria fever. Well, back then the only thing the doctors knew was quinine they gave for malaria and of course probably if I would've taken the round of treatment that the doctor gave me and a-taken it like he said, and not try to overdo myself and go back to work too soon, I would've been all right. But I knew we needed to work, for we didn't have much and it was comin up fall of the year, comin up time to gather the crop.

The next year, all I done after I did get up was just walk around out in the field and sorta supervise the gathering of the crops. My grandfather wasn't able at that time to even get out of the house. I worked the whole next year in the plant. Course I was just a-draggin myself down workin that way, and so he wanted me to forget farmin and go ahead and work in the mill. Which I was makin more than I could on the farm back then and so I did. But I finally quit the mill in 1939.

I went down to Gadsden, Alabama, went to work in Alabama Cotton Mills, worked a couple of weeks, and I didn't like it there in the mill there. They had this danged ole rotten machinery that wasn't no account in their plant at that time. And they couldn't make the production on the machines, they couldn't pay for it all. So I told this boy—I knew him very well, Bobby Smith—I said, "Bobby," I said, "let's go down to Mobile and work the harvest." We pulled out and went down to Mobile, and went to work at that potato harvest over at Foley, right out a Mobile. Then I didn't like the way the grade machine worked. We worked there I reckon about a month, played around there and over around Pensacola. That's just less than an hour from Mobile, only about thirty miles. We'd go back over there every night. A lot of these night clubs at that time were in there, you see. We was at them, goin wherever them girls was, seein them night clubs. Oh it was a good time.

We decided we'd take one summer, decided we'd go up to Kansas and work the wheat harvest comin in. We was travelin on to see what the country was. We cut up to Kansas City, went into that wheat harvest, runnin combines up there for about four months. It was a good racket, good money, but I didn't like it. It was too much ramblin.

We made our way into Independence, Missouri, where ole Truman was from. He probably didn't want to see us, and we sure as hell didn't want to see him! Hit all them night spots there for about a couple of weeks, and went from there over to Nebraska. And this wheat harvest man, this man that we was workin for, he told us to come on, he needed us. So we went over to Sydney, Nebraska, around near Cheyenne, Wyoming, where he was at at that time. And he give us twenty dollars a day, for runnin the combine, and hotel and meals. We worked a little over three and a half months, but we decided to quit. So we cut out, we cut out back down South again, and went back into Kansas City. Spent a couple a more days, and then we cut in from Kansas City to Chicago; from Chicago then straight into Indianapolis; from Indianapolis to Louisville. We was just more or less killin a year's time. Havin a good time. Livin on what we made from the harvest. We killed nearly a whole year, just out travelin the country, just to see what it was, see how's people doin in different parts, how they act and how they treat you. Good life, man; I liked it.

I'll have to say for the West, we got mighty nice treatment out through the West. I never run into no people out there in the West that thought they was better than anyone. Out in that part of the country the people are just a lot different, altogether different to what they are here. You go in the restaurant and everybody was friendly. It wasn't like here: people afraid to speak to you, unless you got the right kind a clothes. Here that's the only time they'll speak to you. But they weren't that way out there. All I wore out there was just a pair of pants and just a short-sleeve shirt. Course I had other clothes in the car, but I just don't see that because a man's not got on a suit of clothes, that he's not as good as that next man.

You go in a place down here in Chicago, right here on Randolph. It's just a common tavern is all it is, common bar. I stopped there when I was comin from the freighthouse, and I stopped down in the Loop to get somethin, and I decided I'd go in that place and get me a beer. I had on clean clothes but I didn't have on no tie and no white shirt. I walked in, I said, "Give me a beer," and this guy said, "You'll have to go home and get you a tie, if you don't have one in your pocket to go into the washroom and put it on." And I said, "If I got to go home and get me a tie to put on," I said, "I'll just buy me a beer some other place. I don't want to spend my money with you in the first place." I told him right to his face, I said, "These guys that got these ties on," I said, "they's a lot a them," I said, "probably ain't got enough money to buy the next beer that's in here." I said, "A lot a times when you turn a man down cause he ain't got a necktie on or a suit of clothes," I said, "you might be turnin a man down with the money." And I turned around and walked out.

That's like Ralph Cordell, man down home. He was a rich man, but I'll say one thing for him. He was for the poor people, he wasn't one of these rich classes that was against poor people. He had money but he wasn't selfish with it. He found out my grandmother was sick. She was gettin worse, and about a week before she died, he just closed his business, he stayed down there at my uncle's, him and his family just almost completely stayed there day and night, just to help them out. Wasn't nothing in the world he wouldn't do. He didn't buy no three-, four-, five-dollar wreath. When he sent it, it was a fifty- or seventy-five-dollar wreath he'd send to the family. Well, a man like that you couldn't complain cause he had plenty of money, for he'd help anyone that needed it. I've even known of him goin up there to this county work camp where those guys had got thirty, sixty days, ninety days in jail or a fine; he'd go up there and pay them out. Some of them'd go down maybe work a couple of days with him, never see them no more. He'd try to help out the poor people.

He had money in every bank in the state of Georgia but people never thought about that. Now, he didn't steal this money. This guy didn't steal this money, he made it the hard way, he worked the hard way. He made that back durin the years when it was hard to make. He made it back in wood stoves, used to cook with wood. He hauled stove wood by the load, he'd take it out and sell it by the dime's worth, the quarter's worth or a dollar's worth. Now he built his business like that then he went into haulin lumber, went into haulin fertilizer. He kept buildin his business and every dime he got he put it in or he invested in some more equipment.

Well now that was a good thing. He was buildin up somethin for his family.

Now the mill, as I said, was against my health, and so I decided I'd better get outside and work, it was more healthy for me. I went to work for the railroad in 1940, and I went with steel gangs. I worked my way up through the section. I wasn't one a them guys that got a section foreman job for goin out there and givin some big shot a good time. I learnt my job, I knew how to do it. They was payin accordin to what you went to doin. Back then they didn't have too much automation machinery and such as that. If you could learn, you could make a good spiker, it was a dollar-seventy-five an hour. If you was just what's called a regular laborer at that time, it was a dollar-fifty-five. And of course, I was tough as the devil, come out from the country; in about a week or so I could take that spike, you know, and spike as hard as the next man could. And I went from one-fifty-five to one-seventy-five. So when I left in '41 and joined the army I was makin two and a quarter an hour.

Yeah, I enlisted in the service. I knew I was goin to get drafted so I figured it would be best to get myself in service. I first went to Fort Mc-Pherson, Georgia, for examination. I stayed there three weeks, I went from Fort McPherson to Camp Hood, Texas. I taken eight weeks' training in Camp Hood and transferred from there to Camp Wood, and we just set there for three weeks. I transferred from there back to Fort Benning, Georgia, and they sent me into an armored outfit which I had applied for. I had applied for the 2nd Armored Division.

I just wanted to get with a rough outfit. I thought I was rough and didn't give a durn about things. Well another thing too, I realized that the infantry was goin to be rougher than being in an armored outfit where you didn't have to do all that walkin. I went into the armored and I taken nine weeks training there and I went to Fort Knox, Kentucky. We stayed at Fort Knox four weeks, then went on to what's called the Alabama-Florida-Louisiana maneuvers. We stayed on maneuvers for six and a half months with actual trainin, rough trainin, terrain trainin. That was rough but it paid off when we went over there in Europe. We went to the swamps and everything else. Came back from there and went back to Fort Benning, from there back to Fort Knox. In Fort Knox they come out and asked for volunteers to go to England with the Coast Guard. I said, Well hell, I done in it, I'd just as well volunteer. I landed in Liverpool, England, and I stayed over until 1945. I had been over there three months when my division that I'd been with at Fort Knox came over there and they put me back in my outfit and I went all up through Germany, Italy and everywheres else on through there.

Damn right I did plenty a fightin, but that's something I don't do much talkin about, for you hear people a-braggin about what they done in combat, that man didn't do it. A man don't talk too much about that combat if he's a man's been through a lot of it. Which I can take my discharge and show what I have been through but I know I'd ruther forget that stuff. It was pretty rough at times and you wondered whether you were gonna see the next day or not, or not the next day but the next minute. A person that's been through it, actually been through it, they don't do much talkin about it. You hear a man: "Oh me, a lot of things that I've been through, it's just a joke to go through it, don't think nothin of it." But then you get those major battles and when you actually knowed that you had killed people then you wonder. You don't know how you made it through without you gettin it yourself.

And of course we were put into the war just like a lot of the people were put into the war over there. We wouldn't have been a-shootin at either one if it hadn't been for our leaders. Hadn't been for Hitler and it hadn't been for Roosevelt and all of those that got us into it both ways, we wouldn't have been in.

If the main thing is to ever have a world peace, I say take all the leaders that this country has, the leaders of all the countries, put them in an airplane, give them M-1 rifles and one bandoleer of ammunition, take them over there and parachute them out, say "Now, dammit, fight!" I'll bet there'd never be a shot fired and I bet the war would end. They'd get together right there in a bunch and stop it. Hell, if they can go all the way to Germany and kidnap people and take them all the way back to Jerusalem, why can't we? Why can't the people kidnap the presidents of all these countries and get them all in a bunch? I would be willin to bet my life you wouldn't have more wars.

Well, I got to do something there that I surely enjoyed, after the war ended, which I never would have had the money if I hadn't went in the service. Even re-enlisted for three years. I got to tour Jerusalem where

Christ was born and crucified. They had a chaplain's tour that went over there and so they came around asking for volunteers to go in there and drive these jeeps for chaplains, and I don't know what hit me to do it but I just said, Well, I believe I'll volunteer for it, be a good tour. And I got to tour Jerusalem and I saw the cross where that they read and tell about today that Christ was crucified. A poor person would never have had that kind of money. And there's a lot of other places that I went while I was in service that I probably wouldn't've had the money to went—but I probably wouldn't've had no interest in goin, that's another thing too.

And I know I've met people that couldn't speak a word of English that would've been as good a friend to me that anybody here in this country would have been, you know. And I have met some very nice people here in Chicago and I've met some that they wouldn't be worth the powder and lead it'd take to shoot em.

As a whole I can't say that I was mistreated in service. I wasn't; I was treated very well, for the outfit I was in we had very nice officers, very nice NCO's. I made NCO in the outfit and they didn't try to run over us. You know what I mean, you made it what you made of yourself. Oh sure, our company commander he was strick on leaves but he was just carrying out his orders, and as long as you went along with him and cooperated with him he'd cooperate with you in every way. I know they was some outfits that they said you couldn't even *talk* to your company commander, he wouldn't even let an enlisted man talk to him, but we didn't have none like that. Gen'l Patton believed that a captain or a lieutenant was supposed to cooperate with the enlisted men cause Patton hisself would cooperate with the enlisted men.

And all the time I spent in the service I finished up high school at night. And I was actually glad that I had the opportunity in the service for me to do that. If I hadn't done that, I'd a been hurtin.

When I married the first time, I was in the army. I was home on furlough. This girl, we'd been goin together for a long time fore I went in the service when I married. Mistake from the beginning. She was a sonofabitch, the truth about it. Hellfire couldn't get along with her, the devil or nobody else, her or her damn people neither one. Them people cost me, boy. She was the only daughter in the family and, honest truth, she had two brothers that was too damn sorry to work. And she'd been a-workin in this Rome Cotton Mill and feeding the family, so when she married, hell, they figured I was supposed to take care of the family. I let em know right quick that that wasn't gonna work, that I didn't marry the whole damn family, I just married her. Well, that's when the trouble started. That was the main thing. She knew I had money in the bank, she knew I had a good job at work at that time, and another thing she knew at that time that I was a-haulin whiskey, and was makin good money on that. I was averagin three to four thousand dollars a month clear money, haulin whiskey.

I'll tell you right now, when you drop about fifteen, sixteen, seventeen thousand dollars out of a bank all at once, you feel like stoppin free spendin. When I came back from Germany I went to that Ford Motor Company, bought me a new car. Good thing I did win seventy-two hundred dollars in a poker game comin back from Germany; if I hadn't I would've been hurtin. I wrote a check for the car. A couple of days later Mr. Millan called me up out at the house. He told me that check bounced. "What do you mean, it bounced?" I said. "I'll be by to see about it in the mornin." I went on down to the bank. A fellow Palmer was president of the bank there, a very nice man. Went on back in his office, I sat down, I laid my bankbook on the desk. I said, "Mr. Palmer," I said, "I would like you to give me some information here." I said, "Here's this check that bounced." I says, "Funny thing is, I'm supposed to have nineteen thousand dollars in the bank." He said, "Johnny"—he always called me Johnny —"you made one of the biggest mistakes I ever seen, fore you left here and made that joint account." He said, "Which it wasn't none of my business to write you or tell you nothin." He said, "I thought you knew the money was bein drawed out." He said, "As fast as you sent a check to the bank, your wife was drawin it out."

I said, "Well how much have I got?" He said, "You got sixty-one dollars in the bank right now." I said, "Well, there's one thing about it," I said, "I'm gonna stop that right now." And I said, "If they's any other checks wrote, I'm not responsible for em." I told him, "I'm responsible for my debts and my debts only." I said, "No checks and nothin else with Beatrice Dawson on it, it's not good to me." I said, "I want it published just exactly like that now." I went back up to the Ford Motor Company, I walked in and I paid the man for the difference on the car—course I'd traded cars, but I paid the man on the other car. But boy that was a devil of a lick. Boy that makes you feel funny too, havin that kind of money in the bank, turn around and write a check and you know it bounced. You don't know how hard that hits you all at once.

I stayed drunk for over a year over that. I mean I *stayed* drunk for over a year. I said, "Well, she spent nineteen thousand, I might just as well spend seventy-two hundred." And I did. I mean I spent some money there. And I stayed drunk at Fort Benning for a year. I had two assistant motor sergeants and it's a good thing I did have too or I'd a probably got—not a summary court-martial, I'd a probably got a general court-martial. For I wasn't there: the only time they'd see me was about twice a month. I was there for the middle of the month when they had the inspection, and on payday. I had a permanent pass and they didn't see me no other time. They didn't worry about me. I had my job to do and that was it. All I done is come in sign the inspection papers and check them over to see if they was right, and turn around and get back in the car and cut out back to Columbus or Phenix City or some other place.

Well, in 1946 when I came home from service, from Germany, this natural gas plant blew up there in Gadsden, Alabama. I had called my sister in Norfolk, Virginia, and I had told her I was goin to come and see her, and so I had my car loaded and was goin to leave and I got a telephone call from Norfolk, Virginia. They said it was an emergency call. Well, I went to the phone and it was my sister had passed away. And they shipped her body back to Gadsden, Alabama, to bury her there with my brother-in-law and a couple of babies that was buried there. And they brought her home there and my dad's house over there, they didn't have a big enough house to bring her casket into, to bring her corpse into for a funeral. So they carried her over to one of my aunt's on Fourth Street in Gadsden, Alabama, right next to Tuscaloosa Avenue.

The funeral was due on Monday, but that night, Saturday night, this natural gas plant blew up right behind the house. You might've read about that, burned up all that Tuscaloosa Avenue there. And that was a mess there that night, and it blowed the house in on her casket there. We had to take the body out of the house till they got the fire out. They was afraid that the building was gonna catch on fire. And we carried the casket back up to the funeral home for a chapel, for about two or three hours, till they got the fire out in that part of town, where we could get back in there. And then we carried her up to another of my aunt's later on.

But the next morning, my dad he said, "Well, let's go over to my house for breakfast, fix us a bite to eat." And my first wife, Beatrice, she went over there and carried my two boys over there, and naturally she needed some place to lay out and rest. And so we went over there, it was about six in the morning and he walked in and he said, "Fay," said, "you been in bed all night, get up and help me fix some breakfast," he says. "I know Johnny's give out," he said. "He's been up all night, been up travelin, comin in from overseas." Said, "Let's help em get some breakfast." And she got up out of bed and she said, "Well, I want to tell you right now this is not my damn company, it's your damn company." Said, "If you want his breakfast, fix it yourself."

Boy, that flew all over me. You know I'm just the type of person that I don't take that kind of stuff. I've just got a temper that I don't take it. I just came up and told her right in front of him. I said, "I'm not company in the first place." I said, "I want to tell you something. I wouldn't be here visiting at all if it wasn't for my sister laying over there dead." And I said, "I'm the one that saw that her body wasn't brought here." I was, "for," I said, "that was a request that she made to me a long time ago." And I said, "I don't have to eat off nobody. I don't have to eat nothin that you have in your house for," I said, "I got money in my damn pocket, I got money in the bank." And I said, "As for ever comin back in your house again," I said, "I don't imagine I'll ever come back unless Dad's dead or somethin like that." I said, "I've always tried to get along with you, and tried to treat you halfway right," and I said, "you've always had a smart remark to make every time I've ever come around or any of the other kids have ever come around," I said.

So I just turned around and walked back to the bedroom where my wife was and told her, I said, "Bea, just get up and get the kids dressed. I'm goin down and get something to eat." And I went on down to my aunt's, where my sister's body was at, and I don't know how that the word got to her, what had happened over there, unless my daddy called, but when I went in Aunt Mary-Lou she said, "Now if it's up to you," she said, "if you don't want Fay to come to the funeral, just say the word and I'll see that it won't happen." My daddy's sisters now, they always treated me nice. I have to say that for em. And they didn't like Fay. I said, "No, I'm not that hardhearted, but I'm just hardhearted that I won't never go back in the house again." And I wasn't back in the house until he called me. I'd come back from Korea and he called at my aunt's in Rome and told her to tell me that he needed some money, that he'd been laid off, didn't have nothin. So, I don't know, I'm always the type that regardless of how anybody'd done me if they was in a tight spot and they needed help I'd go and help em regardless. So I just made up my mind, I said my daddy never did do anything for me but I'm just going to show him that I'm not that type of person, my granddaddy didn't raise me that way. So I just got in the car and went down to Gadsden and sure enough he owned a little home there, but that's all he did have. He was just completely down and out. He'd been sick and laid off from his job so I pulled out five hundred and just give it to him. Well then I wasn't back in the house no more until after he passed away. That was about seven years.

I went by there and so I seen that Fay still just got the same attitude and I don't never intend to go back in the house no more. In fact if she was to die and they was to call and if I had the money to make the trip on, I won't make it.

Late 1946 I was put on that Alaska deal. They organized a task force unit, what was called the Special Forces. What they done is they checked through the records to find out men that had been in special units like I'd been under Patton. And they organized a unit of nineteen thousand men, sent us to Fairbanks, Alaska, testin government equipment, in '46 and '47. We was testing in solid ice to see in case the United States had to go across solid ice into Russia, if we would go across in tanks and stuff. Which I did. I drove a tank across that solid ice. We went all the way over to the Russian border. Yeah, they knew we was up there testin, they was doin the same thing at the time that we were doin it. We was also a-testin out in the solid ice, I forget how many hundred feet they drilled in this solid ice up there, but anyway they loaded it with TNT to see if they could blow it out and block it off. They were testin that too.

And then I came back from Alaska. And I'd been home, I think about a week, and the damn police walks up to me and he said, "Let's go. Got a warrant for you." And I said, "Good, let's go." So I said, "I'm not going to walk up to jail." It wasn't but a block there. I said, "I ain't walkin nowhere." I said, "Come on, hell. Get a car. I ain't gonna walk. You arrested me, you got to haul me." He called for a car, they sent the car down, and I went on up to the city jail and I got there. And I said, "I ain't gonna stay over here at the city jail. You can transfer me to the county," I said. "If it's a warrant, any time on a warrant," I said, "I can ask for a county change."

He says O.K. And they just carried me right over to the county, and I signed my bond. And my first old lady had taken a warrant out for me. Claimed she wasn't gettin enough support for the kids. And her sayin she divorced me in 1941! Well, I had been a-sendin the kids' allotment but not hers. So I went before the judge, hell I wasn't worried about beatin her but what made me so mad, she called me a goddamn liar and started bitchin in the courtroom after the trial. And when she did, after the judge done turned me loose, it made me mad. And she come up and pressed me and I just taken my fist and knocked her plumb across that Superior Courtroom right there in Rome, Georgia. Well, the state solicitor, Parker, wasn't tryin to fight me, I found out after, but I thought he was. He was tryin to git the fight broke up, keep me from hittin her again, and when he did, I slid him out plumb over in the jury box and so it made the judge mad and he said, "I'll give you twelve months in the work camp out there." And I said, "Well, I'll tell you one thing, if you'll come out from behind that desk and from off that chair," I said, "I'll give *you* a slide across this courtroom." So they was hollerin at the sheriff to get me offa the solicitor. And the sheriff said, "I didn't get it started and I ain't gonna stop it."

He said, "The boy's in the right," and he said, "anybody's in the right," he said, "they's in the right, and I'm fer the man's in the right."

"Well," I said, "it ain't the only time. Now," I said, "I got twelve months and I wanna tell you one thing, Parker," I said, "I'm going to whup you every time I see you on the damn street." I said, "I'm gonna tell you the only way that you can keep me from whuppin you." And I said, "You better get them charges lifted off me for them twelve months," I said, "or I'm gonna whup you, and I mean next time I whup you I'm going to leave you where they're gonna carry you in with a ambulance or in a hearse, one."

We made appeal bond and three days later they called me and told me there wasn't no case against me. But that's just how crooked that mess was. That shows you there was a crooked court goin on at that time.

In fact the sheriff offered to hire me when I first come back from the service, and I started to run for sheriff, twicet, at home. I could a been the sheriff at home if I'd a run in 1946, and I could a run in 1955 when I was home. About the time I started runnin I'd back out. Don't fool with it. I always said, if I got low enough to go in the sheriff department, that I'd just take a .38 and walk out and shoot one a the sonofabitches.

I came out of the service in '48. I worked in New Orleans, I worked in Houston, I worked in Dallas, I worked in Eugene, Oregon—I was working on a railroad in Oregon—and I worked in Salt Lake City, worked in Cheyenne, Wyoming: I mostly worked West. I enjoy movin around. And then in '49 they started calling the men back for special training for Korea and I was put on inactive duty status.

They didn't call nobody that hadn't been in service until '50, but all of us men that had special enlistments during World War II got called back in '49. They knew the war was coming then, and they'd been so many men that had got out of service like myself that knew how to operate tanks.

And so they sent me to Fort Benning and transferred me to Fort Jackson and I said the hell with this. I didn't want Fort Jackson, South Carolina, I didn't like Columbia, I didn't like the damn camp, so I went to the regimental commander's post in Jackson and I told him, I said, "I want a damn transfer to either Fort Benning or Korea." I said, "I don't want a damn thing to do with this camp, I got no use for it, I want a transfer." Which he gave me a transfer to Fort Benning. Well, I went to Fort Benning. This outfit that I went into, it was the 3rd Infantry Division and they was gettin ready to go to Korea and I went with them to Korea.

I was in them damn rice paddies, them damn slop holes in Korea. I slept on the ground when these big shots was sleepin on a damn feather bed, probably. I wasn't with no damn rear-action-line outfit. I was with one of the highest decorated infantry divisions the United States Government's got, though decorations ain't worth a damn to a man when he's dead. They ain't worth a damn to him when he's alive. People in Washington think that a GI or a poor person is nothin but a damn dog. I don't see how in the hell they ever get elected. They'll waste money to build guns to kill people with, appropriate money to kill people with, but there's little kids in this country that's hungry, they're barefooted.

These wars is all rich men's wars. Poor men's fight. How many in history, actually, how many rich men have you ever read about that ever was actually on the front lines? Very few. I figure that Eisenhower is a rich man. I can't actually say for sure, but I believe he's a rich man. But I'll have to say now there's one, that he was on the front lines, and I'll tell you another one that was on the front lines, that was his son, Major Eisenhower, in Korea. He was our regimental commander in Korea, and was damn sure he stayed with us on the front lines, he didn't stay back in no rear-action lines.

I say this: if a man's on the front lines a-fightin, if a man's supposed to be the commander-in-chief of this country like the President is, if he puts you out there on the line and he only gives you so many rounds of ammunition and says, "You stand here for twenty-four hours," he's not much of a commander to put a man out there on a line like 'at and do that. Truman's one that done that. He expected you to stand there like 'at. Well that's not much of a commander-in-chief, of a President. And when a man that would say what he said against the armed forces, his armed forces as commander-in-chief—if you remember when him and that guy got into it, he made that remark about Margaret singin, you know. You remember they had a run-in about that and he told this marine, said the Marine Corps wasn't nothin but a—let's see, how did he speak that?— nothin but a parade outfit noway. He made a bunch of remarks, but that durned general of the Marines like to made him eat them words about that. He didn't give a damn if he was a commander-in-chief or not. And our President would say such as that—he's just nutty.

And hell, there was never nothin said, why we was in Korea. I've asked that question myself. We give up more land over thar than we taken when they signed the peace treaty over there. We lost more lives in Korea than we lost in World War II. What did they gain by it? That's still a good question that's never been answered in this country today. Ain't nobody ain't never give a answer to that question. What are they tryin to gain over there right now? Now I mean I don't approve of war. I got a boy over there in Vietnam with the paratroopers. But if we gonna have a war, let's don't stand over there and let China and Russia come over here first. Every day and every month is a waste of this country. I don't think we should be over there in the first place, but if we're gonna be over there, let's get it over with. I know that we got the stuff in this country to do it with. It's like Senator Dirksen told the President—him and President Johnson had a fallin-out last night. He said, "I'm gonna ask congressmen next week when they meet to either take over and ask them to do somethin, or either make a pull-out."

It's a hard decision to make. We've lost about fourteen hundred men over there in lives, I mean that's not countin now, that was last year. We lost a lot of money, we lost a lot of equipment. China is a country that can't be trusted. When I was in Korea, I was in favor of what MacArthur wanted to do, goin on to China and takin over Manchuria and liberate them people. They's a lot of good people in China, just like there are in this country. Then was the time to've done it. They've had all these years to build up, and the only way we can do it now is to bomb the livin hell out of em. But what do you want to bomb just around the edges for? If you want to do any bombin, do it where it hurts worst. Bomb those factories, those bomb plants, those ammunition factories they got over there. If we're gonna go over there and fight, 'n I say this: let's stabilize a country over there and have an independent country. Let's stop that foolishness. Right today, there's a lot of straightenin out and stabilizin in this country we need here too, mighty bad.

I checked into that GI Bill when I got back and there's so much red tape goin through that, goin through schoolin or any other trades. They give you a runaround bout all that stuff. And you try to go through one course and they want you to run right around and do what they want you to take. In other words they try to force you on just like Illinois does here in the welfare, sech as that. That's just the treatment bout the government on that schoolin. If you want to go through some kind of school that didn't cost you nothin, they was pretty welcome to that, you know.

So I started a trade of moldin in the stoveworks and that's finally went out of business. I had a couple of uncles that was moldin there, had a uncle that had been there eleven years and he was listed as one of the goodest molders as ever went into a stoveworks. And I went and talked to my uncle about different trades, different learnin of parts, patterns and all of that. You do not go in the moldin room and learn the trade in one day, or you don't learn it in no one year. I worked about eighteen months under him. Well, when wood stoves, wood heaters, and things commenced to goin out and gas commenced to comin in, the Chamber of Commerce went around to these stove foundries, the owners, and they paid them a big bunch of money to not change over to gas and electric stoves. We was makin stoves for Sears and Roebuck, right there in Rome Stove & Range. If they would've changed over to gas and electric stoves they could still be a-makin stoves right there in that stove foundry. There was I'd say about fourteen hundred hands at work there in that stove foundry and molding room and melting room and everythin, shippin department. Well, that put people out of work. You could make four dollars an hour right there in that stove foundry when this happened.

This Chamber of Commerce was to blame for people had been out a work. They're still to blame. That's the one thing that ruint that city: the Chamber of Commerce. That's one of the crookedest Chambers of Commerce a place has ever had. That's the only thing there about Rome that I hate. When I was down there last year, at home, the American Thread Company, which is union, up in Dalton, Georgia, they was supposed to come in there, which would have been a very good thing for the city, put a lot of people to work. Next thing you know, chairman of the big-shot Chamber of Commerce—I can't think of his blamed name—here he come out, and all that bunch that belongs to the Chamber of Commerce: "We don't want the American Thread Company here." It's a trick: it's stealin. That Chamber, they want all the money theirself. If they can't get us money out of it, the Chamber of Commerce ain't gonna let em come in. See, they ain't got a mayor in Rome, Georgia. They got councilmen, city council, and county commissioners, and they're members of the Chamber of Commerce. They *are* the Chamber of Commerce. If you run for county commissioner, then get elected, then you have to join the Chamber of Commerce, or they'll throw you off. That's automatic.

I went to Detroit after they closed up that foundry, went to work. I went up there with a friend of mine, his brother lived there in Detroit, went up just before the Fourth of July, '55. He went to this construction company and they was wantin two truck drivers to drive this water truck, buildin an extension of that Ford Expressway. Also they were payin four-fifty an hour to drive that water truck to spray the road. You'd work twelve hours a shift. So I helped build that Ford Expressway. I worked five months. Then the work ran out.

I worked in stoveworks, Detroit, Cleveland, and I worked at the Ford Motor Company there in Dearborn. Had two parts there on the windshield wipers to control. It was the worst work you ever seen except that you got good money for it. You had to keep your mind on the job, and it drove you half crazy. I stayed on just till I had me enough money to go on back home with.

I came back to Rome and I got married to Etta. I'll tell you, the first time I ever met Etta I hit her on the toe with a hammer. I'd been over to one of my cousins there that lived on Twentieth Street. He tried to lay some block, underpin his house, and he didn't know how. So I was out there showin him how to lay them block and make up that mortar and he called his wife and told Delia to bring some ice water out there. And I was in under the house at that time knocking some blocks, settin some block up and I actually thought it was Delia up there, standin there with her toes out of her shoes you know and I just reached up with that mortar hammer, hit her on the toe. It was Etta. That's the first time I ever met her.

If I'd a had the money when I married this time that I had when I married before, I never would a thought about goin to Chicago in the first place, never would a thought of goin on the railroad. I could a made it a lot better with Etta. Seem like I get started out and soon a bunch of sickness start to hit me, high blood, everything else. It makes married life harder. And I've always been able to support my family and I don't like this damn welfare. I never did like no kind of welfare. I don't like public assistance no kind for my part and I'd rather be where I got a payday comin in. Well, if you got a good payday comin in every week or every two weeks you know what you can spend, you know what you can save. You know what you can give your wife, you can let your wife have some money to go out and spend extra. With this damn welfare you don't have extra to spend. When you pay your damn rent and buy your groceries you ain't got nothing left. Well, we don't fight over it, we know there's no use in it but it's just not like it would be if we could have some left over.

Etta Dawson, 28

I was born in Rome, born and raised there. They say it's the city of seven hills. It's got seven big hills there in Rome, on each side. We lived out in the country but it wasn't a farm. Dad built us a rock home, porch and everything, and we went to country schools. He was a brickmaker, brick and rock mason. It was a good job till he got too old to do it. I don't know how much he made an hour. He was too old to get into the union when he found out that he could do rock-masonry work—he was in his fifties. Then he was pickin up odd jobs, and he used to make moonshine. After we got old enough to know what Daddy was doin, he wouldn't bootleg no more. My mother went to work when I was a year old and she worked in what they call a spread house. She made bedspreads and rugs and different things like that on a machine. Back then I think it paid a dollar-twenty-five an hour maybe, if it paid that much. We were always poor up till my sister was big enough to go to work and then we went to work just as quick as we got old enough to go to work.

Daddy worked and we got what they call commodities. That wasn't gettin a check, you know, it was just goin up and gettin food. You get canned meat and go oncet a month and pick up groceries, that's what it is. They've got canned meat that tastes just like ham but it's not ham. You can bake it or make sandwiches or fry it. The only thing I had against it, they give plain meal and plain flour and I couldn't make biscuits out of it. We never was on welfare down there. Mother and them tried to get on it while I was in high school and they told em at the time that they had too many kids big enough to support em. They was four of us, I was the baby.

We had to tote water from the spring, right at the edge of a creek. It just sprang up right there. We kept it cleaned out. See we wouldn't let no kids get in it and muddy the water or nothin like that. If the leaves went in it, Daddy'd take a hoe down and clean it out. Had to go outside to the john and that was one reason why Mommy and Daddy moved to town: they was gettin too old to walk on out in the back.

I started keepin house when I was about eight or nine years old. We went to town on Saturday. Mother'd usually take us to the show, and that was our weekly amusement. And then we had our usual playhouses and stuff like that. Out in the country you can have a playhouse where you can't have one in the city.

Out in the neighborhood where I was at, there wasn't too many white families, and the biggest part of em was bootleggers. That's what they moved out there for, to make whiskey. I knew one family there, he put his two oldest boys through school, seen em graduate, bootleggin. And when he got where he had just one little girl left, he told his boys, he said, "Y'all can put her through school." He said, "I'm through with it." He quit.

There was house white, house colored, house white, and house colored. I played with em a lot and this one colored man I'll never forget as long as I live. Daddy was buildin the colored a schoolhouse. I was about five and this colored guy came by and asked where Mr. Fred was, that was Daddy's name. He said, "Where's Mr. Fred?" I said, "He's over at the niggers' schoolhouse workin." And you know a lot of people get mad, you know, bein called nigger. He just laughed. He said, "Well," said, "that's what I am." And they had a cow and they always brought us milk, butter. This one family, they made hominy oncet a year. We'd always have fresh hominy, fresh sauerkraut.

Their school was made of rock, where ours was just wood. They didn't have but just one teacher in the school where we had eight. They just went to the sixth grade where the country white school went to the eighth. Then we went to the Lyndale School. We had separate grades and separate rooms but if you didn't want to go all the way around the schoolhouse you had to go through the different rooms.

They never did say too much about the colored people when we went to school, they wasn't havin this thing about colored folks then. Our teachers just said it wasn't right for them to go to school with the whites is all. Which now there in Rome, from the first through the sixth they're goin together, goin to school together now. My kids have to go to school with em up here. I don't see when it makes any difference. I think it's all right, but the people that live there, they don't like it. Well, some people thinks if you don't like the colored, you know, somewhere back in your generations they may be colored in your family.

And another thing my parents don't like about me now is the thought that they don't have a place for a colored. Well, they like em in their place. Back home they don't have a place for the colored to eat, to sit down and drink, or anything. They have to take their stuff out and take it to home or sit on the street and eat it and that's not right. They should have a place for em to sit down and eat it. My mother accuses me of bein in the North too long.

Well I think this-a-way: if the white people would let the colored alone they wouldn't a started the civil rights. Biggest part of it is the cause of the whites. Now a colored person's got to make a livin just like the white. I may be wrong but that's what I feel of it. Most of the colored people down South, they work for the big rich white people, and naturally they think they can get them for nothin, which isn't right. They should pay more. And these rich people has started downin the colored people and that's one reason the colored people starts out. A lot of places down South, they've took the farms and everything away from the colored. You know one place it showed on TV in Mississippi where they'd taken their farms away from them. They didn't have no place to go, no place to stay or anything and they just built these little ole shacks up close to the river where they could get water.

We used to go to colored churches. Back home, when the colored comes to the white, they sit in the back. When the white goes to the colored, they sit in the back. The one I went to, they don't believe in cuttin your hair or wearin make-up or anything like that. It's what they call a Far Baptist Holiness. It's far stricter than the Church of God. In fact the Church of God is now started lettin them cut their hair. I went to it practically all my life. But we wasn't too religious, except my sister's got so now. Up here I started goin to that little church up on Sheridan. That was the first Free Will Baptist I'd ever been to. But I don't believe their belief no way. You know Baptists believe that Jesus, God, and the Holy Ghost was all one. Which I was brought up the different way. I was brought up, they was three different ascents. What I can't understand is that they say Jesus and God was the same one, the same person, and if God and Jesus was the same person Jesus would never have been born. And they say Jesus is the Holy Ghost. Well, you know, when he went to the river and was baptized and the Holy Ghost fell on him. Well, that proves that it's three different people.

I was thinkin about goin to another church on Eastwood, it's the same church that used to be on Leland. A lady came up to the door, handed me some literature and said she was out invitin people to go to church. But they had a colored man there last week runnin the revival. I told Johnny if I wanted to hear a colored man I'd come down there on Leland to the colored church. Because that's puttin a colored person too far out of his way, up in front of a white church like that, especially a Southern church. And then I told Johnny that I won't be able to go at all now, after I seen the way they dressed. I saw a whole crowd of em wearin their big fancy hats and twenty-dollar dresses. I can't go up there with those people.

We moved to Rome city area when I was seventeen. I had started my twelfth year the year we moved and I was supposed to have went to this high school uptown. And they told me that if I changed over that I would have to start back in the ninth grade, which I was already in the twelfth, because my credits wouldn't count from the country school. So I never did change schools. I just caught the city bus and went on to the country school and they didn't catch me till the last day of school and they had to give me my diploma.

I couldn't stand it. They couldn't keep me in it. I laid out every day that I could. It was full of snotty people, this highfalutin school in the suburbs of Rome at Lyndale. I think that four years that I went to school there about three or four people spoke to me. They just thought they was better than me. See, their parents worked in a mill down there.

In my home town they start hollerin, if you look for work, "You got to be experienced." And right out of high school I wasn't experienced, and the only kind of job I could get was baby-sittin. That's what I did for a while, and then I went to work in this old people's home. I was supposed to clean, but what I did was I had to cook, and I'd mop the floors and wash dishes. I would work from six till two and then go in and help to cook supper, and then I'd go home—for forty-five dollars a month. I stayed on there, livin at home, till John and I married.

I guess I got married to get out of the house. Although I was twenty-four years old, my sister and my mother thought I should be bossed, like comin in certain times at night and curfew at night and all that. So I just got out of it. I met John at one of his cousins', and he was down there helpin her husband build a house. My sister and I fought over him to see which of us was goin to get him, and I got him, married him three months later.

John Dawson

I hadn't been a-workin much after I came back from Detroit. Then just after me and Etta married there was that freeze, and I worked with Georgia Power there on extra help, puttin up those power lines for four weeks. Well, I had to go to Atlanta to get my check, and I was gonna go up to Lockheed, see if I could get a job with Lockheed Aircraft. And we got in Atlanta, course the weather had opened up, pretty weather then, and a big carnival, Kapp, just opened up out there at this colored shopping center, and I seen, as I come along on the bus, I seen he was advertisin for help. Big sign. I just stopped and got off the bus out there, so I just went to runnin the ride. Of course I always knew how to run electric motors or diesel motors, I learnt that in service. I worked out there with him, I was runnin the merry-go-round and Etta was workin for this guy in the glass pitch. She got fifty percent of what he taken in, and you talk about somethin about the colored people—if you want to make your money, go to these colored shoppin areas and have a glass pitch. Those people goes crazy over them glass pitches. You can take one of those glass pitches on those big shows and in a year's time you could clear fifty thousand. Me and Etta worked there in Atlanta for about three weeks. And then I found out Hunt was there, and grabbed Hunt.

Hunt was payin more for the merry-go-round than Kapp was and I heard about him. He was just a straight kind of a guy with his help, and he pays you just like he promised to pay you, you didn't have no trouble with him and he had a mighty nice bunch of people that was on the show with him. He didn't believe in that cutthroat one another, he wouldn't allow it. When he left Atlanta I pulled a tractor and trailer from Atlanta to Muncie, Indiana, for him, and I run the merry-go-round in Muncie. We was only supposed to be in that shoppin center one week, two weeks, and they let im stay three and he stayed three and he moved from there to Cambridge City. I helped him play the street fair there. He was supposed to been there two weeks and he stayed four, and I said, "Well, Ralph, I'm going back to Chicago to go back to the railroad."

At that time I hadn't worked with the railroad since I came out of the service and I decided I'd go back. Etta was pregnant at this time, I knew I couldn't keep travelin without a car, we was havin to rent a motel or place like that to live in. Course I could a used one of these big trailers but I didn't like that kind of livin.

When I first got here I lived out on South Carson Avenue. I got me a job at the freighthouse and it was closest to my work, right off Ogden Avenue. I think one of the best men I ever worked fer was C. R. Williams, down at Freight House 9, Cicero, Illinois, Burlington Railroad. That's one of the best foremans, best agents, or any kinda guy that I've ever been under yet. He just believed in treatin everybody right. He didn't want the dock foremans to mistreat nobody, he didn't want to mistreat nobody hisself. And this guy that taken his place when he went down to the main office and went to work in the Loop, George Mays, he was a good guy but he was long-strung. And that operation out there just changed over all at once after George taken over, just altogether different out there workin. He wanted the foremans to drive you. He wanted em to push you all the time and Williams didn't believe in that, he believed in your doin an honest day's work and that was it, and leave you alone. Now if you didn't do your work then Williams'd come by and get on you, and he'd come by and he'd eat you out, if you didn't do your work. But Mays he just walks in flatly, just keeps goin runnin round just lookin to see here and there, like everybody was dumb or somethin.

I never did like the freighthouse myself, I never did like freighthouse work. I was always out on steel-gang, section work, I like steel-gang work. After I quit cotton-mill work, I got disgusted workin inside, see. I'd rather be out on a job anytime, where it's air, fresh air. I mean you might get on a little harder job than what you do at the freighthouse. Then another thing, it's more money on it, that kinda job, too. I just always felt better myself out where it was fresh air.

Well, you take out there in the freighthouse, you're inside a big dock there, and now if you work down on T-section out there, both sides a the doors is open all the time. They call it the T-section, the trailer sections, where the trailers back in and unload on one side and then load on the other side. The wind blowin straight across there—and of course that L-section down there: they back right on in under the dock and close the doors. Well, you're back in there in the summertime, that hot sun comin down on top a that steel grill; in the wintertime that cold wind comin out on that cold steel building. Buddy, you catch it. I worked out there when it's thirty-one below zero on that T-section, where that wind, buddy, it was cuttin. You put in eight hours out there in that T-section when that wind's runnin about, that kind a cold weather, I'll guarantee you, you don't go overtime, uh-uh. Hell with that overtime. You say I'm ready to go home where it's warm. Or the first bar where you can get you a shot of whiskey.

I slipped across every day and I'd go across to Mary's Bar there; I got there in no time. I got to have me a good drink a whiskey. See, you couldn't carry nothin back over there. Bunch a them pimps, you know, they's always a bunch a pimps for the company everywhere you work, and especially on me. I was dock foreman, see, they was some of em waitin on me to catch me anyway to turn me in to the union or turn me in to the office. Specially some of em that wouldn't do the work and I had to get on em, see, and I was just as wild as they was. Lunchtime I'd go and have me a drink, come on back. Then have a break in the afternoon, I'd go over and get me another drink. Well, they couldn't do a dam thing about that. But they could if they caught me while there was a bottle on me on dock.

They's always a bunch that they figger they won't work theirself, won't work a honest day's work without having this drive on. And so I wasn't the type a person to just get out there and say, Well, I want you to keep goin, go on, go, go. I wanted em to do their job without havin to stay over em all the time, and I know I never was the type a person that liked for a foreman to stand over *me*. Durn foreman tell me what to do and go and leave me alone, I'll do it. But if he stands over me I won't do nothin on the job, I'll just completely quit workin. Well, them kind a guys, some of em they got em out there, they don't care. All they're out there for is to make a day, a couple a days a week, come out there work a couple a days and you didn't see em any more for maybe a month. Well, they didn't care whether they done a day's work or not. All they cared for was that twenty-four dollars out there. Down on Madison Street they could drink wine for a month. So that bunch up there, they caught you drinkin, they run and tell em, Hey, or tell one a them railroad dicks and then he'd turn you in to the office out there. And some a them pimps they'd go to the foreman—"Listen, I saw so-and-so takin a drink." "Oh?" Well, the next thing you know, your name's blasted over the loudspeaker to come to the office. "I saw you. You been down there drinkin. Where's your bottle?"

You had a certain job to do. I'd get in there and throw that freight out. I'd say, "Get that yonder outside and let's get it moved"; say, "I'll put it to you, just listen to the numbers." And I'd throw it outa them trailers. But these transistor radios, these clock-radios, we played ball with them out there. You ought to see them loads come in out there. They have a fifty-foot trailer come in out there. They already got the numbers stamped for the different stores, but you got to separate em—maybe there'll be for all fifty states, there's so many radios goin to all fifty states, to their stores. Well, Los Angeles, California's just got forty-five stores, bet you didn't know about that. Every one of em's got a different number, different street, that's gotta be loaded for a trailer that's goin direct to that store. You got to have a couple a good callers that's a-listenin to what they a-sayin, a couple a good stackin men to do this, what's called play ball with em where they can hear you. You get back there into that trailer and get two men out the door, stackin, and you hollerin off numbers as fast as you kick em out there. Well, these two stackin men got to remember somethin too: they got to remember what number they throwed that. Just clockwork. Well, we played ball with the radios, stuff like 'at. Pitchin em. Well, you ought to see em with televisions. Oh God, they take them televisions and roll em all over the freighthouse, out a them boxcars. Especially when the guy's done about give out, about quittin time, got maybe four-five more to go in his trailer, he's wantin to get his trailer unloaded, he'll take that television, start rollin it up through that boxcar and trailer, get tired of pickin em on up, puttin em on them dollies. Imagine we broke some. Why hell, you didn't care unless they'd caught you. We'd always have a lookout if we was playin ball.

Been livin out on Carson Avenue, and the building caught fire out there, and we thought we'd move out to Berwyn.* But the landlord give me two months a my rent money back. Course my apartment wasn't burned, but I didn't want to live in the building where the other apartments was all burned out and they wasn't nobody there. So I moved way down on West Jackson Boulevard. And I moved from down on West Jackson Boulevard to another place out on Carson Avenue, and then I moved to Cicero, and then up here, on Wellington.† I give up a 'partment down here on Wellington that just made this place here ashamed of itself—all these buildings in Uptown. I went home on vacation, and that's when I should've paid my rent, a month ahead, in place of givin the apartment up. Then when I came back I moved on up to Uptown, up here on Winthrop, 4836 Winthrop. Like a damn fool. I oughta had went the other way.

At that time, when I first moved on Winthrop, it wasn't too bad a street, it was a pretty quiet neighborhood. Five or six years ago it was pretty quiet. You didn't have all that damn much of police runnin around here,

---

*A suburb just north of Cicero.
†A half-mile south of Uptown.

right behind you every time you turned around. Fact, you seldom saw a police unless you walked out on Broadway or maybe you'd see one go out Lawrence, but they wasn't just one car right after another.

I didn't know the first soul when I moved into the building. They was a boy that was living in the building there that was from down close to my home town, I knew him back home, but of course I didn't know he was living here. He was working at that Motorola television place. And I saw one that I knew, then, when I went in the tavern down here on Sheridan Road one Saturday and I guess I'd been here maybe a month, and I walked into the tavern and I run into a boy that was from Engle-wood, Tennessee, Leon Teel. He's about the only one that I know now that's actually been here as long as I've been here. They were livin over on Ainslie Street at that time, managin the building over there till his wife gave up the building.

But that's about the only people I knew. Oh, Bill Hardin and Ray Hardin, course I knew them back home. They just come up here in the spring and they go back in the winter, both of em. Them and Limey* and all them got caught gamblin. Bill's the redheaded guy comes in there, that's got his fingers off his right hand here. Had that Plymouth. They'll probably be back when it warms up again, stay here during the summer. All they do is trade cars. Trade cars, take em back and sell em. When it gets cold they cut back to Georgia.

Then we had a fire up at 4836, so we moved to 4746 Kenmore down there, lived there about eleven months. One month I paid the rent, a month's rent, and this old sonofabitch, he wouldn't pay the gas and light bills. He was s'posed to, it was supposed to be a furnished building. And so he had a little ole cherry farm over here in Michigan. He'd go off over there and stay. So it was on Friday that I paid the rent, he cut out on Sunday. Monday mornin I went to work. I come in Monday afternoon and the gas was all cut off. His old lady lived there. I got up, went in and jumped on her cause there wasn't no gas. "I can't, John, he's got all the money." I said, "If he's got all the money, what the hell, he's not payin the damn gas and light bill?" So anyway it was too late to get anything done about the gas bein on at night. And so I called the next mornin, the

*Limey is a very black cigar-smoking junk dealer, used-furniture merchant, renowned and assimilated in his section of the neighborhood. He was always good for odd jobs for young guys, lived with a white woman, and claimed in a Mississippi accent to have immigrated from a British possession ("Angola"). His store was just down the street from the JOIN office until he moved to larger quarters; he came to some JOIN demonstrations with his troupe of hired hands and played Santa Claus at JOIN Christmas parties.

gas company sent one out and cut the gas on, made him pay it, cost him all that extra money. But anyway the stove wouldn't work, couldn't cook no bread on it. So I told him, I said, "You better get me a damn stove or else I'm gonna nail both of you Jews in here one of these days. I'm gonna come in here about half drunk and," I said, "you're gonna look out."

So I came in there that afternoon and he got me a stove but he hadn't put it in. It was sittin out in the hallway. That was doin a lot of good, you know, settin out in the hallway. So you could tell the gas stove was leakin, so I said, "The hell with it. I know how to cost him fifty dollars right fast." I just walked down the street there over to Whitey's Tavern and I called the gas company. I said, "Would you please come out here and cut off this damn gas stove that's a-leakin gas, 4746 Kenmore, apartment so and so, Mr. Nunno's buildin?"

"We'll be right out."

Fifteen minutes later here come the gas people. They cut the gas off from the stove. This gas man told me, he said, "That's just cost them fifty dollars."

I said, "I don't give a damn if it cost them five thousand."

He said, "When you get your stove hooked up," he said, "call me and I'll come back and turn it on." He said, "That'll be another fifty dollars against them, turnin it on." So I said, "Good, thank you." He said, "We don't like this buildin no way, we don't like these operators here."

Me and Leon put the stove in. I went back and called this man, he come back out and another fifty dollars he charged for comin back out and turnin the gas back on.

So here the landlord come back a couple of days later, you know, they'd notified him there was a hundred-dollar bill, you know. He was a givin a damn fit, one of these damn fido fits. I walked in from work, I was hot as hell I didn't give a damn what I done. Worked like hell at that freight-house and I didn't give a damn no way. Leon was workin' out there with me, he was workin on daily pay at that time. Me and him stopped down on Kenmore there, for a few beers anyway, and had a few, two or three shots out in Cicero. And I walked on upstairs and I said, "You got dinner ready, Etta?"

And she said, "Yeah," she said, "the old man had a fit about that gas deal."

I said, "That's good, that suits hell out of me." I said, "I'm havin a damn fit cause I didn't get to cook no bread here for about a week and no damn gas on for three or four days too." I said, "I enjoy that." So I meant to get my money back some way. I walked out in the hall about that time.

"Mr. Dawson," the landlord said, "I just don't like the way you done about that stove."

I said, "I don't like the way, by God, you done at all. In fact I don't even like you, to go with it. And," I said, "what the hell you gonna do about it?"

I said, "You can't whup me." Well, that's his brother-in-law that was there, see.

He said, "We both can."

I said, "You both can't do it," cause I knew if I couldn't whup both of them over there Leon'd help me whup em. I just reached and got em both by the damn collar, I jerked em over together and taken their heads and just bounced them together right there in the damn hallway, and throwed em both down the damn stairs from the second floor right to the first floor. I walked in there and told them both, "You sonofabitches, get in your damn office and stay in and don't come out. If you do, I'll jest kick your damn sorry ass right down Kenmore down through here. And I want to tell you somethin, I ain't payin no more damn rent while I live here." I said, "I dare you or your old lady or your brother-in-law or anyone else to come up there and ask for that rent."

Hell, no, he wasn't comin up there and ask for no rent. I stayed three more months, then went back home. We'd be off there at the railroad in the wintertime about a couple of months. That's when we'd generally go down home, was in the wintertime. I was three months behind in rent.

Me and Leon loaded the car. I walked right out and loaded my stuff in the car and dared him—he was standin there in the hallway. I told him, "Git out of the goddamn way for I'm bringin my stuff out and put it in the car." I said, "Hell with you." If I'd a known my baby right then had that lead poisonin, I'd a probably picked him up and batted him against that wall.

For the last month she didn't eat very right, but you know a lot of times a baby with a cold or somethin, they're not goin to eat. Well, she taken sick on the way home and she started vomitin just before we got into Terre Haute, Indiana. And so I guess about a couple of miles out there on that expressway goin into Terre Haute, I pulled over to the side of the road. We had some water, a jar, we washed her face and got that vomit off of her and I went on into Terre Haute and I stopped there at this restaurant and she commenced throwin up again, so I asked this lady in the restaurant if she could tell me where there was the closest hospital, if they had a hospital. She said yeah, they had the Baptist Hospital and the Catholic Hospital up there. So we carried her over to the Baptist Hospital and I went in the emergency room. He said, "Oh, it's just a cold." And he give her, I guess it was a penicillin shot and gave her a little ole bottle of green-lookin medicine and told us to give a couple doses of that. And he said if the fever don't break when you get into Nashville, he said, stop at Nashville and have this baby checked at the Baptist Hospital in Nashville. He give me a doctor's name right there. But anyway we stopped at Fort Campbell, Kentucky, at Jimmy's place, Etta's brother's. And we spent the night there. And so the fever didn't seem like it was breakin much and she was vomitin and he said, "Let's take her over to the hospital here at the fort here," Jimmy said. "Well, hell," he said, "there's something wrong bad with that kid," he said, "it ain't none of this cold. She's burnin up with fever." And we taken her over to the Army Hospital. This doctor, government specialist that they called in there, he said, "I don't like the color of that." So he checked her over for about four hours at the hospital and he said, "There ain't no use in goin any further with her," he said, "the kid's got lead poisonin." He said, "I ought to just put her in the hospital."

And he asked me where I was goin to and I told him, I said, "I'm tryin to go to Rome, Georgia." I said, "I got laid off from my job and tryin to get on home."

He said, "When are you goin to try to go?" He said, "Don't leave here tonight." He said, "If you are goin to pull out of here tonight with that kid," he said, "I won't let you." He said, "Now in the mornin," he said, "I will, if you'll go straight on in; if you'll give her this medicine and guarantee me that you'll put her in the hospital in Rome when you get there, if you got a doctor there who can do somethin for the kid," he said. "If not," he said, "we're just gonna have to do somethin here." And so I told him about this Dr. Hackett there and this doctor knew him, you know, he'd been in the army and I told him he practiced in the service and he said, "Well," he said, "I know Walter Hackett," said, "he's one of the good ones as you can get." So they called the hospital at Floyd County and told im the kid was comin in there the next day.

Well, we kept givin her that medicine that night and Jimmy had some baby medicine, aspirin and stuff like at, you know, tryin to get the fever cooled down before it was the next mornin. So we went on in to Rome and she kept vomitin on the way in, over to the hospital. Naturally Hackett was there waitin when we come in with the baby. And they just put it right on in the hospital and he went to doctorin it. She stayed twenty-seven days over at Floyd County Hospital and that's when they checked it out, what was already been checked at the Army Hospital, that it was lead poisonin. They said it was from paint, peelin paint. She must've ate it, it was bad down there, that buildin we were livin in. I didn't saw her eat it, but it's the only damn place she could've got it.

LEAD POISONING

Seventy-five percent of the poisoning deaths among children in Chicago result from lead. Much lead poisoning is not diagnosed as such, but as "unfortunate" mental retardation. The cheap paint and plaster peeling from walls and window sills tastes sweet, and in Uptown is very available. Though the maximum lead content in interior paint is now specified by law, many slum owners simply paint over the old paint, saving the money it would cost to scrape the walls clean first. When the weather changes, both paints peel.

Medical caseworkers at Children's Memorial Hospital believe that the paint-eating "syndrome" is caused by "bad parent-child relationships." Sometimes they will refuse to release a lead-poisoned child until its parents move, but they decline to notify landlords that their buildings are still lethal.

It was just lucky that we caught it when we did. If they hadn't caught that on Lila when they did, she'd a probably been brain-injured, or, you know, somethin wrong. She was just a little over two years old. And it's lucky that I got her home and got a hold of that Dr. Hackett. Course they got other good doctors there in Rome besides him but I just knew he was a real good doctor. Hell, he didn't ask me whether I was workin still on the railroad or what my insurance was, he didn't ask me when they released her what I was gonna do about the bill. He said, "You take the kid." Course I'm gonna turn the insurance in but they didn't even ask me nothin like this bunch here. This bunch here, they're crazy. First thing they start askin, you got this? you got that? They don't care. They'll let you set there all day. Wonder what the man does that's cut all to hell, I reckon they'd have to have a chest X ray down at Cook County Hospital, huh, before they done anything. They'll give him a number down there for a chest X ray and they're so upset it'll take em half a day to give him a chest X ray. God. Shit. Stupid. I guarantee you you'll see the difference in people going through the emergency room there in Rome. You won't be there five minutes before you have a doctor, I don't care whether you got a penny in your pocket. It don't make any difference whether you're from Rome or whether you're from Chicago or where you're from.

A leaflet, September, 1966.

TEEN AGERS PROTEST!

We of the Girls' Streets Project of the Hull House Association want to help people in our community of Uptown. We want to work to end lead poisoning in our area. We want to work to get stop signs on streets where children get killed. We want to help take sick children and adults to the hospital to get treatment.

But Hull House won't let us. Hull House wants to teach us to answer the phone and to be good secretaries. If that is what we wanted to learn, there are many training programs we could go to which would teach us to be secretaries. That kind of training isn't going to help solve the problems of our community: the problems of lead poisoning from slum buildings, of bad health, and of inadequate traffic signs.

We have been working to end lead poisoning in Uptown for the last eight months. We have saved the lives of six kids already. We have gotten 500 signatures on a petition to get a stop sign on a dangerous intersection at Kenmore and Buena. Now Hull House tells us that we are not doing our jobs. Our wages have been cut to $1.25*an hour and our jobs have been limited to office and business work and "beauty culture". That's not why we are working for the War on Poverty. We want to work to help solve the problem of our community.†

*From $1.65.
†Hull House and the Urban Progress Center apparently deemed the eleven girls too close to JOIN. They lost.

They closed up one hospital in my home town several years ago on account of them refusin service to a man. The Health Department did. The guy didn't have no money on him. You don't walk in no dog pen and see a bunch of police standin there, askin you a bunch of silly questions at the hospital. You don't see no bunch of people layin out there in the hall, people sittin out there waitin all week to see a doctor. They's people go there at this Cook County Hospital, you know how long they been there? They been there a couple of days, still waitin to see a doctor in there. Hell, the hallway, the emergency room in Floyd County is in better shape than any part or any place in Cook County. And another thing, there's no sech a thing as you can't visit your people in Floyd County Hospital. Any age, any time of day or night. And that's somethin they just stress there in that hospital, is to visit people that's sick, and any minister that wants to go in that hospital to see anybody, he can go. Or you, if you say you know someone, you got a friend there, you don't have to be kin to im to go to see im.

They's no comparison to Cook County. Cook County's a dog pen.* Now that's the rottenest place I ever seen in my life. I've had experience there, Etta bein at that hole down there. And you ought to have saw the food them people had. They had some potaters that looked like they had maybe been put on the stove and heated a little, you could tell they wasn't cooked. They had some English peas, just a few little English peas, tray like the army has, you know, metal trays. And they had a little spoon of gravy, you know, maybe a little teaspoon maybe twice full of gravy. And the bread, one of these men, these old men, I asked him and he said, "It's so damn hard, I can't eat it." And you could tell that. They dropped it right on the floor. And some of em was half naked in there, together. Well, now, that ain't operatin no hospital. Well, I never see no such in my life. Why Cook County's so damn far behind in their sanitation and their Health Department it's pitiful. I'll tell you, I think Martin Luther King should make a drive on this Health Department here. Him tellin about some of the slum housin, I think he's good in that, but I think he should make a drive on this Health Department here, and the way these hospitals operate.

When Lila taken down with that lead poisonin I had a pretty good

---

*A Chicago newspaper reported the case of a thirteen-year-old black girl who was taken to Cook County emergency room complaining of a pain in her right side. She was given a penicillin shot and sent home. That night she died at home of a ruptured appendix. A hospital spokesman, when questioned, stated that teen-age girls from "ghetto environments" are assumed to have gonorrhea when complaining of such symptoms as a pain in the lower right side.

little bunch a money in the bank then, and while I was down home I just kept spendin what I had, hopin that she would get more of her health where I could get back on the job. I was down about four weeks, I got called back to my job, but she was still in the hospital and I didn't take her out. I just wired in and got a leave of absence. Time she did get able to go back, my money had just went. That's been my main downfall, just not bein able to build back up.

Come back up to Chicago and run into James Williams from Chattanooga. Me and him run around, he worked up at the freighthouse. Anyway, he got his income tax back and pitched a big drunk and went and got him a gal, right straight across from where he lived at. Rent a damn five-room pretty basement apartment. When he sobered up he realized he was straight across the street from his old lady. Could look right out the window and see him. Him and her had their fuss. He gave me the place.

At that time we had a very nice manager there, when we moved in. We stayed there about four months, very nice manager. This woman she was from Kentucky, had some kind of sickness and the doctors advised her to go back to a different climate, you know. And she left and went to a different climate. So they got one of these damn smart-asses in to manage the buildin. And she had the attitude that Southern people was all dogs. So I had the attitude that she was just a sonofabitch. And I just told her there in the hall one afternoon, she was runnin her damn mouth and I just told her in the hall. I said, "Well, what in the hell you think you're talkin to?" I said, "I ain't no dog." I said, "I'm makin more money right now than you make." I said, "I ain't askin for a damn thing." I said, "I ain't got to rent in this buildin."

I moved back to Kostner Avenue, but we didn't have room, so I moved back to Jackson Boulevard then, right straight across from the St. Andrew's Hospital. I was livin there when Lila had pneumonia. I carried her over to St. Andrew's. They have a foreign woman over there that all she does is supposed to be a-specializin in babies. Have a clinic over there that you have to pay five dollars to first get in the clinic before a doctor ever looks at it. So anyway, we went over there and paid the five dollars, got the clinic card, and then they went to examinin the baby. Had the baby in there about six and a half hours. This woman and about seven or eight other doctors checkin the baby. Still hadn't found out what was wrong with the baby. That's supposed to be specialist now. Went on back home, givin the baby baby-aspirin to try to cool her fever down and I'd been out from work for about three days on account of the baby. Etta'd just been up so much she just couldn't stay up, tendin the baby by herself. So I went out to the freighthouse that afternoon to get my paycheck and this colored guy that works out there, he said, "Somebody said your baby's sick."

I said, "Yes, pretty bad off and I can't find out what the devil is wrong with the doctors down here."

Said, "Which one did you carry her to?"

I said, "Over to St. Andrew's, supposed to be a specialist there."

He said, "Yeah, they're good to let em die over there." He said, "I got a friend of mine," he said, "if you ain't got no prejudices about your baby goin to a colored person," he said, "I got a friend of mine that works over at Illinois Research, doctor over there." He said, "Will you meet me down there in the mornin?" He said, "I'll take off from work myself, you meet me down there." He said, "I'll make arrangements for him to be there. Bring that baby over here." I said, "Yeah, doesn't make no difference to me." So he made arrangements. The next mornin we went in, this guy was there and he checked the baby over. He said, "The baby's got pneumonia." But he said, "I'm goin a still examine the baby, find if there's anything else." Examined the baby and he said, "It's not just strict pneumonia, it's bronchial pneumonia." And he knowed exactly what to do. There was no assholin about this doctor there, he knowed his stuff and he was a good doctor. I don't remember his name, but that's the best doctor that I've ever seen in Chicago yet.

Must've been over two years ago now I got hurt. I opened that boxcar out there at Freight House 9, it was the deep freezer, and they didn't have it blocked on the durn door where they were shippin from. And when I opened that boxcar—the blame thing came right on top of me out there. And they okayed to send me to the hospital and I stayed two days in the hospital, and they wanted me to take a hundred and fifty dollars to sign a release, and I said, "You take a hundred and fifty dollars and go on back down the road with it." I said, "The minute I sign that release," I said, "that's the minute I lose all my benefits." I said, "I haven't been workin the railroad for about eighteen years now for nothin." I said, "No," I said, "I ain't gonna lose all that retirement pay and sick leave and all that stuff like 'at." So when I signed up for my sick leave they sent me a letter, said they disapproved it cause I wouldn't sign a release. So I went out to the union. I said, "Now here, just a minute here, what the devil's comin off here?" I said, "There ain't no law to make a man sign a release." I told em what I *would* do. I didn't want no law suit with em, but I wanted some settlement out of it, and I wanted a settlement the right way. So this union steward said, "Well, we'll take it up with the union." I said, "All right."

So I hung around there about three weeks and I still hadn't drawn no sick-leave check. I knew I couldn't sign up for unemployment fer the doctors wouldn't let me go back to work. If I went and signed up for unemployment, see, they could automatically disapprove me, fer I wasn't able to work. So I went down to Rush Street, Railroad Retirement Board. Boy we tangled. I said, "You're gonna write me out some checks today, not next week." I said. "I'm due two checks right now." I said, " I want my blame checks. Got to have somethin to live on." I said, "I ain't got to sign no blame release." So he did finally write me out two checks, for sick leave, handed em to me. A hundred and two dollars apiece, two hundred and four all together. Well, he wanted me to sign a paper. I said, "I ain't signin nothin."

That's the way you got to be with them people. Just say we ain't a-gonna do it, we ain't a-gonna get along. Never give in to a company. I seen too many people mistreated by workin for companies and givin in to em. Like my cousin, her husband got his leg pulled off there in a cotton mill at home and died and they went down there the next morning while my uncle was up in town helpin make arrangements for the funeral. And while she was all tore up there over it, they went down and told her, said, "You sign these papers right here," said, "you'll be gettin so much a week and your little girl'll be gettin so much, and we'll take care of all this funeral." Dadburn if she didn't even sign her rights away till even the insurance paid for the funeral. That's just how crooked these companies are, and if it hadn't a been for a lawyer there just takin it up for her own and helpin her out, she never would a even got a dime for this kid. She didn't get any money for this kid till she was sixteen years old, and that was so durned low it was a shame: twelve dollars a week. I mean that was a lot!

You can work for one a these companies, work your life away, kill you, work every day of your life. If they get a chance they'll stick it *to* you right about the time you get to retirement time. That's to keep from givin you anything to live on for your family. That's these companies this day and time in this country, always has been. Well you can talk about Communist and dictatorship, this country's under the worst dictatorship than Communist ever has been in the world, right here.

And I think that the unions are one of the best things in this country that's ever been. Just look back several years ago when John L. Lewis chartered the coal miners. I have a sister that married a boy from Bluefield, West Virginia. Gibson boy, his daddy was a miner out there at Beckley, West Virginia. And at that time, when they pulled that strike those coal minin companies was tryin to put those people out where they done worked theirself to death, done worked years in those mines. They were tryin to throw those people out without any kind of a pension to live on or anything else. Well, if it hadn't a been for John L. Lewis, people like my sister's daddy-in-law—what the hell would he have to raise his family on?

I went into the union, went all day and night for it, in the summer of 1939. For I've been raised to back the union. I'd heard about the coal miner's union and the railroad union all my life, for my grandaddy and my daddy both was railroad men, and actually the railroad had a union ever since their history, the Railroad Brotherhood. The unions started comin in there in 1937, '38, and '39, in the textile industry. Nineteen-forty, '41, they really made a drive there in the South, in the textile industry. Well, then while I was in the service they made another drive there and got all these other plants in. And they had several bloody killins there over the unions. Guys were tryin, some of em were tryin to work their help without unions, tryin to fight the unions. And a lot of those durn little stove companies, these guys that owned em, they didn't want to sign the contract after people had done voted for the union to go in. Well, that caused killins.

But one thing, when I went into the union we had no trouble there at this plant. They called an election, we called an election and when we had our election we won over the majority for the union to come in. And the company didn't give no hard time at all, they just signed the contract and they didn't have no trouble at all. That was thankful, that they didn't have.

I'll have to come to this, I'm in favor of the union doin the right things same as the companies. It's just like the Rome mill. The union wanted the company to sign a contract that the union could sue the company if they made a mistake, but the company couldn't sue the union. Well, there's no company here, nobody else gonna sign such a contract as that. I know I wouldn't, if I was runnin a company. Now I thought that was stupid in the president of the union that they had there at that time, which it was, and they got shut of him and got a new president. And then they got a new contract, company signed the contract without any trouble. And I know they not leakin' out much of that, on that strike in New York right now, but it sort of seems that that's what's comin' out in that traffic strike right there in New York right now. I mean you can go too far in anything.

I can't complain on the union operation, you know. Only thing that I got against some of the unions is you have some crooks in everything. It's like Hoffa. Yeah, that Jimmy Hoffa's as crooked as a barrel of fishhooks, but look what Hoffa's done for the country too. I do think that he got a dirty deal in Chattanooga in them trials. I think he got a dirty deal here in Chicago in that trial too. To start off with that was Robert Kennedy, and Kennedy and him had a grudge before he ever got into the union. This whole business is just between them two, you know. When Robert Kennedy got appointed Attorney General by his brother, President Kennedy, you know he made a statement about three or four days after he was appointed. He said, "I'll get Hoffa." He made those remarks. If he goes to jail I wouldn't give a nickel for Bobby Kennedy's life. But I still don't think Hoffa will ever serve any time. I think his lawyer'll hold him out till this administration gets out. And when this administration gets out then he'll get turned loose.

You never had a head man or nothin like that, he wasn't gonna take money if he could get a chance to put it in his pocket. But good God, if it hadn't a been for him the damn workin man wouldn't have nothin. I remember when in the textile industry you worked fourteen hours a day, six days a week, you drawed seventeen dollars a week. Well, people's only payin three and a quarter a month union dues in the textile industry. Well, that three and a quarter a month helps better than that seventeen dollars a week they used to make. And anytime you work over eight hours in one day in one of them textile plants it's time-and-a-half. Well, I thought that was a mighty good deal that they got set up.

Every once in a while you run into one of these presidents of the locals that he's not out there for the people, he's out there for the money. And course, there's a way to git shut of him, you can call a special election if you catch him and kick him out. They's some people have a lot of gripes about different locals and I have heard a lot of complaints, you know, these different locals and what they was doin. So when they come and complain to me about the unions I just tell em, I say, "Hell, it's not the local, it's the people that's in the local lettin the president of the union get by with it." And it was. It's like us—if we could get organized right here in this neighborhood just enough, why, hell, Mayor Daley couldn't budge us to save his life. That's our biggest trouble: they're brainwashed, they're brainwashed to death, the people are.

The welfare has got people scared, the city police has got people scared to death that actually lives here, it's actually their home. They're afraid to to make a move. Well, why should people be a-scared to stand up for their rights? If you go to jail for standin up for your rights, there's somebody gonna get you out. They ain't gonna let you stay there. They ain't gonna keep you there and feed you. They don't want to. It costs em too much. When we go out here and picket a place for the right thing we should get together. And we go and ask to go into one a these meetings and they refuse us, we picket that place. We should stand right there until every durn one of us goes to jail, if it take that.

You remember we struck the railroad in 1950? The government seized the railroad. Yeah, soldiers were runnin the railroad. What did we give a damn about it? Let em run it. They seen they couldn't run it and operate the world too. Right now is the best time in the world for us to strike. That's the reason they're comin on across with the rest of this pay raise on us. They got too many men in foreign countries to try to run the world and run that too. That's just like now, the reason the President hasn't sent men into New York about this transit strike. If he didn't have men all over the world, don't kid me that he wouldn't have soldiers in there running those buses and guardin those buses.

Oh yes, they's graft in the unions. We understand that. There's graft in anything that's in the world. You know it's gonna be somebody along the line's gonna make some money. There's nothin you and I or nobody else can do about that. But I had rather pay five dollars a month union dues and draw a decent wage than to go out here and work fer daily pay.

Some a these labor companies thinks you're a dog a some kind, just think you're a straight dog workin. They'll say, "Good God, you can work for that price out here and look at the money you're makin me, and I'll just put all this dirty work on you." I mean some a them jobs you're doin work that the regular employees won't even think about doin. They will work these people at a dollar-twenty-five an hour, they're gettin union scale from these plants.

Say for instance that you go on a job and you're gettin a dollar and a quarter and the cheapest they're workin you for is two dollars. They're makin seventy-five cents on each hour's work that you work every day. That's pretty good interest, settin on your settin down place all day long.

REWARDS OF A PUBLIC SERVICE

	NET SALES	TOTAL ASSETS	NET EARNINGS	PROFIT AS PERCENT OF ASSETS
Manpower, Inc. (1963)	$28,919,331	$7,701,284	$1,159,861	15
Work for Men, Inc.* (1963)	622,916	71,739	15,713	22
Jobs Unlimited, Inc.	†	†	†	†

*Names of day-labor companies have been changed.
†Secret. Dunn & Bradstreet reported in 1964 that on November 6, 1963, the Secretary and Treasurer of Jobs Unlimited "declined a financial statement." He stated that "volume has been increasing moderately" and estimated sales of $2 million for 1962. "Operations believed profitable."

Say these jobs are payin two and a half or three dollars an hour, they're makin a killin. The people should get their decent wage out of it. That's the way I feel about that, about somebody settin down there and drawin it. Why should we work for those offices that are makin that money and takin our money away from our families and then they holler poverty and poverty and poverty—what the hell do they expect the people to be on? Poverty, that's what they're gonna get. They're the ones smokin the cigars and drinkin all the good moonshine whiskey. We're the men doin the work.

They's a poor class of people that come to Chicago and come to different cities like Detroit, Chicago, New York, Los Angeles, and places like this that they thought that when they got there that they could just walk in and get a job of work that would pay em big money, but places like these slave-labor markets hurt a lot of those people tryin to make a decent livin for their families. There's a lot of people that comes here with a family and they find out they can't get a job where they can make a livin and don't have enough money to pay for theirselves. All right, they hop over here and they think, "Well, I can make a living on this place here," and they don't know that the place is only paying one-twenty-five, one-thirty an hour till they get out there. Well, in fact they wind up with about a dollar an hour when they get off their job. They cain't feed their family. Well, they get the attitude, the hell with it, and that's the cause of a lot of people from the South that just don't give a damn.

There ain't no better guy in the world than Leon Teel, no better, freer-hearted guy, do anything in the world for anyone, but when he goes out and works a couple of them days and knows he can't get a good job, he gets disheartened about working all day and then not getting nothing for it. Especially go out on one of these jobs and you're doin the job right along with this guy, the guy's gettin say three dollars an hour and you're gettin one-twenty-five, one-thirty. Well, you say, the devil, you work out there two days and you got ten dollars and look what that damn guy's got! You're doin the *same work* or maybe even doin more work than he's doing. He'll come in, say, "The hell with it, I ain't going back tomorrow." Disgusted with it. And he won't go back, he'll get drunk and won't go back.

LEON TEEL, A DEFEATED MAN

This first day labor I went to was in Evanston, they were payin a dollar-twenty-five. It really costs you when you don't get to work. Forty cents each way, that's eighty cents a day. Get there at six-thirty, maybe you spend half the day settin around and then you don't work lots of times.

They want you to be there every day whether they send you out or not. That's not the way I figure a daily pay job ought to be. It seems they get a little miffed at you if you miss a day. You could get a better job. Say like they wanted you to work the next day and somethin come up, you could make say twice as much if you take that. You go back the next day, you probably won't go out. That's just their attitude. Can't get much ahead, wages like that.

JOHN DAWSON

It wasn't like it is back home. Most of the class back home, you walk in a plant whether they know you or not and if they give you a job you can explain to the personnel manager that you had to have some money at the end of the week or had to have some money the next day after you work. Well, he would make arrangements for you to get money to live on till you drawed a payday. Well, these plants here won't do that, for they've got this cutthroat with these slave-labor markets here, they get their labor to them much cheaper.

There's none of these slave-labor market offices, daily-labor offices, will pay you time-and-a-half time or overtime unless you work forty hours at the same plant. They'll work you a couple of days at one plant, then they'll transfer you over to another plant, so that's to keep from payin it.

The business people is so stupid, I don't know what's the matter with em. If I was runnin a place a business, I wouldn't even allow one to send me a man. I'd go out on the street and hire me a man, say, "Come over in here, buddy, I got a full day's wages fer you." I would pay union scales on that job. That's robbin from the poor. They're robbin from the poor. I'll say they have to be a kickback through their personnel offices. Don't tell me that these personnel offices, a-payin Jobs Unlimited the full scale, that they're not gettin a kickback through Jobs Unlimited to get that. Or either they'd be willin to hire you or me or whoever it is comes up 'ere and pay them when they get off from work, full scale.*

*An Uptown resident who called day labor a public service, guaranteeing the freedom to work day by day for drifters, moonlighters, misfits and alcoholics, went on: "And for all I know they perform a service to the unions too. There must be some union connection. Because Jobs Unlimited down here on Broadway handles all of the work, so far as I know, at McCormick Place and these hotels downtown and the International Amphitheater. And I was at McCormick Place one bitter cold night when we had a hundred and forty-six trailer trucks to unload, and I'm sure they were all driven by union men. But there were not

I started messin around these places around '62, times I was laid off. Some a this work was lumber work, some of it was factory work, some of it was unloadin pipes, in fact they even had ditchdigging. Some places it was supposed to be listed as $1.25 an hour. Course when I went to work they was only payin $.75. Then went to $.90, they went $.90 to a dollar, they jumped from a dollar to $1.10, $1.15, then $1.25.* Well, that's what they's supposed to be payin. Some a these places you'd go to, you tell em you didn't have transportation, they'd let you have $.60. You come in that night, they'd charge you $.60 interest, which they don't have no license to be a loan office. That's a violation of the government law, not only state law but the government law. All right. In place of takin out your right amount on social security, which on me should be $.26 on a ten-dollar bill—before the new raise went in in January—they would take out $.65 or $.70. On income tax, which they should not even touch me on a ten-dollar bill, on eight hours, $1.25 an hour, should not even touch me a penny on income tax, with the dependents I had, they taken out a dollar, dollar and a half income tax. I'd come out with four, five dollars out of ten. Some a these places even tried to get me to go to work without signin a W-2 form, and some of em wouldn't even ask you for a social security number. I told em I didn't have to work that way.

Service, Inc., now, in Evanston, you go up there and work for them, they pay $1.30 an hour. They're sending men out to General Foods way out in Des Plaines, warehouse handlin help out there, and they send em to this Flood Manufacturing Company, which is a government plant, they have a government contract there at this plant. The least wages that's paid there is

---

union men working the docks. There were men from an outfit called Amalgamated Exhibits, doing the dock work for a dollar twenty-five an hour. And I was told by a member of Jobs Unlimited's staff that they are in some sort of a partnership agreement or a corporate agreement with Amalgamated Exhibits, who seem to handle all the loading and unloading for McCormick Place.

"We were waiting for the doors to one of the trucks to be opened, and I saw one of the bosses on the docks, so I asked him, I said, 'How come all these trucks are out here and there aren't any dockworkers?' And he panicked a little, he thought I was some kind of a union spy, I guess, and he said, 'Oh, I'll show you my card, I'll show you my card.' I said, 'I don't want to see your card, I'm just curious, that's all,' but he insisted on showing me this card. And I thought it'd be a Teamsters Dockworkers' card or something, and instead it was a union card, I believe the name of it was the International Brotherhood of Heating and Air-Conditioning Unloaders. It sounded like an Amos 'n' Andy type name. For all I know they might have a pocketful of union cards."

The unions implicated in these expositions—Teamsters, Auto Workers (auto shows), etc.—have not struck against this dummy unionism.

*In 1967, the minimum went to $1.40.

$3.80 an hour, the employees get there, runnin machines. I was a-runnin a machine out there that was payin four dollars and eighty-somethin cents a hour, that made these little taps, some kind a little taps that goes on these airplanes. I was a-gettin $1.25 an hour. That's the kind a place that Flood is.

And say you work up there where you live here in Chicago, it costs you a quarter from here up to Howard Street, it costs you twenty more cents to go to Evanston. All right, the same thing comin back. Time you get to the job and back, it's $1.50 a day for transportation it costs you to make that $1.30 an hour. They have a restaurant and a drugstore set up there in Evanston, that you can get your checks cashed. They don't try to make you go to a tavern there, but you have to pay $.20 to get your checks cashed at any one of these places. Now one thing, say you needed a dollar in the mornin, they'd let you borry a dollar, but they don't take no more'n that dollar out of your pay that night. I guess they figure, Hell, they chargin that $.20 on cashin the checks, and you know they's a deal there between them restaurants and that to get it cashed.

Now this Work for Men, they pay $1.25 on labor jobs and they've got men a-goin out to run punch presses, drill presses, and they pay them $1.35 an hour. And say for instance, say you got a car, they'll give you a load of men to haul out. They'll give you $.40 a head for each man you carry out to the job. Work for Men don't pay nothin—the company where that you're workin actually pays it to Work for Men for you. But the trouble is that you'll go out on these jobs, and a lot of these jobs, you'll drive plumb to Des Plaines and you'll work two hours and you'll come in. They'll tell you before you leave, it's a all-day job. When you get out there, the man'll say, "I didn't send for but two men." All right, you get out there and maybe you got four or five men beside yourself in your car. All right there, the rest of the men, they either got to sit there or he'll tell you, "Won't be over two hours' work." Well, you done drove out there, you almost got to work the two hours to pay expenses back.

Leon Teel and me went up there and he carried his son's car, and he told him, "Now I got a ten-hour job," and we went plumb out to the other side of Des Plaines to a plant out there. We worked three hours, that's all we got paid for was three hours' pay, but he let all of us work three hours, this foreman out there. He was a very nice man, but he showed us right on his record where he'd only called for two men. And he said, "I know exactly y'all's situation." He said, "I don't go for that kind of stuff." But anyway, we got back on the expressway, and we blowed out a tire out there. And we called Work for Men, he's got a couple of service trucks up there, asked him to send a service truck. And so the next day Leon carried out a whole load, just to see what we could run into. Anyway we got a whole day's work, and when we come in he charged Leon five dollars and a half for that service: his own service truck!

There's one other thing about them. Say you go out on a job and the damn job ain't fit for you to be on, some dog pen, and you come back in up there, and because you didn't do the job, or you wasn't a kind of a dog to just do his dog work for him, he'll tell you to not come back in his office no more, for he ain't got any more work for that kind of people.

One time he told me it was a clean job and we got out there and you know what we was a-handlin? Cowhides. Another time they sent me up to a place in Evanston, up near Skokie, where they make these carbon papers for the government and they make carbon paper for people all over the country. I had on clean, nice clean clothes. Went up 'ere. Godalmighty, that blue ink was all over that place, everything, them machines just kickin it out there. The regular employees had rubber clothes to wear. I said to this foreman, I said, "Ain't you got no coverhalls?"

He said, "No, I can't furnish no coverhalls for you guys out a these offices."

I said, "Well, I'll tell you what." I said, "You get somebody else to do your work over here." I said, "I ain't foolin where the ink's flyin all over this floor." I said, "Look at all these people here in these coverhalls, they look like they's a blue wall a some kind."

"Well, I cain't help you."

And I said, "Well, that's good, thank you." I said, "You can take your job and go to hell." I said, "I ain't workin here like that, I ain't got to work for a dollar-twenty-five an hour."

Now Leon and I came back in and told em, told old Bob up there at Work for Men, and he wanted to know why we didn't work the job, and we told him, and he said, "Well," he said, "You'll accept any kind of a job that I have in here."

So I told him, I said, "I'll tell you what, you can go straight to hell. I ain't got to work for you or no other sonofabitch like you." I said, "You do your own jobs up there, somebody else do it." I said, "I ain't goin up there and ruin a pair of pants that I spent about seven dollars fer." I said, "No sir, gimme my four hours' pay." I'm just plain with anybody like that.

This Jobs Unlimited bunch, here in Uptown, they're not doin the people right. And they have several other offices. If they can get a hold of em every day they send out 200 men, each one. They take out money down there, they charge em for a lunch that's been a-setting there two or three days. Sixty cents for two little pieces of thin baloney. It's done stale, the bread's stale, the meat's stale. And you can only draw $7 every day. They pay off the rest full on Wednesday evenin, after 4:00. If you're not there, they leave your check up at this Club Lounge on Wilson Avenue. If you don't buy a beer there, he'll tell you he ain't got the money to cash a check with. But they's a thing about the checks, any of these places that this check is made, I don't care what kind of check it is, they's no currency exchange in Chicago will cash those checks. That's true of all of em. I got a currency exchange card; and they don't cash those daily paychecks. They don't trust em, that they got enough of money in the bank to cover that. You can't even get one cashed at A&P.

And say you lose your ticket, say you've been out workin all day in one a these plants, and you lose your ticket. You can't get no money for it, you just done done your day's work, and that's just it, either way with Jobs Unlimited or Service, Inc., either one. Or any of these offices that you lose that ticket they give you, they won't let you check through these offices. Course you could do it, go and get you a lawyer and get it, but well it would cost you more for a lawyer to get that day's work, for you wind up with about six, six dollars and a half anyway. And a lawyer ain't gonna take no case like that noway. You'd have to go to the Labor Board and it'd take six or eight months or a year to get anything done about it, or State's Attorney's office. You go to the State's Attorney's office and it's the same thing bout somethin like that.

Then I pulled a good un on Jobs Unlimited down there. Me and Bill Hardin went down at this office, we went out to Niles and worked at this plant. And they done cut us, as cheap as they were. We supposed to got $1.25 a head for carryin out this carload. Come back in and got $.60 a head for carryin em all the way to Niles, Bill did. He cussed em out in the office and that's why I think how come the guy forgot to stamp my check. They give me a blank check but they signed the check. Well, the check was good up to $50. So what I got Bill to do, I got him to take a pen and write in $48.85 on the check. I didn't say a thing, I seen what they done. Bill just taken a pen, he wrote it in, which they do on a lot a checks. I just carried it on over there at that tavern over where they cash them checks, went on out. "Thank you!" Old Bill said, "That's the best un I seen pulled down here on Jobs Unlimited for a pretty good while," and I said, "I'll learn them to hand me a blank check and it already signed." I didn't forge nothin! I just put in the amount I wanted for a day's work. I told Bill, I said, "Damn right I deserved it."

You get hurt on the job through one a them places, they'll tell you the hell with you right quick. They don't give a damn whether you went to a doctor, they don't care whether you do nothin. So it *has* to be a bunch a these insurances that's a-backin that, and the syndicate backin that, or either they'd be scared to hell with that.

This Jobs Unlimited, there is as dirty a damn place as there is in the country. They send me up to this J. R. Crew Company in Evanston, and I got my arm broke on the job. They sent this guy that was drunk with me on this job. We was workin this paint machine up 'ere, this automatic paint machine where you put this paint in and it paints these toys. You had to lift these boxes of toys up over your head, and dump em in this machine. And I was up on the machine, a-pourin some paint in one of the machines that we had filled up, and I told this guy, I said, "You wait till I get this paint in here, where I can get started, and I'll help you dump that over in the machine"—in place of him doin it, which he was drunk. Which they had no business sendin a drunk man on a job, and he was so doped up on this wine and stuff that he didn't actually know what he was doin. Well, you can't blame the man, you can blame Jobs Unlimited for sendin a man out in that shape. And you can blame the damn company for lettin a man like that even try to work.

He dropped this box on top of me, knocked me off, down in between these machines on the floor, caught my arm, throwed it back in one a these curlers on the machine. And I asked this foreman to send me to a doctor. He said, "You can go back to Jobs Unlimited, and they'll send you to a doctor." He told me right in the face it's left up to Jobs Unlimited. I said, "Well, how in the hell am I goin home?" He said, "I don't know and don't care." I said, "Well, that's good then, by God."

So I come on back on the el, come back to Jobs Unlimited. I went in and asked this damn little Joe down there, I said, "How bout this arm messed up?"

"Oh, nothin wrong with it, you sprained it."

I asked Joe and I asked Horace both to send me to a doctor, and he said, "Aw, you're not hurt," he said. "You're just a-puttin on."

I said, "Well, that's good then."

I went over to the house and then I went over to this lawyer's office, and the blood was comin out of my shirt sleeve, and he said, "My God, what's wrong with your arm?"

I said, "I got it hurt and I think it's broke, the way it feels." So him and his secretary carried me in the washroom there and he cut the sleeve around my arm and he said, "Yeah." He said, "Where'd you get that?" And I told him where it happened at. He said, "Does Jobs Unlimited know about that?"

I said, "They do," I said, "that's the reason I come in your office, to see if there could be anything done about this, if I could get to a doctor."

And he said, "You mean you've contacted them?"

I said, "I have, and they said there was nothin wrong."

And he said, "Well, we'll find out." So he picked up the phone and he called Jobs Unlimited.

"Well, you know there's nothin wrong."

He said, "Well good. You know who the hell you're talkin to at this time?" And it must've been one of them told him that they didn't give a damn. Then he told them who he was, and then they begged him to bring me a doctor. He said, "No thank you, by God. You done refused him." He said, "We will get it done though." So he brought me to Ravenswood Hospital there. At that time we filed law suit.

That was in '64. At that time Jobs Unlimited didn't have no insurance. They called the compensation board in Springfield to be sure. They didn't wait and write, they called em. Since then Jobs Unlimited has taken out insurance on all their factories, all their offices. But we come to find this out too, that that insurance don't cover every man they send out a that office either. Certain jobs it don't cover that they've got assigned. So right there you'll see that these lawyers has got them nailed. In fact they called me, they tried to get me to take $3,000. They called the lawyers and offered the lawyers $5,000 to get em off em. The lawyers told em, said, "The next time you call me," said, "it's gonna be worse'n that in court." And so actually he's got the company up 'ere sued for not takin me to a doctor, and he's got Jobs Unlimited sued for not havin insurance, and got Jobs Unlimited sued for not takin care of me. In fact J. R. Crew Company up 'ere has begged the lawyers to get off em. They didn't know what they'd run into. No, they didn't expect that. They thought, Hell, that's just one a them damn bums out a them offices down there, see.

And I'll be a-fightin these slave markets as long as I stay in Chicago or any other city where they're at. I just can't be fer such as that. I'll probably wind up with I guess about $20,000 out a Jobs Unlimited, myself, and out a J. R. Crew, my part of it, and in fact I'd be willin to give my settlement just to bust up Jobs Unlimited. And that takes a whole lot for me to say that. I'd rather see a man make a decent wage that he can live on, just like I asked the legislator at the meeting,* that why couldn't they be a bill put in the Legislator and that passed in Illinois General Assembly and have the governor sign it, to do away with the labor offices? Now it can be done.

*JOIN meeting of January 26, 1966, at which sharp questions were put to Alderman Robert O'Rourke.

I know it can be done. And if the state of Illinois can operate one employment office that people goes and works out of on South Jefferson Street, and they get daily pay and get their full wages out a these plants, I think that the state of Illinois could set up a employment office on the North Side like that.

They keep hollerin poverty, poverty, poverty, that's all you hear every day in the papers. Until they do away with slavery, they'll never get shut of poverty. That's slavery no different than it was back when they had Nigras on the slavery. Strictly slavery in the country. And as I said, and I still back it up, until the people gets behind it and busts it up, busts up sech as that, it's gonna be that way.

That's how come I was one of the first members in JOIN, little over two years ago. I'd just got laid off from the railroad and I was fixin to go home, down home, draw my unemployment money a while. I'd come up there on Broadway to cash a check, my last check from the railroad, and I was goin down on Cicero Avenue to buy me a car. And I don't remember this boy's name, this student who came by at the time, but he come down the street there and he handed me one of these leaflets that JOIN was settin to organizin, and they was goin to have a meetin up at Hull House. There was a phone number there to call and I seen it was against these labor offices so I called and told em if they'd bring me some or let me contact em where I could get some I'd pass em out in the office in there. Well, I went right in there, Jobs Unlimited, and passed them out that day. Of course I was already a-fightin em, the labor offices, I'd been a-tryin to fight em for years and years.

So I went up there to the first meetin they had. You ort to have seen Jobs Unlimited. They had four detectives up there tryin to find out what was goin on, cut it off. We just told em hell with em, that they weren't allowed in there, that all the men that worked out of em was allowed but there the door was for them. They had to go. Of course we understood that they went back and told what was some a the things that was said. But we didn't mind, we didn't care a damn, we just wanted to let those detectives know that we knew they were detectives from Jobs Unlimited. We let em know exactly what we was fixin to do.

I went home and then came back, and I didn't do much work in JOIN, for I got called back to work, and I didn't have much chance to do much. Then I got hurt on the job, I stayed here about three months and then I went back home and then I came back. I'd been laid off about three months at that time and I had to go on welfare.

Etta Dawson

When Lila came it wasn't quite nine months. I was accused of *havin* to get married, but I didn't have to. Mine, the way they come, she was two weeks early, Trudy was a month early, Clarence was two weeks late, and J.T. was a month and a day early. This un's due I reckon the last of this month or the first of the next. Johnny says it'll be when the moon changes.

All of em been born in Cook County. The only thing that I've got against Cook County, they don't give you nothin to knock you out. They say that they have too many comin in through there, see, and if they knock you out you're capable of fallin off the table, and there's not enough nurses to catch you. Specially before they carry you to the ward. And a lot of times you'll sit out in the hall, before they have a chance to carry you to the ward, for maybe a day or a night. And if you go in at night, you don't get in the ward till the next morning, in time for breakfast. With Clarence, I set out in the hall. When J.T. was born there was one had a set of twins out in the hall. They was tryin to get a delivery room, and they couldn't get one. And she kept tellin them it was comin and the doctors wouldn't pay her no attention. They said, "Now, you got about two more hours." And they were born out in the hall. And there's been several born not in the delivery room, but the room you go to before, labor room. Well, it's not so bad while you're in there as it is to get to the ward that's next to it, because it drives you nuts listenin to em holler. You can hear em all the way down there. See, with Trudy the afterbirth busted, and I had to stay five days, so they carried us down in that room. For two days we didn't have a nurse come down there. All we had was our food come there, and we went without water. They didn't change beds or anything. Because these other nurses, the day nurses didn't know we were down there. And the kitchen, they just had their orders filled out, see, for em to bring the food down, and we would have to walk clean out to the big ward before we could even get a glass of water. And if you was bedfast, you couldn't. If there was an emergency in there I don't know what would happen. Like back home they give you a light, you know, that you can turn on to call the nurses, but over here it's not.

Johnny worked good till he got laid off, he was makin two dollars and somethin a hour. The first time he was laid off was about two weeks before Lila was born, and he got laid off and we got emergency check from welfare, and they gave me a layette with her. I hadn't been to a doctor or anything so we had to go to County and I hadn't had no chance to buy no clothes up for her. The social worker over there at the hospital sent him down to welfare and he'd been out of work two or three months then.

They called him back to the railroad after she was born and he worked out there till last year, when he got hurt. They stopped the checks and everything. Well, we went down and got on it again. My landlord carried us down. She kept gripin about the rent and gripin about the rent and she took us down and got the emergency check. We stayed on it for two months and they sent John through this school, cab drivers' school. And when he came in one day we went out and cashed the check from welfare and got groceries and when we got back to the house they was a telegram sayin mother was real bad off sick and not expecting her to live. We had to get there some way so we bought a car, a '56 Chevrolet. It'd be kinda rough takin all four of these kids on a bus. That's one good thing about welfare down South, they don't care whether you got a car or what.

She got out of the hospital though. Through the State Employment Office in our home town we got a job pickin pickles in Michigan. These little bitty ones, I guess you'd call it kosher pickles, cucumbers to pickle. And when we got there they had already got their quota in and there was no job and we had to get back home the best way we knew how. When we started out we had money but when we started back we didn't have none. John borrowed ten dollars off of the guy we was workin for to get some groceries with and we got through Michigan, through Ohio, just as far as into part of Indiana. And when you get into Indiana you can hit this place you go and get gas and food, I don't know exactly what it's called. They give you enough just to get to the next big town. Then we stopped in the last town in Indiana and got gas which carried us to Nashville, Tennessee, which we was out of gas and oil both. We had enough gas to take us from Nashville to Comfort, Tennessee, to the American Legion, and they filled the car up with gas and give us oil and give us a ten-dollar grocery order. We pulled in Rome at ten that night.

Well, he worked at pulpwood for a while, haulin pulpwood, while we were down there, and then he decided he'd come back up here. So we came back, had to sell the car when we got here, to live. He just couldn't find no work. Railroad wouldn't put him back to work and the labor offices was slow and we thought we couldn't get back on welfare till we'd been here a year. Which we didn't stay out of the state a year, we was just out six months and we had been here about five years then.

We hadn't been here three, four weeks when we got a 'mergency check off the welfare through the Urban Progress Center,* and I was thinkin that we was put on ADC-U† but we never did get another check. So I called down there and they told me—not the head man but that one next to him, Wells, Mr. Wells—he told me to come down and he'd talk to me personally about renewin the emergency check. Well, when I got there he said he was too busy, so they turned me over to a caseworker. They said that John would have to come down, sign the papers. Well, he done told me he wasn't goin down. He was havin pains around his heart and he just didn't want to go down. They said, "Why don't you take a warrant out for him?" That's why I cussed em all out down there. And they offered me two dollars to feed six off of, till I could get him to come in, and I said no, I said I refuse the two dollars. I said, "That's not even enough to feed em," I said. "That wouldn't even be one meal, much less three or four."

So Mr. Brown from the Urban Progress Center, he came out and talked to John, he finally went down and got a check, and they was supposed to have sent us another check but they didn't do it. Caseworker came out and everything, we never did get another check. That was when they got Johnny the job at Illinois Christian Hospital. And he worked day and night. Drew twenty-four dollars for it. And we paid twenty dollars rent, turned right around and had four dollars to buy groceries with—not four dollars, because he caught the bus from Illinois Christian Hospital up home.

And I went up to Friendship House,‡ and I asked the Reverend, I said, "Do you know whether I can get some groceries?" And I showed him the pay stub and everything, and he called the Little Brothers of the Poor. Which they brought enough food out to last one day. One little shoppin bag full, which would probably, you know, last a smaller family for a week or two, but it wouldn't last us that long. And so next day I went down here to Winthrop, where this little church is, and I didn't have any milk for J.T. so I went and all I asked for was bread and milk. And they brought out

*The local center of the war on poverty.
†Aid to Dependent Children of the Unemployed.
‡A church-supported neighborhood service office.

ETTA DAWSON   101

two big boxes of groceries. So that's what we lived on until Rennie* got Johnny back on welfare.

Johnny had already met Rennie—see, he belonged to JOIN a long time ago. While they was out on Kedzie I believe it was, when he used to go to meetings. I walked up and talked to Rennie about him not gettin the check. So Rennie called up the caseworker and told her, said he's sick and he can't come in that office. We never did go up to the office. The caseworker came to the house and he just filled out the papers right there at the house.

And when they finally got us on it, we got one full check, $229, and then we've already got two checks this month, supposed to get another one. If they don't send that other check I don't know what we're goin to do. They sent us a notification that we was supposed to get $212 a month, which we just got $125. See, they sent out food stamps and we hadn't never wanted them. For $105 food stamps you have to pay $73 for it, and to pay two weeks' rent we couldn't afford all that $73. So John went up at JOIN and called her up and asked her why food stamps was sent out. Well, she said that she would see that we got that other check. And we haven't never got a clothin check, which we are supposed to get.

But this caseworker's probably a pretty good one, because she's German and they've already went through that: you know, the starvin to death from overseas.

But if it was up to me I'd get off it. A family can't hardly get enough to live off of, and you ask for anything they don't never let you know whether you're goin to get anything or not. And then they told us to move cause the apartment's too little for six. That's another thing—if a person don't think their apartment's too little, why should the welfare bother about it?

And at that JOIN meeting the other night this woman she had a little boy in Stewart School, and she said that they'd send a note around and tell em to come to the basement—all that was on ADC, ADC students— and they would give em the clothes there, outfit em in new clothes and everything. And the subject was brought up, why should the child be embarrassed like that? Why couldn't the mother go get the clothes? The mother knew the size—why couldn't the mother go get em? And this colored girl, Sarah, she said that she wouldn't let her kids do it. She told em if they told em to go to the basement, for them to come home. Said if they wanted her to come and get the clothes, that she would come and get the clothes, cause it was too much embarrassment for the child.

*Rennie Davis, then a JOIN organizer.

Join's a good organization but you'll have to ask John about it. That's all he talks about. He used to stay home a lot before he started goin over there. I just wish he'd stay at home more. I wanted to go over there some myself and finally I just got up and went to that meeting. I told Johnny, "You stayed gone four nights in a row and I'm goin out tonight."

I think somethin else: a lot of these organizations like the Montrose Center* and the JOIN and the Southern Mountaineer Council† and the Indian place‡ and the Hull House, you know, and all that would work together, they'd be a lot better. That Southern Mountaineer Council used to be a pretty good organization but now they're not much help. I didn't even know they was such a place until John got laid off from the job, that railroad out there. They wouldn't give him his check or anything and we was out of groceries and this family upstairs told us to go down there. Well, they gave us some soup and stuff and then they told me to come back Monday mornin and they gave me ten dollars to get some groceries with. Which now, I don't think they do that now. And you know they used to have clothes there that they'd give away. I mean they wasn't these dirty clothes or nothin else, you know, that'd have to be cleaned or anything; they was new clothes and if they *was* dirty they'd take em out to the laundrymat and wash em. Now when Clarence was little he got this little girl's outfit— you stick him down in it and zip it up and a little coat and cap to match that goes with it. Now they're chargin ten cents each piece of clothes.

You ever listen to the Jerry Williams Show on the radio? That program is really good. They don't play music or anything, they just call in. WJJD§ goes off at eight and I was huntin ball games the other night—the Cubs was supposed to play and they were rained out—and I turned it, I had it on WGM or whatever station it is, and he started talkin to people. They have some interesting subjects on there. There's one woman called last night and she said that people on ADC was crooked. And Jerry Williams asked her, said, "Well, what's crooked about it?" She said, "They ought to get out and get a job of work." He said, "Well, that's why they're on ADC, because they can't find work." They have some really interesting subjects. Anyway, he's a Jew, Jerry Williams is a Jew. And the other night this guy called in and asked him, says, "Are you a King Jew?" In other words, was he a Negro Jew. Jerry Williams says, "No," said, "I'm not no Negro," says,

*The Urban Progress Center, which is located at 901 Montrose.
†Council of the Southern Mountains, another Uptown office offering minimal service.
‡St. Augustine Indian Center.
§Country-western music station.

"I'm white," but said, "I feel like the colored should have their rights." I'd like to meet him in person. Just sit down and talk to him.

All I ever read in the paper is the funnies, and look at the magazines. I hear enough news from Johnny. If he sees something in the paper that's interesting, he'll read me that. Most of the time he only buys the paper for sports, and the coupons for the bingo games. I have to agree with him about the war though. He's been through it, he was a sergeant, and he's got one of his sons in Vietnam now, the other's at Fort Benning, Georgia.

Don't Read the Papers Much: I

Slum Dwellers Need to Be Taught, Daley Says

Some 600 workers have been working in slum areas trying to help people adopt good housekeeping habits, Mayor Daley announced. . . .

daley's slum education

by Mrs. N.

Mayor Daley made some very swift comments on these poor people who pay his taxes so he has a high salary to live on. He thinks he has to start classes so the poor can learn to make beds and make better housekeepers.

He may not know it but we people aren't as dumb as he thinks. And I figure he will learn that much when the election comes up. Some of the people couldn't make beds if they wanted to because they have no linens or anything to make

them with. They are too busy trying to pay their taxes so that Mayor Daley can pay his servants to wait on him hand and foot, while he sets in his office crying for more money because he isn't making enough.

We poor people don't need any of this slum education. All we need is enough money to keep our families comfortable, and taxes down enough so we can afford to pay them.

A bold new experiment in slum prevention is being tried in Uptown. . . . The unusual part of this experiment is that code violations by tenants as well as building owners are being noted. If a tenant is to blame for an unsanitary condition in a building, he is given a "cafeteria court" ticket, which makes him subject to a $10 fine.

"They ain't comin to my house if I have to go buy a gun."

Launch Uptown cleanup

Campaign goal is to make Uptown 'cleanest community'

By LEONARD DUBKIN

Breakin rock in the hot sun
I fought the law and the law won

Two youths charged in burglaries

TWO YOUTHS were charged of b...

New school program 'introduces' police

The policeman is your friend'

RUTH ANDERSON ... was rewarded with presentation ...

"Where would you be without the cops?" "I'd be a nice boy."

The current economic boom in the Chicago area, which makes it the best job market in the country, has not wiped out unemployment. While there are thousands of job openings, he said, there are tens of thousands of unemployed.

Shriver: 2 Million No Longer Poor

Kentucky Family Johnson Saw Is Still Burdened by Poverty

Commissioner of Urban Renewal Hill conceded that thus far the private housing resulting from urban renewal clearance has been out of the economic reach of many middle-income families.

Chicago's biggest sports betting center was raided Thursday by FBI agents and police who said it was handling $150,000 in bets on the second game of the World Series. The bookie room at 4750 N. Clarendon . . .

I needed money cause I had none
I fought the law and the law won

U.S. Hits New Peak In Per Capita Income

WASHINGTON ... although some gained ... In eight states: Connecticut ... Alaska, New York ...

"We must urbanize the people who live in Uptown," O'Rourke stated.

The emphasis in the poverty program will be on training for the new jobs that Vietnam spending is creating. . . .

I fought the law and the law won

106   UPTOWN

John Dawson

The Cook County Public Aid and the state of Illinois, they don't believe that a person, because they're disabled to work, they don't believe that they should have somethin to live on. They think that because a person's disabled to work that you're just some dog or somethin. They sure keep you in hot water half the time, that welfare. If it ain't one thing, it's two.

First thing you got to do for general assistance is you got to go to this office and get a little blue card. After you first go to Damen* they'll send you back down to this other place. You set in there all day and then you got to go back down to apply, and you done had papers from a social worker to go right in there. That's a good one. You go in there and they give you a little ole blue card. They got about fifty workin in there, just settin in there givin out little cards, and they'll give you out one after about three hours. Well, they send you down next door to get a chest X ray. I fooled around there and waited for about three hours. Then you get back down to the Damen office, you walk in there and hand the papers in. "O.K., have a seat." They got all them offices setting there full and both ways you look, they're settin there drawin good money, smokin big cigars and drinkin whiskey and beer, that's just the truth about it.

Maybe you'll be in there at two, you'll sit there till about four-thirty. They'll come out and they don't call you by name, they'll call you by number, like you was some prisoner or somethin. "I'm sorry, number so-and-so, I can't see you. You be in here in the mornin at eight-thirty, the first one." Well, they tell maybe five hundred that. Go in there next mornin at eight-thirty. . . . It takes you about six days to get through there. Every day the same thing, set there all day. They've got about fifteen hundred workin in them three offices there, the X ray and that other and Damen, but it takes them about six days to get a person through that office.

*General assistance office on South Damen Street.

You go down to Washington,* this big-shot labor office they've got down there. They try to get you to go out in these factories like Spiegel's† that don't pay nothin. You go down there at eight-thirty in the mornin, you turn in your card or letter or whatever you got, 'n—"Well, we'll call you in a few minutes." Twelve o'clock comes, still ain't no call. Maybe they've called three out of seven or eight hundred in there. "Well, we're taken an hour for lunch." You come back after lunch, set there till about five. "Mr. Dawson, we just couldn't get to you today. Let's see, you come back tomorrow afternoon at two." You go back in the evening at two, walk in, you turn in your card, they don't tell you then you can't see em. "We'll see you in just a few minutes, some one of our counselors now will see you in just a few minutes now and have you fixed right up."

They got this punk settin back there from First Cab. You'll be there about twenty minutes, he'll call your name. "We would like for you to go through this First Cab trainin, to drive a cab."

Then I said, "You'd like for me to do what? I ain't drivin any damn cab." I said, "If I wanted to drive a cab, I'd borrow the money and buy me a damn car and drive my own cab."

"O.K., then. All right, you won't accept." Boy he made me mad. Back there at the front, he turns it in to that desk. He'll let you sit there then till five again. "Well, you come down tomorrow, we'll see if we can't locate you a job."

I said, "You needn't tell me come down tomorrow, I won't be back to-morrow."

"Well, how bout you takin this and goin to Spiegel's?"

And I said, "I ain't goin to Spiegel's." I said, "I'll tell you what, though. You let Spiegel's go to hell." I don't feel like that a man should go to any welfare, and kiss their sittin down place—to get nothin. I think it should be give to the people, not make them do somethin that they don't want to do.

Spiegel's called me for three weeks tryin to get me to come on a job. I got mad last time they kept callin at the house, you know? Etta said, "It's that damn woman from Spiegel's." I walked to the phone. I said, "I believe that I told you about three weeks ago that I wasn't takin your job." I said, "You want to pay me two-fifty an hour?" I said, "Which I know your wages are not that, and you don't pay that kind of wages." I said, "I'm not takin your dollar and a quarter an hour and pay two dollars a week union dues." I said, "If you call me in the mornin, I'm gonna sue you for botherin me, molestin me." I said, "I'd rather be a-layin on the bed, restin. In fact,"

*The Welfare Rehabilitation Service on Washington Street.
†A mail-order house.

I said, "I might have some other woman here in bed with me, and I'm gonna be enjoyin myself." I'll guarantee you I ain't had no more calls from Spiegel's.

But this cab school, out here at Thirty-fifth and Cottage Grove, the state and the government together is payin two hundred and fifty a month for this buildin out there, to be a-runnin these people through what's supposed to be a school. I don't feel like I need no damn schoolin to go to drive a damn cab or a damn car or truck. I got any kind of driver's license or chauffeur's license a man wants. I believe if a man can drive a damn ten-ton wrecker or tractor-and-trailer he ought to be able to drive any little old cab. But I went out there and went through school alongst one week, and quit. I just done it just to aggravate em, just so I could draw that money off of em. Course you don't get nothin while you're goin through the trainin. You just get half the amount of general assistance—plus nothin. See, that's a big feather in them sonofabitches' pocket, to try to pull somethin over you like that. And I found out what the deal was, and I wasn't gonna drive no cab nowhere.

The first thing they set in on out there: "Remember now, every one of y'all are gettin general assistance. We want you off of general assistance. We're gonna show you where you can make a hundred and fifty a week. We want you to set here twelve weeks." I think it was a Public Aid guy. They're payin twelve Public Aid men to get out there and speak, shoot the bull all day. They try to beat it in your head out there, to brainwash you that you can make above fifty or a hundred dollars in tips every week, to make this hundred and fifty a week. It's impossible.

Then this First Cab Company man come down—he'll be honest with you. Here's what he actually told you. He said, "You can average about fifty dollars a week." He said, "We guarantee you forty-five." He'll say, "Now listen, I'll tell you how you can make it. Just don't let the city catch you." He said, "If you want to sell whiskey for us," he said, "you can make it. But," he said, "I'm not gonna get up there in front of you boys and tell you that you can make a hundred and fifty a week." He said, "On the average it's fifty to sixty dollars." He said, "That's after you've been with the company for maybe six months."

Here's somethin else now. They pay for your chauffeur's license, the county does; they buy you a cab license; they pay for your uniform, that's fifty flat dollars for a First Cab uniform and a cap. All told to get a man through that school, just one man out there, will cost the Cook County Department of Public Aid at least $4,000. And I don't get that much in a year, drawin it.

Let me show you a point. On ADC-U I'm gettin $2,731 a year. Just to run me through that school costs em over $4,000. Why don't they give me that $4,000 to live on? How do they figure that they've saved anything? That's the stupidest one damn thing that I've ever seen in my damn life. Why, if they had a railroad man, the foreman for the railroad job, just wastin money like that, what would they do with him? I want to tell you the damn truth. You waste a goddamn crosstie with the railroad and they're ready to fire you.

Then I was supposed to have got this emergency check. They give me the runaround. I'd done been out there and got them school papers—I still got em down at the house. I made shit paper out a mine, part of it. Meantime I wasn't intendin to go back to school, all that runaround. The old lady Shea, she was a caseworker at that time over on Clifton, she come and told me, said, "I'll tell you what." She said, "If you go out there to the cab school, I'll give you any kind of trainin you want."

I knowed she was lyin. I said, "Miss Shea," I said, "I was assigned a check today and I ain't got it. What ya gonna do about that?" Well, she was a pretty good cooperator, try and cooperate with you. I said, "I'll tell you what. I'll take the schoolin if you'll get my checks to me." I said, "Y'all promised to pay the rent here and y'all ain't never sent me the money to pay it with."

She said, "I'll get you that check tomorrow." She said, "You come over to the office in the mornin, I'll get you all of it."

I went over to Lincoln Avenue at eight-thirty the next mornin. She give me a voucher, and the one thing was to get it cashed. I walked up there and I wasn't three minutes. Fastest I ever did go through the Damen Avenue office. I walked in and I started to set back down. "Mr. Dawson, John Dawson, here's your cash, emergency." I said, "Yes, emergency, very emergency. We haven't nothin to eat in the house." She went and marked on it, "Special Emergency." I told her, I said, "Yeah, I'll be in school this afternoon, two o'clock." I went right back over to South Drexel Avenue and bought me a car. Came back up, got my stuff, and went south.

Well, I'll tell you, when I start talkin about this bunch I get mad. They're so low-rated over there at this welfare, it's a shame. Got called back on the job and I come back and I couldn't work on account of my stomach and my heart. I've had trouble with my heart for the last three or four years. So I was supposed to went on welfare in September. Well, they thought they had me scared to death, but they didn't have old John Dawson scared to death.

A caseworker told me I had to go down to the Illinois State Employment Office at the Urban Progress Center and go take a job. She was one a these smart ones, she thought she owned the world. So I went through there and tried to cooperate with em. They sent me down to the Illinois Christian Hospital to work, to be a cook. They were supposed to've paid me a dollar-eighty an hour. I worked down there ninety-six hours, I drawed $24.08 for it, which the Cook County Department of Public Aid was supposed to have made up the difference to general assistance. I worked two weeks and I quit, and in three months I still hadn't got no money. They didn't give me no emergency check, they didn't give me nothin. I never received a penny. So I called over there and they said that the caseworker had been assigned to Damen Avenue.

All right, just look at the runaround. You get over there at Lincoln Avenue and they take out and make out all them papers, a bunch of papers there bout your life history. You go in at eight-thirty when they first open. It takes you to one-thirty to get to the adviser, right? The intake will take you, then they'll assign you a caseworker, this intake will take this up to the caseworker. The caseworker will mess around and she'll come back, or—"I'll have your voucher after while." She has to go back to the supervisor, the supervisor has to go back to the other damn half-breeded sonofabitch back there. All right, then he'll come out—"Well, I can't get this approved. . . . So much is all I can do." "O.K., you'll have to wait till one-thirty, you can go on down the street and get yourself a cup of coffee." Well, how in the hell are you gonna get a cup of coffee when you ain't had a damn penny in a month? I told that 'un over there. She said, "You can go down and get you a sandwich and a cup of coffee."

I said, "I just got through workin' two weeks at ninety-six hours a week and I got $24 for it." I said, "I got a rent receipt where I put $20 of that on the damn rent." said, "I bought $4.08 worth of groceries two weeks ago." Course I had some money, but it wasn't gonna make any difference where I got it from. I said, "I got a lot of money to go down the street and get me a hamburger and a cup of coffee!" I said, "You had me over here at eight-thirty this mornin. I've been settin here." I said, "I think you better buy me a sandwich for I got to wait till one-thirty. Cause if you don't I'm gonna go to dinner with you. I'll follow you right upstairs and when you go to dinner I'm goin with you."

She said, "O.K. then." She got me a dollar out of her purse and handed it to me. I went down the street and got me a couple of beers with it. Well, in fact I brought me another can of beer up there and set in there and drink it. Just to show em I didn't give a damn about them. I was done mad at them for the way they done me.

I walked back in there at ten after one. About twenty-five after one, here she come a-prancin, though she didn't have nothin at all to prance with. "Mr. Dawson, it's gonna be tomorrow evenin' before I can get this voucher."

I said, "I guess I just as well go home with you and let you call, go by and pick up my wife and kids and get em somethin to eat tonight."

"I can call the church and you can go over and get some canned food."

I said, "I'm tired of eatin' damn soup." I said, "I told you that today." I said, "I was gonna go home with you and eat dinner if you hadn't given me that dollar." I said, "I'll go home with you, by God, tonight when you leave here." And I said, "When you get home I'll let you call my wife and make arrangements for them to come over to your house and stay all night tonight."

"Well, let me see what I can do."

I said, "I don't care what you can do," I said, "you better do it."

So she finally got the voucher about ten minutes after two. I went to the Damen office. I sat there till ten after five before I got the check. I said, "It was two-twenty-five when I come in here." I said, "I'd hate to be havin a baby, waitin on y'all to make a telephone call for a doctor." I said, "I coulda probably had fifteen babies for myself for by God y'all could've made a telephone call in this place."

"Well, we doin all we can."

I said, "I don't believe you eat soup for supper last night." Right there I wish I had a damn gun, I'd just shoot the whole damn bunch and walk on out. That's just the way I felt.

Well, then that money was spent up, payin ninety-five dollars a month rent on this buildin that's not fit to live in. So I went back to old Hutchins at the Public Aid Office in the Urban Progress Center, and he said, "Well, we'll just see about it." Claimed he called em. Course you know that sonofabitch'd never do nothin no damn way for nobody. So I went back and got on im.

"Well," he said, "I'll call em."

I said, "Well, another thing," I said, "y'all promised me money to go to work on." I said, "I've been a-walkin from Kenmore to the Illinois Christian Hospital, back and forth to work." I said, "I done ruint my damn shoes for walkin." I said, "Look what I drawed for it."

"I can't do anything about that."

I said, "No," I said, "you can't never do a damn thing, but you can promise people things, can't you?" I said, "Well, there's one damn thing about it," I says, "I belong to an organization, and by God I think we can get something done."

And he says, "Well, you can just go to your organization."

I said, "Well, that just suits hell out of me, for," I said, "I got no use for you or nobody else down here the way you operate." I said, "You're not for the poor people in the first place." The next mornin at nine, I guarantee you she was there at ten minutes till nine. And so we gee'd her in from the start off. And I think if all caseworkers was like that, there would be a lot better public aid.

She come to my house down at 4240 North Kenmore, and she inspected the buildin while she was there. She found that it wasn't fit for people to live in. You had to take water from the sink and throw it in the bathtub to take a bath, and no way to get the water out, had no handles on the bathtubs. Showed her the kind of holes that was in the wall. She said, "I can't understand why these people here in this buildin that's on welfare and the Cook County Department of Public Aid is payin for it." And she said, "If they put me out here as a caseworker, like they assigned me," she said, "I'll have to work for the people. I just can't work for the Cook County Department of Public Aid."

Me and Rennie talked to her. She set there and talked for about two hours with us. And Rennie and I just explained what JOIN was tryin to do, and that we wasn't workin against her if she'd work with us and work with the poor people. We wanted caseworkers that would work with the poor people, and not try to get out here and tell them a bunch of stuff. But we don't need caseworkers that come out here and try to tell you what to do. I think you should be allowed to run your home like you want to. That's just like the money that they send you. They claim they've got a right to tell you what to do with your money. They have no right to tell you what to spend your money for. They have no right to tell you where you got to live.

So she asked me about goin through the cab school, and I said, "Miss Barth, I'm not goin through no cab school, I'm not workin Spiegel's for a dollar-twenty-five an hour." And so I asked her about this Standard Oil trainin, when it first come out. It first started in November of '65, at the Cook County Department of Public Aid here. And Rockefeller, he owns all the Standard Oil, you know, and he's the man that was sponsorin all this damn stuff. And so they was advertisin, wantin men to accept this Standard Oil trainin. Well, I asked Miss Barth about learnin to operate those pumps out there at East Chicago and over in Gary. And she never give me no answer, just said that she didn't know, couldn't do anything about it.

But I'll have to give her credit, she's been very nice. She's never talked smart from the first time I ever talked to her, and every time I called her on

the phone it's always "Mr. Dawson." She comes out to your house, it's "Good morning" for you—"Anything I can help you with?" Probably she'd lose her job if they knowed a caseworker was makin a donation to help us out with at JOIN.* And this supervisor of hers, she's always been very nice. If I called and asked for Miss Barth, she'd say, "Yes sir, Mr. Dawson." They know me I reckon by my voice; I've been over there and raised so much hell with them at that place.

And at the Damen office. When me and Rennie had to go straighten out the mess up there, I went down there and WSO† was picketin em that day, tryin to organize that welfare union. I walked right into that, me and Rennie with JOIN Community pins on. I told that guy from WSO, I said, "Hell, give me a bunch of em." I said, "I'll pass em out all over the damn buildin here." Me and Rennie and about three or four others, there was a bunch of us passin out our newsletters and their newsletter. Along come one of them damn punks: "You can't pass them out!" I said, "I can't? I am. I don't know what you're gonna do about it and I don't give a damn." That ole guy from WSO, he said, "Just don't worry. If he goes and tries to get you in jail," he said, "we're standin by." They had all the doors covered; hell, the police never would've got in there to get us. We just filled that damn place.

All right, then they sent me through all that medical checkup, records and everythin. Miss Barth filled out them damn medical papers and sent em in, and they charged me off of general assistance and put me on ADC-U on account of medical records. So then in December when I could've went to work at $3.78 an hour, the welfare wouldn't help me on that. Yeah, they knew about it. I had that job at the railroad, foreman job for the CB&Q Railroad, and my check was supposed to be deducted off of it. They refused. They wouldn't give me no assistance to pay my rent and take care of my family for a month till I could draw a payday, so I had to turn around and quit.

I moved over on Clifton, supposed to be a furnished apartment over there, and they assigned us a different caseworker, this sonofabitch Steinberg. A person never gets his check on time when he has got a caseworker like no-good Steinberg. You can call up no-good Steinberg about your check and also about your medical card, and he says, "Well, you'll get it

*Shortly afterward the welfare bureaucracy did transfer her, suddenly, to another neighborhood.
†The West Side Organization, a black group JOIN worked with off and on.

later." I was to go back to the doctor one time but my medical card was out of date so I had to wait on this sorry rotten welfare to send me a medical card before I could get any more treatment from a doctor, and I know of plenty of people who are that way.

I walked in one day and Etta said, "The caseworker's here." I just wish I'd a-been half drunk when I come in. I'd a-thrown that sonofabitch plumb through that damn window. I wouldn't a-kicked him down them stairs, that's too good for that sonofabitch.

I said, "I'm glad to see you, fella." I said, "I've been tryin to get a hold of you ever since you come on this case."

He said, "What is it?"

I said, "I been a-tryin to get a hold of you, to get some furniture out here in this place." Nanci called him twicet, two or three times, for a baby bed and a crib.

He said, "I don't know."

I said, "We don't even have chairs in there for my family to sit down at the table." I said, "Look at this chair over here, this furniture that's in here." I was payin ninety-five dollars a month. I said, "You people don't care nary a thing about that."

He comes to hollerin around how he didn't have anything to do with that.

I said, "In other words, the buildin inspectors don't never come and check nothin." I said, "All he does is come out and see the landlady and walk out. But," I said, "if you get a decent place you people don't want em to live in it. And," I said, "the first thing, you damn caseworkers, the most of you is tryin to drive the people around."

Well, he jumped up. What caused him to turn mad, he asked me when I'd been down to Washington Street, and I told him I hadn't been down there and, by God, I wasn't goin. And I won't. I said, "Here is the tickets for the damn job that I could've got $3.78 an hour, where they said they couldn't do anything. But they can turn around and send me down to Illinois Christian Hospital."

He said, "Well, that happened a long time ago." He turned right around and wanted me to take some no-good job.

I said, "Why won't they send me through that Standard Oil school to operate a pump?"

He said, "Why couldn't you get a job driving a cab?"

I said, "I ain't takin no $1.25 job, a man like me about to have a nervous breakdown."

"Well," he said, "I'm gonna try to do what I can, but you know I have my own rules."*

Well I just told him flatly he wasn't tellin me to do a damn thing, he wasn't drivin me around. I told him they already got all that medical examination on me. He said, "I ain't got nothin, gonna have to get some more."

"Well, O.K., if the records went in one time, what have they done with em now?" I said, "I want to know where your records go when they change caseworkers." I said, "I'm gonna be contrary as hell Monday when they send me them papers. I ain't gonna sign them. I ain't signin a damn thing."

If I was a caseworker, I'd find out the people's problems. That's what you're supposed to do. You're not supposed to go in and try to tell somebody how to run their home. Just like he was askin me, tell me, tryin to tell me how many children I was supposed to have. What damn right does that belong to the state or the county to tell you how big your family's supposed to be? I told him it wasn't none of his goddamn business how many kids I raised and what I done.

I asked him how old he was. He said he's twenty-two. I told him I hope to hell they draft him and send him straight to Vietnam without any damn trainin. I said, "I got a boy in Vietnam." Like I told that little four-eyed devil, I wonder what he thinks I put eight and a half years on the front lines for. I killed people I didn't even know. I killed men and I killed women, probably even killed a kid sometime, and what have I got out of it? You know some people thinks when you go on that front line, you was fightin for just one person. You wasn't fightin for one person, you was fightin for the whole country.

And I told him right flat that I'd go and get a damn job at $3.78 an hour, but the damn minute I got it I'd sue hell out of the Cook County Department of Public Aid. And I said, "Don't think that I ain't afraid to tangle with you any damn time in court." Now it's a Federal program, the government puts 85 percent into the State of Illinois, and the Constitution says that you're supposed to have a lawyer to defend you regardless of any kind of case. If you don't have money to pay, the State's supposed to furnish you a lawyer to represent you. The Cook County Department of Public Aid does not have a setup where they have a lawyer to defend you. They have a hearin officer, they have a lawyer on their side. He'll get up and tell you in your face, "Oh, I'll help you, but naturally I'm gonna be

*Looking on, John's five-year-old daughter Lila said: "I wish he'd hurry and leave. He's tryin to get my daddy to go back to school. That's no good."

on the Department of Public Aid's side." They have no money set up to pay a lawyer out of.

But always appeal it up to another court, you can always win a case that way. The trouble with the Uptown neighborhood here is people that are afraid of the law. They're afraid of these syndicate lawyers here in Chicago. Now I wouldn't get one a them, I'd get that Harold Frye from Rome, Georgia, and I'll guarantee you he'll bust this damn mess up here. He's not tied to some syndicate, he's not tied to some Ku Klux, and he's for you, he's for the client, not for the damn city. I heard him in a case back home there. He told this guy—first-degree murder now—he said, "Always operate and paint your facts up and then if you have to tell a lie go ahead and tell it." He said, "That's the way you win a case in court," he said, "as long as you lie together." I think a man is that good if he can win sixty murder cases. They just don't know that I can get some good lawyers and make that damn Cook County Department of Public Aid just bounce.

That's exactly the reason Mrs. Simpson* is messed up on her check, just sech as that. She's afraid to talk back to em. I'm like Dovie,† I'm not afraid to stand up and talk back to them sonofabitches and I'm not afraid to tell them to take it and go to hell with it either.

That apartment now, the plaster was all fallin, the windows broke, door locks couldn't lock the door, the furniture wasn't fit for a dog to live in or own, the couch wasn't fit for a dog to lay on, much less a human bein have to sit down on it. You had to have the table propped up, no chairs to the table. We had to come in, set down, eat like a bunch a dogs in the livin room. The back porch fallin through, the garbage stayed out there for a week, a couple weeks at a time before they'd ever get it out. One garbage can for the whole buildin. They wasn't nothin that wasn't wrong. Manager'd come in, if you could find one around—you could find him when the rent was up—and he said he'd throw your stuff out. Course I just cussed him, flatly cussed him out. I said, "The first time you lay a hand on my stuff, you *are* a police. You throw it out," I said, "I'm a-goin a kill you." And I said, "You're gonna fix this buildin one way or the other." And he just determined he wasn't gonna fix it.

One night here he come over about eleven to fix this lock on the door. That's a good time of night to come to work on a door. Very good time. I started to kick him down the stairs then, hadn't been for Etta, for I was

*See p. 336.
†Dovie Coleman, a black JOIN organizer.

afraid I might be off somewhere and, you know, she couldn't lock that door. Anyway, he fixed the lock. Here he come over with two old junk chairs. He said, "Now you come out, Mr. Dawson." He come out with a little piece of paper, statement. "You sign this that you'll pay my rent, and you take these four gallons of paint, you buy brushes—now you have to buy brushes, you have to buy plaster and fix this. I'll give you ten dollars to paint this." With four gallons of paint I was going to paint that apartment! That was pretty good.

And then he tried another good one. "Well," he said, "then I'll have somebody from Jobs Unlimited come up here and paint."

I said, "You won't have nobody from Jobs Unlimited come in *my* house and work." I said, "You just send the first man from Jobs Unlimited up here and," I said, "he's goin out that door." I said, "I'll tell you what I'll paint it fer." I said, "Two hundred dollars, but I don't sign no kinds of statements with a landlord, I don't sign no kinds of leases on no buildings. I'm no Commonist, and I ain't under no Commonist, and," I said, "you people ain't goin a run me." I said, "You're not *gettin* no rent," I said, "till this building's fixed." And I said, "I want to tell you I got a damn new pair of shoes and," I said, "I'll put em in your damn ass or I'll put em in that damn Jew's ass that owns this building, if he come up here." I called im everything but a white man. Well, you didn't see him come up there.

So then the next mornin I went up to the Uptown Commission,* and I got them to send that VISTA boy down there and he fell through the back porch. I thought that was a good un! That was a real come-off, and the thing of it, this case was dismissed against this joker in October. Claimed they wasn't nothin wrong with that building. A welfare building, with people's tax money a-payin for something like that for people to live in.

I had a hard time gettin another place.

*The Uptown Chicago Commission, a business-financed "civic improvement" group that pushed for urban renewal and city receivership of bad buildings.

Ras Bryant

Well, I'll tell you why I came here. Hit's just times got so hard out there I just couldn't make a dime, you know. Nothin a live on. Just had a work for my board, that was all.

A boy Franklin lived here in Chicogger. He's kin to me, about third or fourth cousin, maybe, somethin like that. I'm his great-uncle, see. And he came out there, says, "Ras," says, "I want you to go home with me." Said, "I'll take you out there, buy you clothes, board won't cost you a cent, your room or nothin won't cost you a cent."

Yeah, but I asked him another question. I said, "What if we get out there and the landlord wants a raise a thing bout me stayin there, me not supposed a be there?"

Said, "Well, I'll tell you what I'll do. He do that," said, "we'll just get another apartment."

I said, "Well, that's fair enough."

So I come out here with im, seventeen months ago, you know. Got out here, I started off, he'd buy me anything I wanted. Send me out to get beer every night, you know, feed me when he come in. I need any clothes, I need a pair of shoes, something, he'd find em. A course, I brought plenty a clothes here with me. He bought them shoes right there. They cost seven dollars and ninety-five cents. I done weared em for over a year now.

We got us an apartment over on Beacon. Then I went back to West Virginia for a while, you know, and when I come back the landlady said, "Why don't you stay in West Virginia while you were out there?

I said, "Yeah."

She said, "Now I'm gonna raise your rent."

I said, "And I ain't gonna pay it."

And then here come the old man Greenberg sayin, "Oh," he said, "you can stay right here."

I said, "Nooo, we're gonna move." I said, "We're fixin to move already." My cousin come in that night, you know, and I was stayin with him. Jest as soon as he come in the landlord was all ready to catch him, you know. "Don't you leave here, don't you leave here."

He said, "Wait till I see Ras."

And about that time I come along. I said, "Yeah, we're leavin here." I said, "That old woman gone all over me this mornin, Franklin, told me I had to pay more rent."

He said, "No, we don't have to do it." Said, "We're gonna move. So I'm gonna give you one week's rent but that's all." Said, "Then we'll get us a place and move next week."

We went out and looked us out a place and moved the next week, out there on Beacon, the next block out. Oh, he come back up one time, a-beggin us not to go. I said to the old woman, I said, "Why don't you go back to the old country or why didn't you stay over thar while you was over thar?" She came from the old country somewhere. I don't know. You know, some kind of furrner. Boy, she like to blowed up then. I didn't care either. The old man, then, he come up, seen me, oh man, I cussed him, a fly wouldn't light on it. I give him a genuine good one.

I'd just went around to people's houses I knowed. That's all I had to do. Set around, talk to them durin the day while that boy was workin. Just walk up and down the streets, you know, and talk to people and try to get acquainted with em. That's what I was doin before I got with JOIN. Met Pop like that too. Oh, there're a lot more of em yet, you know, that I've met. They wasn't workin, you know, and some was.

Then I'd go down to Jobs Unlimited ever mornin too. Lot a times with my brother when he was workin down there, you know. Set around and talk with them guys tryin to get out to work, you know.

Never would send me. I got four hours out at Nation-Wide* and they cut me off. I was cleanin up office back where the men set a-waitin, you know, to get sent out. Back in the washroom, you know. Take me three hours the first day to clean it up. It was awful filthy when I went in there, you know. Then I went back the next day and cleaned 't up in one hour. All I had to do was sweep up and mop up a little bit the next day, you know. That was easy. They paid me a dollar. They paid my brother all the time a dollar and a quarter. Hit's a wage law, you know. It ought to be brought up in the Senate and Congress and be a law made agin them a-treatin people like that. I believe it could be done. Now the wage law is done raised, you know, from $1.25 to $1.40, and then it's goin to $1.75. See, you understand now, *I* don't get no raise to take care a my groceries

*Day-labor agency.

like they're takin care a theirs, you see. Therefore it just ruins me. I draw a little old check, you see. And before they get this raise, now, groceries in the store gonna go sky-high.

I went out in West Virginia oncet, where they had them strikes in the mines, you know. The stores would raise everythin around the stores, see. And one boy come down from work in the mines, you know, Ben Baxter's boy, his name was Thomas. He said, "Ras," he said, "what do you think about that raise we got?" They just had got a two-dollar raise on the day, then.

And I said, "Well, I don't think nothin about it."

He said, "You mean you don't appreciate us gettin that two-dollar raise?"

I said, "Lord no!"

"Well," he said, "I want you to tell me why you don't."

"Well," I said, "here sets your dad, now, drawin a little ole social security check. Here I am, I been drawin thirty-six dollars a month to live on. And," I said, "they done raised groceries in the store already since y'all got that raise. They done raised groceries in the store. You know that?"

"Yes," he said, "I know it."

"Well," I said, "now y'all get that two dollars to take care of that raise. Here sets me and your dad, we're drawin a little ole check, and we don't get no raise to take care of that."

"Oh," he said, " 'tis agin you-all, ain't it?"

I said, "Why sure it is."

"Oh," he said, "I never thought about that."

"Yeah," I said, "but I thought about it, right quick."

My cousin, though, he was makin good money. Die-caster. Bringin over a hundred dollars a week—hundred thirty-five dollars a week. Then he got married, you see, and now he's got a wife and a baby to take care of. Well, tharfore he's heavy in debt. Bought him a new car and everything. Everything he sees he's got to buy—it beats everythin ever I seed in my life. And since he got married he's got that trouble with the horses, always bettin on the horses. Why he lost a hundred dollars in one week! Franklin doesn't realize the horses got to eat; he's feedin em. I seed he wasn't able to keep me. But he would, you know, right on. "Why," he said, "you don't have to leave here." Said, "You gettin along all right." I hated to leave that place, you know. He was so good to me. But I went and got on a check and then I had to leave, then. They won't let you live with nobody else and still draw a check, you know.

They pushed me around here for about six weeks, wouldn't give me no check—wouldn't give me a dime.

I went up 'ere, they told me I had to get a sworn affidavit, that I was sixty-two years old, you know. Well, there's nobody in Chicago that I know that's older'n I am. How'm I gonna get a sworn affidavit to that? And I had to get landlords or store merchants to sign my papers that I had been here a year. Well, I went and got that done. And they went back and told me there wasn't anything they could do for me. And I just gave it up, till Mae and Ray* come round one day, start talkin to me. Met em on the street, you know, on Racine over there one Sunday. Didn know either one of them. And I got talkin with em there, and tole em, I said, "I tried to get on welfare but I couldn't do no good."

They said, "Come on out 'n work with us. We're workin out in JOIN, out here."

I said, "O.K. Be out tomorrow."

Said, "If you can't do no better we'll find you a place to sleep and somethin to eat. Come on and work with us."

I said, "O.K. I'll do that."

I came out the next day. Me and Jim Day† come out together. (I just happened to run into Jim Day on the street, how I met im.) Found the place, and we just went to work for em. They went to work for us, too. They didn't change a word, buddy. They was ready to go to bat for us there.

I've met some nice people since I've come around, I mean *really* nice ones. I like em fine. When I first come out and got friends with Rennie and Richie,‡ I like them boys real good, you know. And got acquainted with Harriet,‡ and first one then another just kept comin in, you know. And I ain't found no bad ones yit. They've all been nice to me.

Rennie went with me the first time, Rennie, I believe it was. And Richie, he taken me back up there a time or two. "Yes," said, "Mr. Bryant," said, "we'll sign you up right now." Didn't have a bit a trouble then. They didn push me around that time.

Oh, I had got the nicest caseworker you ever seen. She didn't give me no runaround. She sat there and talkin just as nice as anyone I've ever talked to yet.

I been to the office to talk to her a time or two, you know. I went up there one day, you know, and I told em I want a see Miss Ginsberg or Mr. Dunne, one. That's the man who filled out my application, you know. Mr. Dunne. And they said, "Buddy, you cain't see em today." Said, "They're out in the field."

*Uptown residents no longer active in JOIN.
†A wino who spent time with JOIN.
‡Richard Rothstein and Harriet Stulman, then JOIN organizers.

Well, me and Rennie went back. We figgered out what we wanted to do. Went back up and said we wanted to see the manager there. We's from JOIN. Didn't tell em that to start with, you see.

"Well, we'll let you see the manager," she said. "I'll call him just in a minute." This lady at the desk did, you know. He come out, talked with us. Said, "You, one at a time, come back here."

I walked in and sat down and I was talkin with im. Mr. Dunne walked in there, you know. I said, "Hello, Mr. Dunne."

He said, "Hi."

And the manager sits there and says, "Mr. Dunne," said, "this man wants to know about his check, bout whether he's goin a draw and all." Says, "Could you get his file?"

"Lordy yeah, right now," he says. "What's your name, now?"

I said, "Erastis Bryant."

He said, "Yes sir, I can get your file right now."

"O.K."

He taken right off, you know. In just a few minutes he'd come back with Miss Ginsberg.

Just a few minutes, here in come Miss Ginsberg. "Hello, Mr. Bryant."

I said, "Hello, Miss Ginsberg."

She said, "What'd you come in to see me about?"

I said, "About my check."

She says, "Come back in the room with me and let's talk about it." She talked just as nice as any lady I ever seen. Said, "Mr. Bryant," she said, "you'll get a check," she said, "on Tuesday, for forty-two dollars. And your case hasn't been figgered out yet, what you're goin a get on the month." Said, "You'll get a 'mergency check for forty-two dollars."

Well, on Tuesday, shore enough, the check came in, you know. Well, then hit wasn't but about maybe a couple a weeks when I got another one, for fifty-seven. Got no rent, you know, and I went up and told her, you know, again. I said, "Miss Ginsberg, I want to know what I'm goin a do about my rent."

She said, "Well, I'll tell you what you do." She said, "You go ahead and move, and have your landlord call me, see. And when your landlord calls me, then I will pay the rent for you, see."

Well, I called back up there a couple a times, you know, wanted to know what was wrong with this rent receipt. But hit finally come in. It was sixty dollars, and they sent me a check for sixty-one. I don't know where that one dollar come in there, but they sent me a check for sixty-one dollars.

I went down and signed the papers, rent it for a month. Kitchenette, that's what they called it. The landlord started a-gettin worried about it. She comes ahead and tells you she's kinda gettin worried about it. She says, "Wonder why that check hasn come in yet."

I said, "Well, I don't know, but it'll be here."

She says, "Oh yes, I know it'll be here."

Then I got another check, was for sixty-one dollars. They tell me that was my month allowancement, you know. She told me I probably just allowed twenty-seven dollars a month for food, see. Twenty-seven dollars for food, and the rest of it for like shavin lotion, and razor, blades, and stuff you have to have, you know. All that, it come to $99.35. I don't know how it's figgered out, you know, just exactly. But it's all figgered out some way or other.

Twenty-seven dollars a month's what I get for food. You can figger that for yourself. Not too much, is it? But you can live on it. You can have beans and potaters and stuff like that. You ain't goin a get too much meat and things like that, you know. But it's pretty tough sometimes along the last of the month. Not much things I can fix but I do the best I can. For the rest a what I need, sometimes I get along on nothin, sometimes I don't. I pick up stuff where I can get it. I sat over on Wilson one mornin and a woman come along with this electric blanket in a shopping bag, you know. And she opened up the bag and it was nice and clean and everything, you know. She said, "You know where I can get three or four dollars for this blanket?"

I said, "Why Lord, lady, you can walk your shoes off, you couldn't get three or four dollars out of it." I said, "I know what you want." I said, "You want a pint a wine." I said, "I can get you a pint a wine."

She said, "Go get the wine."

I walked right across the street and paid forty-eight cents for the wine. It was nearly a brand-new blanket.

And another time I was up on the street there and a man wanted three dollars and a half for an electric clock. Said it was his wife's clock but he had to sell it to get him a drink. She was workin that day and he didn have no money.

I said, "Well," I said, "I'll tell you, buddy, I couldn't pay you no three or four dollars for that clock. If you want a dollar for it, I'll give you a dollar for it."

He said, "Would you give me a dollar and a half?"

I said, "No, a dollar's all I got to spare." And I pulled it out a my pocketbook. And I had more money in it, you know.

"Well," he said, "yeah, look at the money you've got in there."

"Yeah. But," I said, "that might be rent money. You don't know where that goes."

"Could be." He taken a dollar and he went on. I reckon he got him a couple pints a wine, I don't know.

And I run into a man that had a radio, and he wanted to get him a pint a wine. Course the case didn't look good now, it was busted up around the bottom, you know. But I can get as high as twenty-three stations on that little ole radio. I gave im fifty cents for it to get him a pint a wine. It done me just as good as a new one. I didn't care how it looked, just so it plays.

Now this report that come out, said we should all get three thousand dollars a year. I read that in the paper. I think it's swell. I was settin over at John Dawson's house and listened to two guys sit and talkin over there, you know, over the television. They was senators and congressmen a-talkin, you know, too. They said every man should draw three thousand dollars a year, see. From there on, said, "President Johnson is sending money over to Vietnam where he's got people here a-starvin to death, and he won't help his own people here." Oh boy, they told it to em. I set and listened to that, you know, all on through.

John said, "What do you think about that, Ras?"

I said, "I think that's a hundred percent good."

This man said, "Listen," he said, "we're gonna put a law in front of Senate and Congress, and we're hopin to get it passed, that we could get each man three thousand dollars a year." He said, "A man that lives in a house that's got to pay rent or either owns a house, and the tax people takes all their money a year for their taxes, they should be allowed three thousand dollars a year. And if they've got a family, it runs up to seven thousand dollars a year, see? So much for every member of the family." I set and listened to every bit of that.

But boy, wouldn't that tickle heck out of you if it did pass like that? See I don't get but very damn little over a thousand dollars a year, by golly. There's twelve months a year, you know. But I was gettin $99.35; now they raised it to $100.02. I draw $1,200.24 a year. Now if they get this three thousand dollars started, oh boy, I'll be settin purty, then, won't I? Oh, I'd buy myself to eat. By God, buddy, you can't get nothin but beans and potaters, somethin like that for a hundred dollars a month, you know that. And pay your rent sixty dollars a month. You can't get much out a that. When you ain't got nothin to eat but beans they get pretty rough, you know. If I eat any more beans, I'll turn into one. Now if I had me some green beans out of a garden, you know, I'd just as soon have them for breakfast as any other time of the day. But they cost too much up here. And you have to have other things too—you've gotta have soap powders, and you've gotta have this, that, and the other'n, you know. Well, it'd pretty well take three thousand dollars a year for you to live on. Yah, you take three thousand dollars a year and you say, fer instance, that you go eat like the big man eats. It's gonna cost you a hell of a lot to eat like he eats. Well, you should eat the same food he eats. If a man has a lot of money I think I should have some. But you shouldn't go a place and pay a hundred dollars for one dinner. No, but buy your stuff and bring it in the house. Buy you some good ham, buy you some good eats, and everything. That's what a man should have, you know, to live on, ain't it?

I wouldn spend too much on the movies, you know, things like that. I've been to the movies a few times, and what burns me up with the movie is just to see two people standin there and talkin. There's two people sittin there—yick yack yickety yack yickety yack yickety yack yickety yack—and that's when I leave out. I say, Oh shit, I ain't payin my money out to see that, I can see that on the street any day, you know. If somebody-or-other's comin and goin every few minutes, I like all-stars, comin and goin every few minutes, somethin like that, why that's not too bad, you know, but boy, when they get down to two—yickety yack yickety yack yickety yack, then boy, I want to get out of there. I git up and leave right then. Don't have to pay my money out for it. It's free.

Don't none a them caseworkers think very much a JOIN, I'll tell you the truth about it. I was up there and passed out leaflets, you know. Right up in front a the office. Tryin to give it to em when they go out to lunch or for a coffee break.

"Uh-uh, I don't think we want one a them."

I said, "What's a matter with em, lady?"

"Ah, don't think we want one, we work here."

"Well," I say, "ain't y'all supposed to help the pore people?"

They said, "That's what we're tryin a do."

"Well," I said, "that's what we're after. Maybe you can get an idea if you take one a these and read it."

"Nah," she said, "we don't think we want one a them." I don't see why they wouldn't take these papers. Maybe they could learn somethin about it.

Oh, of course we go up—Jim Day went up and laid em on every caseworker's desk, everywhere. They run him out from up there twice. I laughed at im. I said, "Well, Jim, you goin back again?"

Said, "I don't know."

I said, "Well, they run you out twice. Wouldn make no difference get run out a third time, would it?"

He said, "No, I don't reckon it would."

Now, I don't have nothin agin caseworkers, you know. If you was my wife, and I loved you, and I was a caseworker, I couldn't do nothin more for you than for anybody else, you know. You got to do what the boss says, you know, or he'll just tell you to go on down the road. I think we should all be in this together. Them caseworkers don't make nothin anyhow.

In later months, checks were frequently late, particularly when Ras moved: with each move he was assigned a new caseworker, a new tie-up. Should he be one day late in reporting his new address, the check would be returned to the impenetrable Audit Bureau; the former caseworker would discharge his or her function with a mechanical "His case has been transferred." The new caseworker could not break the check loose in less than a week.

When his glasses broke one time, Ras ordered a new pair from a welfare-approved optometrist, who said that welfare would take six weeks to approve the order. I* called the optometrist: he was very sorry, welfare required six weeks. I called the caseworker, Mr. Steinberg. Could he call the doctor, assure him the glasses were both permissible and necessary, and speed the process? "It is not our procedure to call the doctor," said a shocked Mr. Steinberg, sounding as if he'd been asked to abandon principle. "That is not our function."

Ras could later say, at one and the same time, "I haven't had any problems" and "We like to aggravated em to death till we got my checks." That he believed both at once revealed how little he expected.

More'n a year now I been workin out in the field, out a JOIN's office. Just walkin around, talkin to people, stuff like that.

Like I go in every night, maybe have a meetin out there, went till ten or eleven o'clock, I put my beans on, cook em about two hours. I don't ever sleep much. I cook my beans maybe till one o'clock. And I'll lay down. And I always wake up about four. I'll get up then, finish cookin em the next mornin, see. Then I've got em ready. I'll let em cool down. I always leave out about seven o'clock. Soon as it gets daylight, you know, I'd leave out and go on the streets and get to handin out leaflets and talkin to people, you know. Ketch a lot of em going to work about that time. Maybe some a-comin in, worked on the late shift at night, you know. When it's warm enough so I can get out, you know, I work sixteen, eighteen hours a day, sometimes I've been out to two o'clock in the mornin. Winters it'd be too cold, you know, nobody stirrin out there. But I got shut a most a them leaflets. Had a big old winter coat I got off a guy for seventy cents.

When you go out on the street and a man tells you his problems, that's what you got to work on. You got to get behind em. With this one building I could get the people together in one, two times goin around. Cause most of em's my people livin there—some of em anyhow, and the rest of em I know. In fact I used to live there myself. That's where that this woman told me I orta stayed in West Virginia. Had rats and roaches runnin around—I even stomped a rat to death down in a basement over there—and no screens on the windows. In the summertime they got to

*T. G.

keep the windows closed 'less the kids blow out and kill theirselves. I don't think JOIN should fix up these apartments. That's the landlord's business, we got to get the landlord to do it. He collects the rent, you know.

So I got on the housin committee, and we went up there one day lookin for all the kin, give em some a them leaflets. But he had painted it since I'd been around there. You know it was cause I made so much noise about it. I said, "I'm gonna see that these damn apartment houses are built up now." And a man went and told him and he said he had to wait to see his lawyer. And I told this man to come and see mine, I had two, smarter than any damn lawyer that he'd ever seed yet since he been in this country. "I got two in the Loop,* come down and see both a mine." Goddamn, he got busy on them apartments and he went to fixin em up! With some with no locks on the doors, you know, and he went right straight to get new locks to put on them doors, he went right to work on it. Now he really fixed it up, too. Paint—man, he throwed it on wide and handsome on them banisters and places.

One time we went down to Springfield, talked to the legislature,† told em how poor people are gettin along and everything, you know. I think they're all right providin they will coal-operate like they say they're gonna do. They said they was a hundred percent behind our organization—Jobs or Incomes Now. They said that's what they wanted.

Course all these politicians is all in together. When you go to one politician, you mention somebody-or-other, "Oh, that's a good man, that's a good man." So if one of em wanted to say anything about Mayor Daley down in there, "Uh-uh, no, not Mayor Daley, he's a good man." Yeah, they know Mayor Daley's a good man. Well, I guess we do know it. That's for sure.

I never got in there. Mary was the one talked to em, you know, Mary Parker. And I never got in—they wouldn't let me in, there was three of us, we never got in till it was purty near over. She done just about had her speech when we got in there, see. They just let so many in, you know, Dovie‡ talked to some of em, not much. The least colored woman, she's the one that got up and she talked a little bit about welfare and such, you

*A lawyer, Irv Birnbaum, and his assistant had set up a legal clinic in the JOIN office, a very popular service. Even after the Urban Progress Center set up a legal-aid program Irv remained overwhelmed by cases, the petty and the potent, so many were they, so timid were almost all the federally sponsored lawyers. (They could not, for example, consider a suit for more than $600, or take a politically "controversial" case.)
†A committee on welfare.
‡Little Dovie, niece of Dovie Coleman.

know. Other than what Mary was talkin about was mostly in leadin up to herself, you know. She just talked about herself all the time and didn't say nothin about the rest of the people. I mighta told em a whole lot when I got started, I'd a told em about these food stamps and things, but I didn't get any chance to. Cause they said they was runnin behind time, then, and they wouldn't let the West Side* in to talk to em. But, you see, on account of us a-goin down there, and makin a arrangement for them to come here, that's why they come here. They said they was a-comin to Chicago just to see for theirself how poor people was a-gettin along, and we told em that would be just fine, that that's what we wanted em to do. We got em here all right.

That's why we had to go over there to the West Side that night, see, to see what they said that night. Oh, they was a lot happened there. Colored man, he got up and told em, he said, "You people have been fair here, promise us you gonna help us." Said, "We're gonna give you about a week or maybe two weeks." Said, "If you don't help us then we're comin after you." He told em! And they mean that over there, boy! They stick together and they mean it. Oh, they was about sixty or seventy of em down there, to see that legislature that day.

I just think JOIN's a good organization myself. Reminds me a lot of the United Mine Workers, when they was organizin in West Virginia.† Organizin, goin around talkin with people, gettin em into a notion to go out with a picket line or getting a notion to j'in up, you know—it don't lack too much difference. Cause this union was out to help the poor people, that's what we're out for, you know. It's about the same thing. I'd go out organizin, and went to their meetings they had, and everything. They was somethin like JOIN's meetings only—oh heck, they was more of em. Well, they was three or four thousand at one place one day. And every man had to wear his black cap so he could be recognized, you know—a cap you prepare your light on.

Man, the miners turned out. It was a sight the way they turned out.

Oh yeah, they all stuck together. Better than JOIN does. They didn't get up raise no sand or nothin, they all talked for a better livin, see, all the time. They didn't none of em pitch off and walk out like some of em does here, you know. They all stuck together. That's what they got to do here if

*West Side Organization.
†His brother Bud, who worked in the mines for twenty-eight years, said about the union, "Well, it's just like JOIN is now, you know, they started small and just kept at it."

they'll ever do any good. You know, John Dawson walked out two or three times over there. And I know more of em walkin out, you know. Well, I don't know why. Some of em thinks they've got it made, I reckon, don't wanna know about, don't wanna help the other poor person. Course I'm not a-gettin what I need, I can't buy no clothes or nothin like that out of it, I get enough to make out on fer somethin to eat, you know, and pay my rent. I get enough like to make out on, but, you know, I like to help someone that ain't a-gettin nothin.

RETURN TO WEST VIRGINIA, OCTOBER, 1965—III

McKinley Camp is just down the Guyan River from Lyburn, where Ras had lived with Ben Baxter. The houses are wedged together like teetering dominoes, but each has a small porch large enough for hospitality. We stop in to see Carolina's daughter, Sarah, and her husband, Tommy Smith.

The house is as neatly furnished inside as it is weather-beaten outside. Everywhere, rows of knickknacks, little doll-statues, and on the walls, plaster casts made by Sarah. Prominently hung, one of John F. Kennedy, framed by four stars. (Ben also had a portrait of Kennedy on the wall.)

Tommy begins with the question everyone asked first in West Virginia: "Got jobs in Chicago? You workin, Ras?"

Ras explains he is working for JOIN, *and describes it.* "We're tryin to get up a union up hyar in West Virginia, like JOIN."

"Be all right," *allows Tommy, barely moving his mouth. To fill what is to him a lull, the stranger asks Tommy what sort of work he's done.* "I've skipped coal, hauled logs, graded roads and railroads; I done a lot of things. There's lots of places around here that'll last after I'm gone."

Ras says, "There's lots of people in Chicago ain't workin. . . ."

"There's lots a people's lazy," *snaps Tommy.* "Wouldn't work even if they found work."

"Oh," *says Sarah heavily,* "there's lots of people hyar needs help, can't even get on the DPA. Old woman lives down thyar, gets thirty-five dollars a month and her rent is fourteen dollars a month. We need somethin here."

The subject and the possibility hang in the air for a moment and then dissolve. Ras asks what has happened to Logan. "I don't know," *Sarah says,* "it's different than it was." *Things for her are never better or worse, only different. Tommy talks about his three children, living in the same building in Uptown.* "I like these hills. Town life's too confinin. Y'ain't got no yard or nothin. Always got some overseer around you."

Sarah does not so much announce lunch as deposit it on the table. Fried potatoes, green beans, pork rind, biscuits, plain flour gravy, all reheated from breakfast. We eat in silence until Tommy begins to talk:

"You know they's draftin young fellers now. Hit's a shame, you know, them fellers have to wait to be called, 'stead of volunteerin. Shame when a man has to be called to protect his homeland." Ras keeps eating, waiting his moment. Tommy goes on. "Hit's a gettin closer, you know. Commonism. I like free enterprise. A man should have a chance to make a thousand a month if he's capable. Under Commonism, you know, they order you around everythin you do."

Ras looks up. "Well, you get in the army, they go round tellin you what to do."

"Well, shore, that's the army. Every organization's got to have a leader, a head you know. Jest as soon have a fish without a backbone as a man without a leader. You take a crew a four men workin out there on a road. If they don't have no leader, one'll go thisaway, another'n go thataway, do whatever comes into their minds. Won't get the work done."

"Well now, Tommy, JOIN don't have no leaders."

Tommy is incredulous. "Why, they got to have leaders, Ras."

"Nope."

"Don't JOIN have a bookkeeper? You know, somebody that spends the money and keeps the records?"

"I reckon they do, Tommy, but that still ain't no leader."

Tommy goes back to his food. The initiative falls to Ras:

"I heard they's a gonna be draftin men that's got babies."

Tommy, grim, shakes his head. "Well, I hope they ends this war afore then."

RETURN TO WEST VIRGINIA, OCTOBER, 1965—IV

To Ras's amazement, the bars in downtown Logan are all gone. In their places, modern stores advertising the standard package of American goods for the small middle-class, and working and retired union-scale miners; a new DPA office and courthouse. "They done changed this place all around, used to be beer gardens everywhere." The best beer joint had been the Hole-in-the-Wall, not six feet from the railroad tracks on the east side of town, but it has been boarded up. On this weekday afternoon the next-door bar, still open, is lifeless, a kind of waiting station with no reason or anticipation. The toothless bargirl says no one comes in to drink any more, except on paydays, and even then not many: "I'll bet Chicago's real nice."

Ras gives her a quarter for the jukebox but declines any other favors—the place stinks of death and memory—and we leave after a single beer. There is a better place on the other side of town.

Walking along the tracks, Ras catches the eye of a florid man sitting on the ground near the depot, hands crossed on his knees, a battered hat beside him. A moment of recognition happens in the casual, unexcited way it has happened with all Ras's relatives.

"Hello Ras. Set yourself down. Heard you been up in Chicago."

"Yep."

"You workin?"

"Yeah, I'm workin out a JOIN. . . ."

"JOIN? What's that?" the man snaps.

"Oh, we're just tryin to help the pore people. You know, somebody needs to go to the doctor, we get 'em to the doctor. Somebody needs to get on the DPA we take em down there—"

"You a Commonist, Ras?" The man has been staring at the "JOIN Community Union" button pinned on Ras's army jacket. His show of strength requires no answer. "I'd rather be called a cocksucker than a Commonist. Any Commonist sets foot in this county, I'll withdraw him. Better a cocksucker than a Commonist, I always say." Ranting, he is plucking at the JOIN button.

With enormous dignity Ras shoves him away. "Don't fuck with my button, man. Don't you fuck with my button." After some seconds the man pulls away, sullen, muttering: "Better a cocksucker'n . . ." Ras is somewhat inclined to administer a memorable lesson to the man but I* convince him he has already upheld his honor.

"Good thing we walked on," he says later. "I'd a killed that sonofabitch shore as hell. Ain't nobody gonna fuck with my button."

That night we return to Bill's house just around the bend from Big Creek, in Daisy Camp, eight or ten unpainted wood structures jammed against a hill near a played-out mine: a ghost town still inhabited. Coal stove; family photos on the freshly papered walls; clean linoleum "rugs" on all the floors. (Next door Bill's younger sister has a TV, the camp's only diversion besides the Free Will Baptist Church). Bill, fit in his fifties, is flattered to be visited by salvageable sinners; then he is positively gleeful at the prospect of our attending tomorrow night's revival meeting. Confident of his impending victory, from the moment Ras walks in, he is more effusive and welcoming than the other kin. He opens with the

*T. G.

standard inquiry, "You workin?" but quickly moves on. Though he had only once been in a city—Memphis—and then only long enough to take freight and return to the hills, his provinciality does not account for the sheer quantity of his curiosity; other relatives, even less traveled, had seemed only politely interested in Chicago. It is as if Bill is so sure of his anchor, Christianity, he can afford to pay closer attention to his guests. It makes him a more genial evangelist, and therefore a better one.

"Got hills like that in Chicago?"

"They have these stamps, U.S. Agriculture Department food stamps up in Chicago too?"

"I heard people are real violent up there."

"Oh, yes," says Ras, but he prefers to talk about JOIN, his extended answer to the question, "You workin?"

Bill does not so much counter as ignore JOIN as an approach to urban troubles. "People has to learn to love one another."

"They used to say you should do to the other man the way you'd like him to do to you. Nowadays you better do the other feller before he does it to you first."

Bill is irrepressible. "Lots of Catholic peoples, ain't there? You know them Catholics is gettin might powerful. People has to turn to the Lord, else them Catholics will take over."

"Well, when I die the devil won't have me, cause I been too mean; and I ain't never done nothin for the Lord. So just put me on a bus out to Shoppers World. They have everything there and handle all kinds of people."

Around Bill and O. C., Ras invokes the Lord, heaven and hell, with an intensity that stops a pace short of conviction. (He came into the JOIN office one day as some winos were joking about long-distance calls, and said, "I'd place a call to Heaven but there ain't enough people up there to answer.") Bill lets the blasphemy pass; so they continue to talk past each other.

"You know, Bill, when people gets baptized I believe they should just be drowned on the spot, so that they cain't get away."

"Everybody should come to church, Ras, to get some salvation."

"Everybody's good, that's what we believe up there in JOIN."

Bill's wife, Gracie, his coevangelist and a gregarious frequenter of church socials, believes that Johnson is "no good a-tall. He don't do nothin for the pore people, and then he goes and gets our boys killed off."

Ras then relates the story of the Logan drunk grabbing at his JOIN button. Bill is confused. "Commonist? What's a Commonist?"

Says Ras, "Reckon it's someone what's agin the government, the United States government."

"Well."

"I say, put all the leaders in a concrete building and let them fight it out."

"Well, hit's a rich man's war."

They go on this way until bedtime. Through agreement and gentle dissidence, conviction and blasphemy, contact and distance, some sense of shared roots and family identity winds like a labyrinthine thread. Says Gracie the next morning, "Ras sure used to be wild. I don't know if he is now or not." But she will greet him warmly and feed him hugely whenever he drops in. "Hasn't changed a bit," says Bill. "He'll always be a sinner."

RAS BRYANT

If you're gonna work for JOIN you gotta be like Jesus and love everyone. I'm like Jesus. I love every one of em in JOIN, coloreds and whites alike. We'd have to love the Indians if we could get them to come in with us, but, you know, won't any of em come around JOIN. I don't know why that is. You just gotta be like Jesus.

Them two colored women called Dovie, I think they're all right. I don't see a thing wrong with em. As far as I know I believe they're straight and square. Colored people got different ways, but they're human beins just like we are. Colored baby looks just like a white baby. You know a white baby looks like red when it's just born. There was a colored guy lived across the railroad, where I lived, and he whistled me one day. I come out on the porch. Held up two fingers and motioned me to come over. I knowed what he wanted—two pints, you know. I got me two pints and went on over.

"Mr. Ras," he said, "you want to see my newborn baby?" Said, "It's jest been born."

I said, "Yeah." I walked in and I kept lookin down, lookin down, lookin down—why, it was red all over!

"Oh, Mr. Ras," he said, "now what you think this time?" He said, "He'll be turnin black in about four hours." I kept goin back and watchin that baby, you know. About four hours, it started turnin black.

A colored man's got anything, he'll use it to help you a little bit—a nickel or somethin like that, you know, if he's got anything. But lots a white people won't. A lot of em will and a lot of em won't. It's like in the liquor store up here one time. I seed a colored guy buy a pint a wine, pay fifty-eight cents for it. And I just had fifty-three. I said, "Well," I said, "is the white port the same price as the red, mister?"

He said, "Yeah."

"Oh," I said, "I can't nary, I lack a nickel."

"Oh," the colored guy said, "I can give you a nickel," and he give me a nickel.

I said, "Thank you, mister, very much."

He said, "Buddy, you're welcome."

I used a help em out, lots of em. Let em have whiskey on time, stuff like that. Any one of em'd beat you out of your money and leave there and go somewhere else, that's all, but they wouldn't hurt you over it. They'd just come around, you know, and talk to you and get so much off of you. The first thing you know they was gone. Maybe leave owin me fifty or sixty, maybe seventy, eighty dollars. Some of em a hundred or more. One left owin me one hundred eighty-five dollars. I didn't pay no attention to it. Well, I was a-makin a good livin anyhow. I got a lot of stuff off of em for nearly nothin. They'd come pawn somethin to me, one guy pawned me a new one-hundred-twenty-dollar suit. Livin in just a little ole coal camp, lived right over the next house or two from me. Buy a quart of whiskey, you know. He never would come back. I'd get the suit.

They get along together a lot better than white people. They'll get together all night, have a big party all night long and get just as drunk as they want to and you'll never hear em raise no sand. There's hardly ever you see two niggers fall out. Well, they've got these here houses out there in West Virginia, very many of em, colored people has, and they have these here Victrolas in there, you know, them dime machines they have them in there. They get in there and play the machines and dance all night. Be dancin next mornin when daylight comes. I went in and stood around and watch em lots of times, buy me a pint of whiskey or somethin-or other and stand around watch em for an hour maybe, dance and carry on. Lots of times there's a lot of white women in there too, dancin with em. I never did dance myself, though. I don't dance any. I never had time when I was growin up to go to no dances or nothin much, you know, to learn it.

RETURN TO WEST VIRGINIA, OCTOBER, 1965—V

In Logan as in all towns of its size, the bus station has been more than a convenience; it is both a monument and a plaza. Ras expects to run across some old friends there, but once inside he is astonished. "They done changed this place all around. Used to have benches all up thar. Colored people used to come in here to set—from Shantytown, Goat Holler, Black Bottom, them other places. Didn't have no other place to set." Late in the afternoon, black and white high school kids in mixed groups are shooting pinball.

Later in the day Ras tells his cousin Orval about the new order of things. As usual on this trip, when Ras engages an old friend his incidental "friends o' mine from Chicago" fade into the background and he resettles into traditional manners of talking:

"Niggers! Set around all day talkin junk. Man comes in to get a bus ride, ain't hardly no place for him to set himself down."

That evening he talks with Bill and Gracie about the rich man's war, the three of them then moving to the subject of race. Ras says, "They should give em their own state, let em live by theyself, and give the whites the rest of the states."

Back in Chicago, we never heard him pronounce on the races in this vein, or revert to the word "nigger," probably the word he had been comfortable with most of his life. In our presence, at least, he reserves it for home use.

RAS BRYANT

Far as I know, we have to have law, but my good God almighty, the police shouldn't be so dirty as they are, should they? Oh man, they'll take every damn dime you've got.

Oh, they get coffee hungry you know around Christmas time, yeah, they got to have their coffee, you know: extra money, for coffee and stuff. And any time they arrest a man they going to take every damn thing he's got just like they did me here, that's what they done me. Trying to make a little extra money for Christmas.

I was standin out in front of the office, you know. And I had seventy-three dollars in my pocket. Just had got my check, you know. Probably shouldn't have carried it on me, but I've studied everything over—you don't know how many keys there is to the door, you know what I mean? People leaves out and keeps the keys, you know. I could a hid it, but somebody come in and search the house, they would find it, prob'ly would.

Me and Bill Irwin had just went up there to Liquortown* and got two pints of wine. Bill paid for the wine. Now I didn't pay for it, Bill paid for

*Liquor store at the corner of Wilson and Racine.

it. And he reached me one of em to stick one in my pocket. And I just stuck it down in my front pocket there. We walked out to JOIN's office, standin right there in front of JOIN's office, and I wasn't a-payin no attention, cause Bill was watchin what he was a-doin and I was standing there busy talkin to him. And he pulled that bottle out a my pocket to take a drink of it, y' see. And it was about half full then, you know, we couldn't a been drunk for the two of us just drunk a half a pint a wine. We didn't have nothin to drink the night before that, see. And he pulled that bottle out, just aimed to take a drink of it, and here come the law up the street, They hollered at him, "Hold it right there, hold it right there, don't drop that bottle, hold it right there." He just stood there and held that bottle, they come up and took it out of his hand.

"Come on," said, "you're goin too."

We got down to the paddy wagon, why they shoved me down and found this other pint of wine, see. It hadn't been opened, now. They took me in too. Took me down there, they shoved me down and taken everything I had in my pocket, they taken it out. Laid it down on a table, you know. Pocketbook and everything. Even taken my eyeglasses off my head, till I couldn't see nothin. Went on into jail and that evenin I told Bill Irwin, I said, "Bill," I said, "Call some of them guys that you know back there, get em up here, and I'll put up bond for both of us." See, I knowed I could get my money back the next day, you know. And I said, "I'll go up there and we'll get out this evenin."

"Well," so he said, "that's a good guy," said, "just walked back up through here now."

I don't know whether there is any good ones or not, but that's what he said. Here he come walkin through. And Bill said, "Say, buddy?" Called him by his name. Said, "Say, what about us makin bond?"

"Why," he said, "you got that kind of money out there?"

"Why," he said, "this man here's got seventy-three dollars out there, see." Said, "He's got seventy-three dollars. He's gonna go my bond and his both. We're both wantin to get out, until trial."

"Well," he said, "I'll go back and check on it." He comes back. "Why," he said, "you've only got twenty-seven dollars out there." Just enough to make bond, like, and get home on.

I said, "Somebody's a goddamn crooked sonofabitch."

"Yeah," he said, "I know what's goin on here," he said.

"Now," Bill says, "there ain't a thing can be done about that."

He said, "I don't think so," he said, "They'd swear damn lies a mile long."

Bill said, "I know you're a guy who won't do that."

Said, "You know I won't do that. But I know what's goin on here." Said, "I get complaints every day, here, what's goin on out there."

And he come back and asked Bill, after I made bail, you see, put up my bond and got out, he come back and he asked Bill, he said, "Did he sure have that money?"

And Bill said, "Yes, sir, he sure had it." Said, "I'd swear it, that I counted it and he counted it too, and he had seventy-three dollars about two or three minutes before they picked us up." Why I knowed to the penny how much money I had, you know.

I don't know what we can do about it, I'll swear I don't. Harriet went and talked to some reporters, but they acted like they wasn't interested. They don't want to go agin these cops, you see. Course when you read anything you don't know whether to believe it or not. Just like somebody that you meet out here on the street and tell you somethin, somebody you don't know, you don't know whether to believe him or not.

Them cops is s'posed to take care of you. Ain't that right? They're supposed to protect you. If they have to take you to jail, well, that's all right. If they don't have to take you, well, they can take you home, or take you to where you want to go to. But they're not supposed to take your damn money, now. Are they? No. But they do it.

Hit goes on all year around, but just a little before Christmas, why they look for everybody to be drunk, you know they going to arrest everybody along the streets. Think they're going to celebrate holidays, you know, they're going to arrest so many more of em then than they do every day, you know. Just like it was out in West Virginia. They paid off a miner's vacation, last day of June, I believe it was. About a hundred or two hundred dollars, a month's time. Oh man, them old cops would grab every one of them miners that they could get, boy. In one weekend they locked up a hundred and eighty-five in one little jail in Logan County, a little old place like that, tryin to get all that money. Well, they fined you according to who arrests you. If the state police get you, I think it's $11.60, something like that. It runs from there to $16.50 off of each man that they arrested. Well, you just figger up how much money that come to.

Oh Lord, the law's the worst you ever seed down there. You go in, sit down and drink a beer like that, or maybe two, and they look through the winders and see you in there drinkin. You come out in the street, they gonna pick you up. The law's got so bad you can't make moonshine up there hardly. Now, they are not too bad about takin all your money like they are here, takin your money and keepin it, you know. Course they do take it.

But the ones that's got me pissed off is the laws in Chicago here. We gotta have law, but we got to do somethin-or-other about that, as dirty as the sonsabitches are. Boy, I'm gonna tell you one thing. I just wish I had the gun I used to have, I used to have a .38 Smith and Western special with a six-inch barr'l. I'd just like to get some of these sonsabitches here. I'll tell you the damn truth. If I had to go to jail from now on. Course I'd have to go for life, cause I done been there twice. I'd have to go for life, now. As old as I am now, you never would get out of jail. Tain't worth it. But I'm tellin you the truth. I'll swear I don't believe that I could hold still. I'd get my nuts off anyhow.

Rennie asked me one day. He said, "Ras, can you tell me why the police fights us?"

"Why," I said, "Rennie, that's easy for me to figger out."

He said, "Well, by golly, I was thinking about this and I can't figger it out."

I said, "If you go to fighting a dog he'll bite back at you, see." I said, "We fighting the police?"

He said, "That's for sure."

I said, "Buddy, anytime you go to fightin someone, he's going to fight back at you, ain't he?"

I don't believe we will ever get strong enough to overcome em, you know what I mean, and make em dance to our music, cause there are too damn many of them, you know. Here's another thing. They can call the militia here if they had to have em, you know what I mean, they could do that or they could call all the state police, they can get every law in the world, you know, around in the state of Illinois, anyhow. If it come up to something like that, we never could fight em with guns cause, heck, they've got too much ammunition for us, they got too many guns that we ain't got, see.

I wish we could get strong enough. I wish we could, for sure. Boy, that would tickle the hell out a me if we could. I tell you what let's do—let's get busy this next election, and put somebody in here by God'll take care of these goddamn police. Is that right? But that goddamn sonofabitch we got in there now, you know he's no good. Goddamn lettin these here police run all over town takin people's money and every goddamn thing. Sheeet! I'd like to shit on Daley's grave the day he dies. That's the best I could do for him. I'd just want to crawl right up on his grave and shit the biggest turd ever I shit in my life right on top of his grave. Damn bastard like that! Shit! Well, there's nothin he'll ever do for me, I know it. Jesus Christ Almighty! If I never vote for a man in my life until I vote for Mayor Daley, I'd never cast another one as long as I live, by golly.

Politicians up here, pretty much like down in West Virginia. Not too much difference in em. There's people lives across from Madison. And they got no way a-tall to get across the river. And before every big election they're gonna put a bridge across there, you know. "Just in a few days, just after election, we're gonna put a bridge across there," and get everybody to vote for em who lives over there, see. They's never been no bridge. That's been a-goin on for the last twenty years, I guess. When they're out electioneerin they'll promise you anything, and after they get elected they ain't gonna do nothin, but they promise. There was one man elected to the county court out there one time, and he went around to all these people, he said, "Now," he said, "this ain't gonna last a lifetime, but let's try to get enough out to do us a lifetime." And he just put all of his people to work, you know. The rest of the people stayed out in the cold. Happens very often. Just before election they'll come around and they'll give maybe fifty people a job on the state road. The first check they get they tax em fifteen dollars, for electioneerin funds, you see. Well, they pay that fifteen dollars. Then the next two or three days after election, probably the next mornin after election, they's a lot of em cut off. It happens every big election out there, you know.

After them sonsabitches took my money, I jest went to drinkin, to survive a little better. I started big around Christmas and I celebrated straight into the New Year.

Christmas didn't mean more'n no other day for me. I told my family not to send me no Christmas cards. I ain't no goat, I can't eat no paper. I'll tell you: when you draw a little old check like this, if you go out and buy a big lot of stuff up for Christmas, that takes all your money. Then you gotta build up the rest of the month. I gotta go on existin, you know. No, the welfare don't give you any extra. No, uh-uh, not a penny extra for Christmas.

So I just went up 'ere and started cleanin up this tavern, messin around— first one thing and then another. I just walked in—I'd been goin in there talkin with the manager around, you know, and a-handin him all these leaflets, and he'd take those leaflets, you know, and I'd go back out in the alley and I'd watch im. And every man that come out a there had one a them leaflets in thar on top of his bag. He put em in thar now! After I got to talkin with him, see, what I told him, I said, "Now listen here, mister," I said, "I'll tell you one thing," I said, "you know that the money you get comes off of the pore people." I said, "D'you ever get it off of rich people?"

"Why," he said, "Lord, no, Ras."

I said, "Now listen. If rich people's gonna drink, they're gonna go to these nightclubs, where they can have a big time, and they're gonna drink there," I said. "They ain't comin in here and spend no money with you."

He said, "That's right."

"Well, if I help the pore people they'll come in here and spend some money with you."

He said, "That's right." He said, "I'll tell you what to do." Said, "Lay a bunch a them up on the counter, and," he said, "we'll put one a them in every man's bag." Said, "We'll give everybody one that comes in."

I laughed about it. I said, "O.K."

And so tharfore, you see, I made a pretty good guy out a him. And then one day I went in, was talkin with him. He said, "Say," said, "what about you comin in," said, "and moppin for us?" Said, "Can you do that?"

I said, "Oh, yeah." Said, "I'll come in and mop for you." And I went in there every Sunday—

"Oh," Bob said, "Lordy mercy, Ras, don't be so particular with it." He said, "It don't take that time."

I said, "Oh, well, I like to do a good job in anything I go at."

He said, "Well, I know, but ain't no use to be so particular with it." They hadn't had that before, you know. I cleaned that place up, buddy, and they said, "That's the best that's ever been cleaned up yet." And that's the reason they liked me there, you see. Three dollars, every Sunday. Just that much, you know, makes you a little spendin money extry, to buy you tobacker and stuff with like that. Maybe sometimes you'd run up some money, you know, some way or somehow, and you could take that and go get ye somethin that ye had to have, you know. I'd generally meet old Pop down there, on the streets, him and Bud. Bud was on one corner, one mornin, and old Pop on the other un, a-wantin a dollar apiece. They've been a time or two that I didn't spend a penny of it myself, I just let them have it, you know. The boys they was sick. One day over there Bud was a-settin there and he was a-shakin like a leaf on a tree, buddy. They wasn't no question to it. He was just about to die. Well, I only had a few cents, about thirteen or fourteen cents, somethin like 'at, and Bud, he had a little bit, not enough to get a pint a wine, you know. My cousin, he come along and he didn't have but about ten or twelve cents. Anyhow I walked up the street thar to borrow some money, see, to get him a pint o' wine. And just right on the edge of the curb thar laid a brand new quarter, with the head of it turned up, you know. I looked down at it, I couldn't believe it was a quarter. And I picked it up and turned it over and said, "Oh, well, I can get im a pint a wine now." I walked back down there, and that made enough to get it, you know.

I don't know hardly myself how I managed, I'm tellin you the truth. Oh well, I didn't make it, I didn't have one-third what I wanted to eat, hardly at any time. It just put me so hard up, I couldn't find nothin to eat.

I got me a little place in the Marsha Apartments, and I went to keepin a bunch a people there. Cooked for em and everything. I couldn't afford to feed em all on the DPA, now you know that. But I didn't know what else to do, I fed em all, they gotta eat, you know. I just had enough stuff to feed em on, that's about all, and not too much a that either. Bryant's Welfare Service, I called it. They'd sleep in these empty rooms, you know, most of em would. There's two of em'd stay with me. I had two beds, you see. I had a big bed and a small bed down there. The rest of em'd go out and sleep in them empty rooms. Had seven of em in there one night.

Never had the least idea how many I'd be cookin for, until it's over with. They was good to me while they was thar, while I was keepin em, cept one mornin I got up, and there were six men asleep in my apartment, all drunk, you know. And somebody stole everything off me—my electric clock, my radio, they took em both. The manager called the law oncet, you see. On the winos. Me and Jim Day layin there in the bed. And this police come in and taked his billy and commenced to hittin Jim right across the toe. She said, "No, don't bother that man in there," said, "they pay their rent."

"Oh," he said, "well, all right," and turned around and walked out. He thought we was just layin out thar too. But he should've knowed there wouldn't a been no sheets on the bed if we'd just been a-layin out in thar. Yeah, they taken a man or two out a thar.

That place was just a damned dump, to tell the truth about it. The door open thar all night, all day and every time. Just anyone could come up. there and knock on the door. And you just couldn't stand it in thar, with that there sulfur in that coal, you see, coming right up in thar. Why, I went through thar one mornin, I swear I couldn't hardly see to get out a thar, to the stairs. Smoke was so bad. And I went and knocked on Jay's door and like to tried to tear his door down. He was the manager, see. I thought it was a mattress or somethin afire, see. And directly I got him out, and he run down in the basement. He knowed where it was, y' see. But I didn't notice where the smoke was comin from when I run down. And the water was runnin down over that light bulb, in the toilet, and over electric wires in that light bulb. Why, when they'd flush this commode upstairs, you see, that water, it wouldn't go through, it run over and come right down through right where I had to take a bath, see. And I was fraid to go in thar and take a bath. Fraid someone would come in thar and flush that commode, then run right down on your head, you know. You wouldn't want that happenin. I didn't take a bath all the time I stayed there. I was afraid to. And the winders, they was all broken out and everything on the other side. I don't think she ever did fix them. She just locked that side off and never rented hit at all, see. I was goin to leave there jest as soon's I got my next check—go somewhere, I didn't know where, but somewhere else. I don't like that junk. But the reason I didn't want to do it was the bunch stayin with me, you know. If they got a place a their own, that'd be different, but as long as they didn't, I wouldn't leave em.

"THEY THREW MY DAMN ASS OUT"

Ras didn't have the chance to move out on his own.

At the JOIN *meeting of December 8, 1965, Ras had stubbornly complained that* JOIN *was shirking its responsibility to tenants. "Now people ask me what we're gonna do about this where they's been livin with rats and roaches and so on, and if we can't do nothin about it then we might as well quit. All we do is talk about it. Let's not put out anything we can't back up." As the meeting drifted to other subjects, Ras stood up periodically: "I still want to know what we're gonna do." In the midst of reports on different activities, John Dawson cautioned against trying to do everything at once. The student organizers, faced with an unexpected demand on their energies, were silent. It was Richie Rothstein, just back on staff after a three-month hiatus, who acknowledged that Ras was on the right track. Meetings, he said, shouldn't simply dwell on the stupidity and venality of housing inspectors; maybe we should become our own housing inspectors. As a result of Ras's eloquence, and what we thought a peculiar default on the part of the staff, we abandoned our pristine status as observers and began to work in the new* JOIN *housing committee with John Dawson, Richie, and a few others.*

On January 19, John Dawson visited Ras and described what followed at a meeting that night: "It's a damn crime, the welfare will approve a building the shape that one's in. I called the health department at the welfare department myself. They promised me that they would have somebody over there in fifteen minutes. If they didn't have, for a couple of us JOIN *people to go down to 901 Montrose, that one a the inspectors there would go with us to see about it. In the meantime, Todd came by there, and this damn furnace, the fumes from this furnace'll run you out a there. It'll strangle you to death to try to walk through the building. . . .*

Anyway we went down, Todd and I went down to 901, went to the inspectors' office. Todd tried to tell em where it was a fire hazard and all that, we did. And Todd said to one of them, he said, 'You gonna go down there?' He said, 'No,' he said, 'it's four-thirty.' Well it wasn't four-thirty, it was around approximately four. I said, 'You mean to say you didn't have no call from the Lincoln Avenue Welfare Office?' 'Oh, yes, we had the call, but it's four-thirty. We'll see about it in the mornin.' I said, 'The landlady there's drunk, don't care anything about nobody in the buildin.' I said, 'That's the way you like to see buildins run in this city?' They ain't answered that question. They said it was quittin time, that they couldn't do anything about it till the next day. But it wasn't quittin time, and I can't see where the government would be wastin money on war on poverty, payin em so much to inspect buildins, when their day's work's not up.

"We wanna make a show of the buildin cause that's been in the courts since 1958. If we can make a show over there and win that, then we can make a show all over town, for then they'll say, well if JOIN can win that and the Uptown people can win that, and get out here and fight for sech as that, then when we go out here on another buildin they damn sure won't bust you in no way.

"Course I mean right now I'd rather we'd work out somethin without havin to pull a picket, as cold as it is. But we asked this landlady to do somethin about it, she wouldn't do anything, so we'll picket that buildin till there's somethin done about it."

John had told Ras, "We'll be makin example out a this damn buildin," and Ras had come right back, "Why you can throw this buildin in the lake if you can, I'll help you carry it."

John and I* arranged to meet at Ras's the next morning. When I arrived, early, Ras's little room was crammed: Ras, another man, and Jim Day asleep on the bed, Jim's legs across Ras's chest; one of Ras's episodic girlfriends and a black man asleep on the couch; John moody in a chair. Everyone was wearing JOIN buttons. In the corridor, oddly enough, an inspector was compiling a seemingly thorough list of violations. A minute after he left, as if obeying the sequence of some propaganda film, three cops stomped upstairs, the manager in their wake screaming that someone had come after him with a knife. It was John he pointed out. The cops pushed us out in the corridor and up against the wall, frisked us, and finding nothing, asked what I was doing there. One always needs a reason to be anywhere. I said I had come to find out if the building was

*T. G.

being inspected for violations. "What do you mean, violations?" said the cop, offended. "There are no violations in the building." He ordered John and me to leave; under the circumstances we had little choice.

Assuming Ras would be arrested, we drove back to the JOIN office to get bail money and a camera. Drunker than he had seemed in the presence of the cops, John confided that he had threatened the manager, who had at first refused to let him in the building. When the cops came in he had ditched the knife—I hadn't noticed.

At the office we ran into a well-known newspaper reporter, of impeccable liberal reputation—the sort who occasionally contributes articles to The Nation—and a photographer who turned out to have a Pulitzer Prize. Since they were preparing a series on Uptown, featuring JOIN, we invited them back to the building to verify its condition and the conduct of the cops. When we got back the cops were gone, and Ras and his buddies were still sprawled out, asleep. The photographer poked around, snapping pictures, but not until we obtained a promise that he wouldn't use any that might humiliate anyone. We returned to the office where John summoned an informal meeting and proposed we "picket em day and night. When I want to picket, I picket." There was no argument. We set to work making picket signs.

Later Ras explained what happened next:

"I just walked out in the hall and the landlady, she just pushed me plumb down the stairs. My arm's sore up there yet, I can't sleep on that side a-tall. Where I hit that wall, you know. Messed my hip up, you know, and I couldn't hardly walk. I blowed blood out a my nose for two or three days where it hit that wall, or the stairs or somethin—I went so fast I didn't know how it was done, hardly. I'll tell you now what the cause was, on account of y'all goin there and takin them pictures, you know, of the place. That's what started it. She accused me of it, see, turnin it in on her. She didn't want to put no money on that building, see. Called mc a goddamn son of a bitch, you know, and then shoved me plumb down them stairs. Said, 'Get the hell out of here and don't never come back no more.' And me with my rent paid up. I got back a check of ten dollars the next day, but she didn't give me anything that evenin. Shoved me out with no place to stay at all. Hit cold weather, too. No clothes on, didn't have nothin on but a shirt. Jim Day brought my coats down to me, this coat here and my overcoat. Then she went in the room, broke and entered the room now, taken all of my stuff out, and carried it downstairs. All my food was gone, all my razor—my razor and razor blades, Listerine, toothpaste, and everything. Lots a food. Fourteen-dollar, thirteen-dollar-ninety-five-cent electric blanket and the tax, made over fourteen-dollar. That big double b'iler I had, cost fourteen dollars, that real heavy aluminum. And all my silverware was gone, seven plates, all my deeshes I had to use to eat out of, to put stuff in, you know. It was all gone—lot a my clothes was gone."

Ras joined the picket line that evening, foot after foot as if on a victory or a funeral march, weeping, "They throwed my damn ass out," but, indefatigable, singing in a high-pitched and quavering voice, the only song he knows: "Will the Circle Be Unbroken?" At one point the landlady emerged with a pair of scissors, and ripped up two signs before she could be restrained by picketers, not the cops who watched on. Neighbors gathered in clumps across the street, watching quietly for the most part—except for one woman who had once lived in the Marsha and cursed the landlady in no uncertain terms. Approval was general if silent and cautious.

After a couple of hours John brought the picketers to his apartment just down the street, for coffee. John burned to picket all night, but no one else could say why, and the warm respite from the cold night came apart as he began ranting, cursing Rennie and a "damn Mexican" for counseling a night's sleep. Etta finally restrained him, with tears, the Mexican slipped out, and the awkwardness was broken by the entrance of Jimmy, another former Marsha tenant and one of the JOIN corner guys.* Knowing we were planning to picket but not finding us on the street, he had gone up to Ras's room. The manager asked him what he was doing there. "Lookin for my friend Ras."

Manager: "Threw him out today."

Jimmy: "You did?"

Manager: "You with that JOIN bunch?"

Jimmy: "I sure am." The manager had kicked him in the ass and Jimmy had hauled off and slugged him—"knocked half his eye out." John roared with approval, we all felt somewhat redeemed, and with the long day thereby salvaged we decided to picket in the morning. John insisted Ras, Bud, and Jim Day spend the night at his place.

The picket resumed uneventfully in the morning, this time without Ras, who was in no condition to walk on the icy sidewalk. On the corner of

*See p. 222.

Wilson Avenue, one old woman with a kerchief over her head said to another, "Did you see them boycotting that building? Carrying a sign saying 'High Rent, Low Heat' . . . Hope they don't let the Puerto Ricans in there. . . . Bunch a bums live there anyway."

Late in the afternoon the landlady capitulated, signing a statement pledging repairs. A few weeks later it became common knowledge on the street that she had installed a new furnace. This was JOIN's first picket of a building in Uptown.

When the reporter's series on Uptown appeared, neither JOIN nor the picket was mentioned. But on Page One was a photograph of a young wino asleep in a sheetless bed surrounded by wine bottles, in a back room of the Marsha Apartments.

In 1967 the building was bought by a real estate management company —they painted it, fixed up the entrance, cleaned the apartments, and hung little pennants outside. Only in the most superficial sense did this buttress JOIN's victory. For in the process of community organization, such small victories matter if they can encourage the victors to win others, and if the movement is in a position to gather new friends with its just-revealed power. By the summer of 1967 JOIN had swung around to face

the more urgent danger of urban renewal, and was unready to parlay its effect on the building into a success. In other words the new tenants did not know to whom they were to be grateful, or why; and there had been other and more visible defeats. The summer of 1966 JOIN had organized a successful rent strike in a large corner building—known as the Bobo building after its Southern owner—down the street. Bobo signed a contract with tenants pledging repairs. When he defaulted, though, there was no recourse, the courts demurring to plunge into the precedent of insuring tenants' rights.

Housing court finally leaped into action and fined the landlord $13,200, but the tenants' organization had meanwhile disintegrated, there being no money to make the most elementary repairs. In an underpopulated (average 15 percent vacancy) neighborhood of transients, progress must be quick and tangible to hold disgusted tenants in a dangerous building. So the tenants moved out, occupancy turned over, and for months the main mark of continuity was the broken windows facing one of the busiest corners in the neighborhood. Since JOIN had loudly declared that collective action could bring improvements, the broken windows were taken popularly as symbols of JOIN's failure. In fact, the trouble was that the tiers of government would not intervene directly to make repairs. Where else could the money come from? But the blame was not apparent to the passer-by.

Walking the Streets: Wilson

The Wilson Club Hotel for Men, $1.15 a night for cabinet and bed, separated from the next cubicle with a partition topped by chicken wire. The winos call it "The Iron Lung." In front of the store called Liquortown, two carloads of police interrogating a wino, knots of older men watching, smoking. Deluxe Market: "Sale. Meaty Neck Bones 23¢ Lb." The Lunch Pail, hamburgers, fried shrimp, crowded with teen-agers, two little kids ogling the pinball machines. A tired teen-age girl missing two front teeth gazes dully out the window of the laundromat.

Deluxe Theater. *Nature's Playmates, The Bad Seed, Run of the Arrow.* Triple features every day. Adults 55¢, Children 25¢. Their brochure shows a man with a revolver to his head: "Don't Shoot! See a Movie First!" Angry kids kick the litter in the rear, unseparated from the auditorium. During the movie a small boy somersaults down the center aisle; a bottle shatters somewhere in the back; no one objects. Three teen-age Indians asleep while two babies wail, and there are knots of nine- and ten-year-olds on their own.

Bars, pawn shops, variety store, Happy Foods under the el. Mr. Adams, fancy coat-and-tie restaurant, located on the corner of Broadway for years. Across the street, Uptown Federal Savings and Loan, with a mural intending to show centuries of progress, displaying these captions:

"Make All You Can—Save All You Can—Give All You Can"

"Every Man Is the Architect of His Own Future"

"Save, and Teach All You Are Interested in to Save"

"Thus Pave the Way for Moral and Material Success"

"Thrift Is a Powerful Force Toward Happy Living"

Down the street another new Lunch Pail, but the old clientele has stayed with Shelly's Red Hots, fries included, pinball, always jammed. On the corner a young guy appears to be attending to a collapsed drunk; he walks into Shelly's and says, "Went through both pockets and all I found was a dime and this radio." Stewart School, its playground occupied by "mobile classrooms" for the overflow: a concerned teacher complains the kids are restless, noisy. Michael Reese Foundation, blood for one of Chicago's fine South Side hospitals, $5 a pint, $15 for rare types. TV repair, shoe repair, grocery, the church and government-sponsored Tri-Faith Employment Center. Two drunks sitting on the steps of the North Side Baptist Church, under the sign:

C H   C H

What's Missing

U R

Storeowner: Why don't you dress decently?
Young Southerner: You mean middle-class, like you?
Storeowner: Why don't you get a job and improve the neighborhood?
Young Southerner: I'm tryin, but they keep firin me cause I'm against the police.
Storeowner: The problem with Uptown is that all you Southerners all want to go back South. Nobody wants to stay here and build this place up.
Young Southerner: The sonofabitch makes all his money in the community, but do you think he spends any of it here? Not a chance.

I'm not a bad kid but they wouldn't teach me what I wanted to learn so I told them to.

Actually I'm from thirteen miles out from Hazard, but you have to say you're from somewhere.

Every time a soldier comes back from Vietnam, he brings some new disease.

1 Dead, 2 Hurt in Wilson Av. Hotel Blaze

Did you hear about this ole woman who got a heart attack out there on Wilson Avenue? Everybody's talkin about it. They brought a fire truck to take her to the hospital. That's right, a fire truck, from the station up there on Lawrence. They brought a stretcher out of the cab and moved some stuff aside in the back of the truck and just laid her on it. And they didn't even turn on the siren, they stopped at all the red lights with the traffic. I guess we don't rate.

**I've got swingin doors, a jukebox and a barstool
My new home has a flashing neon sign**

I cain't work with the niggers but I sure like what they're doin on the West Side.

**A rose in your hair
Four more in a vase
I like four roses
That come in a case**

I was s'posed to get me another car today.

I feel like an old maid already. I'm seventeen but all my cousins are married.

Mother told me there'd be days like this, but she didn't say how many.

At the Continental Lounge, 1028 W. Wilson, government agents seized nine liquor bottles which they said field tests indicated had been refilled in violation of federal law.

Ten, eleven, twelve years ago that place around Lawrence, Broadway, Kenmore, places like that, that was a good place to live. Hit's no good now.

They's too much drinkin, they's too much no-care, they's too much of this here slackness a-goin on. People's gonna have to press down on it and stop it.

Every man his own notion.

I was so sorry, I had to crawl to the toilet.

She was sixty-four and she lived here twenty-five years and she got sick and went to County. Waited all night in the emergency room and they wouldn't take her so she went home and died that night.

I'm going back to my wife and kids in Kentucky. I'm fucked up.

Two months of undercover police work paid off when a longtime mob prostitution figure was arrested in a raid that also netted four young women and three men in the Kitty Lounge, 4615 N. Sheridan.
Unreported fact: the Kitty Lounge was owned by a Chicago Vice Detective.

I don't want nothin fabulous, I just want to be an average American John Doe. I'm happy with a hundred and a quarter a week where most guys ain't. I'm happy with a hundred and a quarter a week and some halfway decent furniture to sit my back end on and a hook to hang my hat on. Money'll make you cut your brother's throat.

Stop by and see me anytime you want to
Cause I'm always here at home till closing time

We were born alone and we're gonna die alone, but we've got JOIN and ought to get movin.

John Dawson

It should be condemned, every building on Clifton Avenue. From Montrose all the way through that thing should be closed up. The Maremont Foundation building there, there's the only ones that's actually fit for anybody to be in. And I would like to see these streets cleaned up, this glass and stuff on the streets. In fact I'm just gettin where I can walk on account a steppin on a piece a glass, went through my shoe, broke off in my foot. I wasn't hardly able to walk about a month on it. And a lot of it goes on with the people livin on the streets. I'm gonna have to say that. Fer the people that come down the street and bust a bottle on the sidewalk or on the street, I ain't got much use for em.

I was lookin right out the winder and this woman came right out of her house with a box of garbage. In place of puttin it in the garbage can somewhere, hell, she just dumped it right out in the damn street down there. I know I was raised better'n that.

I just don't like to live in a neighborhood where your wife can't walk down the street without people's knockin em in the head. In the spring of the year and summertime, when the weather's warm, it's just a knockout and a drag-in there. It's a gang hangout. Children usin the language goin up and down the streets that they use this day and time, it's pitiful. But you can't blame nobody but their parents, for the way they're teachin em. I reckon they act like they're afraid to teach them anything. Well, this damn town is to blame for all this juvenile delinquency. Actually, I may be wrong, I think they need some recreation for the people. I think several small parks would help us out at the time being and then I think they should have some building where they'd have recreation, some pool and things like 'at. And basketball and places inside where it'd be warm where the children and people could go and take the kids and they could play, place of having to be in the damn streets and sidewalks in front of the cars and everything—hell, I never seen a city like this before, about that. The parents are to blame for 90 percent of it.

You got to start teachin a kid when it's crawlin. A kid's like a puppy

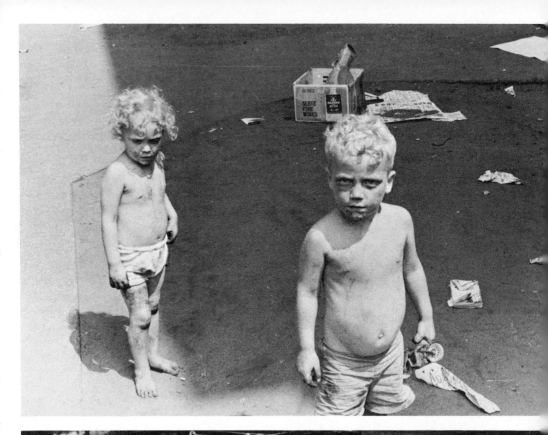

or a cat. You can take a little puppy and you can teach it to stand up and bark for its meals, you can learn a cat to do the same thing. Well a kid's the same way. And every day after they start walkin, they know—the little mean devils—they know just exactly what you're speakin about too. Well you can see that from mine. They know exactly I mean business.

You should raise your children to where that they like anybody in place of hatin a person. Don't bring your kid up in this world hatin among people. If you do, when that kid gets up thirteen or fourteen years old, there's no tellin what the kid might do. Ain't a bit of tellin.

That's the reason they put on Wyatt Earp* and this other guy to walk the street with them clubs at night. That's what they call him! He wants you to call him Wyatt Earp. This big police. Hell, they *had* to. I'll tell you, for an officer he's a damn nice guy. If he catches you drinkin on the street he gives you a break, he tells you to go on. I know that to be a fact, if you don't run your mouth at him, say O.K., turn round, walk on off. But don't give im no sass back: he'll take anybody in. Well now, an officer like that, he's just out there to protect the people. And he will protect you.

This is all like a syndicate operation here. It's Daley's ring, actually the truth of it. The city of Chicago is not fit for a man's life to walk down the street in daytime, much less at night. And it's on account of the police department, and the law here in Chicago has not done anything about it. They're gonna stab you in the back, they're gonna do everythin they can, for they know damn well you're tryin to bust up that big money racket they've got. That's one of the crookedest

*Everybody's name for a certain Uptown cop.

things that ever has been in history. They'll stop you, anybody knows they'll stop you out here on the street and tell you to get in the car and if you got any money they'll take that. That damn slavery and dog stuff, I thought that was supposed to be years ago before I was born.

Well, you don't have that back home. I don't care what, if they arrest you on a warrant or stop you for a violation of drinking—course they ain't gonna stop you there unless you are makin a violation of the driving—if they give you a ticket, you can just get ready to pay that ticket, you better not try to pay one of them cops off. If you try to pay off one of them officers there, city cop, county law, or state patrol, you can get charged with bribery right then. That's a very nice county law there. They don't come out and arrest you like some damn dog, they arrest you like somebody.

Up here, it's a different thing. They'll get you in a car, and if you ain't got no money, you go to jail here, but if you got money you can give them money and that's it. They'll drop you off, say, "You get home the best way you can." You go down here before the judges, you tell one of these judges that they're takin money, the judges here, in place of havin them investigated like they're supposed to be, they'll tell you, "Well, we'll just charge you for slander against an officer," and all sech stuff as that. Course they have their own investigators. As I said it's a ring here, all this ring's been goin on. They call him in and they say, "Why he's not guilty."

The police department's supposed to be for the people, not against them. We need a police department, we understand we need a police department. But what I favors is that we're the ones, the people is the ones that sees that police goes in there. O. W. Wilson's appointed by the Mayor; let's have him elected by the people. We got to learn that police department: we're gonna run the police department. They ain't gonna run it. We should have that police from our neighborhood, not bring im from the Seventh Ward or Fifth District up here in the Forty-eighth.

I had a good run-in with em up here on Argyle, and that was two years ago at this Star Club. I'd come in from the railroad and I had $365 in my pocket. I'd been to this currency exchange on Argyle and cashed a check, and, well, I come out of the currency exchange, they was sittin there. Well, I walked around the corner there to that laundry, picked up some laundry, and this colored guy and this white guy, police, told me to get in the car. And I told em hell, I wasn't gonna get in the damn car, I hadn't done a damn thing. So they followed me on out the street. I walked on out the street there, into the Star Club, bought me a beer, and they parked up the street there and come on in. And this colored guy, he told me he was gonna take what money I had, and I told him, I said, "Well, you'll take it over my dead you-know-what." So there was a fifth of whiskey sittin there on the bar, there wasn't nobody but this bartender in there. And I just taken that bottle a whiskey and I busted it over his damn head when he tried to touch my money. Well this other one run out the door and they called in eleven cops up 'ere, so I left six of em out on the floor fore they got me to jail. They got part of my money off of me before we got to the station, and I didn't get it back. I was still fightin em in the car. I fought them all the way there over to the station, I fought em in the station. And I'd do it again today.

They knew that I worked at the railroad, they knew I was livin here on Winthrop, those two sonofabitches did. And they'd been a-watchin me every time I'd come in on payday. All these cops knows all these plants, when they pay around here. There's no accident about that. For these syndicates tells em what's goin on with these pay plants, and what day's payday, and if you'll just watch it that's when you hear these guys are bein robbed by the police. Or either when some man's on welfare, if he gets his check, they know when that comes up too. And they could be a stop put to that, I think, now, with this civil rights law that's passed, that covers anything in the world of constitutional rights. I think a person has the right to apply on civil rights, his constitutional rights to Washington, D.C., where the government would look at it, I believe, and investigate it. Or Lutheran King and these other ones that's got them here on Chicago now, investigatin schools, well why can't we get the government to come here and investigate this police department?

The Catholics believe that you live your hell here on earth, and they may be somethin to that. We can't dispute them on that. Course now some of their other beliefs I can't go along. They's things that you see along through life, in the last ten years, that actually got me to believe that. What I actually mean is the way that you're treated here on earth. If you need medical treatment, you don't have money to get it, when you got to go home without any medical treatment or sech as that, that's actually just havin to live hell here on earth. Well, it's like today: we carried that baby over to that welfare doctor on Broadway, and he didn't no more check that baby than I did. Give her a damn bottle of medicine and the kid commenced to vomitin all over the place. Well, if it hadn't been for somebody from JOIN we'd've had no way in the world to carry that baby to a doctor who's some account. I don't think that these damn doctors, like this county here's got especially, should be assigned to doctor to nobody, for they will not give you a prescription for the right kind of medicine to do the right thing, that's very few of em that'll do that. And this bunch down on Broadway, that ain't no bunch a doctors. Who ever heared of a woman goin to a doctor for pregnancy and them not examine her? You call that doctorin?

I think that if a person is sick, that they should get the same medical care that a person that's got say a million dollars or a billion dollars in the bank. When a state like this un here, as big as the state of Illinois is and as much money and as much taxes as they take in here, when they can't afford a better medical association here than they can, they ought to just close up their damn County Hospital and their county doctors.

They was some of em, that Cook County had assigned, some good doctors. That there Morales that used to be on Wilson Avenue, that was a good doctor, though he didn't doctor women. He moved to Joliet. You know the reason he left the county doctoring? They refused to let him write prescriptions for children that was sick, the right kind of medicine. He didn't care who you were when you walked in there, whether you had a medical card or not, he'd write you the prescription for the right kind of medicine and see that you get the medicine. Well, the county didn't like that, it was costing them too much, and so they wouldn't pay him, they refused to pay him. Naturally the man couldn't live on nothin when they cut him off from his pay, for he had to move to another district or either just go out of business. And there was a real little doctor. Well, why don't the county keep a doctor like at? They want the money for their big shots, that's why. That shows that the state and the government is not for the poor class of people and they're for the rich class of people, right there.

I called the fire department once when Etta was havin a baby, when we lived right up here at Kenmore Beach Hotel, and they would not carry her to the hospital. Claimed they couldn't do that. I think it's a poor damn excuse for a ambulance service. They carried her to the hospital in a paddy wagon. Hell on earth. Hospitals the same way. It's a big shot place over there at Weiss Memorial. They don't want no poor people coming in over there.

A person, if they out here sick on the street, that's nothing but just hell on earth. You take a guy like Jim Day, walking up and down Wilson Avenue like he is now. Now they's medical care that could be doin something for that man, but get it done if you can. Now every other day that boy, they pick him up and take him down to Chicago Avenue,* turn him loose,

*A Near North Side police station.

he has to walk all the way back. What good's that doin that man, takin him down, puttin him in jail? If they goin to pick him up like that out there and him all wined up every other day, why don't they take him to the hospital and get something done for the man that's fit for him, and not to a damn dog pen? I mean to a hospital. That guy's just livin hell on earth here.

CHILDREN'S MEMORIAL HOSPITAL

It is a private institution on the Near North Side, with a charity out-patient clinic and hospitalization for children of the "medically indigent." The hospital itself is a good one, but the clinic is a clinic in the American sense: overworked, understaffed, dispensing public service on an assembly line: "Next. Do you have an appointment? Is your child registered here? Go through the entrance with the green light. Next. Do you have an appointment? . . ." Long rows of railroad waiting-room benches, a few beat-up children's books, some glossy Kodak ads. Etta need not worry about being late for Lila's 8 A.M. appointment, since half the patients have the same card: "Next Appointment Time: 8 A.M. Tuesday." The other half have 1 P.M. times.

Checked through two bureaucratic outposts, they are sent upstairs, wait, wait; then Etta is told she must have an ADC hospital card, not her old general assistance card, so she must go back downstairs and make the corrections. There is no question of having Lila attended to before then.

Lila's urine is to be tested for lead traces: she has been eating paint again. Around ten the nurse calls Etta to the front desk, hands her a plastic container to take a urine sample, fails to warn her to keep it sterile. Lila is not so easily scheduled: the bottle is not filled until after eleven. The doctor sees her, shakes his head, says something about undernourishment, tells Etta to come back tomorrow. The nurse tells her to wait for test results. Back to the waiting room. Nurses bob around, kidding one another; doctors refer roughly to "kids"; no one notices the waiting ones. Toward noon the children begin to fight, cry, run restless, complain of hunger, but to leave for the coffeeshop is to chance missing your turn and bearing the wrath of the officiating nurse, cackling about Responsibility and Inconvenience. Lila wants to break something. (On another occasion, Charlotte Gibson, unable to wait any longer, prepares to leave, only to hear the nurse bark, "Go back home and eat plaster!") Soon the 1 P.M. patients crowd into the room, hoping to be seen first, their faces dropping as they spot the somber morning holdovers.

Now a nurse is going to find the doctor. She disappears. Another doctor calls to check if the other one is still here, then walks off without thinking to inform the patient. Waiting, waiting, Etta is used to it. At last the doctor walks in, passes her without a glance, then he is gone again. This Etta seems to accept too, but too quietly for the nurses to hear she says, "That's why I hate this place. You have to wait so long." She has not been told why she is waiting, the doctor having said to return tomorrow. Or did he? All information fades and blurs, nothing remains but the pebbled white walls of institutional brick and the vast fact of the waiting.

The doctor appears again, walks toward her, then away, then turns back. He issues a directive: "Come in here." In the examination cubicle he reports that the urine tested negative: good news, but then why is Lila sick? Etta is too drained to ask. The doctor wonders about a throat-culture test. Politely Etta tells him Lila had one yesterday. A phone call: yes, she had one yesterday. "Come back tomorrow."

Etta will not. "They never give you a straight answer," and the place drugs her against pressing for one.

JOHN DAWSON

Now there's another thing too, that's this aid bill, Medicare bill the name of it is. That's something that I think that they didn't pass right, that form of it. I mean I'm in favor, don't get me wrong. I'm in favor of taking care of the old people when they get disable to work and givin them free medical care. But there's people like my wife's daddy never did work on social security. All right, that don't even cover him. I'm against the bill 100 percent on that account. That's a disgrace in this country, if we have medical care for part of the people and not for all. Why is it the socialists, the government in Russia—and we know that that's the biggest Communist country in the world—why do they cover all the Medicare and this country doesn't? All right, they're passin all these bills, but it seems like this day and time they don't pass them for the benefit of the people. It seems like they pass them for the benefit of the big shots, not the poor class of people. You see they're always a-passin the bill to raise the senator's pay, the President's pay, but you don't see them comin out with a labor price no higher, do you?

Why should in this day and time that people be down and out? With as much advantages we got in this country, as much taxes as we pay? They holler taxes, taxes—if they cut off two-thirds of what they got a-workin runnin around the community tryin to tell people what to do, how many family you can have, if they just stop that stuff, how much money do you think they could save a year, to give people to help them? I don't believe that that damn bunch should be settin over there and drawin all that money. They could be a poor person that works over there that comes out to find out what your needs are.

And on this money in Vietnam they spent over there last year, thirteen billion, the people will never know whether there was more money than that spent or not. What the hell is any use in takin money and taxin these people to death, and sendin billions of dollars to Vietnam and foreign countries to fight with to build up arms? I realize it takes taxes to operate, that's true. I'm not against payin taxes, not one bit. Now, I'm in favor of takin this money and feedin people in America first, then takin the money, for the people that needs food over there, send them food. They've got land, just like we've got. Now farm machinery and sech as that's a mighty good thing. But as to buildin arms, airplanes, guns, missiles, and all this country's wastin money on today, look at the little barefooted children that's runnin around.

The standard on what the welfare rated me and my family, my wife, and four kids, there's six in the family, $231.57 a month. That's to pay ninety-five dollars a month rent. Well, do you know what's left there to buy groceries? If you go to the store to buy thirty dollars' worth of groceries, you carry it back in two paper sacks. And clothes? You can't buy groceries and clothes out of that to save your life and have anything to wear that's decent to wear on the street. Do you realize how much money that is a year? That's $2,757 a year for a family to live on. That's not even what President Johnson and the Administration came out with on poverty. They claim that a family should have at least five thousand dollars a year to live on. Make it five thousand at least. We throw away enough of money in this country to see that people gets that much money a year.

You take the price on everything, five thousand dollars is no money a year to live on. You take a pair of shoes that's fit to wear that's from twelve to fourteen dollars, that's about the cheapest you can get. Well, if your wife goes downtown to the store to buy her a dress fit to wear, this'll make fifteen dollars. I done tried it. I walked into Sears and Roebuck's in Houston, Texas, me and Etta and the kids, I got em all a pair of shoes and me a pair of shoes and her brother a pair of shoes and a pair of pants and a new shirt—and I mean this wasn't no fancy stuff, it was just common clothes to wear. A hundred and ninety-seven dollars. Well, if you got children goin to school, it costs you more than that. These blamed old snowsuits that that damn welfare give us, from Goldblatt's, was $14.95 apiece over 'ere. These people give you a hard time, you go over there with a distribution order,* try to give you a hard time on gettin the stuff. They had listed on the distribution order two-fifty for a pair of dress gloves; they want me to take a pair of those old thin fifty-cent gloves for the two dollars. I told em to keep their whole damn gloves. Well, half of the stuff that we got, when you washed it it came all to pieces. Yeah, I got a six-dollar distribution order to buy a pair of shoes, when the glass went all through my other shoes, and the cheapest shoes they got over there was $9.95. Me and Ras went up there to see. I still got the distribution order. The ole lady caseworker, she wondered when I was going to send it to her. I said, "When you send me enough of money to get me a pair of shoes."

They're wastin money every day, the city of Chicago, wastin taxpayers' money every day for nothin. I don't think a man should stay on welfare if there's any way possible he can get off it, we're not in favor of ridin the relief rolls till you're dead, but I don't believe he should be put out in the street on a job that he couldn't make a living on. I think he should have a job, but a decent job where he could take and make a living for his family, and give him enough money that he could lay some money aside for sickness or something like that.

Any city that you go into, everywhere, they's some kind of political deal goin on. Either round mayor or governor or senator or representative, some way or another they's always a cutthroat political deal. It's just a money racket. You can always hear it leaked out. There's never been a politician in the world who didn't tell a damn lie. Never will be. This damn old Carl Sanders, governor now from my home state, I thought he did mighty dirty. Course I think the civil rights bill is one of the best bills they ever passed. But when he was runnin for office there he was against the civil rights. All right then: after he got in office he turned for it. So you can't be two ways. You got to be either one way or t'other. At least be a man from your head to your toes or either say, I'm just a damn dog, and go on and be about it.

Well, politics is crooked anywheres you go, we understand that. But that's one thing I can honestly say about Georgia, you don't have to be a millionaire to run for a political job there. You can get the backin of the people there, just like Julius† did in Atlanter on this Senate there. That's this colored guy that run. You can get the backin. All you got to do is go out and talk to the neighbors there, and explain what your platform is goin to be, and just tell them the truth. Regardless of whether the big

*A welfare money order, good only for a specified item at a specified store.
†Georgia State Senator Julian Bond.

shots want to seat you or not. They gonna vote you in. And then 90 percent of those people that voted for you will back you if you had to come to a case in court to try to get into office. Course I don't see why they should refuse a man because he's against war, fightin wars, and makin machinery to kill people with, and guns to kill people with. This country's supposed to've been raised on religion, not killin. Why have we got all the churches in the country today, preachers runnin around the country, all this missionary work, tryin to get people to go to church and do right, and then they turn right around and back these politicians to turn around and fight?

I'll tell you how I feel about this country. I think we should have a government that just one or two men wouldn't have the say-so to run this country. I think the people of the country should run the country. It's just like these big shots ownin all this property. I don't think that no one concern or company should be allowed to own but just so much.

God Almighty set this world here, He made this world, I don't think that He made this world for people to speculate on and make millions on or billions on. I think it was put here for the people, for all of the people to have a livin. That's something my granddaddy always said, he said he thought the land was put here for people to toil and have em a place to live on. And say for instance you get a place out here in the country, say for instance say you wasn't able to pay that damn tax that they put on it. I don't see that that state or that damn county should be authorized to come in there and take that home away from them people. I think at least they ought to be allowed to live on there till those people passed away.

I don't think that one man should be allowed all of this big life. Look at General Motors, look at Ford Motor Company, look at any of them big companies. Now if God made this world, He said that you shall not live by bread only, you shall live with water and bread. If them guys sits down and they eatin their big five-dollar steaks, why shouldn't the poor people be allowed to eat five-dollar steaks? Why shouldn't that be divided?

Say we set up a business. If we get over a certain amount you'll see them big shots like Johnson and all them big shots at General Motors, they'll go to hollerin that "he's gettin in big business." They don't let him go no higher. They're afraid we might learn some of their tricks, then it would help some other person out. I think that's the whole deal. I've never seen no free enterprise in my lifetime, 'less you're big enough.

Just like the land of this country was supposed to be for the people. I don't think it was put here to speculate on. I want to show you a point in why I say that. You take these cemeteries. Couple of big shots, they'll come down there, they'll buy this land out. They'll start a thirty-, forty-acre cemetery. All right, they'll charge from twelve hundred to two thousand dollars for a grave. I don't think they charged for God's grave when they laid him in the grave. I'll have to come back to the badness in that. I believe that a person should have a free place to rest their old body when they're gone. I think that ground ought to be free for you put in it. And I do think this much, I think that a man that's a-speculatin on the dead like that, I think that hell's got him wide open. I don't think he's got no chance. I don't think he'll ever get no kind of forgiveness.

And I think that if God put his earth here for people to live on, make a livin on, and put people here with enough of sense to make factories and things, I don't think he intended for people to start makin bombs and things like that to kill one another. And I don't believe that he intended for Russia, about they claim they landed that satellite on the moon, I don't no more believe that than I do this house gettin up and walkin across to Sheridan Road. And that's just a waste of money in this country, that's what we're doin, what Russia's doin, sendin that satellite around the world.

Now you take President Johnson. He's makin millions of dollars off this war, billions of it, right in his pocket. I been a-readin on Johnson's history from the time he was a senator. Well, I have never seen nothin that President Johnson ever approved of in the Senate that was any good for the people. It was always for the millionaires. And if anybody'll read back through history, it was always in his benefit where it kept him and his big ranches, and him and his old lady. Why should a man be the President of the United States, and him and his wife owns all those radio stations, all these TV stations all over the country? They own all those farms down South, South Carolina down there, there's people down there livin on those farms, they showed it on TV. Why would you think a man like that would have those people livin there in those houses that's fallin apart, workin on those farms, and then takin it away from them? If they thought anything of them they'd give them the farm to live on, and to work on, to make a livin, and give them the stuff that they made. At least they'd do that.

You can't understand what Johnson means. Of course the Bible speaks of wars and rumors of wars, but it looks to me like he's just one of the rumors of wars that come out in the country and was born. I don't know why his mamma even had him, the truth about it. I hate to say this about a man: I just don't know why he didn't die when he was born. You just look at that Bobby Baker. And he has help for sech as that. Well, is that running the country? I can't see it. I think the people should get off his knee and sit on their own knees or their own tails.

There's some things I like about President Johnson. Course you can't, you don't just come out and say what you actually think about the President. See, you have to be careful what you say. Well, you know they's a constitutional right about sayin anything against the President, you know that. Supposed to be free speech, but we don't have it. There's a lot of things you can think but you have to keep it to yourself.

As for the man part, I think that Goldwater was more of a man than Johnson. And now I'm no Republican, I'm a Democrat, but still if Nixon was to run I'd have to vote for him, I'd have to vote against President Johnson. I think Nixon actually thinks more of poor people, for Nixon was just a poor boy hisself. I don' know whether you know it or not, but he was. He was raised on a farm in California. And his family had no background and still got no background, no millionaires and all that money, and he worked his way through law school also.

I think Kennedy was just actually two faces. I think he was just like that Robert Kennedy, that Attorney General. He'd tell the colored people one thing, he'd tell the white people different. And I think that John F. Kennedy was the same way. Not that he was a Catholic, I had nothin' against that, don't get me wrong, but if Kennedy wasn't two-faced, if we're gonna have a war, we know we're gonna have one, get into it all right. Why should a man turn around and do something and then contradict hisself? This Cuban mess, Bay of Pigs. All right, Sears and Roebuck's, Montgomery Ward's, J. C. Penney's, every big company in this country had business over there, place of business in Cuba. All right, when Eisenhower was in office, it's leaked out since then about it, before Kennedy was elected, regardless of which one was elected, Nixon or Kennedy, Sears and all these big companies paid the United States Government so much money to go in there and stop that mess. All right, Kennedy he agreed to that even before the election even come off. It was a bribe deal. Sears and Roebuck's alone, I know that for a fact, me workin at Sears' freight house over here, Sears and Roebuck's alone, lost fifty-eight stores, stock barrel and all in Cuba. They had put up so many million dollars to that United States for protection of their company. They knew what was comin off. Castro was settin up his rig to take over all that. And we don't know whether Russia carried those missiles out of there or not. That's the biggest fakest deal in the world. Why you can get on a ship, walk on a ship, you don't know what's on that ship. They don't know what was in the basement of that ship. I still say today they's all kinds of missiles leveled right on this country right down there.

And another thing, how can a poor man become President if he ain't got the money to buy the votes? That's the way they've always got in. I wouldn't have the money to run a campaign. They claim that any man can be a President. Yeah, Abe Lincoln was elected President, he was supposed to've been a poor man. But that was a hundred years ago too. If Abe Lincoln was livin today, he couldn't get elected unless he had the money to run on.

Of course I ain't got the education to operate a job like Johnson's got, but I'll be damned if I don't think I can run that President's office better than Johnson operates it. The main thing is havin common sense. You get that from your raisin, comin up through life. But what I'm speakin of on the education is that you would need I'd say a four-year term of college in the figures and the money and the keepin track of what you was gonna have to spend. By rights he's supposed to do it himself. Course I understand he's got a bunch of em do it for him, which that could be a bunch cut off of the payroll right there. That's a bunch of excess. Look there at all that bunch of cooks he's got. How many does it take to cook for him and that bunch? What's his wife doin? Now there's something: I say if a man's to be President and married, his wife ought to do the cookin. What's the matter with her, sittin up there, doin nothin? People payin her way all around the country, flyin here and there all over the country—why hell, cause she's the President's wife she ain't no better than my wife or nobody else's.

And I would lay money right now that Johnson won't be elected the next President. He has ruint hisself right now, already done ruint hisself to the country. In the fust place, why did he get us in Vietnam? I think that actually the leaders is just stupid, of both countries. Making billionaires out of millionaires. Trillionaires or some kind of aires.

And I'll go along with Fulbright and Morse on that, I thought Congress was supposed to declare war. Hell, the President, he just as well take over the country. Hell, when he says, "I'll send you boys overseas, or I'll take you out away from your home, break up your home, I'll send you up and put you in the service," he just does that. Funny thing that he's got all that power. Franklin Roosevelt couldn't get that power in World War II. He couldn't even get the power to send a man back on a strike without Congress approvin. Hell, Truman and Kennedy and Johnson, hell, they got ready to send them out, they just said, "You go." Well my God, I don't see there's no difference in dictatorship nowhere in the world. What the hell's a dictatorship? If Russia's got dictatorship, we got dictatorship. And when it comes to Communists, we got just as damn much Communists in this country as they ever thought about bein overseas.

In fact we ain't had a President in a hell of a long time. I would say that

Roosevelt done more for the country than nary a man in my lifetime. They holler this poverty. At least you can give Roosevelt credit of the W.P.A. The W.P.A. done more for the country than this poverty is doin for the country. And at least the poor people did get to work on it, and they did make some money at it. And hell, it was just much better than the way this is right now. Well hell, why don't this poverty operate that way? I thought that when the Senate passed that bill, that the money was supposed to be spent on poor people, not on rich people. We should not have people down here at the Urban Progress Center that's half-millionaires.

Last Monday their representative came to the house to ask for Ras to come down there, left word for him to come and get him somethin to eat. Well, when Ras came to the house, when I told him about it, so he asked me if I'd go down to the Urban Progress Center with him, which I did. So this old gray-headed devil there at the desk, we asked her if she knowed which one it was come to the house, and so she give us some kind of squeal: she didn't know this and she didn't know that and we'd have to wait. So we set there and we're settin there waitin and Miss Queen came in. She's one of the district reps, they call em. She goes out in the district talkin to people. And she asked me, said, "Mr. Dawson, is there somethin I can do?" I said, "I don't know." I said, "Mr. Bryant here," I said, "one of your reps came by the house." I said, "Well, she came by and left word for him to come down here to see her, and," I said, "we don't know which one it was."

She said, "Let's go upstairs." She said, "I've got a roster up there that does give a list of who does work, so we can find out." So she carried us upstairs. So we were settin there waitin on Miss Queen to check the records, see which one it was, so here come this old lady upstairs—boy, she just jumped all over me. She wondered what-all I was doin up there.

I just kind of asked, I said, "By God, do you own the city of Chicago? Another thing," I said, "I don't think you own the war on poverty here. But," I said, "you act like it, for you're a damn millionaire." And I said, "God be with you if I get on this Advisory Council down here, for," I said, "I'm gonna give you the devil." So anyway she tore out back downstairs. And so Jim Brown came along, guy I knew there, and I told him. "Well," he said, "Good God," he said, "I'll find out right quick what's the matter with her." I said, "Well, by goddamn, I don't like that kind of talk and ain't gonna accept it." So he called her back in the office. And he just reamed her out, right there in front of us, and when I came back downstairs, when he found out who the rep was that wanted to see Ras, we came back downstairs to that intake.

She said, "Mr. Dawson, please take this chair." She called me Mr. Dawson then. And Ras said he thought that was pretty good, to get cussed out and then turn around and have to tell you Mister on top of it.

You know finally when the Urban Progress Center got Ras somethin to eat? Friday afternoon at three. It taken from Monday at one to Friday evenin at three to get that man somethin to eat. I wonder what people's gonna do for somethin to eat while you wait on them sonofabitches. Ras got a good point: he don't want to go from one house to another, eatin.

I was tryin to get on the Advisory Commission down there to work with the people. That bunch of big shots that's on it, all of em's got their nose in this money racket. That's all over the country. Other words, if you just don't go down and kiss them, make them drop their pants and you get down there and kiss them like you was some dog, you ain't supposed to be on the Advisory Council. Well, if we can't have enough poor people in the community to have a voice and a say-so, I don't want nothin to do with it. Fact I'd rather just be down there fightin them from now on. I feel that a man's rights is his rights, and I think that a poor man ought to have a little say-so in the country. When they ask me a question, I'm jest gonna be bound to answer them how I feel about it. And if it hurts feelings, it'll have to hurt feelings. For my granddaddy always taught me the right thing could sometimes hurt people, when you tell em the right thing, the truth about anything. I don't give a damn whether they vote me in or whether they don't, for it don't make a damn no way. We've had meetins, we've had several meetins at the Urban Progress Center, but have we got any benefits out of it yet?

Look at all the people walkin the streets here that don't have work. They claim they have so many jobs at Urban Center, 901 Montrose, they don't have a damn thing. Oh, they have these dollar-fifteen and dollar-twenty jobs, seventy-five-cents-an-hour jobs, if you want to be some maid or kiss somebody's ass, that's just the truth about it. They send employees, men, up there to Jobs Unlimited and Service, Inc., and places like that. Why in the hell don't they take this money and do away with these slave-labor markets and set up their own unemployment office, free of charge, and let a man get a decent job and cut out that big money racket? That's just a thievery, that's all it is, it's just thievery off of the people.

> Isn't it wonderful that in this time of prosperity
> we are interested in helping the poor?
> —Member of the Advisory Council,
> Montrose Urban Progress Center,
> November 16, 1965

THE WAR ON POVERTY

Who Gets the Credit?

In the winter and spring of 1966, John and other JOIN *members spent long days preparing a proposal to the Urban Progress Center for a nonprofit day-labor hall; for where else could the resources be found than in the state? In their plan, the government would subsidize expenses so that the worker would get the full wage attached to the job.* JOIN *brought community people to Urban Progress Center meetings to support the proposal, but the war on poverty, it seemed, had more important fronts. Despite the popular clamor, the proposal was chewed to bits in the bureaucratic mill;* JOIN *could not be accorded the recognition which a favorable response would have implied.*

In December, 1967, the Urban Progress Center, with the State Employment Service, did set up a nonprofit agency. There was not a word of credit muttered to JOIN. *But by that time* JOIN *as an organization had faded, and a ghost is in no position to remind people of the origins of an idea.*

A Tremendous High-Rise Market

Uptown News, January 30, 1966

SBOC? It Spells Success in Poverty Program

By Robert Lerner

IF YOU CALL the Village Maid service for someone to clean your apartment, you will be unwittingly participating in the poverty program, because the service is a former undercapitalized private enterprise that is now being financially assisted by the SBOC, perhaps the leading success agency in the poverty program.

The SBOC (Small Business Opportunities Corp.) is a non-profit Illinois corporation, drawing the funds it used as loans to small businesses from the federal poverty agency, the Office of Economic Opportunity. . . .

The SBOC is a part of the OEO, which was formed in 1964. However, it wasn't until late in 1965 that the

(continued)

SBOC solidified its staff, and got "ready to move," as the saying goes. A limited amount of money was available for these early preparatory days, so calendar 1966 is really the first year of operation. And Village Maid service will be the first organization helped under the program. . . .

WHY, the discerning reader now asks, is an agency of the poverty program so interested in keeping a domestic service in business?

It is because Mrs. Rodger [head of Village Maid] employs people who, in most cases, are otherwise unemployable. She has a training program for domestics, so even if these people don't stay permanently on her payroll, they will have still attained a certain job skill.

"There is a tremendous high-rise market for domestic help," Long [Uptown Director, SBOC] points out. "This market is right here in our community. And, right here in our Uptown community, we have unemployed people who in some instances are unemployed because they have no skills.

"As Mrs. Rodger's business grows, she will need more and more domestic workers. She is hoping to open a branch office right here in Uptown. This means employing people from right here in this community, and having them work right here in—or at least close by—our community.

"Her training program is frosting on the cake. By giving her $13,000 to make her business grow, look at the areas in which we are saving government agencies! She is employing people who might otherwise be on the relief rolls. She is doing job training and retraining. And she is paying these people at the same time."

And an Official Statement

At the JOIN meeting of February 23, 1966, one of us* asked Don Smith, director of the Montrose Urban Progress Center, to name the businesses extended SBOC loans. "Let's see," he said. "Grocery stores, cleaning shops, some auto repair shops, a millinery shop is one. They've made about thirty-six loans, I think, to about $320,000, I think."

I pointed out his omission of the maid service, the business which the Center and the local newspaper, widely circulated on the Lake Shore, had deemed most worthy of publicity.

"Yes, there is one."

"Is that your idea of lifting people out of poverty?"

"It isn't mine, no, it isn't mine. But at the other hand, the areas today in American business that are really growing are in the area of service. And in fact that girl was in the office about a month ago or two months ago, and the results of the number of people hired, the salaries that are paid out, is very high, and it's very small business, but it has helped and it also fills a need. And I don't know if it's the best, you know, I mean, you know, but the range is very broad."

*T. G.

An entrepreneurial and educated JOIN member named Jim Turk sent the following article to the local paper. Introducing it, he wrote: "I fail to show even ten percent of the laughter Mr. Smith generated from the impoverished Southerners who attended the meeting." Its force is even plainer against the background of Jim Turk's Chicago-born conviction that hillbillies rival bureaucrats in ineptness.

How to Generate $4,000,000 Without Really Trying

By J. E. Turk

"That's a lie," shouted Mr. Don Smith, the new director of the Urban Progress Center at 901 Montrose.

Frankly I was stunned by his reply to my question. I had thought that this was to be a folksy briefing of us poor folk by our new general on the war on poverty.

All I had asked was why Mr. Swee, the man who hires community representatives for the center, had told me that the center wasn't a bit interested in placing unemployed persons in menial tasks such as dock workers or punch press operators, etc. Mr. Swee had told me in no uncertain terms that the jobs the center sought for their poverty people were not the type that might disappear in ten years or so.

Mr. Swee said that the great society would rather train an illiterate for two years to become a tool and die maker (while giving him a living allowance) then get him just any old job.

Mr. Smith was correct in his lie charge. He indicated, however, that I was the liar for misquoting Mr. Swee, his faithful servant (who may be recruiting astronauts from chicken pluckers by now), rather than Mr. Swee whose community representatives, it seems, have placed a few recruits in jobs slightly below that of tool and die makers.

Mr. Smith spoke at a meeting in the Hull House at 1257 W. Wilson, on Wednesday night, Feb. 23rd. He addressed a group of the area's poor at the request of an organization known as JOIN, the community union.

JOIN was organized by a group of college students, and recent graduates, who volunteer their time in the Uptown area helping persons with poverty problems.

Mr. Smith listened to complaints (mostly of slum landlords), and fielded questions concerning his duchy of the poverty program. Of nineteen direct questions put to him, he answered five, and said that there was no way at present of determining the answers to the others.

He frequently mentioned that he had spent two years in the Philippines as a Peace Corps representative, where he philosophized that it was much easier to be poor. This statement made everyone feel superior I'm sure.

A man named John asked why he had been sent to work from the Urban Progress Center as a cook in a hospital

(*continued*)

for ninety-six hours and only had been paid for twenty-four hours. John got one of the "direct" answers. He was told that "All that had changed now." (John is still waiting for the "change" in pay however.)

Another questioner asked if any of the program was tied in with politics. He was assured by Mr. Smith that all the politicians have the good jobs already. (Whatever that meant he didn't say. Perhaps Alderman Keane is in training to be the first tool and die maker on the moon.) Mr. Smith then emphasized that absolutely no political ties were required for help from the poverty center.

That balloon was hardly inflated before the next questioner asked who had hired Dr. Brooks to head up the program. He was informed that no other than that old, non-political tree surgeon Mayor Daley had hired Brooks. (At this point Mr. Smith seemed to look sorry that he had ever left the Philippines. It must be as easy to sound silly there as it is to be poor.)

Mr. Smith then waxed eloquently about a new program being set up by a man he identified only as "Herb."

Herb's program was a little short of the tool and die maker bit of Mr. Swee, but a step in the right direction anyway. Herb and two associates are now setting up a program called representative #1.

This program is designed to go out to the employers seeking to place the unemployed with their firms. It's brilliant thinking for a government agency —private industry has been doing the same thing for over fifty years. It also must be a new speed record for government planning because the Montrose center has only been open a year now.

When asked by a Southern newcomer if this wasn't the same thing the Illinois un-employment people did, Mr. Smith replied, "Oh, but this is different. Next question please."

The Montrose Urban Progress Center distributed a four-page pamphlet during the meeting proclaiming the great progress made by the center during its first year of operation. One of the statistics claimed 237 adult job placements—or less than one a day.

The nearest private enterprise, day labor office barely sees a day they don't send out over a hundred workers, and the jobs are comparable Mr. Smith had to admit, as he had no idea if his agency had ever placed a tool and die maker anywhere. He did admit to training maids for service in the Lake Shore high-rise apartments however.

The privately owned employment service offices also deduct income taxes from their employees which must in some way help defray the salaries of Mr. Smith, Mr. Swee and ol' Herbie, so it might not be too bad an idea if the three of them took some on-the-job training at one of them.

Another news blast from the progress center's sheet states that "In its first year of operation, programs coordinated by the center have generated more than $4,000,000. more in income for area residents and business firms, income that is spent in the community and goes to helping it regain its financial feet."

I suppose if Mr. Smith hadn't called me a liar for quoting Mr. Swee in public I wouldn't be so picayunish in mentioning that the "four million" statement isn't quite 100% true either. But I happen to know Joe, the owner of the Lakeview tavern on Argyle street. And Joe does not live in, or blow his dough in the community. He does, however, peddle a few belts to citizens on the dole.

But even Joe is doing his part. Despite that four million dollars generating all around him, Joe has held the price line on cheap wine to fifty cents a pint. And without any arm twisting from LBJ either.

More News on the "Giant Community Effort"

Uptown News, January 30, 1966

"It is going to take time to get results," Donald Smith, new director of the Montrose Urban Progress Center at 901 Montrose, said.

Many significant things can be said about the War on Poverty, but Smith apparently feels that communication is the basis for the success of this North Side operation.

"For the first time," he concluded, "we have people invested with the authority to offer new vistas of help going door to door and talking with the poor person."

Smith continued, "We have 27 community representatives. They are local residents who, one year ago, were either unemployed or underemployed.

"They are screened and hired by Daniel Howard Associates, which is an outside management consulting firm."*

Smith also took exception to charges in the press that the poor are not being allowed to participate in the program as worked out in the government's policy. "This is inaccurate," he contended. He pointed out that the specified section denotes "maximum feasible participation of the community."

Further, he asserted that 1,006 poor residents all over Chicago are participating in the program. The staffs have some 690 persons, who were unemployed or underemployed, Smith said.

"If that is not participation of the community," he declared, "it is very, very difficult to know what is."

*" 'That way we can separate those who really want to participate from those who are just chronic complainers and agitators,' explained Deton J. Brooks, Chicago Committee on Urban Opportunity Director" (*Chicago Daily News,* February 7, 1966).

December 6, 1965, the chairman of the Chicago Committee on Urban Opportunity had made plain what is. Introducing Sargent Shriver to a gathering of 1700 "business, labor, religious, and civic leaders" at the Sherman House, Mayor Daley established the principle of what he called a "giant community effort":

Chicago *Sun-Times,* December 7, 1965.

"To some this is just another forum for them to air their complaints about injustices and inequalities.

"The achievement of this goal [eradication of poverty] should not be the subject of continuing controversy. Let us stop wasting time in arguments over the power structure and in attempts to make political issues where none exists.

"Much has been said about participation. The answer is in this room. All Chicago participates. . . ."

Shriver noted that the conference, called by Mayor Daley, had spilled over into a number of rooms in the Sherman House. It was "the largest conference on poverty ever held in the United States," Shriver said.

"It is also the first to which the dedicated and articulate critics of the war on poverty have been given an opportunity to air their gripes and complaints with the things we are trying to do," he added. . . .

"I'm not saying all these things are right," Shriver said after reviewing the scope of projects. "I am saying if some-
(continued)

body has a better mousetrap, let them come forward and we'll try it.". . .

"Don't prejudge the establishment. The establishment is listening."

Shriver drew applause as he quipped: "These days unless you've got a picket somewhere you're not really making it."

A Good Enemy Makes for Good Friends

Members of JOIN, WSO, and The Woodlawn Organization were milling in the lobby; some had brought sandwiches. Admittance to the gala ballroom was refused, though a side room was offered to the mice so they might gnaw closed-circuit on Shriver's words. This was John Dawson's first demonstration.

That night, as JOIN reconsidered tactics, he said Shriver "talked about how the war on poverty was goin all right, though of course it couldn't satisfy everybody—"

Black Dovie Coleman, two months into JOIN, boiling mad after what was also her first demonstration and her first political rejection: "If I could have got in there, I would have said to him, 'Mr. Shriver, I know you can't satisfy everybody, I just want you to satisfy the poor people.'"

"It was completely Daley machine down there," said John. "All Daley machine. For another thing we made damn fools of ourselves this mornin. Me and Dovie should have gone up there and all the rest a JOIN should a gone up behind us. And we should a gone all the way to jail. We was ready, Dovie and me."

"Yes we was."

"If we'd a had guts enough to went to jail, we'd a had more than the six-o'clock news tonight. There was several presses there, from Chicago and different places, reporter from L.A. was hittin me, and I told all these press reporters, "Why wasn't they givin the money to the poor people instead of to Mayor Daley and his damn middle-class gang upstairs? . . .""

Big Dovie kept a certain wary distance from this man who had emerged her ally, but noted his alliance as she also argued we should have bulled our way through: "Those people was sittin there, lot of people very quiet, and if I had gotten in there and got up and talked, they would have heard me. Let me tell you, he would have heard me. And if they wanted to take me to jail, O.K. I just wanted to tell Shriver just what kind of war on poverty he's got in Chicago. This man said I could watch him on TV. I said, 'What good is that? That's just like sittin home and watchin the

President on TV. All you can do is listen, that's all you can do, just take it like he says it.' "

The organizer who had first encountered John Dawson, sixteen months before, remembers him as an enraged and bitter redneck whose sputtering anger found its clearest focus on "the niggers." Now, discovering that his ally in militance was black, suddenly he became cordial, even comfortable with blacks. His conversion—for that is what it was—seemed as sudden as the moment when a river swells to the top of a dike and, finding the retaining pressure lifted, becomes a flood.

Of course Big Dovie and her niece Little Dovie had to have decided to cross the color line from their side, for John's conversion to take hold. It helped that, as John said later: "You heard what Dovie said about the colored woman that was her supervisor? Said she got supervisor and it went to her damn head. That just shows you Dovie wasn't only fightin for her own race, she'd be a-fightin anybody." In other words race as an issue could not be solved, it could only be submerged, left slowly to decay, by mutual agreement.

When his children misbehaved, John would still threaten them with "nigger Sam," but at least around JOIN, which for more than a year had something to offer him worth more than racism, he struggled with "Nigra," "Nigro," and occasionally "Negro." He knew well our attitude toward white supremacy but was not simply mirroring it to preserve friendship. He had converted before we got to know him, and he maintained his new stance outside our presence, and evangelically.

JOHN DAWSON

You know, after I left home I used to hate the niggers—colored people; I called em niggers. But I don't call em niggers any more and I'm not prejudiced against em. That's been the trouble in this country for a long time, is settin the whites against the niggers and sech as that. You know I'm from North Georgia and they hate the Nigras, but my granddaddy taught me, and he's dead now, but he's workin in me. I was raised up hard. If I was ever heard to say anything against the Nigras, my granddaddy would whup me with this old leather belt. I was taught not to low-rate any nationality, any race of people.

There was colored people lived right joinin our farm, there was colored people worked for us on the farm, but my granddaddy never did pay them no less than he paid the white people. My granddaddy was a Christian,

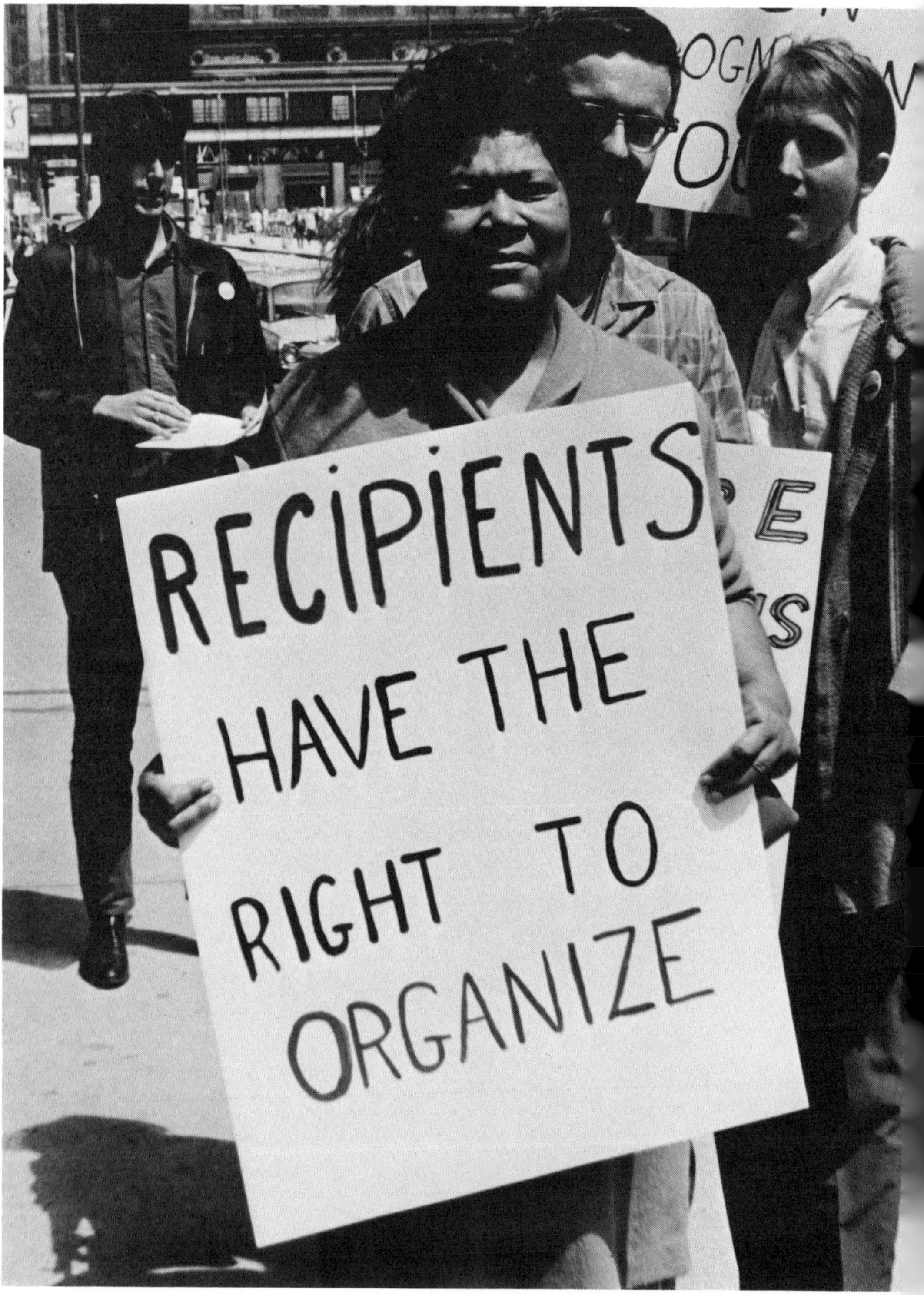
RECIPIENTS
HAVE THE
RIGHT TO
ORGANIZE

and he'd tell you right quick that the Bible said to treat no one different regardless of who they were, or if you did, you had that Judgment Day to pay for it. If we had more of these people like that back then, that had that attitude, had that kind of Christianity about em, you'd have a better world today than what you have.

They was people there back then, they was a lot of people there didn't care. But you know they've not had no trouble in Rome, never had no trouble in Rome, the schools or nothin else. That's one thing that helped the city of Rome about their havin no trouble there: the colored had nicer schools than the whites. In fact the colored didn't even want to mix the schools.

I never could understand why all the North Georgia counties have not had no trouble, and the South Georgia counties have, there. Well, in fact some of South Georgia didn't have no trouble, just two or three spots there. The only thing that you can figure out about it actually is a bunch a people that it was beat in their head when they was raised up, they was a old class of people a-runnin the towns, the cities, that probably they were some of em there when the slavery was there, that they figured, well, cause you're black you got to do as I say. Course it wasn't only that way with the black. It was the same way with the poor class of people. The type like me, maybe I'd been a-workin for that bunch that had the money, they'd figure, Well, you a damn slave, you just like the Nigra. They were a lot of em, just like right here they's a lot of damn people that thinks that the poor people regardless of what your color, or especially if you from the South anywhere and if you're colored, they think that you're just a dog. Now that's the truth and I just don't see it. I don't give a damn if a man's got a million dollars or if he ain't got a penny.

And I'm from the deep part of the South, I'm not ashamed of that. A man should not be ashamed of where he's from. I think that a person should be a man or a woman with a dignity of their heart, a relationship to work with people not against em. It's not where a man's from, it's what he makes of his own self. Nigra, Puerto Rican, Mexican, or American, it's what you make of your own damn personal self. You come across a class of people in all colors that you can't get along with, and you'll come across people in all colors that's just as good as you are. I have no prejudices against no one, from where they're from or who they are. The colored people's got to live same as we've got to live, and I think that they should have a decent job that they could take care of their families, and a decent place to live. I don't see nothin in the world wrong with a colored person goin into a restaurant, sittin down eatin where I eat at. I don't see nothin wrong with a colored person goin into a school, I can't see that. And it's not only down South that they're prejudiced as hell, it's right here in Chicago. And they's so much of it, hit's pitiful.

I mean they's a lot of faults in the South. They's a lot of faults in the North. I don't know if you heard King make his talk last night or not. He's here in Chicago, and this movement that he's gonna call it, it's Breadbasket, they're gonna go around to these plants to ask em to make no difference, regardless of what color it was, about hirin. If the companies and the plants, Mayor Daley and everyone here that was involved, welfare and all, if they didn't cooperate and get some of this prejudice out of Chicago, then he would have to call his main force in and make a march on City Hall. And he said, "We don't want to have to march on City Hall. But," he said, "if we have to," he says, "it'll be a worse march than what we done on Montgomery, Alabama." But he said as to the prejudice, he said there was more prejudice right here in Chicago than there was in any city in the United States. Well, which he told the truth. And until that is knocked out in the North, well, why should they be a-drivin on the South about somethin the North is carryin on their own self and hollerin it's not so?

And as Lutheran King said last night, we all got to work together. And as he said, they's no use in havin violence, we can avoid that violence and we can get somethin done without violence. For you would hate it if you had to kill somebody on account a some foolish thing. Anybody would hate that, rest a their life.

Ras Bryant

I stayed with John a little over a week. Well, John just come and got me and told me, said, "Hey, you ain't gonna lay out." Said, "Come on, go with me." Said, "You can stay at my house," said, "Pack your stuff into my house." He went and helped me pack it over there. Whole bunch of em did.

Oh, they treated me just like a baby. They treated me as nice as any-place I ever stayed. They didn't want me to leave when I left. I said, "Yeah, I'm gonna go."

They said, "You don't have to go."

I said, "Yeah, I wanna be on my own." Course I paid my goddamn way. John got up there and told it at a meetin the other night, that it cost me nary a penny while I was there. I said, "Bullshit, it didn't," to myself, you know. I went downtown and I got three pounds of hamburger down at one place,* you know, and oh, a hell of a lot of canned stuff and two loafs of bread, see—enough to done me a goddamn week, you know. Them runs into money, you know. And I brought that up there, well, we eat it up. Then I went back, you know, and I got a whole load of canned stuff at another place, see, another church. And then I came back, and I gave em that. Well, all right. Then I'd turn around, you know, and every Sunday when I'd clean up the beer garden I give em a dollar, dollar and a half, gave Bud fifty cents. And somebody else I gave the other dollar to, I swear I didn't spend a penny of it for myself now. I really paid for more 'n what I ate there, you know, what time I stayed there. Now you ask me if John would a *made* me pay. Well, I don't know. That's a hard cat to clean after, ain't it? But I figure I paid my way all the time I was there, you know, I was bound to.

Jim Day taken eight dollars off me, you know. Over there, John Dawson's house. We went back in the room, laid down, and went to sleep, me and

---

*The Evergreen Avenue office of the Chicago Missionary Society. To get the food Ras had to listen to the elderly minister preach that since he, in his seventies, was still working, anyone could get a job.

him did in a bed together, and that was the ten dollars I got back from Marsha Apartments, see. And I had spent two of it. And he taken the other eight. And when I waked up he was gone and the door open. And he was the only one was in the room. Now you know he got the money cause there's nobody else in there. Why he done it, that's a mystery to me. I was as good to that man as I was to a baby. I've kept him for weeks at a time and fed him. Oh, he's a mess. And I got on the street one mornin, I got to studyin. I said, "There's got to be somethin-or-other done."

We saw Jim Day about two weeks after Ras's eviction from the Marsha. He was wincing from blister pain, frostbitten feet in shoes forced to last one Chicago winter too many.

"Where've you been, Jim?"

"Oh, out walkin the streets." His tone transparent: the usual good-fellow false aplomb. And then, unasked:

"Ras says I taken money off of him. I wouldn take a penny off of Ras. But I'm goin a give him every dollar he says I took, soon as I get my welfare checks. An a couple a dollars extra. . . . You know Ras thinks more a me than he does his own brother." His face was even redder than usual, gray-cast red; he'd lost his hat and his footing, but some last reserve of pride kept his voice from breaking and his body upright. "Maybe he misplaced that money, or hid it somewhere and forgot where."

RAS BRYANT

Lord, this is the most violent place I ever seed. A man can get killed on these streets; hit ain't safe. You can hear every day, nearly, you get the news every day, somebody's been robbed somewhere. I'm just gettin tired of gettin robbed.

One time I was coming along down Sheridan Road right out there and three fellers jumped out of a car in front of me, they broke my nose and taken eighteen dollars off of me, skinned my face all up. Wasn't no cop around that time. Right in broad daylight it was.

It's white and colored both that's a-doin it. A bunch a three coloreds, they caught my brother out there, just a few days before that, and beat him up, even pulled his pants off of him, plumb off him, left him standin right there in his underwear. He got them pants finally wrapped around him when the plainclothesmen brought him back home, brought him right out there in front of the door, and he come in with his pants, holdin em on best he could. Well, this plainclothesman seed em and run over there, and they run when they seed him a-comin, they run, see, and got away. Why, he orta done em through the leg. I'd a stopped them runnin, I'd bet you a dollar, if I'd a been that law.

This is a much more violent place than West Virginia, that's for sure. You don't hear of people gettin knocked in the head and robbed out there like that, you know. Lots of times you hear of somebody, he'll get drunk and get down on somebody and take it off em, but they don't knock over the head and rob em hardly. I got knocked in the head and robbed out there once. About right close to eight hundred dollars. They was three of em on to me that time, and they hit me in the head with their arms and come down on me with a rod. It hit that shoulder. Oh, it just broke that all to pieces, just tore it all to pieces in there. And this here part wasn't long enough, you know, to put a brace on, and they had to go in there and cut in there and set a new bone in there and then take silver wire and tie this part up here with silver wire. That wire's still in there. Oh, he like to killed me. But just once in a while it happens down there.

SIX BAD MONTHS

For an old man alone on the Uptown streets, drinking and falling prey to robbers and accidents and eviction compose a total calamity, so total as almost to seem natural if you did not know it was man-made. During 1966 Ras had six bad months.

On the night of May 13 he was again beaten and robbed, on the deserted block of Clifton they call Dead Man's Alley. The cops found him lying in the street and took him to County Hospital. The next day two plainclothesmen walked him up and down the street, looking for suspects but finding none, asking one of us* who passed by, "Is he straight? I mean when he was younger did he go for women or men? Get what I mean? Is he straight?" Old Pop, on hearing the news, shook with an unaccustomed fury: "If I caught whoever did it—I'd kill him. Ras is the best. He'd walk fifteen, twenty miles a day, just to help a man out."

Ras was living at this time on the half-black 4700 block of Winthrop. The manager volunteered that Ras would be evicted as soon as his month's rent was up. "All this drinking up there—this building wasn't like this before he got here."

Ras was lying in bed, his nose swollen and his face puffed. Through his left eye he could "just see daylight." His last memory of the robbery is

*N. H.

that a man stopped to talk with him. The "FBI's" who came to see him "asked me what I was doin talkin to this man, and I said, 'You expect me to stay here in this goddamned apartment all day long? I'd go crazy not havin no one to talk to but myself.'"

The "apartment" is a single room—bed, dresser, closet, two-burner range. On the dresser, a scroll of "God's Gospel." I* was surprised. Ras said Jack Lee, a wino he was putting up, brought it, or else the land-lord: "I don't need it." Jack had brought a woman up to stay one night, and Ras thought this was the cause of the eviction; in any case he was sure drinking was not the cause. "All this movin around, it ain't no good 'less you can better yourself, is it? You see one little ole room I've got, it ain't big enough for nothin. I can get a better place 'n that. . . . I'd reether take a woman than start a-movin here. Oh God, you can't move every day, buddy—can you, hardly? You can't move every day." He feared he had exhausted all available apartments by then.

He cursed Jack. He'd been giving him fifty cents each morning so Jack could get to work, but no longer. Jack goes to a certain restaurant, orders coffee, and bums "off of these drunks who come in there." Jack was a "sonofabitch," but he had no objection to Jack's coming along when he moved.

They moved in with cousin Franklin and his family for a couple of weeks, drinking steadily. "I just get pitched off about somethin or other and start drinkin." One evening Franklin looked up from the distorted picture of his huge-screen television to say he tolerated Ras—"I'll give him a bed, I've never turned him down." But his wife didn't want him there drunk. Since Franklin had brought him to Chicago, "all he's done is drink," and besides he might give the baby some disease he caught from the winos. His tolerance was edged with a reluctance that must have glared through Ras's stupor. Ras must have got the point; he moved out, parted with Jack, and moved in with old Pop and Jim Day in Jim's apartment in a crumbling building, now demolished, on the corner of Racine and Wilson. Here mutual aid was predicated on the sharing of wine, and some days there was a woman, naked before all. Ras assured us he would return to Franklin's, to sober up.

He didn't. In the meantime Jim had lied to Ras about "a month's rent paid up." Three days after the solemn promise, Jim was evicted. That night Ras went looking for him and, checking the basement, fell into an uncovered pit. Unable to find his way out, he lay at the bottom until day-

*T. G.

light, when he crawled out and made his way to Franklin's. "I was hurtin so bad Janice* had to help me in and out of bed." But she couldn't care for him, because "she's only a kid"—she was married before she was fourteen, had the baby at fifteen, and was now barely sixteen. "These kids are gettin younger all the time; hit don't make much sense."

It was almost a week before he got in touch with us. He thought his shoulder was broken—the one broken years before in West Virginia. We insisted he go to the hospital.

Frank Cuneo Hospital is small, modern, private, expensive, but it does accept a few welfare recipients. After X rays we went to the clinic, where after a sufferable wait the doctor glanced at Ras as at a fly and told him to come back at 9:30 the next morning. Ras complained, "I been sufferin so bad this week, hit's pitiful, and they didn't even offer me nothin for the pain." Finally he procured a prescription for pain relief. But the nearby pharmacist said he couldn't accept Ras's welfare card since the doctor hadn't used the official welfare prescription blank. We put up a small resistance, but to no end; without the official form he would not be reimbursed by the Public Aid Department.

We returned to the clinic. The officiating nurse was sorry, she didn't have the welfare forms; why didn't we check with the social worker next door. The sign on the door looked promising: "Clinic Office and Social Service." The caseworker was even less sorry, she couldn't help either. Ras was ready to leave in disgusted submission, but something stuck in my throat.

"If someone weren't on welfare, would you still tell him to come back tomorrow?"

Icily she replied, "That's what the doctor said, I can't change it."

I pointed to the neat lettering on her door. I would like to have said, with the proper polished irony, "Why don't you do some social service?" Instead I yelled it. We left. Perhaps we would fare better at the hospital's own pharmacy.

Ras explained the problem. No, the druggist said, he would have to have a note signed by the nurse. I pointed out he could pick up his phone, if he was so inclined, and call her.

"I have to have the piece of paper."

"What if a man was lying right here on the floor? What would you do, still insist on the piece of paper?"

"I wouldn't do anything."

*Franklin's wife.

We walked out. Ras said, "If I had a 'tomic bomb, I'd drop it right on that place. Ain't no good for nothin. Hit's a shame, isn't it?"

"Yeah."

"If the Lord'll forgive me for going there this time, I'll never go again after tomorrow."

At the outside drugstore I told the story of our struggle for the proper form. The druggist was incredulous, sympathetic; but he was reduced to repeating, in the somber tones of a decent, compassionate man "just doing his job," the conditions of his reimbursement. We didn't argue; I paid cash for the medicine.

Walking back to Franklin's, Ras said he had seen Jim the previous morning. He didn't know where Jim was living now. "Maybe an alley. He sure looked like an alley rat. Somebody says he's livin on the second floor of a vacant lot." Why hadn't Jim notified JOIN of Ras's accident? "Jim won't never do nothin for you. Went out to bum him some wine."

Ras went into the hospital for tests the next morning. I went to see Franklin's wife, Janice, a slim and shy girl from Alabama. On Malden the air was thick with the renewing smell of mowed grass, unusual for Uptown. Janice had already done the day's rearranging of the newly bought, overpriced furniture and was cleaning up. Five rooms took her most of the day. Later she would have time to paste S&H Green Stamps in the little book. On the coffee table was the only book in the apartment, a huge, illustrated vinyl-covered Bible, Franklin's engagement gift to her, bought on an installment plan.

She hoped Ras would come back to them. "He's got a home here as long as he wants it. He's good to us and we try to be good for him. Franklin told him, if he wants anything, he'll get it; it might be a little hard but we'll arrange it." She could get him on Franklin's group insurance plan, buy his clothes. "He's good to me, stays with me through the day while I'm home. And he's real good to the baby, he'll set and play with her all day." (Ras had said the baby likes him because "he never paddles her to make her mind," though he used to paddle his own.)

She explained they were having trouble with car payments but hoped to finish in a year and a half. Afterward she could go to work, they could save money and buy a house in West Virginia; Franklin could get a job down there. Ras, she thought, would like to accompany them: "He likes to hunt the mud turtles and farm."

With a kind of concerned vagueness she was of the opinion that Ras would indeed want to stay with them, but you couldn't be sure unless he's sober. She doesn't know why he left them in the first place; he told them his check would be cut if he stayed there. (Welfare had forced Ras to live alone, though from time to time he preferred it anyway. In part, also, he must have thought he would spare her the embarrassment of knowing his alcoholic proclivities. Not least important, he had simply not wanted to be a burden.)

It would be best for him to stay with them. Living there, in one of the better blocks, he didn't drink, except—once in a while—some beer or whiskey. "If he leaves," she said with a concern that was natural despite her youth, "I'm afraid he'll take to bein with those winos again, and he'll kill hisself." She paused for thought, not effect. "I guess we treat him more like a father than we do our own."

Ras stayed in the hospital for about a week. One day, with the Filipino nurses out of earshot, he confided that they had taken eight blood tests. "It's a money racket. They're takin my blood and sellin it for fifty dollars a pint." The X rays proved negative. His pain, he was told, was a matter of "arthuritis," an affliction he had brought with him from West Virginia. "That arthuritis is like a bad check; it just keeps comin back." He also had heard the doctor say he had found "some leukemia" in the blood samples. Calmly, without drama, he said, "I ain't worryin. You know we all gotta die sometime."

The doctor turned out to have said anemia. This reprieve Ras accepted mildly as a stroke of incidental fortune, and he moved back in with Franklin.

But two weeks later Janice told me, "I don't know what's wrong with Ras. He's been drunk ever since he got out a the hospital. When he's sober he's good, but when he's drunk you cain't hardly understand him. Franklin said he hadn't said nothin to him." But Franklin's patience was again wearing thin: "I think a lot of Ras but I won't put up with this kind of junk. He hangs out with them winos and you don't know what he's gonna bring back. I don't see how we can help him."

Franklin offered me a beer and relaxed. He had been in Chicago eight years. "The neighborhood hasn't changed but the people have." The current migrants are "the last ones leavin the South," the dregs with the least initiative, who knock hell out of the buildings. Then, in immediate defiance of these words, he allowed he would have to move by winter, since this rather decent-looking apartment had no heat and no extermination.

He doubted Ras had really been robbed this last time. "You can't believe everything people tell you" about the cops—but "people can't let the sonsabitches get away with pushin you around." Ras should have gone before the police complaint board for justice. Ras should take care of himself; Franklin worked eight, sometimes ten or thirteen hours a day at the Rauland's Zenith color-TV-tube plant—with a lot of other Southerners —over a hot furnace, and had little time or energy to tend to anyone else's affairs.

Ras lived there on and off for the next three months. Once in a while he sobered long enough to return to JOIN, but his energy had gone a little wry. "I give out one hundred fifty of these leaflets this mornin," he said one day in August. "Somebody down at JOIN asked me if I had any trouble with the police and I said, 'No, they're givin me a hard way a livin any-how. What kind a trouble can they cause me?' "

Early in October Janice and Ras had "pitched a big drunk" Saturday night. She had told him to go to bed; he said he'd go to bed when he was good and ready. Then he returned with a wino friend. The next day he came back, more sober, and Franklin accused him of a breach of faith. It seemed to Janice that Ras was calling her a liar in denying her story. "So Frank told him he'd have to get him another place to stay."

A week later he was back, with Franklin's acquiescence. He had stayed the previous night at Pop's, but "he's so crabbed, you know." The next night he was gone again. John Dawson took him in. For a healing month, he played with the kids, chewed tobacco, played a sharp game of 500 Rummy, and stared out the window. Then he grew restless, began hanging out on Wilson Avenue again, and appeared one day with stitches in his forehead—he'd been jackrolled, sleeping in a car with Jim Day.

Not eating well, feeling weak, he went to Cuneo Hospital for a checkup. He couldn't understand the diagnosis—"You cain't hardly make out these Chinese doctors, you know"—but again thought the word leukemia had cropped up. He received twelve pills with no description, and no advice for his drinker's shakes—severe, uncontrollable jerks, after three rare days without wine.

We called Cuneo to diagnose the diagnosis. Again it turned out to be hyperanemia, this time augmented by colon trouble. The pills were vita-mins. Ras acknowledged that drinking was doing him no good, but he had an inexorable logic on the side of his abandon. "On my little ole check I can't make it too good no ways." He drank because "I just got worried about my check, you know. Then I drank celebratin my check comin in."

He didn't know where he could spend the next night. Day was in jail, having been caught as an inept lookout over a game of craps. Franklin had two brothers on his hands, the wife of one having left him. Ras thought he would walk up Wilson Avenue and "hunt me a bed." He found one with Pop; a few days later he was back at the Dawsons'.

We saw him in the JOIN office one cold Friday just before Christmas with his face badly bruised—he said he'd been robbed of forty dollars more. His voice was shaking, he had aged and knew it. Very drunk, he spoke with an urgent self-consciousness I had not heard before:

"I'm goin to church this Sunday. I got to do somethin to stop this drinkin, you know. I'm gonna go this Sunday and I'm gonna keep goin till I've stopped it. Cause I can't do it the way I am now. I'll swear it, buddy, I can't do it now. I got to do somethin cause I can't go on this way, you know what I mean. I swear to God I got to do somethin. I got to get straightened out, you know what I mean."

That Monday Etta Dawson told us she had thrown Ras out. "I took Lila and Trudy to the doctor with impetigo and when we got back he was lyin on the floor, passed out. I told him, you'll have to get out, Ras, and your wine bottle too. I won't let Johnny drink wine around the kids. Beer's O.K. but not wine. It runs em crazy."

It was Christmastime again. The stores in Uptown, like those everywhere, displayed their special displays; Jim Beam wrapped its whiskey in a gaily striped box; JOIN planned a party for neighborhood kids. The night after eviction, December 22, Ras spent in jail:

"I was just comin out of Liquortown, see, and I just had bought me a pint a wine, and they was waitin for me. They seen me goin in, you know. Took me straight off to jail. They was lookin for money, they searched me all over, in my pockets and everywhere, but I didn't have none. Now I hadn't drunk a drop, and the bottle it still had the cap on, but they taken hit anyhow."

He did not get to church; the impulse toward salvation faded like a twinge of memory. But rumbling in him was the fiercer, less repressible, to him mysterious though lifelong habit of finding a new way, getting back on his feet.

As he drank less, he lost less money in robbery. But his friends were still on Wilson Avenue, and so he was with them, and so he was still prey for the police. One night in the spring a local minister saw the cops raid the winos' favored all-night cafeteria, rounding up everyone without clerical collar and heaving them in paddy wagons "for disturbing the peace." The cops had been under fire from the good lakeshore citizens for failing to keep their neighborhood sufficiently clean. Ras, drinking a glass of milk, was one fish gathered in the net. He was released after five days in jail.

With a more secure monthly check (now raised to $101.16), he succeeded in renting a room, only "a dump, not a damned dump like them other places." To escape from solitary confinement without the pressure of Franklin's guardianship, or the dissolution of life with Jim or Pop, he had hoped for a while to find stable roommates:

"There's a feller now wantin me to move in with him, but I can't do that, see. Jimmy Hopps, that's got three rooms over here, he pays twenty-five dollars a week, you know. Well, I can't move in with him, you know, on account of the welfare. But I might take a chance on doin that, you know. To have somebody to talk to every night, you know. Jimmy says, 'I know, Ras, you're all right.' "

In the end welfare had its way. Meanwhile Bud returned from a stay in West Virginia; on his way up he had a minor stroke. Ras shepherded him to the hospital and confided that he didn't think Bud had long to live. When Bud's health picked up he installed him across the hall and unselfconsciously proceeded to support him, as in the old days. Ras no longer drank.

They would sit long hours on the stoop, sometimes in conversation with passers-by, often in silence. When a new JOIN newsletter appeared, Ras would pass out several hundred. They came to Thursday night meetings, marveled at the hilarity of the skits—"Ain't that somethin?"—but they must have known their participation was less central now that JOIN was more sophisticated, and Ras showed less interest in the making of JOIN's decisions. They could still be counted on for demonstrations.

That is, when Ras had the time. The manager hired him to man the rental office in his building and collect rent. It took upwards of ten hours a day and brought him $17 a week, but with Bud as a dependent he had little choice.

Knowing he was at the manager's mercy, he sought an alternative, and found one, at least for the summer. A cousin in Uptown, an occasional plasterer, hired him to help out during the outdoor months, one day a week at $20, for a few weeks. This illicit boon he banked regularly, with us, for welfare would penalize him for fraud if he kept an account in his own name.

I asked him one day what he intended to do with the money. He was saving it, he said, expecting that one of his kin would pass on one of these days, and he would need money quickly to get to the funeral in West Virginia.

Ras, he raised the best lettuce and the best
garden I ever seed. He canned the best pickles
you ever eat. Yes, everybody liked Ras around
here. He never had no trouble with no one.
Everybody loved Ras.
—Mrs. Saunders, Big Creek,
West Virginia

RAS BRYANT

I was born and raised there, in West Virginia. I like the place very well,
but it's just come to where you can't make anything to live on, see. That's
the reason why I don't want to go back.

Oh, I like the situation of it very well, there's plenty a reckeration,
huntin, fishin, but you know what I mean. It's no good there. It used to be a
good place, but it's no good down there now. When them mines were all
goin and everybody had jobs, why, you could get a hold a somethin then,
you know, to live on. But now, you see, there's so many on relief that you
can go into that relief office and Lord, it'll take you a week or so to get
signed up on relief. Then they gonna give you a bawlin out, say you gotta
do somethin.

I just wish I had the privilege to take you out to West Virginia and show
you what kind of barns people's livin in. I don't call em houses. Well, out
in Ohire they got better barns for their stock than we got houses to live in
in West Virginia. Don't get me wrong now, there's some good houses in
West Virginia same as there are everywhere else. But the little ole mines
were worked out and those houses were run down. Hit's pitiful to look at,
just the number a them, you know. I call most of em tin-can alleys.

There's a good bit a coal in West Virginia yet, but there're so many a
them workin out, you know. No more coal to get there. Oh, they'll finally
go down in the ground just as far as they have to, and get it, you know.
Course they'll just have to pay for it, you know—the people 'at consumes
it. But the biggest portion a them out there, now, is worked out, shut down,
and the people has nothin to do. And the mines what are not shut down,
they had men cut off. They got seniority rights there, you see, and you
couldn buy a job out there in the mines now. Not a Chinaman's chance a
gettin a job out there in the mines. Some few of em, they're workin them
truck mines, but they're not payin so much. See, they're truck mines; they
can't pay the union scales, you know, and operate.

Them miners hain't got no chance a gettin nowhere now. Logan
County is a billion-dollar coal field, you see. Been a billion-dollar coal field
for years, but it's runnin down now, see. I'll venture to say it's run down

half. But you know, even if they was hirin, I won't go in no coal mines no more. Too dangerous. When you go in there in the mornin you don't know whether you're comin out or not. You don't know what's goin a happen to you. You don't know whether the props'll fall on you or what's goin a happen to you. Yeah, they been some bad accidents out there in them mines. Isn't anythin couldn happen to you in that mine. Course it didn't bother me a bit when I first went in. I was just a big boy, didn have sense enough to be scared. I'd try anything, you know, anybody else would.

They make a livin now out there in the mines, the ones that work in the mines. They have plenty to eat and everything, you know. They have clothes to wear, stuff like 'at.

Next door to Tommy Smith in Lyburn, West Virginia, Ras ran into a thirty-five-ish man unloading groceries.

"Makin any moonshine up thyar, Ras?"

"No."

"They make everythin else up thyar, might as well make moonshine."

He had worked in Chicago seven months himself, and before that in Cleveland and Detroit. Not long ago, with the war reviving the demand for coal, his old mine had called him back to work. In Chicago he had made $1.95; in the mine $3.48. (He displayed pay stubs for pride and credibility.) Here, his house rented for $12 a month; in Cleveland $30 a week. "They tell you it's no good to work in the mines, but I like it."

But you see, them operators, they gotta pay so high now that they've all kinds of new machines in there now, that's what cut all the men off out there, you know. They used to have to go in there and take a machine and cut around under the bottom of this coal plumb across the place. Then they had to drill holes in that coal, and put the dynamite in there, the powder, and shoot it down. Then go in there the next mornin—you taken your pick and shovel, and you went in there and you load that coal in the car with a shovel. Now they've got machinery in there will dig the coal, shoot it, cut it, and load it right in the car. Three men can do the work that fifteen would have done, with them shovels. Or more.

Yeah, lot of em leavin there. Oh, they's a number of em right here in Chicogger, from West Virginia. And they're comin in gradually. Ever few days I meet a new one, you know. I got some few cousins here in Chicogger. Some other people I know is good friends. They're all kin to me.

It's kinda hard, right now, to find jobs here, ain't it. A man ain't got no experience, you understand what I mean. Well, they don't have any factories in West Virginia, see. Out there they's mostly farmers and dig coal or somethin or other like that, you know. Some of em work on the roads for the state, and some works in the gas fields, stuff like that. What can get jobs, you know. Where I'm from, Logan County, there're no factories in hit whatsoever. Not nothin a-tall.

And I hear from some a my people every once in a while. Thomas, my first cousin, he goes out there pretty often. He brings the news back about how they're all gettin along. Course things don't change much down there.

And I go back there on a visit once in a while, but not to stay. I been back about—seven times, I think, since I been here.

Ras came back from a week's trip to West Virginia aware that welfare might cut him off. (Their reasoning would be this: Since the budget provides no money for travel, presumably his travel must have been paid for by someone able to support him, etc.) But, he said, if welfare cut him off, "We'll throw up a goddamn picket line on em. We done that before, ain't we? I got a right to go wherever I want, do what I want. I got as much right to a vacation as they do."

I just go stay with other friends and people, you know. I got some other people that I travel about with, stayin.

Those people down there, they eat good and they feed you good, too. You don't just get by the way they do up here. I get well taken care of down there, you better believe it. I get offered a lot more food than I can eat—for a short spell, you know, anyways. They're a lot friendlier in West Virginia than they are out here.

I went back to West Virginia and was talkin with a guy.

He said, "Well, Ras," said, "how you gettin along out there?"

I said, "Oh, gettin along good," I said, "you only have one problem."

He said, "What's that?"

I said, "To find somebody to talk to."

He said, "Why is that?"

I said, "Everybody talks to theirself out there." I said, "They go along the street talkin to theirself."

You notice em doin that lots of times, you know. These original ones from here, you know. I told im, "Now if you find somebody from West Virginia, or the South somewhere, down in Alabama or someplace like that, they're ready to talk to you." But the original ones that live here, you can ask em anything. Maybe they'll say something or they'll turn their head and look the other way. I had em do me that way lots a times. Settin in a beer garden, you know, drinkin. Maybe I'll go in and get me a mug o' beer, say somethin-or-other to a guy: it's pretty cold out there, or somethin, or pretty warm, or somethin like 'at. "Yep"—he'll just turn his head over, turn right on the stool, turn and look the other way. They won't talk to you. I dunno for why, but they won't. They sure won't talk to you.

But I like it fine, Chicogger. I like 't real good. Cause I can get somethin a eat, somethin a live on, here. In West Virginia I cain't. Unless you workin all day for your board, and you don't like to do that, you know.

Nah, I don't want to go back home. Too hard a times back there. No, I'd never want a go back there, to home.

> Well, I say we made a big mistake in '45. After we marched on Germany, when we landed in New York there, we ort to have marched down to Washington and ripped that place apart, set up our own government. And I still say that when this mess ever ends in Korea, I mean Vietnam, that's what should happen. They should march right into the White House and tear it apart and set up their own government. That's the only way to ever change this country. Poor people could run the government a lot better than the way the big shots is runnin it this day and time, a lot better. If ever this government needed overthrowin, it needs overthrowin now.
> —John Dawson

John Dawson

My daddy was a minister. And my granddaddy was a deacon of the church. Course they's a different religion there. My daddy was a Holiness and my granddaddy was a Methodist. Well, I don't even believe in either one of their denominations. So actually in religion when it comes to denominations, our family was all spread apart. I believe in the Baptists, I got a sister who believes in the Baptists, I had a sister who believed in the Catholic. And I just don't see that fightin one another on that church denomination. We can't get along like 'at. What makes me mad about these landlords, I told one a mine that Hitler should've killed all the Jews, and I know there's nice Jews, Etta's best friend's a Jew, but these landlords got the evil of makin you say things you don't mean.

We're out here to help the people and we'd like the cooperation of every church, every pastor. And we'd like to work with the churches and we'd like the churches to work with us. But the people in our neighborhood at the present time, it's so many people that will not work with no one. Take this Peoples Church over on Lawrence. About once a month they have these little boys goin around puttin these little ole pamphlets under your door, in your mailboxes. And they say, come to our church or call this number and we'll give you any assistance that we can get you. But you can go out there and they'll never give you no assistance or nothin. Well, when JOIN got burned out we asked em and they said, sure we could meet there. Then not more'n two hours before the meetin they called and said that they had a meetin, their board of directors or somethin had a meetin, we couldn't use it. I can't figure it out, unless it's some of that bunch that's down at the Urban Progress Center causin us to not get in there. Now that could be a cause right there.

And they claim the church is for all, they got a sign that says the church is for all people. Well, what kind of a meanin is that? And we sent Ras down to St. Thomas the other day, the Welfare had his check on welfare all messed up. JOIN was burned out and we didn't have no way to get him no food and anything. One of the guys carried him down there and they wouldn't even talk with im. And I think that's wrong.

Now don't get me wrong. I'm not throwin off on no Catholics, no denomination, for that'd be wrong. My wife went down to this Catholic church down on Buena. We didn't have a bite to eat in our house to feed our family, and this priest told her, he said, "If you're not a Catholic," he said, "I'm not gonna even spend one penny to buy you and your family nothin to eat." Well, my wife was plain and she told him, she said, "I'll tell you," said, "you'd better check it a little bit," she said, "you ain't gonna get to heaven like 'at." She said, "I think there's more ministers in this country that will help me out, and my family."

In fact, my wife went up there to the Hull House and we didn't have a bite to eat in the house, and she offered to give her two little ole cans of some kind of soup, expect us to live from Thursday to Monday on it. The two cans of soup wouldn't even of fed one of my little girls, much less have fed the family. So my wife just told her to take it and go straight to hell with it. Don't think my redheaded woman ain't a tiger!

I'm like my wife. My estimation of a Christian's supposed to be a person that lives right, and that will help anyone regardless of belief and religion or regardless of their color, who they are or where they're from.

Until this country stabilizes itself—which we're supposed to be on a Christianity basis, right? Free religion, free speech—until they come back to free speech and free religion, we're gonna have one of the hellaciousest messes here in this country. And until the people of the city of Chicago, regardless of where they're from, make up their mind to just have a solid union in the city of Chicago, all over the city of Chicago, and the suburbs and get together, it's gonna be this way in Chicago. If they don't do somethin contrary, the riot in Los Angeles last year is not gonna be nothin to what it's gonna be right here in this city. And the only way to stop it is for the people to have a word and a voice, and what their word and what their voice said is what goes. And until the people in this country comes to think and realize that they can run, rule this country, it's gonna be in a hell of a shape. If the people here in this neighborhood had of woke up to what was goin on ten years ago, this neighborhood wouldn't be like it is today.

It's our politicians that the people has elected in office that's to blame for this country bein in the shape it's in today. The people actually represents the world if they'd get together and back theirselves together. As JOIN, we go around and try to get people to show them the right from wrong, but we have to have more cooperation. They's people in Uptown that don't even know what's existin in the Uptown neighborhood. Well, you know what you and Ras run into on goin around them taverns.*

They've never had a election in Chicago. Never been one. I happen to know that when President Kennedy was runnin for President, when him and Nixon run, they had all these debates all over the country, that this state has never been give to nobody. In this state there's been twenty men that has been sent to prison for fifteen, twenty years apiece on account a this vote racket they have here. The government caught em. Why sure, they was people that was votin, how could they vote? They've been over there in the grave for ten or fifteen years. There's never been elections here in Chicago. It's a money deal, a money deal.

If I was Daley I'd never get up and open my mouth about Alabama or Mississippi and them down in there when they wouldn't let the Negro vote. What are they tryin to do right here? I just don't see that that's right, the way they operate this votin in this country today. It's one of the ungodliest things that ever has been. I'll tell you somethin I'm not in favor of, I'm not in favor of these damn votin machines in this country. They're too damn crooked. A man can go in there, and he can run up just as many votes on em as he wants to. I still think the old ballot way, you have a ballot, you mark it yes or no, is more safer than the votin machines are.

And another thing, I don't see a man sellin his vote. That guy across the street, a politician'll give him two dollars, that guy's gonna take it to get him some soup bones. That's what's the matter with this Daley machine right here now. I'll tell you somethin that I done this last damn election. I went down the street and I taked their money in and I didn't vote for nobody. If they're that dumb, I'm gonna get drunk that night on their money. There wasn't a sonofabitch runnin that I wanted to vote for. When I feel like votin up there, I'm votin because I know he's for the people, not against em.

They ain't no sech a thing as a man can't be beat in politics. And this

*While asking for contributions to help JOIN open a new office, we were told by several bartenders that we had better check with the Democratic Ward Committeeman—who sells insurance to the bars.

JOHN DAWSON   201

Mayor Daley—Mayor Daley can be beat. Ain't a man that cain't be beat if the people works together.

So if we have to we'll run an independent man, some way or another, without this write-in, which we know is no good.

My granddaddy was a mayor of Etowah, Tennessee, for about three years, and course he left that and went back to the railroad. He was a big politician but he wasn't for no party, he was always independent. For he said that if you represented the Republican Party or the Democratic Party that they wanted you to stand for what they believed, and he thought that the independent man had more say-so for the poor people than a man with a politician's belief.

We'll put up a candidate of our own. The parties, they're gonna start humblin to you, try to get you to vote for em. But when they start humblin, say, "Hell with you, we still ain't gonna vote for you. We gonna pick our person to run." Which we know we're gonna lose before we run, but there's one thing about it: we'll show this Daley machine that the people of Uptown's not afraid to get out there and say, "Well, we're gonna bust this one way or t'other." And another thing, I don't think we need a rich man to run for office no way. I think it should be in a lower class of people, that runs for office to represent the people. He's the man that needs the job, he's the man that needs to get the money out of it. Well, that's all those rich shots is runnin for anyway, to get the money out of it.

You know you're gonna have some crookedness, but the main thing about it, you get a man in on the platform we're tryin to get him in there on, is that he knows if he don't try to go in the legislature and get some a those bills passed, just look out, buddy. The next year, you know, there's another election comin. If you can one time break the ice of this machine down here, there'll be a hell of a machine change.

We're gonna have to get out here and let the people know what we want and what we need. We want to know from a man that's gonna run regardless of alderman, mayor, senator, representative, whoever or whatever politician office is open, whether he's gonna come up before the State Legislature and have a bill put in to abolish these slave-labor offices and set up a free State Employment office or a city office where you could draw every damn penny that these companies pays. Let's set up a nursery in the neighborhood for people that wants to work, their mothers can work.

Another thing is that we would like to see a health inspector in the area, and that inspector *from our neighborhood*. Not bring em from the Seventh Ward or Fifth District or First District up here in the Forty-eighth. What the hell you need this joker here, this inspector, he's no good. For all he's gonna do is walk in this buildin, say, "You got ten dollars, fifty dollars?" "I got it." "Thank you, I'm gone." But if you got that sonofabitch settin there in one a these blocks where you can walk over here and punch him in the nose, say, "Now, you go up here and do it, buddy, you ain't gonna stay in this office, or we'll take you down and whup your damn head," you'll get some action out a these people. We want em people elected. And when these landlords don't do anything we want a stiffer law where it don't take no eight, ten years to do somethin about it. Hell, when it's turned in down there, have it done the next day.

And another thing, we need a rent control, a ceiling price in the city, 'specially in the city of Chicago, and a reasonable rent people can pay. Why should a landlord have a right to charge one man two or three different prices because he's got a big family, and another family can move upstairs over you with more rooms, and they pay less money? The rent control is still in effect in Georgia, New York still has a rent control, and why can't these other states go along with that? In fact the poor class of people should have one year's *free rent* from the United States Government, paid. The reason I say this is they're bringing these damn Cubans down here—now don't get me wrong, I'm not against nobody—but they're bringin them damn Cubans to Florida down there. They give em a hundred and fifty dollars and six months' free rent.

We want good schools for the people, we want good schools for everyone, not just one person. And we lack a lot of havin that in this country. We should have more science, we should have more of everything in this country right today than we've got. I know if the schools was operated now like they was when I was a boy, we would have so much more opportunity. I know when I went to school you didn't set there all day in your seat and nobody teach you nothin. If you asked the teacher anything you didn't know, anything, the teacher would at least explain it to you. They wouldn't dare grab you in the hair a your head and whup hell out of you or tell you to go home, or all such stuff as that.

A poor kid don't have the opportunity. They claim they do, but a poor kid don't have the same privileges in school a rich kid does. A poor kid don't get the same teachin that that rich kid gets. A poor kid can ask the teacher a question, she'll ignore it. That rich kid ask that teacher a question, she'll answer it or she'll see that there's an answer for it, for she knows if she don't the rich kid'll go home and tell his mother or father— well, there's a big stink about it. A poor kid can go home and tell its mother or father, and you come over, you can't even get to talk to the principal.

I say that the public should have a say-so, the parents should have a say-so over that school. Hell, you can't call them public schools unless you do have. If you don't have a right to go over there and tell them people that that school's not bein run right, I don't call it public school. If you want to have a dictatorship, that's what you call dictatorship, and that's all they've got in Chicago with these damn schools. I went over here, I was going to start Lila in this kindergarten over here. I went and got her birth certificate, I went over there, I asked to see the principal over there. You think I saw that principal yet? Told me, said, "You can see the room teacher, someone." I said, "I tell you what, you can go straight to hell." I went over there, I wanted to know what she had to have in school. If you can't find that out in school, my kid's not goin to a damn school like that. My kid's just as good as the next un.

And also we need another school in the neighborhood for the children. There's children goin from here all the way over here on Montrose. Walkin. Little bitty children. Their mothers got two and three kids, they can't turn loose to take that little kid on the streets. It's a shame. It's like Mrs. Simpson here, she's got a little boy that don't need to be down here at no school down here on Kenmore. They have buses runnin around here to pick up kids like that, take care of em. Hell, no, she can't get it because she's on welfare.

That's one thing I liked about Wallace. He thinks that a kid should have the equal opportunity goin to school and have the same privileges a goin to school, havin the same books. That's one thing I do like about that man, right there. There's nothin else I like, that's the only thing I like. I just don't like him no other way and there's no use in me sayin I do. But that's what I was sayin while ago about independent. If one man in the state can pull what he's pulled, how come the people cain't get together and have a independent President? If you recall, Wallace and his wife either one have not run on Democrat or Republican ticket, that's independent direct.

You got to get it across to the people, the neighbors in this Uptown neighborhood that if they'll do somethin about it, it can be changed. Didn't they change Montgomery, Alabama? If they can change one damn town, Chicago can be .changed. The colored people organized, that's how they got somewhere. Some people say Uptown can't be organized but I say it can be organized. Listen, do you know what Lutheran King started off with? He started off with a raincoat and overshoes and two colored guys a-workin with him. That shows what a person can do if they want to.

But I don't know if we'll ever have enough people. We should have had seventy-five people picketin that Marsha Apartments. We need more victories or there's no point in picketin again. For the last six months I think we've done very good with the organization. The first six months was pretty slow, for people didn't believe that we were out to work with the people, they thought we were against the people. Some people was afraid to come into the office. Like us goin to the houses, knockin on doors, tryin to get people to cooperate with us. A lot of times it's accordin to how you talk to a person whether they'll speak to you, whether they'll cooperate with you or not.

And we've got to have an organization that don't fight one another, we got to get together on some kind of a form of what we want done. You take like we are right now, it don't take but three or four, they could tear us all apart. When I was in Alaska, the army, the marine corps, the air force, everything, it was all up there together and we was all tryin to operate as a team, not against one another like it had been during the war, operatin as a separate unit. We was operatin as a team. Teamwork is more than a mob at all times. I could take twelve men in a squad of men, take one machine gun and the rest of it, small-arms fire, and we could hold off a mob out there with teamwork, with those twelve men, mow em all down. Cause a mob's not trained to know what they're doin, they'll walk into anything. And that just shows we are runnin our organization in JOIN, if we will work as a team, we'll get something done, but if we work cuttin one another's throat, we can't get nothin done.

But I think that JOIN's made a lot of difference in this neighborhood here, of a lot of the attitudes of a lot of the landlords. Well, they's a lot of landlords, that they don't want to see their buildings taken away. They figure, well, if we don't do this, this bunch of people'll be in here on us, give us the devil, like when we pulled a picket on the Marsha Apartments there. We got cooperation. I'll guarantee you that it cost this woman $2,200 to fix the boiler. Oh yeah, we made a difference. That's the reason right today that that real estate company bought it out. That's the reason they fixin it up. Them lights they put up there, they got them big white lights that shines all out there in the streets at night now, and they put in new stoves, new refrigerators, new furniture and everything in that buildin. And they completely redecorated every apartment there. You wouldn't even know it. You know back up there where Ras was? 'At just looks like a big nice livin room, beautiful how they got that decorated in there. And they're rentin two rooms there, two rooms for nine dollars a week, that real estate company is.

Course there's still a class just like that damn landlord where I live on Clifton, he don't give a damn about the people. That's the reason my kid's sick right now on account of that damn heat system there. If you can turn on that furnace, it'll keep heat up there, if you set that thermostat. I learnt to operate a boiler in the service and there's no man'll stand up and tell me that you can't set that thermostat to keep a certain temperature.

I wasn't raised to live in a place like at and I don't like it and I ain't gonna put up with it. I just meant business. I'm just like that. Maybe it's the Indian in me. I don't care if it's President Johnson that owns the damn buildin. You know I'm so bullheaded I'll stand in the way of a circular saw and try to stop it.

IN AND OUT OF JOIN

A few days later his nine-month-old infant was in Children's Memorial Hospital with bronchial pneumonia, the hospital refusing to let her out until the heat was turned back on. There was no heat for several days in subzero weather, the oven serving to make the kitchen barely habitable. Then someone threw a rock through the living room window. When Dawson asked for action the manager proceeded to turn off his electricity. Dawson then activated a single lamp with an extension cord to the hall-way. He called the Health Department one twelve-below-zero night. They sent a man over that night, and the furnace started up, only to go off the next morning.

Dawson began to talk rent strike with his neighbors one floor under. The next morning these index cards were taped to his door:

LANDLORD WILL HAVE TO FIX UP OR NO RENT.

JOIN   JOHN DAWSON

BILL—YOU BETTER NOT COME UP HERE
IF YOU DON'T PUT THE HEAT ON.

JOHN DAWSON

But the Mexicans across the hall didn't speak English, the people on the first floor—though "they're from Alabama so we can talk to em"—turned out to be four parentless teen-agers, and JOIN was in disarray. Dawson was besieged by agencies: a friendly but impotent welfare housing consultant, an Urban Progress Center representative taking a survey of housing conditions. Getting the baby back had to come first. He moved.

In the next weeks he came closer to JOIN, attracted by the prospect of getting criminal charges filed against his previous landlord. The Illinois General Assembly in a liberal mood had passed a yet untested Criminal Housing Management Act providing that in cases of "gross carelessness or neglect" endangering the "health or safety" of a tenant, where prior notice had been given and the landlord made no attempt to correct the dangerous condition, the landlord is liable to penalties up to one year in prison and a $1,000 fine. In this case and one other (also involving a JOIN activist), all conditions had been met for prosecution. The alderman proclaimed his willingness to press for use of the virgin statute. An Assistant State's Attorney began "investigation." No charges were ever filed.

John had in the past periodically stormed out of JOIN meetings at what he took to be personal slights, insulting some other member, lurching into a long drinking binge, but returning time after time with "no hard feelings" and a readiness to atone by redoubling his work in JOIN. This time, the state's failure to move against a clear criminal, and the injury to his own baby, coincided with a lull in JOIN activity. He found no way to focus his frustration but the traditional recourse of the poor white.

Five months after his comments on JOIN's successes, he made the first of his departures which was charged with a political finality. Sputtering alcoholically, he began to denounce Martin Luther King at a meeting for making money off the poor niggers, and when Little Dovie asked him to desist, he burst outside and tore up his JOIN card. Railing at "niggers" and "draft dodgers," he was concluding at a higher level of bitterness that organizing was probably futile. His drunken sense of impotence ground him down all the harder by contrast with the past year's periods of organizing momentum; impotence released its formula for cheap redemption, brute racism, with a new force.

He was to return to JOIN yet again, but the old purpose seemed to have cracked, and JOIN, in the throes of reorganization, preoccupied with relations between "students" and community people, turned into itself, was in no position to put the pieces back together.

I'm goin to Georgia. . . . My mommy and daddy
don't even treat me like a child. They treat me
like a dog. I'm goin to stay at my Aunt Clara's.
I ain't never comin back. . . . They don't care.
My mommy don't care. My daddy don't care.
Let me out the door. Let me out the damn door
—I mean the door. I'm goin to Grandma's. I'm
goin shoppin.

—Trudy, age four

Etta Dawson

Well, John was a pretty good man till here lately he's a-drinkin, drinkin,
drinkin. He's still pretty good about takin care of the kids if I take a
notion to go somewhere, but after the last check came he went off before
he paid the rent. I don't mind if he spends it after he pays the rent, but
this was the first time he ever went off first. I went lookin for him all afternoon, three currency exchanges, and those bars he hangs out. Finally he
came home. Then he's done it again.

He come back drunk with Leon the other day and I asked him, "Do you
know where home is?"

He said, "I'll come around when I'm good and ready," and stormed
on out. That made two days in a row.

Nerves starts it. Well, see he's been in the Korean War and the Second
World War too, and one time they didn't have nothin to eat for about
three-somethin days. He got shot in the shoulder, shot in the foot, and
when they had that breakthrough in Germany, his feet froze. Got his
tonsils froze in Alaska. It was snowin so hard they couldn't see and he
held his head out the window and his tonsils froze. He couldn't even speak.
They had to operate and take his tonsils out before he could speak.

I'm gonna break him of drinkin one of these days just like Mamma
broke Daddy. I've never been drunk but twice in my life. But I'm goin
to do just like Mamma done. She wasn't drunk, she hadn't been drinkin
the whiskey, we'd been pourin it out. She goes out on the porch and sets
down on the porch and she says, "Fred," she says, "see that snake goin
up that post?" Daddy said, "What snake?" She said, "There's snakes
goin up that post." He says, "Well, that's the end of my drinkin. I ain't goin

to drink no more." He'll drink a beer every once in a while but he won't get drunk any more. What makes me so mad though is him start hollerin, "Shut up, shut up, shut up"—and there ain't nobody sayin a word.

They ought to ship all the men to Africa and let them give us our checks so we won't have to worry. Right now the check's completely in his name. The only thing my name is on is on the medical card. If he was in the hospital or somewhere I'd have to send the check back, I couldn't sign it. Where some recipients are gettin it, you know, as a family, he gets it himself. They won't give it to me in my name because I won't take a warrant out for him. I'd have to put him in jail before I'd get anything. That's what hurts so bad.

Let em go to Cook County and not give em nothin to knock you out. They knocked me out this time though. You know why? I wouldn't stay down for em, so they gassed me. They gassed me when she was bein born and when the afterbirth. And then that doctor shook his finger in my face and said, "No more!" Said, "I better not see you over here next year." This colored lady laid beside me there and they told her, she had four, this was her fourth one, and the doctor told her, said, " You better not have no more. Better get you some birth-control pills." And they come up there with a list, passin it out, you know, where you can get them. So they gave me the address. So I started up to the clinic to get me some and Johnny said, "Nooo," he says, "they'll damage your health."

I'm tryin to talk Johnny into lettin me be operated on but he won't do it. Well, I normally take orders from him. He don't do too much bossin but if he says don't do somethin I usually don't do it to keep from havin trouble. But my old man's got seven, I think that's enough. He's got five by me and two by his first old lady and if that ain't enough, I told him when I come home from the hospital, I said, "If you want any more, you'll have to divorce me and marry somebody else." I said, "I'm through." Trouble is there's no door to my bedroom! Nothin to lock.

One time I went down to the Urban Progress Center to ask for a bus ticket home, and they said, "You and your husband have to stay together for the sake of your children." And the thing that got me, when I got back the dishes hadn't been done, the floors hadn't been swept or nothin. He had fixed up his bed in there and that was it.

Well I'd a-done left him if it hadn't been for that young-un, the oldest one. She'd grieve herself to death for her daddy. They all think a lot of him, even that baby. But they're gettin old enough to realize what their daddy is.

I'd rather live in Georgia, you got more room to play, you ain't got to worry about the streets or the roads, kids gettin hit by cars, kids gettin picked up. You can let the kids out in the yard and play, where in the summertime here I wouldn't even let my kids play out there in the court. John used to say he wanted to go to Oregon—I don't know. He knows some contractor out there. Now he says we'll go back South after he gets a settlement. Johnny says it's for good. I don't know. He says he'll stop drinkin when he gets down there. We are always sayin, "Yessir." When are we goin to start sayin "No sir" to them?

I'm no Christian but I believe in this that the Bible says: "Don't taketh what you can't giveth."
—John Dawson

John Dawson

Yeah, I been in some fights. I can get in one in a minute and a half. I remember Twelfth Street back home when you had to fight. Guys wouldn't take your money, not at all, but they would flatly see if you'd fight. Them guys wouldn't knock your head, they'd just call you and say, "Hey, let's fight." If you whipped em, they'd get up and shake your hand. Yeah, it was a sight, get up and shake your hand. But if you wouldn't fight em, they'd jump on you every time you came down Twelfth Street. It ain't like this gang here. This gang here that's out on the streets, they're out there knockin heads to take all the money you got. I don't back off from em, ain't no sense in backin from nobody. You ain't got but one time to die.

If you don't stand up for your friend, ain't much of a man to you. And I'll stand up for JOIN too. Ain't twenty people in JOIN'll do what I did a few weeks past. Well these guys in a tavern, they didn't like us, said they's somethin wrong with JOIN. They said that our place was crummy. So, he said, why didn't we run a better place? He said we're just a bunch a goddamn guys goin around tryin to tell people a bunch a bullshit.

I said, "Well," I said, "I'll tell you one thing," I said, "how bout you runnin this damn tavern here chargin three or four prices for your beer and things." I just run it right back in his face.

"Oh," he said, " you're some Southern guy that thinks you own the city up here."

I said, "I might be some Southern guy that owns the city but," I said, "you and your whole damn bunch in here, that's the way I figure about you too." I said, "You don't own a goddamn thing." I said, "You might own this damn tavern, but you don't own the whole Uptown neighborhood." And I said, "As I told you," I said, "if you don't like our place up 'ere," said, "why the hell don't you pay us the rent on a better place?"

"Well," he said, "you just a bunch of winos hangin out."

I said, "Well, I'll tell you about the winos," and now I said, "guys like you is what's called winos." I said, "You get em here when they spend their last dime, you put em on the street but," I said, "we take em in." I said, "If the right thing was done we would have a clinic for those guys but," I said, "people like you wouldn't back it up." I said, "All you care about is their last penny." So anyway they didn't like it, see, and they go and jump on me. Well, I fought to win.

Them Indians are the worst. You know I heard that the colored people was bad at that but I been in colored places in this city all over, never been robbed around colored people. Now you could go in down here at Eddie's, and I guarantee you, now there was a rough bunch of colored guys come in there and I mean they got rough. They'd fight one another on Saturday night and Friday night but they wouldn't never bother you or open their mouths to you.

As I said, I don't like to have trouble but if you're gonna have to have it the best thing to do is just have it and be done with it. Sometimes it takes that kind a stuff to make good uns out a people. That's just like a guy goin out here to the tavern. If a guy wants to go in here and sit down at the tavern and drink a few beers and act like a man, he can do it. I think these guys that goes down and drinks a few beers and show theirself, I think it's just a showoff. I think that's just a little bit of lackin what they should have a whole lot of. When it comes to goin in to one of these places or actin a fool, I don't think that. I like to get along. I'd rather have a friend. Like a song I got at my house, it says, "I'd rather have one rose while I'm livin as to bring a truckload when I die." For you're a lot better off. If a person actually wants to be a friend to a person, they can be if they try to be. A kind word a lot of times means more than some smart word to somebody. I know I'm the type of person that if somebody talks smart to me out there, that it just be hell with em. I just won't take it for I don't believe in sayin anything to nobody or botherin nobody. I believe in goin on and tendin my own business. Person asks me to help him, if they's anyway I can help em, I'll help em.

I've helped a lot of people that—hell—they've stole from me, picked the stuff from me, come to my house and we've helped em out, and then they'd leave and clean us out. Well, I didn't hate that person for that, I hated their ways, the way they done. And that should be all the way through life. Course that's one thing I'd say my daddy and my granddaddy taught me, to not hate nobody, but some people, their ways you couldn't like no way. And they's a class a people that you can't get along with, I don't care what you do for em or how you try to cooperate with em. They's people that'll cut your damn throat wherever you go to. Course I lack a lot of havin damn good sense myself, at times.

I know I drink. I've worked hard since I was a kid when I went to work in the factories and it's ruint my health. Now I'll be honest with you. I drink cause I got so many worries on me. I had *never* touched a drop of nothin before I went in service. I lived in a Christian home and we had a Christian life and, I don't know, I went to church, there wasn't a Sunday I didn't go to church. And I lived right, done right, and I reckon after I went in service was when I left the church just completely. Only way that I could figure that done it was the crowd I got to runnin around with in the service. Well, I always said if I ever got to where I went to clubs, that I wouldn't go to church and claim to be a Christian for I think that there's nothin no worse than a two-faced, I mean it's all right to go to church, but don't then get up there and tell people you are a Christian when you not a Christian and they damn well know that you not. That's not right for nobody. So I wouldn't call myself a Christian no more.

I don't know, when I came back to the United States from Korea I slacked off, I just quit. Well, then I hadn't touched a drop of whiskey in three years when me and Etta married. About a week before we married, her brother came home from Germany and me and him went over to Cedartown where they made whiskey and got ten gallon. That's the first drop of whiskey I'd drank in been over three years. Well, then I slacked off again, started up again, slacked off again, started up again. You get somethin on your mind, you get worried about somethin n'other, that'll cause me to drink. When I'm not disgusted about anything I don't give a durn whether I can see a durn drop whiskey, beer or nothin.

Workin keeps my mind contented. When I'm workin every day, work regular and when I had my paydays regulated, comin every two weeks, I'd go down here at the Club Lounge and drink a couple beers, I'd get up, walk out up at that package store there across from the el tracks there, I'd buy me a carton of beer and go on to the house on a weekend and watch a ball game. Maybe I wouldn't even drink that whole carton of beer the whole weekend. But when I'm not workin, and there's a lot of people that way too, like me, I'm just like somebody lost. I think a person should have their own free choice as to what they want to do, but as for me I just would rather be a-workin if I'm able to work. I got nothin against nobody that don't want to do it, don't get me wrong there: hell, let him lay up if he wants to. But if I had to lay up all the time, I'd go crazy, I'd just flatly go crazy I guess—in a place like this here I'd go nuts.

Right now I get disgusted settin around the house just all the time. That'll cause me to go in a tavern if I've got any money and get drunk. Actually if they closed all the taverns it'd be the best thing they ever done, in my estimation, and very few people say that that drink it. Say you get off the el there at Wilson Avenue. Say you stop there at that Club Lounge there. Well, if you drink two or three there, you get across the street, there's another one. Well, if you didn't have them two taverns there right in your face like that a man wouldn't drink half as much.

If it hadn't been for me a comin to Chicago huntin a job, I would never have come to this city to live, I would a stayed in Rome. It's just much better livin conditions than it is here. Course I wouldn't be around a furnished apartment if I was there, but you get a furnished apartment there for fifty, seventy-five a month, that would make these buildins up here ashamed of themselves—if I wanted to live there. But I just don't like it back there no more, and you know if you ever get turned against a place, you are turned against it. I got turned against it on account of my own people there. I just don't like livin with my people. They upheld my first wife, what she done, takin money and stuff, her and her family. Well, they got mad at me because I stopped it. So I don't get along with my people and my wife don't even get along with her people. Etta and her daddy would be into fightin in less than a month.

Oooh! He's such a grouchy devil. Now I can get along with Etta's mother, she's got a good mother, but Jesus Christ couldn't get along with her daddy. He didn't speak to me for over two years after her and I married. He hadn't spoke to me until Lila was about fifteen months old and we went home for the first time from up here. The trouble was that he had always knocked them girls around, bossed them around. He just didn't want em to marry nobody. He'd always mistreated his kids and he just thought that he could do that after they married. That's what me and him had it out over. I just don't believe in livin around your people no way. If you try to live around your people, there's gonna be an argument goin on between you. If you're away from your family your folks can't say, "Well, you do this," and her folks can't tell her what to do. We do what we please and that is the best way to be.

When I wind up livin here, for good, I'm goin either back South or out West, one, for I think the climate'd be better on the health. I got a lot of friends out there in Eugene, Oregon. It's either out there or down South. I'd like to find me a small town where I can buy a house, place with a yard for the kids to play in, not like this damn city. It ties the kids up, their not havin a place to play. It's dangerous to walk down the street in the day.

Soon as I collect one a those settlements, from the railroad or Jobs Unlimited, I'm gone and I ain't comin back. I'll miss JOIN for a while, I'd like to see the neighborhood built up but I don't guess I'll be here when they finally get it. You know I'd like to build this thing, but—the main thing that I want to do is just have a decent livin, have a good place of business that I can make a decent living. I think that's the only thing I'll ever be able to do, and that's exactly what I got full intentions of doin with this settlement I get. And I could help somebody else.

I don't know, I always had this attitude, I always wanted to have enough money to put me up say a grocery where the people that I was makin cash on, I could take some of that and those people that didn't have nothin I could help em, give em somethin. As I said, my granddaddy always taught me to go and help the person that didn't have, and that's always stuck with me. I mean that builds a man's business up to help people that needs help, and you get to know a lot of people. Course naturally if you own your business you still got to make enough of money to live on, enough of money to pay your taxes and exist. But I don't want no place of business that would bring in no two or three thousand dollars a week. They's a lot of people in life that they want to get more money, more money, more money. Course if I had my business I would like to lay back some money for my kids or somethin like at, you know what I mean. Well, say for instance something happened to me, Etta and the kids could run that grocery store and they'd have somethin to make a livin. And that's my main attitude right there.

I'd like to see my kids go through school, for this day and time if you don't have the education a job ain't nothin no more. Say one of my girls wants to go through nursin school, I'd like to be able to help put em through there. I think it would be a mighty good trade, especially I do know that this surgical nursing pays good money. And I'd like to see the boys have some kind of good education, whatever they want to learn. And of course if I was gonna go back over, and I had my life to live over, course which I won't never have, but if I had my life to go over, I would go through engineer's school. I think that's a mighty good trade. At one time I would have liked to have went to doctor's school, if I'd a stayed out of the service and if I didn't have to quit school. Then I had different ideas. Oncet I thought of goin to law school. You know, hot air comin up through the life of a young person; you change your mind. And then after I went into the service there, I didn't have no opportunity to go to law school then, I just completely forgot about it. I wouldn't've come up so dumb, anyway, like I am.

Right now I can go down here and ask for a government job and they'll say, "Well, you ain't got enough education for the job." But I had enough education to drive a tank in World War II, I had enough education to use a damn M-1 rifle or drive a tank in Korea. And I mean course you can't say what you would have done years ago now, it's too late to talk about that. You got to hope you make the prospects ahead of you, and anybody else. And that's my main attitude in life, is to see the kids get the schoolin that they need, and whatever the kind of course they want to go through, I hope that I'm able to put em through it. I hope that's one thing I live to do. And then they won't have to sweat it out like I've sweated out through life. And that's about all a man can hope fer here. When you're dead, you're just dead. A lot of people holler you meet hereafter but I don't believe in that no more. I think that man lives his hell here on earth and that's it. They's no such thing as "Well, you goin to meet hereafter if you do this and you do that." I don't think that's true any more. I think that's all a mistake.

In the summer of 1967 John Dawson received his two settlements and moved to Florida. Six months later, the chairman of JOIN got a letter from him, asking help in founding a new JOIN in the South. Then he returned to Chicago, and once again threw himself into the fight against urban renewal. Thinking it hopeless, he went back to Georgia, but not before appearing briefly in a film showing an alliance between Uptown insurgents and the Black Panther Party.

In the summer of 1969, he attended an SCLC meeting in Atlanta, when he was recognized from the film by a racist white man. A while later— information is scanty as the book goes to press—he was murdered.

Walking the Streets: Racine

A scattering of grass remains on the lawns. Three-story buildings, apartments from three to seven rooms. Average rent: if by the week, $6.50 per room; if by the month, $17.50 per room. If the houses are rehabilitated under federal funds, leases for six months or more will probably be required. A *VISTA* worker surveys one block, Sunnyside to Wilson, asking if tenants would sign leases. Of 111, 64 percent say no, and of them, one-quarter give as their reason, "Not enough money," the other three-quarters, "We wouldn't stay here that long." It is a very Southern block. The black-bearded manager of several buildings wears a miner's helmet, dozens of keys clanging from his back pocket.

On one corner of Sunnyside, three public telephones, at least one always out of order, kids in and out looking for forgotten change, retrieving pop bottles, taking them to the grocery store across the street, emerging with more bottles, candy, bubble gum. Young guys leaning against the fence, sometimes joined by girls, sometimes by a motorcycle gang stopping for cigarettes and Cokes.

Saturday afternoon three men wash or repair their cars, talk of engines and carburetors, lean back glaring as a car races too fast down the street. Girls hang out the windows, watching for friends. Young mothers push shopping carts of dirty clothes toward the Wilson Avenue laundromat. WJJD, The Country Music Station, one-one-six-oh, blares from the open windows, from an occasional transistor radio. You can hear a song start at one corner, catch up with it down the block. (Even many blacks in Uptown listen to WJJD.)

Near the Wilson corner, old people sit quietly in the lobby of the pseudo-rococo Wilson Hotel, like retainers in a Tennessee Williams play. Across the street, Free Will Baptist Church, screened by a velvet curtain.

Crippled man dies in fire on Racine

THE BODY OF ⌐ genrader⌐ He was apparently a crip- ⌐ches

I get $92.40 on social security. It's not enough, for a lifetime of work.

I've lived on Clifton and this buildin down here and down on Kenmore and this one over there, they're all the same.

Amazing grace, how sweet the sound
That saved a wretch like me

You know these colored people are always complainin about their homes, but their houses wouldn't be so bad if they took care of em. . . . I have a colored friend, I've stayed with her a couple times. We were workin together at Rauland's. She said it might not be good for me if they saw us together but I don't care; that job's not worth all that much to me. They start the white people at $1.87 an hour and the colored at $1.67 an hour. That's not right to do people that way.

If I can get me a second job, construction, I'd have it made.

LAW AND ORDER ON RACINE
by a woman on Racine

Last Wednesday night three detectives found a friend of mine just walking down the street. They drew a gun on him and sent him down the alley. This one cop said, "I've been waiting two years to do this to you." Three of them surrounded him and beat him with billy clubs—his shoulders and arms were all sore. They tore some ligaments loose—he has to wear his arm in a sling. He went over to the police station to swear out a warrant for the cops and they wanted to lock *him* up.

This friend of mine had beat a rap in court about three years ago and so one of these detectives had gotten suspended for about thirty days because of it. This is why they were after him.

Every time I get disgusted I want to go to West Virginia, but it's so lonesome there.

I was workin as a grill man at the old restaurant over here on Sheridan Road, fifteen hours a day for fifty dollars a week. He knew he had me over a barrel, he knew I needed money. And I've had jobs workin for guys where one day you get paid and the next day you don't. A lot of people say, Why did you quit? or How come you got fired? They never stop and look at the employer.

They say that hillbilly music'll die. It'll never die. Don't know why I like it. I'm a hillbilly, I guess.

I once was lost but now I'm found
Was blind but now I see

I could eat breakfast and whup your ass at the same time.

Sometimes your plans don't work out right. You try to better yourself, but never plan ahead. Plan day by day.

You know, those people down home are a million times happier than the people up here. They may have wood stoves but they huddle around em *together.*

If a colored man moves into this buildin that's all right, but he ought to have a colored wife, that's the way I look on it.

How'm I doin? I'm doin on nothin, that's how I'm doin.

I'll probably get drafted, I guess I'll have to fight.

I like for a woman to do what I tell em to do.

Woman Who Rented Flat To 3 Little Girls Arrested

During the day, the girls said, they went to Riverview Amusement Park and then earned the six dollars they paid for renting the apartment by carrying packages for shoppers and merchants.

Here the guys, they don't feel sorry for nobody, have any pity on nobody. Like if they had a guy down, and the guy started, "Please let me up," all this, well he wouldn't feel no sorrow for that guy, it'd just make em hit him that much more, seems like.

Did you ever see the government do anything for you? Ought to be raisin pensions 'stead of spendin all these billions to get to the moon. What do we want to get to the moon for? What'd the moon do to us? The Jews are behind this moon business. They already run the world and they're lookin to run the moon.

My brother-in-law came first and he kept writin, you know come up here to live. He was workin.

I'd like to go back home, but my husband wants to stay here cause he couldn't find no work in Louisville and here he has a good job. He's a punch-press operator—he's makin it good now.

Riverview Sold, to Be Industrial Park

I wouldn't wanna be buried up here. Seems like, I don't know, it's like I don't belong. I was born in the South and that's where I was really stabled at. It's a good place to be from.

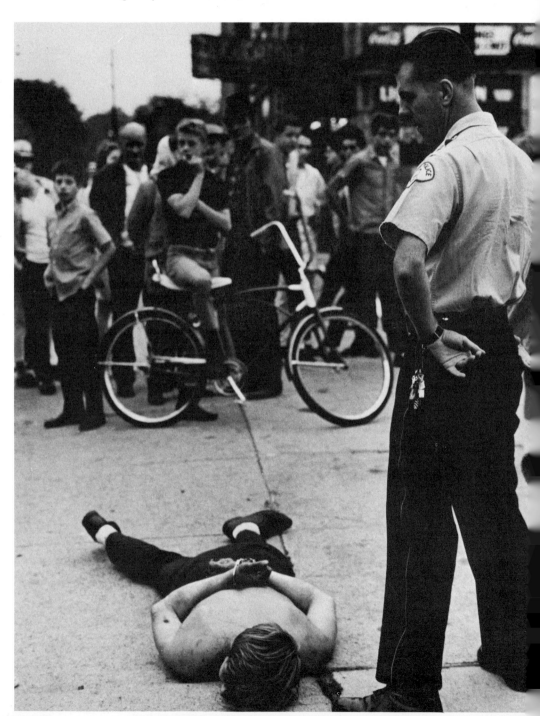

"A Certain Amount of Freedom"

Policemen, 19th District, which includes the southern part of Uptown, over to Lake Shore Drive:

Patrolman: "By instinct, a police officer knows who he's stopping: whether it's a sticky-slimy character or just someone coming home from work. If he proves he's honest, if he lives on the 3600 block of Lake Shore Drive and he has a business, you apologize and thank him. If he's a shady character, you take him into the station."

Sergeant: "A police officer should have a certain amount of freedom, not that he should abuse it. But if you talk harsh to a kid you shouldn't be reprimanded. It's sometimes best for the kid. . . .

"Today the police's hands are tied. A lot of things that you used to be able to do, you can't do today. Some of these small groups of kids should be kept off the streets, kept moving, harassed in every way they can be harassed, because they commit most of the petty crimes.

"Lower-class people, they feel they can walk all over the police a little bit because they can always write a letter of complaint. . . . No arrest is made unless there is grounds."

Patrolman: "I think this country is wasting too much money sending rockets to the moon. If you took the money spent for just one of those rockets you could build a prison big enough to hold every person in the United States."

I'd like to be a truck driver. Tractor and trailer. State to state. I like to move around. I mean, you meet a lotta people and everything. I'd just like to drive from state to state, and work on cars. I like to work on cars. Mechanic.

Ever since I can remember, I guess, I been workin on em. Doin this, that. Sometimes it gets pretty rough, but get the right kinds a tools and stuff, it's easy. It's dirty but—say a car's out there that won't run. Say you work on it. Then you get it runnin. You know you done accomplished somethin. Right?

—Popeye Adkins

Popeye Adkins, 23

Popeye was one of the young Southerners whose base turf was the corner occupied by the old JOIN storefront. "If some woman come by," said another of the group, "we'd make wisecracks at her and stuff like that, and if she goes and tells her husband about it, four or five of us jumps him, whup him, bunch a junk. There was all the time somebody leadin us on into it. If somebody didn't lead us on into it, we'd make up somethin to do, like throw beer bottles at windows, and stuff like at." They had the corner first, had settled on it when the storefront had held Teen Challenge Chapel, and when JOIN intruded they were affronted. During the summer of 1965 they beat up several organizers who were carrying antiwar signs. Over time they were involved in JOIN activity, with the results Popeye describes. This was the awkward, haphazard first phase of JOIN's work with young guys.*

Got up to seventh grade in McGraws, West Virginia; quit. I stayed around home about a year and then I left. I went and registered for the army, left home, went to work. That's when I got my thumb shot off, in a fight. Army wouldn't take me. Lucky.

Down home, where you pay twenty or thirty dollars a week rent up here, you can get a damn nice home, a house, for that a month down there. It's cheaper and everything down there. People up here is just tryin to make a

*For the lessons learned, see "Peacemakers, Goodfellows and the Police," p. 375.

damn killin on these houses and shit. So I did work down at home three dollars a day, workin in the mines. Punch mines. They's a lot of these little punch mines, you know, down there. Owner a this 'un, guy drives a new car every different year; he's got a brand new car and a new truck. Bound to be makin money somewhere. Got a bunch of colored guys work for im. Gives em a dollar a buggy. In a big mine they two and three dollars a buggy, and he was sellin to them. Dump it in his trucks, would haul it to the big mines. Union mines. They pay good money in the union mines, but they ain't too many *of* em. I know of four down there. For the people they ain't none of em. That's why everybody's left from down there. Just can't find no jobs.

Stayed in the mines bout three months all together. Then I went to New Jersey. I worked for a dollar and a quarter up there and then I quit. It's a pretty good state but I wasn't makin nothin of it. I wanted to come up here because all my people, you know, I knowed from down home was up here too. Been up here since. I knowed Randall, a guy that lives up here, he was doin pretty good. Stayed with him till I got a job at Wells, same place he was workin. Started off one-ninety an hour. Got to where I liked the town. You walk around on the streets, you can *see* somebody at ten at night. Down there you don't see nothin but a cop—and you see very few of them. I'd never go back down there to stay.

It was a week after I got up here I first run into the cops. I had an accident up on Foster, Foster and Broadway. At first they was pretty good till he found out I didn't have no insurance. And he says, "Well, if I gotta buy goddamn insurance, you gotta buy insurance." He says, "I'm just gonna see how many tickets," said, "I can write you."

I says, "Well I just don't give a damn how many you write me." So he wrote me out four of em. And I went to jail. Got out and I had to pay for the guy's car, I had to pay a hundred and four dollars for tickets. In a way, cause it was my fault, but hell—this guy shot around this other guy, and I was turnin through and he hit me. Shit, I run into police five thousand times since. Every time they'd ask me for a operator* I'd show em to em, and I'd get away, give em five dollars or somethin, they'd let me go. I've been took to the station twice in five years. Like the night I was stopped out here on the block. This cop asked me, he says, "Where's your operator's?" I showed it to him, he says, "I don't wanna see these kinds a operator's"—was from West Virginia. He says, "I wanna see some operators with Lincoln on em." So I give im a five-dollar bill. He says, "Now you got a Illinois operator's." Pulled on out!

*Driver's license.

Was in the paddy wagon one time. This pal and me got took to jail—had a wreck. Cop asks us, "What're you in here for?"

I told him, "I was in on an accident."

He says, "Oh hell," says, "I know you stoled somethin. What the hell are you in here for?" I told him I had a wreck. He didn't believe us so he kept talkin and puttin things together. So finally he said I was a sonofabitch. And I told him I wasn't no more of a sonofabitch than he was. So that's when he broke my teeth. In the back of the paddy wagon.

I think they're rotten sonofabitches, I'll tell you what I think. They'll do that shit when they've got their damned badge and gun on, but you get one of em out by hisself, when he's just off duty or somethin, he won't say a goddamned word. Rotten bastards.

I never been hit by a cop in West Virginia. Yeah sure, if one of em stops you and you hit him or somethin he's gonna hit you back, but I think they're just nice down there. And I've been stopped down there a hell of a lot.

Up here these damn people's smart as hell. Just like I went to the store over here the other night, right up there on the corner. This woman started cussin. I just stood there and took it, like I knew that I ort to have done. I don't know what brought the subject up, she was standin there checkin out and I was standin behind her. She just started talkin about these people from the South: "I wish these goddamn hillbillies'd go on back where they come from." And I still stood. And then finally I said, "Well, if we would, you wouldn't have nothin but a goddamn ghost town up here."

A lot of places won't hire people from the South. They say, "They won't work." If they paid a little bit more money they might damn work a lot bit better. Like Chicago Cork, you know what they pay an hour? A dollar and a quarter an hour. And I wouldn't work for no sonofabitch for no dollar and a quarter an hour. Shit, I'd steal off the street first. Can't pay your rent on it. Now down home I'd work for a dollar and a quarter an hour, but that's different.

You know what they should do? They should take some a these damn factories, say from Chicago, and just spread em around, you know. Not just only in this state but in different states, or make more in different states or somethin. People from the South down there, they have to leave to come up to this shithole. They don't *want* up here. That's the only other place. You gotta realize these goddamn people from the South is the ones run most of these plants—most of their employees is people from the South. I can't understand them sonofabitch factories.

I can't understand this war either. Actually there's bound to be a reason

or the United States wouldn't be over 'ere. But they're not solvin a goddamn thing now. If they're gonna fight, I think they ort to send everything
in there and fight and get it over with, win or lose, or just pull on back out
a there and say the hell with it.

I don't even know what it's about. But I figure it's over—well, say the
U.S. wants that country. If they don't get it some *other* country'll get that
country, and if they ever do go to war that'll be another country they'll
just have to fight with. But there's a reason, or they wouldn't be over there.
I don't know the reason, you don't know, nor somebody else. At least you'd
reckon they'd tell somebody.

The people should make the decisions. That's what I think. Not this
other bunch a damn people behind a desk. I really don't have no idea what
they're like, but they're bound to be pretty smart. They know what they're
doin, I guess. They're available for the whole United States to put their
trust in, they're bound to be pretty smart some a the time.

But they're not doin shit for the poor people.

I just started goin over there to JOIN about two months ago. Well, I've
knowed about it, but I thought it was a bunch of shit. I just did, I don't
know why. And you know, when they had this marchin up here,* where
Wallace is, these colored people did—well me and Gerald† we went down
to that one. I didn't like JOIN, he didn't either. So we stuck our head in the
door and told em why didn't they go on there to join the rest of the niggers. I used to hate em, niggers—ummm-um! They was a JOIN‡ there, I
started messin around there a lot. I taken a likin to it, so when I got back
to Chicago Harriet§ and them they just invited me down to the West Side.
I said, "Well, I think I'll go."

Harriet says, "No, I don't think you should go."

I said, "Why?"

She said, "Cause there'll be a lot of colored people down there."

I said, "Well, I don't think I wanna go." So they went on down there.
When they come back to JOIN there was Harriet, Jimmy Collier,‖ that big
nigger named James,‖ and this other guy. They got up there and started

*The Selma march, April, 1965.
†One of the leaders of the corner gang, from Anniston, Alabama.
‡One of the Selma black groups.
§Harriet Stulman, then a JOIN organizer.
‖A young black folksinger and organizer for the Southern Christian Leader-
ship Conference West Side staff in 1965.
‖James Orange, a former gang leader in Birmingham tapped by Martin Luther
King first for the 1963 Birmingham demonstrations and then for the West
Side. Built like a fullback; an evangelist for nonviolence.

singin around, you know. I liked the singin, you know. I got to thinkin—shit, they got as much right as I've got.

Now Gerald talks to em too, they come up here and talk to im. They won't take shit. They've got just as much right as I've got, or you've got either. Color just goes skin-deep. They been done so damn dirty, which a white person has got a better chance than a colored person. A man can't help it cause he's black or white, you know? You meet good and bad anywheres you go. They're O.K. I'd just as soon work with a nigger as work with a white person. But used to, I wouldn't work with em, unless I really had to. And I didn't have to.

But I still don't think they should mix. But if they do, they do; that's their business. If my sister married a nigger I'd leave it to her. Now I don't think I would marry one right off. I've done a lotta thinkin. Now I'll admit I went with nigger girls before, but not to marry. Most ever I been around the niggers is after I started goin around JOIN. When I was down home, now, when I was growin up, there was colored people livin beside of us. I liked them, I went to their house all the time, or they'd come over to our house. Gotta be around em, particularly when you live right beside of em. I heard everything about em, like they're sorrier 'n hell, they was sorry and they stunk and everything. I've heared all kinds of stuff like that. You know I just never did take a likin to runnin around with one. If somebody'd said to me I'd be hangin around with niggers, I'd have said, "No, I doubt it."

But now, I don't mind the niggers now. If I did, I wouldn't went down there with Eric* and James this weekend. Or I wouldn't a went over on the West Side with Eric after. Which I was a fool. We went in this joint, well, it was this church and it was all colored people. I was in the back there. They asked what was I doin. I told em I was messin around, so he said, "Oh, we don't like you white people." I said, "Well, I can't help that." So this one colored boy come around. He was in the same gang that come over here oncet. And this guy just kept talkin, kept talkin, said he *hated* white people. We started talkin. So we went out and we got drunk together. And then he started callin me white trash, and I started callin him nigger. Then we was pretty good friends then. But I don't think I wanna go through it again. Son of a gun had a Magnum pistol and got up

*Eric Kinburn, at the time a white Southern SCLC organizer. He and James Orange, along with JOIN, had arranged a weekend gathering of West Side and Uptown gang kids, at a suburban camp. The political talks, if any, seemed to have made little impression, but Popeye, awed and a little hurting, reported afterward that Orange did not simply look like a fullback, he charged like one.

there and started shootin it in the street. And this Pete, he had a knife bout that long. This other guy had a gun. So we go in a wine store and get this wine. And this cat didn't wanna sell it to im. Now this boy was twenty-six years old. Now Pete pulled out this little ole balled-up birth certificate, throwed it down, and told him open it up hisself. So the guy said, "Well, I'm still not gonna sell to y'all." So he pulls out his gun. . . . Don't think I wanna go through that shit again, though. And I ain't if I can help it. If I ever go over there again I'll get me a gun too. I might meet some more of em—that I don't know!

Right now the way this neighborhood is, I don't think JOIN should bring a bunch a them colored people up here, you know, from down there to talk over about welfare, housin in the neighborhood, cause it won't work now.

You can organize the white people too, just got to do a lot more than what's goin on now. Just like here—and I did it myself—me and Harriet and them, we had a meetin with this Urban Progress. Now you can't tell somebody you're gonna be there and then not show up. Cause they got other things to do besides set around and wait. Well, we finally got together on it and went down there, but I didn't stay, I hadda go to work. I just went down and stayed a while. They was talkin bout Harriet tellin what the situation was and what we wanted. But we ain't got it yet. Eventually I think we'll get it.

It was about these alcoholics over here. Before they go to the hospital, I think they need a place to go and they need a place to go when they get back. When they get out of the hospital, say they got thirty cents to ketch the bus. They ain't got nowhere to go or nothin to do so they start right back out on the streets, drinkin again. I'd like to see em get a place, you know, somethin like a store or somethin. Let them get somethin to do besides stand around on the street. Cause it's gettin cold now. That sleepin in a car ain't no good. They're all fit to be froze to death.

I got friends. I know some of em from down home. And the boys I took a likin to em, and I just started hangin out with em. We just started drinkin around together.

Now some a the others around, they always fucked me and I always fucked them. Was just like this guy who's comin up to JOIN tonight, the guy they call—he calls himself Jesse James. Now he thinks he's bad-ass but he's gonna get cooled down when he comes up 'ere tonight. Rennie invited him over there and Rennie just better not step out there and help him or I'm gettin out there on *him*.

Some people come up and tell you Jesse James said he's gonna whup you and he's gonna do this—Jesse James ain't gonna do shit. I don't even know what he's got agin me, and I ain't looked. I don't even know the guy, I just know im when I see im, from this restaurant right over there. The minute he steps on our corner I'm just gonna pop him with a damn ball bat and get it over with. I'm gonna bet he ain't gonna whip *my* ass. Cause he told Dobie* they use chains and pipes. So I got a pipe *and* a ball bat in my grill. I'm keepin it all the time.

There don't *have* to be a fight. Not if Jesse James don't come over there. If he does, there's gonna be one. He's done started it. By tellin other people he's gonna whip this certain boy and this boy and this boy's ass.

Now Rennie and them can talk to em and try and get em in JOIN. I hope they try, myself. The guys might be O.K. if a person'd get to know em. But I don't want this now, for he done said all I want to hear him say. He's just a goddamn punk-ass kid. All he is.

Here's the way I feel about it. If a person says he's gonna whip my ass, I want him to do it, just to show him that he can't do it. That's the way I feel about it. I ain't done nothin agin the guy, I don't even know im. But if he wants to whup somebody, I like to fight myself. I don't, but I don't take no shit off nobody. My mommy slapped me once and I hit her. I'm goddamn sure I'd hit somebody else. I just don't believe in bein pushed around by nobody—shape, form, color, anything. If he wants to fight, I want to fight too.

People's gonna fight, I don't care where it's at. They're gonna fight each other. Can't find anybody else to fight. It makes more sense to fight the things that's keepin everybody down. . . . But some people you can't tell nothin. Ever think about that?

"SOME PEOPLE YOU CAN'T TELL NOTHIN"

Word of an impending fight blanketed the neighborhood; the meeting was lightly attended. The JOIN corner guys showed up early, Popeye with a bat and a metal pole, anxious that Jesse James show up soon to get things going. Rennie had invited James Orange, who showed Popeye how the bat could be grabbed and used against him. On the spot, Popeye fumed the more. Rennie, he said, wanted to call off the meeting. "I'd just as soon take him on—bust these windows all up, it would give me pleasure." But reveling in their tenseness, and their cause for everyone else's

---

*Another corner guy.

tenseness, and wanting to challenge the students' ability to run the meeting without them, they came inside when the meeting started.

Rennie introduced Orange: "Maybe he can tell us how they deal with this on the West Side." Popeye chortled: "How can they tell us bout the West Side if they don't know nothin bout the North Side?"

Orange stood up, "in case I'm not big enough for everybody to see me." He said the causes of gang fights are the same everywhere—we're fighting ourselves, leaving no time to think about who's got power in Chicago. "I'm not goin to tell you not to fight, I'm going to tell you how to fight. Go out and fight welfare and police brutality. . . ." His eyes narrowed, Popeye ostentatiously went outside. Nothing happening outside. He came back with a pack of cigarettes. He listened with detachment to this goody-goody social worker he had thought was someone else. As long as Orange went on in an abstract political vein, he still paid a mote of attention. But when Popeye became for him an object of the power structure, a reference point for a lecture, then Popeye was on the spot.

"We're going to tear down the ghetto," said Orange, "tear down the slums, get everybody an education. See, the Board of Education has somethin to do with the fact that Popeye wants to stand out on the streets

and fight. The political machine's got somethin to do with it. He wants to fight over this corner—but who owns the building?"

A car whizzed by, screeching around the corner. At this, Popeye and Dobie jumped up, dashed outside, came back in, picked up the bat and club and two other guys, and left again. Their mufflerless car shattered the night.

Orange acted as though he didn't notice, but a couple of women drifted out. The meeting relaxed. The usual speeches piled on top of one another. In a few minutes the guys drove up, got out, milled around the lamppost, banging it furiously. The war dance settled their lesser victory: no fight, but Jesse James had been kept away. They came back inside, sullen.

Rennie gave a report on the Urban Progress Center. Mrs. Alexander, a short, distracted woman with glasses, asked what they were doing about housing. Nothing.

"They puttin all the money in the roads instead of in the families," said Mrs. Alexander. "Fixin up Lake Shore Drive the way we're doin. The cars don't eat."

Jimmy Hopps, an older one of the guys who had been listening with a reluctant attention, interrupted; he thought the meeting should be run by "one of us."

"If you want to run this show, let someone run it who knows something about it. I've been beat up twenty times on this corner right here, and I got the bond papers to show. And Popeye's been beaten to death."

Popeye chuckled. "But I burned my papers!"

"Every time my old lady comes to get me out, I've got a bloody mouth or either or a bloody eye. Ain't that right?"

Mrs. Alexander plucked up. "They're snakes."

"You're damn right they're snakes."

And a woman said she was in the movement because the cops ganged up on the kids. But nothing more could happen; energy was spent in violence and relief; the meeting ended by default. Some people were shaking their heads, others simply hugged the thought that the worst had been averted; Popeye and his friends were, more than anything, puzzled.

Ras Bryant commented:

"I wasn't there that night but they had a big fight out there one night, run in there and got iron pipes and run out with em and all that junk, and scared a lot of people. They said they'd never be back, and they hain't come back yet either. They had about sixty or seventy comin there every meetin night fore that. I know it wasn't JOIN's fault, but see they just got afraid to come back there, fraid they'd get knocked in the head or shot or somethin-or-other.

"I'll tell you just the truth about it now, that they just allow too much drinkin around that office. Course it's kind of a problem to stop it but I'd stop it one way or the other. I'd just tell em plain, flatfooted, we wasn't gonna put up with it and then if they come in there with another bottle I'd call the law on em. Rennie tole em all the time and first one and another'd tell em that the law's done told us if there's another bottle in there they're gonna close this place. But still they come in there and sit right in front and drink it. I've seen quart bottles pitchin back and forth, one and another, across from seat to seat. Now you know that ain't no way. Pull out a bottle and just pass it on, just same as they'd do if they were home.

"Hit's pitiful, I'm tellin you. I couldn't say it was the parents' fault or whose fault 'tis, but now if somebody come and tell me there was somethin wrong with one a my kids, they'd sure know they was gonna get a correction. Whenever I found out it was the truth, you know."

POPEYE ADKINS

I like this place. I like this life up here. I know everybody up here, you know. I just like it, don't know why. But I ain't goin to jail for somethin I didn't do.

There was just this girl ran around on the street. I don't know whatever started her comin over to the house, but she started comin over to the house and all them boys used to take her out. Then I started taken her out too. I was bullshittin.

But finally she messed around and she got pregnant. Then I got the blame for it, cause I was goin with her at the time. So they got a warrant for me. I left and went to West Virginia and left there and went to Virginia, right out a Washington. Got a job in construction, buildin houses. The hardest work I ever done in my damn life, carryin bricks, and 104, 105 degrees out there in the middle a them fields. Man can get two dollars an hour. That's no money, as hard as the work is. My damn hands was so sore they bled. I stayed up there four months and come back. I was just homesick I guess.

I met Patty Jenkins, comin down the street. Different girl. I knowed they had that warrant for me. And she was drunk. And I thought she was over twenty years old. And she had six cans a beer. I give her the money, she went in and bought it. I didn't even buy it. We was sittin over here on the alley and the police come by. They got me delinquent to a minor and they got me for disorderly conduct. I guess that was for makin fun of em. I weren't drunk. It's funny in a way, though. In a way it wasn't.

See, I run. That's what made em mad. I was over in that graveyard. Soon as I seen em comin I jumped. That's when they got mad. They couldn't jump that fence.

This guy Richard come with us, and Richard couldn't get across the wall. So he told em it was my car and stuff, which the car ain't even in my name anyhow. He didn't have to mention my name. That's a true tale.

I come back to get my car and there they was. Taken me to jail. And they tore my seat. And shit, I'd spent three hundred and some dollars for that upholstery. Tore it on the side and I told em, I said, "I didn't put that goddamned stuff in there for you to tear." And he hit me up beside the head. They found some aspirins and some other kind a pills, I don't know what kind it was. I ain't never did see em that close. The car had sit out there for three months, easy as hell to get in and out of. Tried to get me for dope and then they finally found out it wasn't dope.

Went to jail. And they've got the sorriest goddamn jail I ever seen. They won't let you hardly make a phone call or nothin. They wouldn't let me make one that night. I got in there at about nine, and I didn't get to make one till the next day, when I was down at Cook County.

That mornin I got a old salami sandwich and a cupful a water, was supposed to be coffee. Didn't get nothin else to eat all that day till sunup sometime. Late that evenin they give us some kind o' old stew down there. Shit and slop. Then Randall come down and got me out. He brought me $150; I had a $150 bond. See I been livin with him over here bout two months, since I worked last. He works at Wells, where I used a work. He's been workin there for five years now.

Then they got me on that warrant too, see. I've been to court two times already and got a continuance. This guy in the courtroom, you know, this clerk, he pointed me out to this lawyer. And I went down to the lawyer's house and he started talkin; said he knowed the judge good, cause he played chess with him three nights a week. And if I'd come across he'd, you know, fix somethin. He said six hundred dollars.

So I said O.K. So we went to court again and I didn't have the money. I thought I'd sell my car; couldn't sell it; or I wouldn't sell it, I don't know. The girl didn't appear. But the state done take it over. She had the baby and the state had to pay for it. But I don't know whether she's gonna show up this time or not, I haven't seen her. I hear she left with some man.

Which I ain't goin. I don't think I'll go back to Virginia, I think I'll just go home. Split on down there a while. Hunt and loaf. I been back there three days last month, squirrel-huntin. Huntin season just lasts another month, and I'll just loaf around. Cause I know there's no jobs down there. Ain't nothin down there. Ain't too many people down there now; I mean all the young people. I'll hang around, stay around until I get tired of it, I guess, and then cut out somewhere else.

I'd like to come back in five or six years, after this, cause I don't like goin to jail. For somethin that I didn't do. And now when I leave, it's gonna make it worse. I'm jumpin bond. Well, I think I'll come back after a while. Unless I get up there where I'm a-goin and get me a bunch a money. See, if you got money you can get out a anything. That'll be all right. It's the only way I'm comin back.

A month later Rennie and Harriet and another organizer, Alice, got this letter:

> . . . it isn't so good down here, I am pulling 30 days in the country jail, for fighting and was fined $20. Tell —— hello for me, and the big niggar, tell him I'm getting along just fine.
>
> I'll be up after Xmas if I don't get a year Probation. . . . I would send a Xmas card if I could get one. It is lonely down & I am home sick and I wish everyone up there a happy Holliday. . . .
>
> P. S. I wish I had a match so I wouldn't have to fight. Learn Baby Learn.*
>
> Answer real soon
POPEYE

A week afterward he sent for busfare back—for two.

Then he showed up for a JOIN *meeting with his wife of two days. Judy was thin, frightened of a hundred things at once: the subzero weather, dial phones,* JOIN *(which might be Communist), Popeye's rage, houses obscuring the sky. "I never been around a big city before." Popeye was as casual about the marriage as she was bewildered: "We didn't have nothin else to do." His friends were mystified. Stapling* JOIN *newsletters a few days later, one of them said he didn't see why anyone would get married —you can "get everythin" without it. The other nodded; he was married himself for four years, his divorced wife lives on Racine. You get a wife, she starts giving you orders.*

Popeye went to work in a suburban steel mill with a mainly Southern work force, making a little over two dollars an hour. Somehow he avoided

---

*A play on the words from "Burn, Baby, Burn," a song commemorating Watts, written and sung by Jimmy Collier.

the police: Ras heard "that Popeye's case was done fixed up. I heard Jim Day talkin about it. Now Jim's such a big liar I can't believe him." But in the manner that ordinary troubles are taken care of, patched over, paid off, so was that one.

Judy worked for a while but Popeye stopped her: "I didn't marry her so she could work." As she gained the nerve to explore the city, he kept her in the apartment—it was too cold for her, too dangerous outside. Her fear sharpened, focused more concretely on him. It didn't help much that he respected her fear of JOIN by staying away, for he complicated her life by bringing his parents to Uptown and installing them in their building. He tried to accommodate: they moved away, but she remained the object of his violence.

He resumed hanging around with old buddies. Motorcycles for a while diverted him from the monotony, the crashing dreariness of his job; finally he quit the job and began odd-jobbing and house painting. What money he and his buddies had was shared around.

Six months later he walked into the JOIN office. His parents had re-settled in West Virginia; he'd been living with them in McGraws, driving a bulldozer for $2.50 an hour, courtesy of his father's position on the state roads. As for his wife: "I left her right where I found her—with her mother."

We went to the bar next door and drank a beer. Popeye asked about a number of the organizers, Big Dovie and others. He knew about August's march on the police station* and was glad of it, but the young guys now active in JOIN were not his bunch, and his bunch was scattered in jobs, its corner was no longer JOIN's site.

He grinned quickly as he said he didn't know what he would do next. He was not desperate; he had never been desperate. He never came back to JOIN.

*See p. 391.

"Makin' It" in Uptown

From *The Firing Line,* a JOIN newspaper, October 28, 1967.

Interview with twenty-four-year-old Fon Madden, from Pikeville, Kentucky.

F. L.: Where are you working now?

Fon: I'm managing a building right now. I hurt my leg out at Harper and am still getting treatments since the knee operation.

F. L.: Tell us a little about what it's like at Harper (H. M. Harper Steel Co. in Morton Grove, Illinois).

Fon: It's hard work. It's hot and it's dangerous. They push you a lot. I was making $2.37 an hour. There are three shifts. About three thousand guys work there. Most are from the South. A lot from this neighborhood.

F. L.: Is there a union out there?

Fon: No. The company has tried to keep it out. A lot of the guys working there think a hundred and ten dollars a week is good money. They think they can get by, y'know. See, they don't realize that they're really supposed to make more. Guys who are in factories that have a union, doing the same kind of work make $3.60 to $3.75 an hour. But guys think that they don't have the experience or something. So they put in more hours and work harder, trying to make more on the bonus.

F. L.: What's this bonus?

Fon: You get a group bonus, according to the amount of work the group turns out. Sometimes it's good, sometimes not good. Maybe I work hard, and another guy doesn't, so I don't get the bonus. Sometimes the company don't give the bonus because they say there was bad pieces or something.

F. L.: You said it was dangerous work. Tell us about that.

Fon: Well, they don't tell you about the safety rules. One time I cut my finger, cause I had a ring on. Then they tell me you're not supposed to wear a ring. They just say there's a job to do—go do it. They should have more safety rules.

F. L.: What happened to your leg?

Fon: I was cutting steel, and a piece dropped on my leg. There was no cut or bruise, so I didn't go to the doctor. The next day I told the foreman. He said it would be O.K., but finally I went to a doctor. I had to go a lot, and finally had an operation on my knee. I got fired for missing too much work. I'm suing them now.

F. L.: What other places have you worked since you came to Chicago?

Fon: When I first came to Chicago I worked at Warwick Manufacturing Co., in Morton Grove. When I started I was bringing home fifty-two dollars a week. When I left after three years I was bringing home fifty-seven dollars a week.

F. L.: Where else did you work?

Fon: Landreth in Evanston. They make insulation for boxcars.

F. L.: What was it like working there?

Fon: I made $2.57 an hour. I got messed up out there. They laid off guys with low seniority. I wasn't supposed to be laid off, but I was. I was out two weeks. Then the union president calls up, says it was a mistake. He said come back to work and I could get my back pay.

The personnel department said I could get my nine days' back pay, but I'd have to get it by working four days and getting paid for five. I said O.K. Then the president of the union said I was going along with the company. So I told the company I wanted all my back pay at once, like the union told me.

I kept asking for money. My wife was going to have the baby. My insurance was paid up, and the company was supposed to pay the hospital bill. They fired me. They said I hadn't worked there, even though I had check stubs to prove it. Maybe if I had a good lawyer or a good union I could have beat it, but I didn't. I paid the hospital bill myself and never did get my back pay.

F. L.: You started buying a lot of stuff while you were working?

Fon: Yeah, I'm pretty much in debt. That couch cost $927, and that rug about $100. I'm still paying.

Seeing the Rules

1916: Franz Kafka, an employee of a welfare program, wrote:

> On the table, which still stood on the platform as before, several books were lying. "May I glance at the books?" asked K., not out of any particular curiosity, but merely that his visit here might not be quite pointless. "No," said the woman, shutting the door again, "that isn't allowed. The books belong to the Examining Magistrate." "I see," said K., nodding, "these books are probably law books, and it is an essential part of the justice dispensed here that you should be condemned not only in innocence but also in ignorance." "That must be it," said the woman, who had not quite understood him.*

*The Trial (Modern Library edition), p. 62.

1965: JOIN press release:

On June 22, a delegation of nineteen JOIN members, about half of whom were receiving public aid, accompanied Mrs. Dorothy Perez to the welfare office on South Damen Street. Her checks for the past three months had been short of the standard set for her family. And she had failed to receive her most recent check because of bureaucratic errors.

Upon arriving at the public-aid office, the delegation sat down in the main auditorium while Mrs. Perez and a JOIN staff member went to see the supervising caseworker. At the interview, Mrs. Perez got written agreement that her check would be mailed and that she would be paid the amounts she was due for two of the last three months. She was told that a "rule" of the public-aid office prohibited retroactive payments for more than two previous months, even though the aid office had erred for three months. Mrs. Perez asked to see this "rule" and was told that there was another rule which prohibited recipients from seeing the rules.

Outraged, Mrs. Perez decided that she would stay in the welfare office until she was shown the rule under which she was denied retroactive pay-

ment. The denial of a recipient's right to see the rules supplied to him was, she felt, typical of the indignity and dehumanization suffered by one who has asked for public assistance.

Mrs. Perez asked three JOIN staff members, Richard Rothstein, Casey Hayden, and David Wheeler, to accompany her. They remained in the welfare office until they were arrested at 10:30 p.m. that night.

The following day, after the four people had been released from jail, about forty people surrounded the welfare office with a picket line. Mrs. Perez, her husband, and Richard Rothstein were finally shown the rule on retroactive payments. It turned out that Mrs. Perez could be eligible for the amounts owed her; the inaccessible rule quoted to her the day before was not even applicable to her case. The director of the public aid office, under the pressure of the organized protest, agreed not only that Mrs. Perez would be given the money owed her but that recipients would be entitled to see the rules applied to them and that there would be third-party rights at the welfare interview. In view of the errors of the public-aid office, the director, Paul Peifer, agreed to consider dropping charges against Mrs. Perez and her three associates.

However, within ten hours of Mrs. Perez's interview with Peifer, thirteen JOIN staff members were arrested on trumped-up charges of narcotics possession and disorderly conduct. Police pushed their way into a staff apartment without a search warrant and arrested everyone there. Mr. Peifer, in an interview the next day with a minister friendly to JOIN, indicated that he had a file showing that JOIN and SDS were "subversive" and would not under any conditions drop the charges against the four sitting in.

At the trial on July 2, the four people were sentenced to forty days in prison or a $200 fine each. The sentence, handed down by Judge Saul Epton, is the maximum for the disorderly conduct charge and is ordinarily never meted out to first offenders. Judge Epton read from a sentencing statement typewritten in advance of the trial. Almost the entire supervisory staff of the public-aid office appeared at the trial to testify "what kind of a rough pressure organization JOIN is." The prosecuting attorney, from the legal department of the Cook County Department of Public Aid, walked around the courtroom displaying irrelevant though recent newspaper clippings which attempted to smear JOIN staff members with charges of "subversion" and narcotics addiction.

*At this writing the convictions are still on appeal.

The Gibsons: Harold, 40
Charlotte, 32
Janey, 15
Carolyn, 13
Kathleen, 12
Jimmy, 11
June Bug, 9
Debby, 7
Peter, 6
Lynn, 5
Tommy, 3
Billy, 2

Charlotte Gibson, 32

We met her Christmas Eve, 1965, when she came into the JOIN office
—a half-block from her house—for help: "The landlord accused me of
owin rent that I didn't owe him. He come up and gave me a notice to
move out and said that I owed him two hundred and eighteen dollars'
rent, and I didn't even owe him a hundred dollars' rent. I had the receipts
where that I had paid him rent and I didn't owe him that much rent.

"He never gave us a receipt hisself. Then finally he got where that I
guess he got afraid to come to the buildin, that people was just gettin
tired of the way he done, and he sent Lee, this woman that helped take
care of his business. And she'd come, and every time she'd write me a
receipt she would date hit wrong; she was makin my rent come sooner
than what I owed. I kept a-tellin her that it was wrong and she'd just
keep on. And finally she come and knocked on the door and asked me for
a month's rent, and I owed her some rent but I didn't owe her that
much. I told her I wasn't payin another dime's rent until I seen the landlord, and I wanted that receipt straightened up, I didn't owe that much
rent. She got real mad when I told her, and then when she left, he didn't
come by, and about two hours after that his brother come knocked on
the door and handed me a receipt for two hundred eighteen dollars' back
rent, that was a house notice to move.

"And then I got Todd to call, and he told him that he couldn't put me
on the street with my kids, ten children, and he talked real hateful to
Todd, he threatened to tear Todd's tongue out. I guess that they seen

that they wasn't goin to get me out so finally I paid the month's rent, and then I moved, that was when I went home then."

The dingy, stone-gray three-flat building in which Charlotte was living seemed squashed by the brown buildings around it. The front steps were cracked dangerously, the iron pipe inserted as a banister wobbled. The minute yard, though bare, was fenced in: the forms of private property outlast the functions. The hall was dark and the steps darker, and not until the eyes adjusted could one see the potato chip wrappers, Coke bottles, dog shit. During the winter, when the kids lacked winter coats and boots to play outside, they made the stairs their field, swinging from the banisters, scooting up and down.

Charlotte's third-floor apartment was the cleanest in the building. Two or three of the older girls would be mopping the floors or cleaning the younger children; when not busy they moped. The younger children would be watching TV. Plastic curtains, no pictures. A worn "Jobs or Income Now" sticker flashed its unnoticed message onto the street. A new overpriced living-room set covered with bedspreads, another TV, a sewing machine. In her bedroom, a leak through the ceiling over the bed. Two wringer washing machines in the bathroom. Eggs boiling, beans cooking in the kitchen, Charlotte checking their progress or folding clothes, feeding and changing the baby, brushing somebody's hair, fixing a broken toy. She had the high cheekbones of her Indian ancestors (her mother was half Indian), her skin stretched smoothly over them, but she was somehow not gaunt, not prematurely aged, no Dorothea Lange portrait. Her very attractiveness raised her agony to its true proportions: she liked being a mother.

I grew up in a place they call Ackeville; it's in West Virginia and hits about twenty miles from Logan. My father was a coal miner; he spent about all of his life in the coal mines. He got disabled from work mostly caused from the mine. This rock dust I guess they call it, from the coal minin, got on his lungs and that caused a lot of his sickness. He worked in the mines when he wasn't really able to work. But he did anyway cause he had a big family to support, but he just got to where he couldn't go any farther, so he had to quit. Then he went on DPA, they call it back home, and then he finally got on this government pension and he were on it and they took him off the DPA then—before he died. It's been ten years ago.

It was really rough; I had some pretty bad times. Actually I tried to go to school. I couldn't keep shoes to wear and we had to walk a long way to school and we didn't have warm enough clothing and it was really hard. My daddy just drawed a little check and hit wasn't enough to even buy clothing for us. At this time the welfare gave kids clothing but they had a limit. I think it was only two dresses a year, and if you wasn't there at that time to get the clothing, well, you didn't get any. I just went to the fifth grade. I think I went to school a little while after I met Harold. I was fourteen years old when I first met him. I got acquainted with him and we just started talkin to each other. I were real young and I hadn't ever really went with no boys and I didn't know if it was O.K. by my mother or not. So I asked her and she said she didn't see why not, that he was a good boy, that she knew the family, you know, and they were good people and I just started goin with him then from that. And I dated him three year before we married, the 26th of October in 1950.

He was real good to work, he worked in the coal mines and he made good money and we both were just young back when we first married. We just spent it for mostly foolishness I'd call it, now that I can look back and see. Harold is eight years older than me. I was sixteen when we married. He started workin in the mines, he said, when he was fifteen or sixteen years old, and then he went to the navy when he got old enough. I think he spent about three years in the navy. Well, he worked until after we had had two kids and then after I'd had the two children, Janey and Carolyn, he wanted to go to his mother's. We just broke up housekeeping.

I don't know why. She had moved about 230 miles from Logan and he wanted to go over there where she was livin. So we went over and tried to make it over there but it was real hard. It was just farmin work and they only pay three and four dollars a day and we just couldn't make it so I just got where I didn't want to stay over there and live with her, because I didn't think that we should live with her. And we came back to Logan by me nearly forcin him to bring me back to my mother's and I stayed there a while and finally we just broke up. Right then I was expectin another kid and we were separated then for seven months. Harold came to Chicago and he stayed out here without us and never sent me no support of no kind.

Well, finally I got on DPA and after I got on it, it were two months before I got any help, and actually my mother and father kept me. And then I got where that I felt it was a bother to them to stay with em and I got out, after I got help from the welfare and moved to a place they call Lyburn. And then I had my baby, it was a girl, Kathleen, and I stayed there about a month and I moved back to Logan. I think she was about three months old when Harold come back then. It was during Christmas and the children didn't have anything for Christmas. I never will forget—

they didn't have a toy or I didn't have anything and he asked me to take him back and things was gettin really rough on me then. I had three children and it was just so hard. They cut my check down to forty-seven dollars a month, which I hadn't never signed the baby on it. They said that she would have to be six months old before they would sign her up down there.

I took him back but I didn't go right with him right away. I waited for a while to make my mind up whether I would take him back because I had went through so much. And at that time one of my sisters had three children and she had come to my house and started stayin with me too and I just couldn't keep em all. So I made my mind up by that, that I just couldn't go on with the kids, tryin to raise em, and they needed clothing and things I couldn't give em and I just came to Chicago then on a bus. One of my nephews come and help me—at that time Carolyn was fourteen or fifteen months old and she couldn't walk by herself so I had to have help. I had the three children and I had the small baby so he helped me out here. Harold had come back here to Chicago and started workin. When I come out here he was a-workin real good, he worked at this boat yard and he were makin pretty good money but I don't know why he didn't send me nothin. But anyway I had to take him back.

First time I ever was out of West Virginia in my life—except I went to Ohio for several visits, you know, but not to stay for very long—and I really didn't know what to think. It was really scary more than anything else. I could just look out and see these big buildings and I never saw anything like that before and it just really seemed frightening.

When we first come to Chicago they were really hard on you, I mean the Chicago people just acted like that they didn't want to have anything to do with the Southern people. And they really treated the Southern people like they were dogs, worser than they were dogs, because they would take dogs in a building, which they still will in a lot of buildings, before they'd take a child in.

I remember us goin to the stores and people from Chicago would get in line and you know Southern people believe in eatin and I think they buy more food than Chicago people do and they would really get mad because they'd have to stand in line an wait for their turn. Then they'd start throwin off on the hillbillies, which they call us the hillbillies. As far as that, we knew we was hillbillies but to be called that, the way they put it, they just made a nasty word out of it. They just kept shovin the Southern people around till finally the Southern people showed em that they wasn't gonna be shoved around no more by em. Well, they just started fightin back with em. In one way, I guess they showed em that they couldn't have this city all by theirself. I think they have got to live with us because they knew that they couldn't push us around and they got where they had to convince theirself they had to be friends with us.

I got to like Chicago. We stayed here for a while and then finally my mother took real bad sick and I had to go back and they were lookin for her to die. But she didn't die right then, she got over it, and we stayed out there I guess about five or six months again and we came back and I started runnin a apartment buildin over on Winthrop and we lived there, I guess about four or five years. We lived there till after we had Jimmy and June Bug and then Harold wanted to go home again. He was workin, a-makin three-ten an hour and he took a notion to go home. We were takin care of the buildin, we had a four-room apartment and we were gettin our rent free and the man were payin us for takin care of the buildin too and he was makin three-ten an hour. He just quit his job and wanted to go back home. I guess that's really when our trouble started about him over not workin so good. At that time his mother still lived in the same place so we just packed up and got a car and we just went on back to his mother's again.

I don't know exactly how long we stayed there but I know it was for a pretty good while and it was gettin so bad. He signed up on unemployment and at that time he didn't get anything for eight or nine weeks after he'd signed up. He finally got his unemployment and he got all of his money that was comin to him, and when he did me and his mother just couldn't get along. I don't really know why, I guess I just took it out on her because Harold wouldn't work. I really blamed her with it, but I don't know if that was her fault or not, now. But anyway I got where I couldn't take it and I went back to Logan again. My mother and my father both was dead by that time and we went back again to try to make it. And he worked around there a little bit and really couldn't find a job in Logan or nowhere out in there. Works were real bad then and finally we sold out everything we had again and we come back to Chicago.

He finally found a job here and he started workin again. I think we moved on Kenmore, I don't know exactly the address, we lived so many different places. Well, I had got pregnant again and I stayed until after we had Debby and then we moved back into this building again, 4829 Winthrop. We stayed over there until I guess she was about six or seven months old and we went back to Logan again.

Then it were gettin really rough on the kids. We didn't have em all in school at that time and he thought it would be better if we take em back there and put em in school. And we went back to try to make it and we stayed I guess about three months that time.

After my mother had died I went back to her home and lived. I knew he would just go in and out all the time but it was a home for the kids. But I had so many it was gettin really crowded—it's only a three-room house. I had six then and it was gettin so crowded so we tried to find another house. We did find one—we paid thirty dollars a month rent and it was gettin really bad, we couldn't even pay the thirty dollars a month rent, and we had to move back into my mother's home again.

At that time the mines didn't hire—they didn't need nobody. The ones that had jobs held on to them cause most of the mines had all shut down and the work was really bad back then.

He worked for one a my uncles with scrap iron. They worked these old mines that had been worked out. They'd go in there and take this steel all out and sell it for scrap iron and he had several men workin for him. We moved into another house and we had started to buyin hit and at that time they had put Harold on ADC. They call it a road program out there. He worked out there for a while, stopped that, and then come back to Chicago again. I didn't want to come back because he was workin on that ADC. Hit wasn't very much but still I could keep the kids together. I drug em around so much that I thought it would be good if I could just keep em there for a while. And we'd stayed there for a little while, we sorta

liked it you know cause the kids could get out and play and it was really good. But he decided he was comin anyway so wasn't nothin I could do.

He come out here and he got a job workin for this Bone Boats it was. It's workin on boats and they took boats in for storage for the winter and I don't know exactly what kind of work they call it but I know he was doin all kinds of work on em. He kept that job steady for three year. I came out here to try to make it again, then. I had eight kids and then I had two more after we came back out here. Well, he stayed for that three year and when hit was up we went back to West Virginia. Actually hit was only summer work and then when the winter comes hit shut down, from November on until sometime the last of May, before it starts again.

During the rest of the time we were out here we usually went on welfare. We had a time gettin on it at first. We had to have references that we had been here a long time and actually they asked us for more reference than they really needed because they didn't have to have all of that. They wanted us to have a letter wrote that we'd been here five years and you don't have to do that. This caseworker that we had, she was really hard on us, and we had been here a year already when we signed up and I was expectin Tommy. Well, I think I was about eight or nine months, it was just nearly time for him to be born and we were really havin it rough then. Harold, he had been laid off from work at that boat yard. They don't pay in no unemployment and he couldn't draw that and she was really just givin us a runaround. Well, one nurse that worked over there at the Boys Club I got acquainted with her, she was from West Virginia and she was pretty good at that time to help me with the kids, and so she just kept onto me and finally I got Harold to go down to the welfare and ask em for help and I'm tellin you it wasn't easy. Well, it wasn't easy to get him to go down there, and when he did this lady just kep a-givin him a runaround for two weeks until he got signed up—two weeks.

Mostly what we lived on, I had a friend that lived in Chicago here that helped me and they gave me food for the kids. That's what we had and we didn't pay no rent at all until after we got it straightened out. But the landlord was real good and he knew us and he knew that we would pay him.

They had started Harold off a-goin to a school for to drive a taxi and he didn't go very much and finally they called him back to work. It was gettin just about time for him to go back to work at the boat yard because they had pretty good weather that year and he didn't finish out the schoolin to take the taxi job. Really he didn't like it because he knew how to drive. Hit was different rules, you know, they had and he just didn't approve of it and actually he wanted another job; they had told him to go and ask this man for a job. It was workin on radiators, car radiators. And when he went in and asked this guy for a job, he asked him where he was from— it was real funny. And he told him that he was from West Virginia and the man told him to get the hell out of there, that he didn't want no people from the South a-workin for him.

I went with Herman for two years. Me and Harold had had so much trouble. I told him I wanted to marry Herman. I asked him for divorce and he wouldn't give me a divorce and he wouldn't leave. So we fit I guess two years or more. I didn't live with Herman, I still stayed with Harold but I tried to get Harold to leave, cause actually I just got fed up and I just couldn't take no more from him. I finally got where I really thought a lot of Herman and I thought if he would leave me alone that I could marry Herman and make another start, you know, but I still would keep the kids. And Herman were really good to my kids, he acted like he was crazy about em. And I believe me and Herman would have really been together today if it hadn't been for Harold, the way he done. He just wouldn't give me up and he just held on to me and the kids and I finally got tired of fightin and I quit Herman myself.

One time me and Harold was havin real bad troubles and I had went to Herman's sister's. Harold had grabbed hold of the baby and tried to hurt Tommy and I got mad at him and I took out the door and I stayed for two days with her, and him and Herman fit while I were gone. I don't think it was really bad; I think it was just more arguin than anything else. He claims Tommy's Herman's and he really ain't good to Tommy. He'll never believe nothin else, I don't guess he ever will. Except Tommy *is* his child.

In the winter of 1966, Harold was again laid off by the boat yard. The Gibsons had tried to get on welfare but the Department of Public Aid objected: if Harold could work before, he could work now. He went back to West Virginia to try again, this time leaving the family behind, leaving Charlotte to weave in and out of the welfare maze, to fight the truant officers who don't understand that snowboots cost food money, to fabricate some sense of domestic normality for ten children. She feared that someday some blank-faced, power-hungry caseworker would take the kids away because she couldn't get them to school, and often complained of her nerves. "The kids worry me to death. Yesterday I was shakin so much I just couldn't hardly stand it."

It took a long time for her "case" to be accepted by the welfare department, which calculates humanely in such cases that the husband is more likely to return if the wife and kids are desperately in need. "The purpose of Aid to Dependent Children," says an official brochure, "is to keep the family together and to provide a good home for the children." "Well actually," said Charlotte, "the caseworker was takin it out on me because Harold wasn't with me at that time and she helt my checks up to see if he'd come back home; that's her statement. But she wasn't considerin what we was gonna eat during that time. She didn't really care, I don't guess."

JOIN helped Charlotte get an ADC check in her own name. The checks came every two weeks. But the welfare department required her to purchase a month's food stamps at once to qualify for what was meant to be a money-saving program; it was impossible. Just before Christmas a "community representative" from the Urban Progress Center came to survey her problems: Charlotte asked help in getting her checks on time. A few days later, Hull House sent some canned goods. Then she got the five-day notice. Helpful Hull House called Public Aid, asking them to intervene to hold off the landlord, and they mentioned they had brought food to Charlotte. Public Aid, having calculated to the penny the family's needs, is regulated to guard the taxpayers' money: what the family can obtain elsewhere must be deducted from the public's aid. Thus the caseworker, figuring that Hull House had provided about two weeks' food, withheld Charlotte's food check for two weeks.

Most of the kids are behind with their grades an awful lot. I had em out on account of this bad weather. They didn't have nothin but gym shoes to wear and they couldn't go to school like that. I've had em off from school, I know for the past two weeks anyway, waitin for my check to come in so I could get em shoes. I had to buy two of the girls shoes and actually the other ones needs em but I couldn't get em—I had to let em go. I've spent about twenty dollars for food and I have to save money back to buy milk for the baby until I get another check. They gave me a card to get the food stamps, was $122 for food stamps and I only got a $125 check. I couldn't get it, that's all. I couldn't take that $125 and buy food stamps with em, which I know would mean a lot more food for the kids. That only leaves me three dollars and I owe the milk man twenty-five. I just don't see how I'm gonna make it.

Once that winter Harold asked his brother to give Charlotte a message. He wouldn't tell her where he was, but he was sorry he'd left her alone.

*He knew how hard it was on her and offered to take five of the kids as
soon as he found a good job. He just wanted her to know that he didn't
leave because he didn't love her, but because he "just wasn't doin no good
for anyone." Charlotte was bitter: "If he comes back I don't know whether
I'll take him back or not. It'll just happen all over again if I do." She
could not bear the prospect of the children split: "Those kids may fight
and everything but they love each other too. Kids is funny like that."*

*Sometime during those months she took in a man. Wilburn was a slight,
rather sullen type from rural Michigan, not unlike Harold but younger.
He had a job managing several laundromats. No doubt he added to her
welfare pittance, he had a car, he could be counted on to take a sick child
to the hospital, and he was company. Charlotte's hard-bought gaiety
seemed to surface as after a long trial. She waved from the window more
often and her face reclaimed a few years. We could not tell if she "knew"
she was only buying time; from her position time was a wraith, a bogey-
man.*

*Spring came, and Harold found a job in a mine near Logan at union
scale, with full medical benefits for the family. He was working a big
seam with a substantial future, and now found himself within five years'
working distance of retirement with a union pension and continuing
benefits.*

He came back and threatened me. He did, he really did threaten me
because he wanted me to go back to West Virginia, and he said that if I
didn't go back that he'd kill me—that's what he said. And he really had a
gun, and he meant it, and I knew that he had went out there so many
times and we had tried to make it so many times that I was afraid. Hit
wasn't that I didn't *want* to go back. I was afraid.

He took the kids. See, I took off and went to Michigan with Wilburn
and we stayed at Wilburn's sister's. I thought if I leave that he wouldn't
take the kids; I never would a dreamt that he'd take the kids without me.
I just can't help it; I been hurt too many times by Harold. I try to stay
with him, you know, for the kids, but I really don't need him. He just
ain't no good for us—me *or* the kids. I tried to live with him every way I
know how. It just seems like it gets harder and harder.

I had to follow him to West Virginia, for the kids. Harold were workin
good. We decided to buy a house, really we didn't have a hard time. So
we finally found this house and then we went ahead and started to buy it.
It was $2,700, and we were makin it pretty good until he quit work again.
Well, they started them garnishees in there on him too. That made it

rough. He'd got old cars, back when me and him was first married, and they turned it in on him—I think it was five garnishees. Actually two of em he didn't even owe, three of em he owed. One was a gas bill, it was only eleven or twelve dollars, but they still turned it in and they turned it *all* in at one time—*five*! They took fifty dollars out of each pay until the last one. I guess they got em all cause that last payday that he drawed—well, would have drawed—they helt it all. What the company didn't get, they did. He didn't draw nothin out of it.

They do that, they don't care. See, we owed the company and they had the right to take it. The drier I got and the kids some school clothes and they helt it all out on us, for the company store. They'd hold it out through the office. I needed a drier so bad, I really should have waited before I even got it. But I just kept a-waitin until I just thought, well, I ain't gonna get none and the weather was gettin bad and I needed one and I just convinced myself to go ahead and get it from the company store.

They give you credit. If you're workin for that company, no matter what they got, they won't refuse you if you want it. They're really good about that. Yeah, they hold it out, but they don't hold no down payment, and that's one thing that's good. Then the next two weeks they hold that payment out on you. And from then on then until it's paid off, every two weeks.

They still had a garnishee to come in there on him, $250 for a old car that they had done took back. That was thirteen years ago. And they had

took the car back! So I guess he just got disgusted and he quit. Actually I wanted to come back out here, I was gettin tired, the kids were needin clothes and I was afraid we was gonna lose our home and we were gonna lose everything we had if we stayed there. He worked every day. Hit wouldn't help anyway because they would hold every bit of them garnishees and then they was holdin thirty or forty dollars out on him—that's every two weeks—at the store. And by the time we got groceries we just didn't draw anything. We was just gettin behind with everything. There just wasn't no other way. But actually he didn't want to come back. He wanted to stay out there. I don't know why but he just kept sayin that he could do better out there, he could do better out there, but I don't know.

You can't get no help down there. It's not like here. Everybody's down and out there, but if you're down and out you just stay down and out. Nobody's goin to care. At least up here I knew I could find someone to help us if I had to walk all day long to get food for these kids. I'm not goin to let my kids starve. It's not their fault that their daddy won't work. They shouldn't have to have his worries or mine either. They're just kids.

I just finally made up my mind that I were comin back and he could stay out there if he wanted to. And he knew that I was comin back and I guess that he just thought, well, there ain't no other way. But they's no use. Just look like every time that we start to try to have anything it just goes again.

Yeah, we come up here in the night and we spent that night just chasin from one of my sister's apartments to the other one. I was just actually on the street when we come up here. The kids had laid on the floor at Olive's apartment, my sister's, and the next day Pearline let me have the thirty dollars to rent the apartment from this man Agee. He promised a rug and he never did give it; when we moved out he still hadn't got the rug. We lived in the apartment I think it was goin on the fourth week before he put a bit of furniture in the living room. He didn't have anything in there but an old piece of couch and he told us to throw it out, and if we had've, we'd just been sittin on the floor.

In this place they's rats and roaches and they don't do anything to the building, they don't do *anything*. Whatever gets wrong in the building, something gets tore up, why it just stays that way. We been here, this makes the second week, they finally did fix that switch to try to get it to stay on for the light. The stove is settin in there in the living room and he told us to take it out but we'd have to put it back in when we got ready to move. All they furnish is the couch, dresser, and bed. That's furnished apartment. I believe this is the worse one I've lived in since I been in Chicago.

"Okay, Mrs. Gibson," said the welfare officer, "you come in tomorrow morning at eight-thirty and you will be interviewed."

"And what are my kids gonna eat tonight? They're home without nothin to eat right now."

"Mrs. Gibson, I can't talk to you about that now, your appointment is for tomorrow morning. You come back in the morning and the case-worker will interview you."

"My husband came in here last Monday and then I waited for two days at the Urban Progress Center and they told me you people would give me some emergency aid so I can feed those kids."

"Mrs. Gibson, we are already making an exception in your case because really our next available interview date is March 7. Come back in the morning."

"My kids can't eat appointments; how are they gonna eat tonight?"

"They ate last night, didn't they?"

"How do you know they ate last night?"

"Well, they're not dead yet, are they?"

"I don't know. I been waitin up here all day."

"Mrs. Gibson, you will have to talk about this tomorrow when you are interviewed, that's all."

It was now 11:30 A.M. Three hours earlier Charlotte and I* had come to the welfare office armed with a letter from the Urban Progress Center verifying that the Gibsons were residents of Illinois, having been out of the state less than one year. It was Thursday, six days after they arrived from West Virginia. On Monday Harold had gone to this same welfare office. An all-day wait left him with a letter to the Urban Progress Center for emergency food, but the Center was closed by the time he got there. So Tuesday morning Harold went to look for a job and Charlotte went to the UPC: forms to fill out, questions to be answered. After, they gave her some bread, milk, and soup and told her to come back the next morning. Three days of sitting, waiting, telling caseworkers again how many children she had and when they were all born and how much her husband was making (at the job he didn't have) and how much they paid for rent; being advised to put her children in school right away; "tell the landlord you need more heat." By Wednesday night she had a $10 food order for her family of eleven. Harold got a job but he wouldn't be paid for two weeks; he quit.

*N. H.

On Friday morning it was 10 degrees below zero as Charlotte and I set out again for the welfare office. Charlotte had no stockings, no scarf, and only one button left on her spring coat. I hadn't been able to locate a car that was running in the subzero weather and we would have to walk from the subway. What did she want to do? "Ain't got no choice; I have to go try to get these kids some food. I've froze before." We arrived at the welfare office at 8:30; at 2:30 Charlotte received a $30 check for rent and another $21 for food, calculated at slightly under the standard rate of 22 cents per person per meal. The regular check "ought to" arrive Monday, but the caseworker said, "We can't be sure." Clothing would require an investigation of what she already owned. Presumably she had walked in subzero weather without boots, gloves, or scarf to trick them: you can't trust these people.

But indeed she had lied. She told them all her children, but for the now-married Janey, were with her. Janey at fourteen had married in West Virginia during the last stay and was living with her husband in Ohio. The baby had been sick when Charlotte left for Chicago, so she had left him with Janey; besides, Janey was forlorn without young children in her new house. But had Charlotte leveled with welfare they would have assumed that she was "an unfit mother"; or that Janey could support Billy, therefore Janey could support other members of the family; or that Charlotte was trying to get extra money; or some combination of these suspicions. When the investigator came to count heads, she would have to compose a new lie, her only choice a choice among lies.

Monday Charlotte called to say that the check hadn't come. The truant officer had come, though, wanting to know why the kids weren't in school. They were out of food, the three days at 22 cents a meal having elapsed, and some of that money had gone for washing, since the kids had very few clothes to rotate. (Later she spent $33 for a washing machine: "I'd rather starve than to have dirty clothes lyin all around," said this slum mother. Consider whether she should be callous or unkempt; that was her choice. If she "qualified" for a laundry allowance, she was not told.)

Tuesday a check came for $62 (still more under 22 cents a meal, this time for nine days), and a bright-eyed investigator to check the number of children and the clothing they needed. "I just kept talkin and talkin to him; I didn't know what else to do till I got him confused. He gave up countin em after six. I just kept talkin and talkin to him and after he got to six he just put his coat back on. I said, 'There's one yonder you didn't get, and here's another,' and he was so confused he just quit askin how many there were and asked me what clothes did they need so they could all go to school. He was real nice and he told me not all caseworkers were bad. I said, 'Well, maybe they aren't all bad but those I get sure are.' "

Charlotte finally began to get checks regularly; the kids went to school; these were the only regularities. They were not "settled." "Home" was still West Virginia. They had left most of their belongings in their house, pending the mythic return. Harold could no longer dream of working in West Virginia, with the prospect of more garnishments to steal the first decisive paycheck; not with the family to feed. The social security number that was his ticket to a job was also a tipoff to the bill collectors.

But they reached him even in Chicago. The big Buick that had taken him to Chicago was plucked away a month later. Harold said he had put $1,200 into payments. Standard business practice is to count these payments for the use of the car, but ownership is something different, something special, all or nothing. Without the car, he lost the chance for most industrial jobs, located in the suburbs where public transport doesn't reach. Fitfully he sought jobs that would pay enough, but the demand for his skills was sporadic. "I went out to this place in Evanston," he said one day, "but they told me I didn't have enough experience in factories." Finding no place in the market, he let his impetus to resume "gainful employment" waver and then crumble. An unsalable commodity, he spent more time at home, drank more beer. His hard, no-nonsense look glazed. The unmistakable self-esteem we had seen in him in West Virginia, his brandishing of pay stubs, his expansiveness as breadwinner and householder, his pride in arduous work, all decayed with disuse. That intolerance of being "made to do something," which exploded in a work world foreign to Charlotte's domestic world, also stalled his search for the necessary job. Charlotte's understanding of his need for self-respect went on shrinking, as it had to, under the pressure.

"It's the same as before," she said. "He'll work just for a little while and then he goes off. I don't think he cares if his kids go hungry." Her nerves were bad, her blood pressure high, she sometimes felt faint and thought she might be going crazy. She was aging. The despite-everything gaiety she had held intact in the margins of her struggle fell into shadow, an impossible, an obsolete luxury.

At this higher pitch of despair, her cycle resumed.

I thought that we could stay in West Virginia, after I got settled down that we could stay there, that it would be home to us, we wouldn't have to go no more. And then after we came back out here and we lost our house

I don't know if we'll ever have a home again or not. Twelve hundred dollars is all we owed on it. It'll go up for auction and the highest bidder gets it. And the owner told Harold on the telephone that he was goin to put a bid in for $2,500 hisself. And they'll have to go over that $2,500, to get it. This makes the fourth time that the house has been sold since he started to sellin it, and he just keeps makin the money on it. It's really a shame.

The mostly thing I want for my kids is a home, which I don't know if I'll ever have. Cause I've been drug from here to there with em so much that I would really like to settle down and have a home where I wouldn't have to go no more.

Cases

Lincoln Avenue Welfare Office:

"Why didn't I get no check this month?" asked Mrs. Richardson. "My rent's behind, there's no food for my kids."

"We found that you have been living with a man who is not your legal husband," said the Agency.

"But he's the kids' father. He came to see his kids."

"At five in the morning I would say he came to see you, not the children."

"He pulls the kids out of bed when he comes after workin all night. He don't think about what time it is."

"It is indecent, a bad moral influence on the children. We are responsible for the children."

"But he *is* their father, whatever else he may be, and he'll be a-wantin to see them."

"It's right here in the record: Caseworker arrived at nine A.M. and was greeted at the door by a barefoot, shirtless man who said he would wake Mrs. Richardson."

"But he just came to see the children and I had to let him in. He threatened to kill me. See where I'm missin these teeth? Hit's him that done that."

"What I can't understand is how they live with them all those years and never complain about cruelty. Then suddenly they are always being beat up. It isn't logical for a man to change overnight. . . . Mrs. Richardson, did he beat you while you were having three kids by him?"

"Oh no, he never would hit me while I was carrying any of them; he never would do that."

"Mrs. Richardson, I think you want this man around; I think you let him in your house."

"I threw that man out of my house, do you understand that? *I* threw *him* out!"

"Mrs. Richardson, I'm not going to pretend that I believe you because in all honesty I don't. But the Agency must be concerned about your children."

"If you're tryin to get around to sayin that you're gonna take my kids away you can just forget it. You can get off that, mister, because nobody gets my kids."

"No, Mrs. Richardson, I'm not saying that—not yet."

"My kids are mine and you get that straight."

"Mrs. Richardson, I'm going to release your check but I want that man out of your house and I want him to stay out. So don't say you haven't been warned."

"He'll beat the door down to see his kids."

"Just tell him he can't come in, that's all."

JOIN *Newsletter,* May 1–10, 1967.

welfare rights

by Peggy Terry

If you are on Public Aid, you are entitled to the following items of furniture if you do not have them or if yours are in bad condition. This is listed as a "Special Allowance" and you will not get these things unless you demand them.

One bed for every two persons of the same sex 8.00
Springs for each bed 8.00
Mattress in good condition for each bed 14.50
One crib and crib pad for every baby 25.00
A rollaway bed for individual children 20.00
Bunk beds if room is too small for regular beds 55.00

A studio couch (hide-a-bed couch) can be allowed instead of a bed ...35.00
One dresser for each three persons 15.00

One kitchen table for each family 10.00
One chair for each person 3.00
A stove if the landlord doesn't provide one 75.00
A washing machine if a doctor recommends one 35.00
A space heater if there is no central heat (at least) 65.00
A storage cabinet if there are no kitchen shelves 10.00
A floor lamp if there is no ceiling or wall light in a room 5.00
Linoleum if the floors are bare6.95

This pathetic little group of items and figures tells a lot about the injustice of our "way of life" when we remember that Gov. Stratton had wastebaskets in his office that cost $90 each.

... almost every accused man, even quite simple people among them, discovered from the earliest stages a passion for suggesting reforms which often wasted time and energy that could have been better employed in other directions. The only sensible thing was to adapt oneself to existing conditions. Even if it were possible to alter a detail for the better here or there—but it was simple madness to think of it—any benefit arising from that would profit clients in the future only, while one's own interests would be immeasurably injured by attracting the attention of the ever-vengeful officials. Anything rather than that! One must lie low, no matter how much it went against the grain, and try to understand that this great organization remained, so to speak, in a state of delicate balance, and that if someone took it upon himself to alter the disposition of things around him, he ran the risk of losing his footing and falling to destruction, while the organization would simply right itself by some compensating reaction in another part of its machinery—since everything interlocked—and remain unchanged, unless, indeed, which was very probable, it became still more rigid, more vigilant, severer, and more ruthless.*

*The Trial (Modern Library Edition, pp. 151–152).

Lincoln Avenue Welfare Office:

The blue-haired shrew of a receptionist has told the man, "I'm sorry, sir, but you're not eligible until your resources are six hundred dollars or less." The JOIN welfare committee meanwhile has been trying to see the administrator, demanding that special allowances—all recipients' by right—be prominently posted. The administrator agrees to hear individuals with individual problems, but refuses to post the list without approval of the county office: the welfare appropriation would vanish if the helped insisted upon the full measure of their legally available help. She agrees not to force a mother to work, but on medical grounds, not because—as JOIN argues—motherhood is work.

The man, tracing the JOIN delegation with a sudden interest, returns to the desk.

"What are you waiting for, Mr. Andrews?"

"I'm supposed to get a decision."

"She said you're supposed to go *home*."

Instantly a new administrative circuit snaps into place, shunting around the embarrassment. "She said you're supposed to leave here."

"I ain't leavin till I got a decision."

A caseworker at the Damen Avenue office said caseworkers there were told they would get time-and-a-half for spying at JOIN meetings. If a "client" says he is with JOIN, he is to be referred to the supervisor: inexperienced caseworkers are vulnerable to demands.

Early in 1967, the JOIN welfare committee, under the leadership of Mrs. Dovie Coleman, now called Welfare Recipients Demand Action (WRDA, pronounced War-Day), took part in a national lobby against a congressional bill which would force ADC mothers to work. The bill passed and President Johnson signed it into law.

Linda Mullins, 21

Linda made a lasting first impression: unabashed, the "natural woman" of the popular song. She was in the JOIN office talking raucously, laughing in great bursts, surrounded by admiring boys. Her hair was teased but stringy; her pancake make-up was thick and brown, caking to red splotches here and there. Green eye shadow encased her eyes. Her bright-green dress, hitched above her knees, was appealingly tight. She was talking about Harlan, Kentucky; she was new in Chicago.

Linda was in and around JOIN for a long time; she was even elected chairman for a couple of months. But she drifted away without ever really submerging herself. Linda saw JOIN as a place "that helped people." She wanted to help but she didn't feel that she had any real problems of her own: she declared herself her own woman. But she remains a part of the community of friendships that JOIN created.

Right now if Mommy knowed I was a go-go girl she'd kill me. She would, buddy. Now they're old-fashioned in Harlan. A girl, even if she ain't never dated a boy in her life, she was to go out one night or maybe date a boy and the boy would be real nice, you know, and gentle and not say nothin or try nothin with her—if she got drunk or anything that girl would be disgraced in camp for goin out and gettin drunk and havin a good time. They'd think she done everything. I had the biggest name being the biggest prostitute and whore around there and I swear to God right then, you know, I was just out for a good time. But usually most a them girls stay right in the house. I'd go out and get drunk and didn't give a damn what I done, you know; I didn't care what nobody said.

See, Momma was considered a whore too. We double-dated. We'd have a lot of fun and then she'd wear short dresses and make-up too. She worked in Lexington and into Indiana, but I mean they took and they said she takes off and leaves her kids, puts em on her poor old aunt, and a bunch a shit like that, you know, which really she had to.

I was the envy of everybody in school, all the girls. I was real popular at school; everybody liked me over thar. I'd get to wear the make-up and the dresses, you know, the way I wanted to because me and Mamma came from Texas and the styles were different and everything. But I'd wear em the way I wanted to and here they had to go buy what their mother wanted them to wear.

I can say one thing though. People around there, now, they're real religious, they believe in a lot of things. And when I'd walk in the church house the whole thing would seem like it would fall down. I swear! Since I had such a bad reputation, you know. It hurts you in a way to know, even though you don't do nothin, maybe just get drunk or somethin like at, yet you got a name of being drunk to the dogs. And I'd walk in the church house, everybody'd turn and look at me like they'd never seen a woman before.

I first come to Kentucky, I was about twelve years old and I hadn't even had my cherry busted then, and they got out that I was pregnant. How could I be pregnant when I can't have kids? See, I jumped off a motorcycle and I got a tree stump stuck up in me and had to have an operation. I know I can't have kids, but yet I still was supposed to have been pregnant. Boy, I swear! So Momma took me to the doctor and she said she was pressing charges against Ludy Johnson that was takin and sayin that I was pregnant. She was one of the biggest whores that ever walked, her damn self, and I know that for a fact, cause I been with her when she screwed. And anyway Mom was pressin charges against her, you know, for goin out and sayin I was pregnant.

And everybody had that I was pregnant. They was all a-talkin and Momma went and got everybody in that courthouse. Acy Cornblue, the judge, was settin there and Dr. Buttimore was settin there and Dr. Smith Howard was settin there and they asked Momma a big bunch a questions and they got up there and asked me. And I told em, I said, "Yes, I've runned around and I've stayed out until eleven o'clock and yes, I wear my dresses short and yes, I wear make-up. But," I says, "I'll be damned if I screwed." And Acy Cornblue said any young girl that does that is bound to be a whore. And so I just set there and Momma's blood was boilin, buddy! So Dr. Smith Howard took me back in the chambers and he examined me back there and he come back in there and he said, "I am willing to stake my reputation that Linda has never been touched by a man and has never been sexually fooled with in her life." That was just the way he told it, you know. Well, all their mouths dropped open, you know. That just throwed the whole case right out then. Oh, I've been over some good ones.

One time I run away from home. I was about fourteen years old. At the time I thought I was madly in love with this scab, you know, and I took off. I done had my cherry busted and everything, you know, I was O.K. So I didn't give a damn and this other girl went and we was all goin to take off and go up here to Chicago. Momma went lookin for me. And boy, whew, when she did find me though, I was in Frankfort, Kentucky, and she started cryin and everythin, you know. So I got out of that. They told me if I ever run away again that I'd be sent to the reform school, you know, till I was twenty-one years old. But I took and was a runaway again when I was sixteen. I didn't go back home till I was eighteen and when I went home at eighteen, you know, the law told Momma I was of age.

But in Kentucky it's a sin if you go out with a married man *one time*. Now I had took and went out with this married man, but *I didn't know* he was married. Somebody found out about it and his wife come up to the house you know and there was a big bunch of shit went on, but then my name went down to the dogs, you know. But I didn't know that guy was married. It was the next time I had a date with this guy I knowed that he was married. I just didn't give a damn no more because my name was run down to the dogs. I didn't care. I'd go out with a married man and everything else. But then I said, "Well, I'm breaking up a lot of marriages, you know. Why should I do that?" And I quit it. But I mean a lot of the girls keep on—and to spend the night with a man, oh lord, that was the worst thing anybody could do. And also to take and live with a man you might as well die in Harlan. Oh brother, that was the awfulest place, goodness!

I tell you something else that's pretty common now in Harlan. The jail, that's just like being in your own house. I stayed in jail for a year there. I had took and got drunk and smashed some three hundred dollars in glasses right on the main street of Harlan. They had throwed me in jail. I was about seventeen. They got four other girls in there and there was a prostitute in there that got picked up for prostitution. We had this wooden-looking thing for the jail, you know, and them steel bars around at the sides connected with the boys, and they had cut a hole about that big leadin from the girls to the boys. At night here'd come these boys and girls back and forth. I sat there and watched em and the boys would put a chair next to their hole and the girls would put one thataway from the guard so he couldn't see that hole.

You laid down at night and count the cockroaches. You had to go around the back of the jail to eat and I could walk out there naked and there wasn't nobody say shit to me. They wouldn't say a word to me. I mean you could go any way you wanted to in there. I know boys who'd go out there, had their pants about halfway down their waist. You could see their hair and everything on em, yeah. Well, that was nothin new to look at.

I just sat on my ass, that's all, didn't have to do nothin. Some of em boys they'd bring wine in there and everything. We had one jailer, his name was Mack, he would take and bring us wine and yeller jackets* and everything in there. Anything we wanted, we got. I had a bottle a moonshine in my damn purse when I first went in there. They didn't even check it. They just throwed my ass in jail.

But the food was pure slop—beans. I looked at beans for three weeks one time. That was all—beans and bread.

I'm talking about my personal life right now but I mean I'm not ashamed of it. And I've got the most wonderful mother that anybody could ever have. Now, lovin my Momma, I'd do anything. But my daddy—I once loved him better than anything. But when we was in Japan, he was in the army, I was young then, I was about five years old, but I can remember. He come in there one time and my mother she was sick, she had a flu or something. Anyway she was settin on the couch and Daddy walked in the house with a Japanese whore. And she said, "Mrs. Mullins," said, "I love your husband much and your husband loves me and we'd like you to get a divorce." Well, my mother jumped up and like to beat that woman to death, and her as sick as she was, and then she fell and I started cryin. Well, I locked the door on Daddy, and we wouldn't let him back in the house for two weeks. So he come back a-cryin and a-beggin and everything you know.

I know Japan ruined him because he come back, he would sit and he would drink and drink and drink. He would sit on the couch in his undershorts no matter who would come in. And one time he come in and he'd been drinkin, and he went to bed and went to sleep. Well, he woke up—I was sittin at the table, you know, and Mommy was fixin a cake and she was makin the fudge for it. Well, here was my chair and the refrigerator was right behind it, you know, and Daddy come from the bedroom. Bedroom was right next to the kitchen. He said, "Linda, do what your Mommy told you." He got up and he had a hangover and Mommy hadn't told me to do nothin, you know, he was just dreamin that I had done somethin. And he said, "Linda, you better do what your Mommy told you," and he kept on and he kept on. He come in there and he opened his eyes and seen me, he took his hand and slammed me and I hit the refrigerator door and busted

*Pep pills.

my head wide open. Momma had that skillet, that hot skillet that had that chocolate, and just threw hit at him. All I was doin, I was settin there jest lickin the bowl. Well, I guess I was only about seven or eight years old then; I was a little ole bitty thing. And he got up then and just politely slammed me against that wall and Mommy said, "I don't see, Robert, how I live with ye."

Then he was trying to get Mommy made as an unfit mamma because Mommy told im, said we was comin to Kentucky when he went to Korea. She said, "Robert," said, "I been true to you," and said, "I went through pure hell for you." Said, "I'll be damned if I'm gonna be true to you and do it all over again." And we went to Kentucky, you know, where our kinfolks was.

Sure Momma dated, I know she dated a couple of guys you know, but I wouldn't a told Daddy that. And Daddy when he come back and he was in Lexington he admitted hisself that he had lived with a Korean woman when he was in Korea. And I thought enough of him then to come all the way from Harlan to Lexington to see him, a hundred and some miles, after he got in, to see him. You know what? I was a-lyin on the bed one time. Let's see, it was about a week after I got there and I was eatin popcorn and he said, "Linda, I'm gonna ask you somethin." Now I wasn't dirty, you know, and I wasn't gonna think anything. Now, this is what Korea done to him. He said, "I'm gonna ask you something." I said, "What is it?" And he said, "Can I make love to you?" And I'm thirteen years old at the time, never been with a man in my life. He said, "Can I make love to you?" Him my own daddy! I mean if it was my stepdaddy it wouldn't a been so bad but this is my own flesh and blood, my real daddy. And I started cryin. And he said, "You mad?" He said, "You gonna tell your Momma?" I said, "Yeah, I'm tellin Momma." And that's what Momma got a divorce on, cause I stood up in court and said that.

I'll tell ye, Daddy had me so messed up in life that I was put under hypnosis to see what was wrong with me. I started gettin nervous, so nervous that I couldn't even take and drink a glass of water without droppin it. Went on like at for three months and I had to get under hypnosis and find out the reason was my daddy.

Up until I was six years old he wouldn't let me wear a dress. I'd have to run around in my panties. Yeah. That's why right now I'm so conscientious of my body. That doctor told Momma, said, "If your daughter was to ever get married," he said, "I don't care if she was married twenty years, her old man would never see her naked, completely naked." That's what he told her. Cause you know all my life I'd took and run around like that until I got ashamed of my body, I was so conscientious of my body.

Daddy always was oversexed. Even before he went to Japan and Korea, it didn matter who was in the house, if Mommy walked by he'd pinch her or something like at.

Oh, all the time I lived in Harlan people tried to belittle me. Like a person asked me, said, "Would you go with a colored person?" I said, "Yeah." I wouldn't deny it and they'd say, "Oh man, isn't she awful." I never did stay out later, I know for a fact, than eleven o'clock, and then I was at a drive-in movie with a boy. But if I wasn't at a drive-in movie I never stayed out until later than ten-thirty or ten. So me I was considered one of the biggest prostitutes, the biggest whore that ever walked in Harlan. But half the boys I dated, Fred could tell you and Luke could tell you, say that girl is no whore. But it was just the people, you know, that went around and was talkin.

Oh lord, everybody started talkin about me and I said, well, shit, I'm gettin fed up with this, I'll just leave. And I did.

And I'll tell you, the whole Harlan County is nothin but a slum area. It's not a place to live. I mean a lot of the shacks and everything are still there but you can find very few houses over there that's really nice. And the houses that are nice, they're either owned by doctors, by lawyers, or somethin like that.

I wouldn't advise nobody to grow up there. That's a run-down city. Now, I mean everybody from Harlan County they go to Ohio or go up here to Chicago or to Michigan or to somewhere around there cause there's no work whatsoever—any real good-paying jobs—in Harlan.

They don't have very few mines operatin no more over there, you know. Right today there was a lot of scabbin goin on up 'ere and a lot of people was gettin killed. Now, when they was picketin over at these coal mines, you know, all of this scabbin was goin on. And I was fer the miners' union, you know, that was against scabbin, and me and Mom and all of us went down there, buddy. They was more women down there than men. A woman down in Kentucky is considered just as rough as a man. And this one guy tried to get past Mommy and Momma had the end of a broom handle and she just took and slapped right like at at his stomach and he fell. And she said, "You sonofabitch, I dare you to walk over there." And you know that guy turned around and walked back.

But the few mines that was open, that was just for the people in the camps that had to have coal in the winter in order to live. And a lot of people was wantin to close em down. Well, that was the only support of heat, and it probably still is, as far as that goes.

Well, my mother didn't want me to leave, you know. She wanted me to stay with her. But see, I told her, I said, "Momma, I haven't got no future down here, you know." And she said, "Well, go to Indianapolis." Momma had to go to Indianapolis durin the week and then she'd come in back to Harlan on the weekends to see me and my brother. First she worked in Lexington at the tobacco when it was warmer than it is now. Then she worked in Indianapolis, Indiana, at some factory over there.

I said, "Well, I'm going to leave and get a job." She said, "Well, go to Indianapolis." I said, "No, I want to get as far away from Harlan as I can get. I want to get so far that I can't come back so easy." And so I left there. She still writes me and everything.

Mommy was in Indianapolis, you know, and so I hitchhiked from Kentucky to Indianapolis—me and these two other girls. Then when I got in Indianapolis Momma got paid for two weeks. She had I think it was two hundred and eighty dollars on her and I took eighty of it. Well, the other girls had took and done the same thing—got money off of their momma.

We got picked up by this guy. He said, "I know a short cut, take you there faster."

"Well," I said, "O.K." And he took us on a gravel road. Well, I still didn't think anything, cause you know most of the roads in Harlan and around on into Indiana are gravel. So then he cut up goin through a holler and I said, "Oh, wait a minute, where are we goin?"

He said, "If you don't give in," said, "we ain't takin you nowhere." And it was about three miles back to the main highway.

I pulled a gun out on im. I said, "You're taking me back."

And he said, "No, I'm not." He *still* didn't see that gun.

I pushed it right up there and he said, "Hey, Mack, is that real?" That was the other guy in the car, you know, and he was settin there a-shakin in his britches.

I said, "You're mighty, bloody right it is." So I said, "You're going to drive, buddy," and he drove us all the way to Indianapolis. We was right in the city and left em. And here we was in Indianapolis and then we took and wandered up the drive and she said, "Don't let's catch a bus." I said, "Well, what are we gonna do? I'm tired of walkin and gettin rides." She said, "I know a better way." So first car she seen had the keys in it, we hopped in, drove it about three miles, got out. We did that now from Indianapolis to Chicago. We switched cars, you know, whenever we found em. We switched about three or four cars. Got up here to Chicago and had all that money. Hadn't spent a cent, you know, except for food.

Well, I tell you, I come up here and I mean I thought *everybody* up here was rich and I started lookin and I swear there's a lot of poverty people around here. It's just as bad as Harlan to me. Why don't they have the jobless aid here like they have in Kentucky? President Kennedy had it done all over the United States and he said anybody that needed it, that they could be on it, any state.

My opinion, I think Chicago's pretty nice but I think it could be nicer if it straightened up some of the slums around here. I think every one of em should be tore down, every one of these slum houses. And I believe new ones should be built. And I believe the government should be paying for it and I don't think it should take no money out of the welfare recipients' mouth—not a small bit. I think they should be more money though put on the welfare recipients.

But, I mean, as far as getting em completely out of poverty, I don't care if it's a hundred years from now, I don't believe nobody will ever be completely out of poverty. One simple reason, the government isn't workin. I mean I don't think they're workin their money in the percentage right.

When I first come up here I was livin on 4069 Kenmore and I met a man and he gave me his address and told me where to come. I went down there but he wasn't home then so I was leavin his house and I got lost. I didn't know which way to go and I was all mixed up. So here comes Limey* in that black car. You know that ole rattle trap he's got. He said, "You want a ride?"

I said, "No, thank you." I didn't know what to think of a colored person stoppin me, you know.

He said, "Well, I'll take you up to the store and take you on home."

And I said, "Well, all right."

I was scared you know, but I wanted to get back home, so I said, well, if he says something to me I can always get out, you know. But he didn't. He talked so nice to me and then he started tellin me he was from Angolia and this wasn't his country.

He said, "I gotta stop at my warehouse first."

And I said, "Oh, you own a warehouse?"

*See p. 77.

He said, "Yeah." So I went over there to his warehouse and then Bobby or somebody come in there, had that JOIN button on.

I said, "What kind of a deal is that?"

And he said, "Oh, it's just a community union next door."

I said, "Really?" So I went over there and that's where I met all a them.

Well, I tell you, he was the first colored person I ever talked with in my life. I mean my mother had talked to em and I've been around em, maybe talked to em off and on, but as far as, you know, runnin around with em and talkin to em, I never did. And I always had somebody else with me. I was taught to *hate* colored people. I was taught to kill one if they ever tried to make a date with me. Because in Harlan, you know, you never trust a colored person. And I'll tell you, a white man was to kill a colored person there wouldn't be a thing said in Kentucky. But if a colored person was to kill a white man I guarantee you, if the law didn't kill im he would be hung within two hours.

Well, I don't think it's right cause I figure every man's got his freedom no matter what race or color, but you couldn't tell people in Harlan that at all. If I was to walk down the street in Harlan with a colored guy, I got to tell you, me and him wouldn't get two blocks. Either we'd be dead or beat the shit out of.

But since I been up here, I dated more colored boys than I can count. Matter of fact I'm madly in love with one right now. Well he's not colored; he's half Negro and half Spanish—that's Chris. And then I been dating this other boy named Robert. I think a world of him and he's colored. And then that guy I lived with for two months, he's colored. Oh, I ain't dated hardly a white boy. Because I tell you, I have found out that a boy that's different from you, he gives you more consideration and he lets you have you own way. I can talk to a colored person better than I can a white one when I'm datin em, cause they give me more consideration.

Just like Chris told me when I first started datin him. He said, "Now, Linda, wherever we go we're gonna be belittled. We're gonna be blast-steamed all over hell and everything. But all you have to do is just try to ignore it." He said, "That's all you got to do."

I said, "Well, all right, then." I feel it's my damn life and if anybody wants to ever say somethin to me—I mean if hit had been a boy that say something to me, "Well, why are you datin that nigger," or somethin—I know Chris would kill him. And I also know if any girls was to say somethin to me I'd tell her it was my own damn life, it wasn't nobody else's.

Well, I'll tell you, Chris, he won't date hardly a white girl because he told me too many people up here is prejudiced against em. I think from the way he talks that I'm the first white girl he's ever dated. Me and Chris's a perfect couple; we never fight, we never get in an argument. Oh, my feelings get hurt sometimes when he mentions that girl he lives with, but he don't mention her, you know like "I like her" or somethin like that. He talks about as soon as he gets her out of the way and everything then we'll be happy. But I don't know, I get so hurt and then I get so disgusted. You know waitin *kills* me; I'm impatient.

Chris told me, he said, "Linda, I love you more than anything but you know that if me and you was to ever get married we would really have to stick together. Our marriage would have to be stronger than most marriages." I mean he really felt hurt and bad, people being prejudiced. He said, "What would your momma think?"

And I told him. I said, "Well, I know Mother wouldn't like it."

He said, "That's what I mean." And he said, "My mother right now don't want me going with white girls. She wants me to stick to coloreds and my father is the same way."

I find a lot of people up here that's prejudiced but I mean my momma would kill me right now if she knowed that I was engaged and would even marry a colored person. Oh, wouldn't she though! I dread the thought. Well, I'm gonna tell her I'm married when I get married. I'm going to send a picture back of him and then I ain't goin home. No, I'm gonna send her a picture and I'm gonna write her. And I'm gonna tell her, I'm gonna say, "Momma, he treats me good and he treats me like a human being. He treats me better than Daddy ever hoped to treat me." And then she'll probably go right through the ceiling though with hurt. But I'll take him and stay my distance.

You know I traveled a lot. I been around so many people that wasn't prejudiced when I was in Texas and California and Mexico that I just decided, well, what's the use of being prejudiced? There's no need to. I guess that's one reason why I'm not like that. I probably would be if I had stayed in Harlan all my life.

Linda finally did marry a black—not Chris—and to her surprise discovered she was prone to motherhood. The pregnancy and prospects delighted her. Her husband said, "I guess I've finally tamed Linda," and bought her a new convertible on time. She gave birth to a healthy girl, and seemed to settle down.

But Linda wasn't suited to be a good stay-at-home mother. Rumors of the baby's neglect filtered down her block. The car was repossessed, then her husband was convicted of passing a bad check and sent to jail for six months, and Linda was seen with a succession of white and black men. The last time I* saw her was at the Public Health Pre-Natal Clinic. Her dress was tight and short, her hair a new color, her eye make-up comic-book blue. What was she doing there? "Honey, I'm four months pregnant and I just walked out on my old man. Ain't life hell!"

*N. H.

Don't Read
the Papers Much: II

Courts Back Police

"They's somethin dirty every day comes out against the people."

Poor Will Get More Food Money

A 3% increase in food allowances was voted Tuesday for the 400,000 persons on relief in the state. Action was by the Illinois Legislative Public Aid Advisory Committee. The change, effective next month, is the first increase in the food allowance since April, 1963. About two-thirds of the persons affected live in Chicago. . . . Swank said the adjustment is based on the cost of living. Data he supplied showed the federal consumer price index has risen 2.8% overall and 4.9% for home food purchases, mostly in the last six months.

There'll be peace in the valley some day
Some day
When unrighteousness passes away
Away

Mayor Daley now predicts, anew, that by the end of 1967 every Chicagoan will be living in a home that meets at least minimum standards. He is perhaps overly optimistic.

Construction of an underground bunker designed to protect the vital records of the First National Bank of Chicago in case of nuclear attack is near completion in a rural area 75 miles northwest of the city.

Chicago is one of ten cities where $100,000 in federal anti-poverty funds will be provided this summer for a special recreation program for children in slum neighborhoods.

OEO Official Calls Chicago's Poverty Program the Best

The governor told the press conference that foreign businessmen need not worry about a state income tax in Illinois as long as he is in the statehouse. "I do not believe the income tax is a proper tax," he said. "I am against it."

No more sadness, no sorrow,
No trouble for me
There'll be peace in the valley for me
For me

David E. Brown, Uptown Commission president, in a detailed review of the past year's accomplishments, pointed out that nearly $16 million spent last year on Uptown construction places it "among the top areas of the city."

Since 1958, food prices in Chicago have risen 14 percent. The ADC food budget is up 6 percent.

Uptown News, August 2, 1966.

Uptown Survey Shows Jobless

Five blocks of the Uptown area were surveyed in a human resources program by the Montrose Urban Progress center, 901 Montrose.

The report, released this week, is based on a door-to-door canvass of more than 2,248 individuals living in Uptown. It shows an unemployment rate that varies from 27.2 per cent to 47.7 per cent for all persons over 16, depending on the definition used for unemployed. . . .

"This survey has uncovered large numbers of people who have never been a part of the labor statistics before," said Dr. Deton J. Brooks Jr., executive director of the Chicago Committee on Urban Opportunity. "This accounts for the high rate of unemployment unearthed in the survey."

Of the total of heads of families questioned, or 1,189 persons, 619, or 52 per cent, have jobs. Ninety-two are on public assistance. A total of 505, or 42.5 per cent, are employed full time. A total of 482 are unemployed and not on public assistance.

The range in the percentage of unemployment results from differences in definition. Using the standard Department of Labor definition of those over 14 actively seeking work, the unemployment figure for the survey group was 27.2 per cent.

Two other large groups of persons not seeking work but still a part of the labor force were uncovered. These were persons who were not seeking work because of repeated failures in job interviews.

These two groups, when added to the first group, raise the total unemployment to 47.7 per cent. This does not include mothers who had household duties that kept them at home.

Taking the reverse approach, a total of 39.5 per cent of those responding indicated they were employed full time, and another 4.5 per cent said they were employed part time. The remainder were housewives and students.

Even those who were employed stated they had suffered long periods of unemployment during the last year. A total of 18.9 per cent of the employed had been out of work for 15 weeks or more during the previous year. These are the marginally em-
(continued)

ployed, and many will be fired if there is a slack in the economy.

Average weekly earnings for those employed full time was $71.15, and for the part time employed $30.91.

The relationship between employability and years of schooling also showed up in the report. The median number of years of schooling for the entire group was 9.9. For those who were unemployed the median number of years of schooling was 8.9 years.

Of those interviewed, 63.2 per cent had been residents of Chicago for more than 10 years. Another 29.3 per cent had lived here from one to 10 years, while 5.3 per cent had lived in Chicago less than a year.

Bill and Amanda Carter, 25 and 35

We met first at a JOIN meeting, during Bill's brief period of active interest. He had something of the look of the street tough but it was softened by age—mid-twenties—and a certain vagueness in the eyes; a vagueness that might mean abstraction, confusion, or—a later residual thought—menace, in part the product of the murder of Dr. King. The menace of any single pair of eyes is hard to isolate and measure from within a culture that sends menace shooting through the streets, around the corners, seeming to kick up the discarded newspapers; and in fact what first struck us about Bill Carter when he spoke of George Wallace was not menace at all but the soft high timbre of his voice. He walked slowly and seemed to live slowly, not given to making demands on anyone or anything. The sense of menace returned only one day in June, 1966, when we heard on the radio that James Meredith had been shot in Mississippi. "I hope they killed him, he deserved to die," said Bill, and suddenly his voice took on a definiteness, a punctuation usually missing when he talked about his life, his cars, and his prospects.

He had few friends, spent more of his time with his wife than seemed usual for a man his age. Even more extraordinary, the friends seemed to be shared; Amanda was treated as something of an equal, was at least present in around-the-house discussions. Or perhaps it was only that their apartments were too small to permit an easy segregation, or that few of his friends were married. Most were older men. The only time we saw them with a younger friend, the sense of menace flowed back, even for Amanda. A well-spoken man called Junior, from Mobile, was talking about the shooting of Ronnie Williams* under the el track. He had been in Big Mike's bar across the street, "about half drunk. I saw the brains on the sidewalk, went back in, and I got all the way drunk then." Junior liked JOIN's march on the police station but, "I don't know how we'll ever get

*See p. 394.

the cops to do their job. I don't think we ever can. But if the white people would stick together like the niggers, we'd be in a lot better shape. . . . I wasn't raised with prejudice—I'll sit in a restaurant with a nigger, but he'll sit down there and I'll sit here. He won't sit in the same booth with me."

We asked him about "the situation" in Mobile. "We haven't had much trouble with em cept one time Martin Luther King came down. There was some trouble and a friend of mine got three of us and we went down there. I don't know if he killed any but he must've got one cause he fired a double-barrel shotgun right at em—they were right behind us."

Amanda was direct, sharp-tongued, and, when we first met her, quite gay. As suited the difference in their ages—she admitted to thirty-five—she sometimes treated Bill like a kid brother, a role Bill did not seem to mind. At first her oldest son was living down the hall, a huge and quiet blond of twenty, a truck driver, with a nail-biting wife who looked twenty and was in fact fourteen. Until they went back to Georgia, Amanda blamed him for drawing Bill into the bars.

Our interviews with them extended over three months' time. Often Bill and Amanda were present together for parts of an interview, cross-commenting furiously, and even when separate their concerns fell closely together. Therefore their narratives are presented in a jagged form, with the main voices alternating and the other's comments in italics in each section.

AMANDA

I got married when I was fifteen. Divorced at eighteen. Married again, stayed married twelve years, divorced again. Then I went with Bill for a year and married him.

We wasn't the poorest of people but we didn't have too much. Daddy did a lot of drinkin, you know, but they got along pretty good. You know he never had a public job in his life? Always self-employed. He'd peddle, or had his own stand. Boy, he had it built up for years and years, and then he was in used cars, junk and all that. He bought and sold cars.

Any way to make a dollar.

Always paid cash for everything he bought.

He'd go out and buy a car, and then he'd turn around and sell it, make a profit on it.

He went to school about a week in his life, but you couldn't beat that man out of a penny. He couldn't even spell his name but he never did let on like it affected him.

He was what you would a called an alkyholic. He'd get on a drunk, he'd stay on that drunk for six weeks. We'd have to put im in a alkyholic hospital. He'd stay off of it two or three years, and then he'd get back on one. When I taken him in the hospital the night he died, he kept askin me for another drink.

My mother's a practical nurse, she's sixty-three and she worked till last year, but she doesn't do anything now cept take care of my kids, the ones that's not growed. Oh my gosh, she's practically raised all mine. She's been pretty good about that. She stays at home since she sold her home—our home, that's where I grew up, the South Side of Atlanta. Been in the neighborhood fourteen years, in that one house. It wasn't the best class section but it's not the run-downedest, and all of em had to sell their homes. Colored people taken over and she was forced to sell. She stayed there six months till she got her price out of it. She wasn't goin to take no loss on it. She sold it to a realty company, and then the colored people bought from them, I guess.

You show me a place in Atlanta where niggers ain't tryin to move in. Oh yeah. Boy, it's like up here.

Now actually, this civil rights, it's gettin worser than it was. What I mean, the colored people are gettin more bold about it, you know. For a while they didn't have too much of a chance, not in the South, but now they get more of an opportunity than they did have. As far as I'm concerned it doesn't matter to me, cause they got to live too, you know what I mean. I never would want to live right with em, but ain't have much choice. You can't hardly get a colored person now to move in and keep your kids, not any more, not down there.

They got now to where they got em colored and white goin to the same schools, but my children, where they go, they's no colored kids in yet. When it first started they was gonna put colored kids in there. I said, well, I wouldn't send mine, but naturally they got to have an education too, you know. And in fact my kid has the cutest little colored boyfriend you ever seen in your life. They went to school, not the same school but they went to and from school together and they rode the bus in the mornin but they'd walk home in the afternoons. And you know that little colored boy's neat. And Mike was always shy. He wanted friends, he would give anything to find a friendship, and he really enjoyed playin with that little colored boy. When he first brung him up to the house I thought to myself, Well, I don't know what to say or nothin, but I felt that if he wanted him as a friend, you know, let em play.

But my son Robert hates the niggers so much, I hope he ain't got in no trouble with em down in Atlanta. And he hated Kennedy, boy he did. Well I really liked Kennedy. There's a lot of people that didn't, but I did. I mean I don't have anything against Johnson but I liked Kennedy better. Bill don't like Johnson, he didn't like Kennedy either. I think he's just heard people talk, you know. I mean I don't think he cared one way or the other.

> What would you think of somebody who had good enough grades to go to Georgia Tech but instead took to drinkin? That was me. Took to drinkin, cars, and chasin women.
>
> —Bill Carter

BILL

My mother and father were separated and my aunt took my mother and myself in. I don't know too much about my father except he drank a lot. About all I can say for him. He was a shippin clerk for this wholesale outlet place. I never did know him that well.

I lived with my aunt and uncle as long as I can remember, about twenty miles outside Atlanta. Lived out on a small farm. My uncle's a retired pastor. *Mean as an old snake. Hypocrite.*

Well, it's a fact. Only thing he loves is the almighty dollar. A lot of times after I got my license I'd have to drive for im. He didn't feel like drivin. I'd drive im in to Atlanta, he had to go to the bank every day. Every day. He had a good bit of income from selling books and stuff, different literatures. I think he sold Bibles and different books associated with the church. And they passed a plate around at the end of the service. And I thought I was lazy—damn if he ain't a hell of a sight worser'n I am. How he runs down other denominations! Read the Bible, he'd read a chapter a day, yet he can't take a thing that's in it. Only thing he cares anything about's the money.

Went to public schools through sixth grade, then I was put in Georgia Military Academy. Big idea of my aunt's, thought it'd be good for me. I didn't like it. Had a big fence around the place, you wore uniforms, somebody'd tell you "You *will* do this, you *will* do that." Everything had to be done to perfection. It was just about like basic trainin. I was in there the seventh and eighth grade. You had your upperclassmen over you and if they didn't like you they were rough on you. And me, I was just as independent as they come. Somebody's tell me something and I didn't like it, I'd tell em right quick, which was rough on me.

Then at the end of the eighth grade I was supposed to have went back for a third year. Met the president, I told him what I thought of him and the school, so they got me in another military school in Barnesville, Georgia.

I went down there, it wasn't near as bad. No fence, and you had town leave. It was a little better, but I didn't care for it. Stayed there two years, got caught drinkin at the end of my second year. My roommate was a addict football fan and as long as the team was a-winnin everything was all right, whatever the football team done. But right at the end of the year they kicked me and my roommate out. Nothing was said to the football team.

So then I went to a college prep school in North Carolina, in the Blue Ridge foothills of the Smokies, which is very nice. I had to do a little studyin up there of course, but it's a whole lot nicer place. It's a small school, about seventy-five or eighty students, countin the local students that went and come every day. You had closer supervision and the studies were much stiffer, but yet you had the teachers there to advise you, cause you had two hours' supervised study period every night plus an hour and a half in your room. You needed extra help, they'd call you in at night or the afternoons. All in all it was pretty good. I graduated and that was doin somethin for me.

I went back to school during the summer for a third year in summer school, and wrecked my first car. I'd kept it about six weeks. I don't know what happened to cause that car to wreck. This was one night I wasn't drinkin, I wasn't showin off, I was headed over to the county line to get some beer. All of a sudden we were ridin along, the next thing I know I done flipped over. One thing it was partially due to the road, it was a side road, there's a curve there, you come right into a curve, no warning of it. It wasn't banked nor nothin, and loose gravel too. That's the only thing I can figure caused it. Top caved down, busted the windshield. I drove it to the junkyard and sold it, which was foolish on my part. Good engine in it, good rubber. Sold it for fifty dollars, junk. I should have kept it and put it in another body. I didn't know nothin then. If I knew what I know now, I would have. That was a fast little ole car. It was a '52 Chevy, six-cylinder. It outrun a '55 Ford Fairlane one night.

Then I went back to Atlanta in August, I guess it was, and messed around little odd jobs. Then about first of March I got this call from the city to come to work. I had went up, put in application earlier, I guess around January. They put you on waitin list. I went to work for them about a year, drivin a garbage truck. I liked the work all right. There wasn't nothin to it. I like drivin, and you'd be surprised, the stuff you can find in the garbage. Them niggers, a lot of times they'd find radios—I found me one, almost brand new GE. They wasn't but only one white man on the trucks, that was the driver, and the guys that took the garbage out was the niggers. All the white man done, he just set up there and drove that truck. He was boss over them niggers. Whatever he said, they'd better do it, cause he had the power to let em go, suspend em, or whatever.

At the time I was makin $9.78 a day, that was in '60, but one thing about the job, at the time it was security. Cause after you had been there one year they couldn't fire you without goin before the civil service board. I didn't quite make it. I stayed there eleven months. I was off for a while, had a little legal trouble, had to go to court and get some papers straightened out. A guy swore out a warrant against me, he thought I'd got into somethin and I had to get it cleared up. His daughter had run off, I'd been datin her and he thought I had carried her off, cause she'd been seein me the night before. They dropped charges against me; come to find out later she took off on a bus out a town. After he done had me pulled off the job, three days I was off, he comes over to the jail, takes me over to the judge's office, gets me to sign a release. I like a fool signed it. I could've got him for false arrest, but I didn't know it. I was nineteen or twenty, scared. He had me on a kidnap charge; I didn't know nothin about it.

So I went back, the inspector said, "I can't use you." Said, "You've been replaced." Stuff I'd had in the truck had been throwed out. He said, "I threw it away." I said the heck with it then.

I messed around about eleven months and I got a letter from the air force that I had been accepted. Either join that or be drafted. That was with the air reserve. I stayed about nine months down here at Chanute Air Base, downstate Illinois, takin my trainin, after I finished my basic at Lackland. I took tech trainin. The name of the job was ground support equipment repairman, they just called it ground power for short. It was pretty good for a while and then things got bad and then they'd get better.

I wish now I'd went ahead and joined the regulars, I'd a been better off. Probably stayed in. Cause I've tried to get in now several times and they give me the runaround. My career field isn't open on my level—whole lotta red tape. Yet they're cryin for me. I've heard of several others done the same way. That's the rules Washington sets down, that's what they have to go by. They don't pay a whole lot but I'd be better off, more security, Amanda would be drawin allotment plus the baby would draw one, she'd have the best of medical care. And I would know I would have so much comin in each month, and she'd know she'd have a certain amount comin in.

Come out a there, I messed around down home a while, then I took off up here. I got lost and went to this Salvation Army down on Madison Street, the Harbor Light. Old man there said to me, "Where you from?" I told him Georgia—Atlanta, Georgia. He said, "Why do you people have to come up from the South?" and all he give me was bread and coffee, black coffee.

Then I worked about nine, ten months as a relief janitor up here on Howard Street. It wasn't hard work. I had to serve a five-day notice several times on this one particular family that'd be late on the rent. Either pay up or get out. Didn't bother me none, it was just somethin I hadda do. I didn't know as much about it then as I do now.

I stayed up here pretty close to two year. I liked Chicago. I still like it all right. I don't know, I don't like to stay in one place, I like to move. I left Chicago several times, said that's it, but I always end up back here. I'd take off on weekends sometimes, had to make drill every so often with that reserves. Finally they discharged me from that unit, papers went to Denver, and they never assigned me to another one. It's O.K. with me. My duty expires next year and I'd just as soon let it.

I ain't aimin to go over there and get shot at. I'm a peace-lovin man, I never have gone along with the idea of war. And I have to agree with John Dawson, it could be ended in no time. If they put all these heads of state in a field and give em a rifle, tell *them* to shoot it out, I'd guarantee you that war'd end. It's nothin but political action, people gettin rich on it. That's all war is. Greedy—more power, more money. Communists want more power, more people to dominate. U.S. says you can't have it. Says we won't let you. I'm going along with that policy to an extent but I still don't like the idea of guys goin over there and gettin killed when there ain't no excuse for it. I don't see why they can't sit down and talk things out, reasonable-like. Why's everybody got to be so greedy? I believe if they'd a listened to MacArthur at the close of World War II—he said, "Go ahead across the river, take care of Russia." Said, "She'll give you trouble one day." They laughed at him. She's caused the trouble in Korea, from what I understand. Backed Red China, brought Red China into power. From what I understand, she's the head of the Communist movement. I may be wrong on that, but that's my feelin. Any country that's got atomic weapons I say is dangerous. We're a threat to Europe, and Europe's a threat to us.

I saw a picture here a few years ago, it could very easily become a fact. Do you remember *On the Beach?* Just atomic war, set off accidentally by a mistake on somebody's part. One country thought another was shootin at em and they in turn shot back, and everybody was shooting at everybody. Nobody knew what it was all about. Could very easily happen.

Why can't we be a neutralist country just like Switzerland is? Why do we have to go put our nose in everything? You don't hear Switzerland pokin their nose into nothin. Well, why can't we do it? Your guess is as good as mine. I think all they want to do is sit up there and figure out ways to take the money away from us, and ways to spend it. And as far as I think, it's sposed to be spent on other things than goin in somebody's pocket. Peacetime activities and not war. Tryin to improve the country. Now I say Eisenhower was pretty good, cause as I remember at the time, Eisenhower went in, the Korean War ended. He done what he could to end it. He even went out of his way to avoid war. He had been in war and seen it. He knows what it is. I would have thought Kennedy would, but Kennedy didn't seem to be too much interested in whether he went to war or not.

And this damn Johnson, he's not gonna do nothin for the poor man. He's pushin the nigger, tryin to push the nigger in, to overtake the whites, in my opinion. I'd like to have seen Goldwater went in. Not a lot of good it done. I think the niggers're gettin a little more power than we are, yes. I look forward before too awful long, that niggers'll be takin over a lotta these politicians' jobs that whites been a-holdin. You're hearin a good bit about niggers bein appointed to jobs in Washington. The only place I think you got any control over niggers is Alabama or Mississippi, parts of North Georgia, some counties up there, but very few. I messed around Mobile one time, out fishin red snappers for a month, and those fishermen have the niggers sayin yassuh and nosuh. But most places the politicians just turned it over to em. All they gotta do is yell for Washington, Washington supports whatever they say. The government's givin em all kinds a rights where they won't give the whites the rights. Such as up here in Chicago, for one thing: Nigger can walk in a bar, bartender's gotta serve him, where he don't have to serve a white person. That's a fact. I don't think that's fair, but what can you do about it? They go in, apply for a job, nine times out a ten they'll get it quicker than we will, cause in my 'pinion, they're scared not to hire em, cause they'll have Washington down on their back, they'll say they're bein discriminated because of color or somethin.

I ain't got nothin against em, I just don't want to mix with em if I can get out of it. I don't want to go to school with em or live with em. I'm willin to work with em, associate with em, but when it comes to livin with em or somethin of that nature, that's out. And I think most of em are the way we are, with the exception of a few, makes it bad for the whole bunch. I say they got the same trouble we got, bein overrun by somebody's got a little more money, little more authority than they have. I'd say King pushes a lot of this mess, a lot of em are bein pushed into this civil rights mess. A lot of em don't want it and a lot of em don't know what it's all about. Lotta times they live so bad down, they ain't got much, and they're told they will participate in this, and we'll give you so-and-so, and if you don't we'll make it bad for you and this and that. Lot of em down there just live in shacks and pay an extortion rent.

Give you an example, I was downtown one time in Atlanta, I was walkin to get me a beer fore goin home, just right close to the bus station where they hang out. Old nigger come up there and he wanted something, hand-out. He's an old fella, I'd say about fifty or sixty, you could tell he was gettin on up. He said he used to get odd jobs around to work. Said this Martin Luther King's got things so messed up he can't get nothin no more. He just come in from Athens. Said he'd been on a drunk, but said police locked him up, the judge turned him loose that afternoon. Said he didn't want nothin to drink. Said, "I can go down here to the colored section a town and get all I want, but I want somethin to eat, some money to eat on." So I gave him some change I had in my pocket. I didn't have much myself.

It ain't right. King's supposed to be such a big shot, why don't he do somethin down there in Georgia, stead of runnin around all over the country? But he's out after the money. Tryin to make a dollar. And I think a lot of colored people're the same way. And they got a durn mayor down there, he's all for the nigger. If there's any way he can help em, he's all for them. The white man wants somethin, that's your tough luck. He tries for the power. He thinks there's power, because King backs him. You know King's got a lot of money to put in.

That's my opinion of most politicians. A decent politician gets in there, gets into office, what can he do when the odds are stacked against him? Either play ball or get throwed out. We had one mayor serve twenty-some-odd years in office fore he retired. You know how he got in? Bought his way in, bought his votes. This here nigger that worked on my truck when I was drivin for garbage, he said he voted four times for Hartsdale. Five dollars a vote. They carried him from poll to poll and gave him a pint a whiskey. You know most niggers love the whiskey anyhow. Lot of em make it.

We got two good senators up there now, I think's pretty good. One of em is a former governor. You heard of Herman Talmadge? He worked for the people, but what could he do when his hands were tied? Lot of laws he got pushed through, the legislature rejected, overruled, wouldn't pass it. Wasn't able to convert the public schools into private, to keep em from bein integrated. His father lowered the votin age to eighteen. He said if a person's old enough to go in service and get his head blowed off, said, he's old enough to vote. He had the chains done away with on the chain gangs. He tried to get the drinkin age lowered, they wouldn't do it. I never did keep up too much with it, but now I do know he scraped, before he started out, same as you and I. He built himself up. It's accordin to how smart you are. Breaks fall your way, you can make it; if they don't, no. Just like Russell*—he started out with nothin, one of seven kids. He been pretty good.

I could name several senators right now, several men that'd be good to be in there as President, but you try to get one of em in, you can't do it. Can't get the money. You take Wallace. Wallace, he run for a while, but he was throwed out. They wanted a bigger man, but at least he got the issues out in front of the people fore he got drove out. I'd like to see him in there. I'd like to see Talmadge go in. I'd like to see a Southerner in there. Well, there's Johnson, but hell, I don't claim the sonofabitch no more.

I'm for Wallace. He's for the common people and he's against integration. I don't want no part of no integration if I can get out of it. I don't know too much about what he's done, but you don't hear about all this small stuff. But it have anything to do with the Nigra, it's played up big. Different politicians there in Alabama, they don't want it out, they don't want it in the papers. I say they run the papers. In Atlanta a newspaper opened up, just before we left, named *The Atlanta Times*. There was all kinds of opposition to it, political opposition. The judge that was back of it, supported it—well, it come time for re-election, he wasn't elected. The newspaper prints a lotta news that the regular Atlanta paper, the *Atlanta Constitution and Journal* wouldn't print. That is run by the city hall. That's common knowledge down there. Ralph McGill, the editor of the *Constitution*, and Martin Luther King are the best of friends.

No, we don't have no power and no money. If I'd the money I'd try to do somethin; I wouldn't know what, where to start or begin. Get hold of somebody who knew somethin, let them do somethin about it.

Now the cops down home, they'll pick up the poor class, the workin man, for nothin. That's how they support that screwed-up city. All them cops know how to do down in Atlanta is lock somebody up for drunk or give a traffic ticket. They've picked me up numerous times. "Drunk." If I tried to argue the point, "drunk and disorderly." You go down there on a

*Richard Russell, senior senator from Georgia.

drunk charge, or drunk and disorderly, you don't get no lawyer. They'll hold you in jail. Bondsman won't touch you on drunk and disorderly. If you can't pay that fifteen dollars they'll send you out to that city stockade, make you work it out for thirteen days. The city picks up these drunks, puts em on road gangs, makes em clean the streets ruther'n hire somebody to do it.

Well, it's more on the white. A nigger can live like a king down there.

I met Amanda down there in Atlanta, through her son Robert. He hung out some of the places I did. I went home with im one day and met Amanda. I knew her well over a year before we ever married. I started out takin her and the kids out. They'd want to go somewhere, I had a car, well and good. It'd give me a chance to get out somewhere, somewhere to go, somethin to do.

I've always gotten work down there but it don't pay nothin. Just like I worked for this real estate company for a while. He'd buy up apartment units and then turn around, rent to niggers where they was movin in. He was cheap anyway: he didn't want to pay me. Forty dollars a week, and then he gave me so much on gas allotment. But I was gettin my pay out of it. He'd say, "Paint a room." If I didn't have to I didn't, maybe hit it a lick or two, touch of it. He was usin that cheap water-based paint. Some a those niggers come around, they'd want to buy some of it, I'd sell it. I figured what the heck, I'm gonna get my money one way or another.

He kept promisin me a raise, promisin; that was the end of it. He was a Jew, he was cheap, didn't want to do nothin he could get out of. I just got tired of it, so we moved up here and settled in this area. Low rent, lotta Southern people down in this area. I had worked for a fella here on a nightclub up here one time, just general maintenance man. I was supposed a go back to work for him, he never would hire me back, cause I pushed him for wages.

It's not hard to find jobs, trouble is findin a way to support yourself till you could get your payday. Another thing, I'd see a lot of ads in the paper, I wouldn't know how to get to em. Went down to Illinois State Employment, they looked at my work record, seen truck drivin on it, and they said, "Go get you a driver's license and then we'll talk to you, get you a job." I applied for training, was turned down. I thought maybe with this mechanic's training from the air force, I'd get on this automotive mechanic training, but they turned me down on it. They gave me some kind a test, a bunch a these tests. Couple days later they contacted me, said I wasn't qualified.

I had tried this Jobs Unlimited a couple of times and never got out on it. They always took the old hands they knew first. So I went back up 'ere to Service, Inc., and I worked a few different places. I been on this one job, it lasted two months, the one I injured my finger on. I hadn't been there a week before I messed my finger up. They kept me on at this place—I went directly to the job, I didn't have to report to the office. They'd mail my check out. Say I'd work today and Amanda'd get my check tomorrow. Still just a dollar-twenty-five an hour. And then after I filed suit they got to where they wouldn't send me out when this other job ended. So Amanda went to work, odd jobs around she could pick up, baby-sittin. And I went to work at this plastics place, on my own. This feller lives over here at this 4900 building, he was workin there and he told me about it. I used him as a recommendation to get on. One a them places you have to know somebody before they'll hire you. I stayed on there about a month, six weeks, then I collected $975 insurance and I went home.

Now we were talkin about police down home. Police down there wouldn't carry you to the doctor for love or money. Cite one example, back in January Amanda and I was at this beer joint waitin on the last bus. We'd been out shoppin that night and we'd went down to the beer joint, had a few beers, see some friends of Amanda that hung out down there. Couple old drunks come out of this place across the street, and one of em come up, propositioned Amanda. It was a warm night, she had her coat open, and she was pregnant, as big as a barrel then. You could see she was expectin.

The old guy still propositioned her. Amanda don't like me to say anything in that fashion, she likes to handle it herself. She tried to ignore em. So I finally put my two cents in, I said, "Feller, can't you see she's married? So how bout leavin her alone?" Well, they didn't give a damn, they turned on me. I had a six-pack in my hand which I threw at them and then one of em shoved Amanda, and that's when I turned, which was my mistake. And then that guy jumped me and then the next thing I know they were both on me. And Amanda about six months pregnant, that could have easily messed her up. Just luckily she braced herself.

Well, the waitress over there at that beer joint, she called the police, and I bet the police took about thirty minutes to get there. Said they was settin down on another street. They said, "We didn't know where you were." I asked em to take Amanda to the hospital. She was hurtin. "We can't do it. Gonna have to get a taxicab." Said, "We can't carry her." Another thing: up here, if you get injured, they will carry you to the nearest hospital. Down there they got one hospital regardless of where you are in metropolitan Atlanta, that they carry you down to. So you could be twenty, thirty miles to the hospital. They gotta carry you to this one, in case of an accident, and not the nearest un.

You get better police action up here than you do down home. Down home cops come out if they want to; if they don't they forget it. And up here you give em a call, you will get a response from it. Whether they do anything is another matter, but they will come out.

AMANDA

After I met Bill is when I started goin in them beer joints—they don't call em bars in Atlanta, they's just beer joints down there. And my son, one that was ten years old, had a toy rifle, it looks like a .45 gun. Well, Bill always kept it in the station wagon because we were in the colored section, you know. Well, this particular day he had it in his belt. Walked in to have a beer, set down, drunk one myself and same for him. An old woman, after we ordered the beer, she said, "He's got a gun on him. Grab him!" And I turned around, the cops was there, they put him under arrest for a concealed weapon. They were gonna shoot him! They said, "Put your hands up in the air and don't move." Well, my God, Bill was standin there scared to death, with his hands up. They taken him to court for concealed weapon, drunk and disorderly. But here's another thing: he wanted me to take the station wagon home. And he had about fifty dollars' worth of tools, he had all those clothes, a new pair a boots that he just bought, and

I had a 'lectric clock and some vegetables that I was gonna take home. Uh-uh. I couldn't take it home. Cop said, "You got anything in the station wagon that you wanna take home?" There I was, way across town, and I said, "Yeah, I got my 'lectric clock." If I hadn't got it out, it'd been gone. So he gets out the next day, it cost him fifteen dollars to get the car out.

They hadda impound it and steal everything out of it.

Just this mornin I was up on Winthrop and Argyle, and these teen-agers were standin on the corner. They got em a pop, soft drink at the store, and they was standin out there, you know, cuttin up like kids will. They was throwin the pop bottles to each other, just kiddin around like I used to do myself when I was a kid. And then when I came out of the dry cleaners, across the street, that's when this cop jumped out of the police car and come up to him and said, "Commere, fella." The kid walked over to the cop, and he began searchin him, and found this little souvenir, is what it was. It wasn't a whole bullet, it was just a part of it, cause I seen it, I was standin right there. Put his arms behind him and the handcuffs on im, pushed him in the car. And that kid looked scared to death. Probably the first time he'd ever been locked up. He was a nicely dressed kid, you could tell that he wasn't from a family that didn't care. Well, he didn't open his mouth, he looked like he was just shocked about the whole thing. My opinion of it, he didn't know why the officer came up to the corner to even *wanna* search him. He was just a kid, he couldn't a been over sixteen.

Well, I walked up, I said, "What are you lockin the kid up for?" He said firearms. Well, it wasn't my responsibility to say he didn't have no right to, because it wasn't my kid, but if it'd been one of mine, I'd've spoke up right there and said, "I don't see where you can get firearms against him when you didn't have nothin but a partially bullet." But anyway, there was a girl there, I'll say she wasn't over thirteen, and two more boys, and I asked one of the girls, I said, "You know the boy's address?" And she was gonna give me his address, I was goin down to talk to his parents and just see. And that's when the police spoke up and said, "The rest of you punks clear this corner or you'll all go down." He said, "Get off this corner! Now!" That's what I can't understand. A cop can come up and jump out of the car and search you for no apparent reason. I mean I can't see it.*

*Passing by a hotel a block and a half away, a few minutes later the same morning, John Dawson's brother-in-law saw a cop lead a handcuffed teen-ager into the lobby. Curious, he watched, and saw the cop beat the kid about the head with the heel of his hand, leaving no mark. Someone said the kid was the one who calls himself Jesse James.

The hotel is one of those used as a polling place. On election day, voters have been heard muttering about payoffs.

BILL

I just got tired of it down there. We had figured on comin back and never did make it till about a year or so later. Amanda stayed down there and had the baby. I drove a truck for National Woodworks, deliverin doors and window units, this moldin that goes around the edges. Then I got mad at em and quit. I kept sayin I was comin back, I don't know, finally we just up and come.

We moved down to this Castle Hotel and had trouble there back around Christmas. The manager there was usin the pass key to come in on Amanda a couple a times while I was workin. I knew he thought he was a great lover. He made every woman in the hotel and wanted Amanda. She told me several times he'd propositioned her to come up to his room.

New Year's, Amanda was pregnant then, she later miscarried about the first a February. We had a bunch a company over there, some neighbors who lived next door plus some a their friends and some of ours, couple a boys I'd worked with—they's about six or seven of us, we were all playin around. They jumped on Amanda. So she started takin cramps in the lower part of her stomach, so I said, "You'd better go to the doctor." Landlord just said, "You can't call the police to take her to the doctor; they ain't nothin wrong with her anyhow." He was so drunk he couldn't hardly stand up himself. I called em anyhow. He wouldn't put the call through the switchboard. So I goes to the pay phone. Cops come in, and he offers the cops a twenty-dollar bill to turn around and forget about it. The cop said, "You better get out a here before I lock *you* up." And then later he told us to move, and we started to move, take our stuff out. He plugs the door. We went ahead and moved. We had part of our stuff and went back and had to pay him fifteen dollars. I don't know how much we owed, cause I was payin so much a day. They would not give no receipt there. I just took im at his word, cause I got behind when I quit that landscapin. Worked for them I guess about two and a half months. It was easy work, good pay, up in Wilmette, Winnetka, all along the North Shore. Taken care of Max Factor's place, that's just one. Then I think I worked one day in a week's time—it was rainin and the cold weather got a little too cold to suit me. I just quit.

We got this job out in Evanston, nursin home. Amanda was workin as nurse's aide, I was workin in the kitchen: cook, dishwasher, just general kitchen help, whatever had to be done. Stayed there about a month, six weeks, and then I had a row. Wanted to search me. One old man accused me of stealin some stuff, searched everybody: he didn't know who'd stoled it. All the kitchen help had to be searched. That was it. I quit. We had a big row, he called the cops in, was gonna have me locked up. The cops said they's nothin they could do, said, "You can't prove he stole it." He wasn't gonna pay our salary, so we left that day. We finally got it the next day.

Went to Jobs Unlimited, I worked there a few days, and then I seen an advertisement for the Manpower, said help wanted: deliver soap samples, a buck-fifty an hour. So I got on deliverin Bold soap. I delivered soap about three, four weeks. Then the truck driver got fired for drinkin on the job and they put me on. They delivered east to Broadway and then they skipped and jumped over to Sheridan Road, up to Marine Drive. Had Uptown blacked out. I guess it's cause they figured it's a lower class of neighbor-hood, wasn't worth it.

I'll tell you, I sold just about as much as I delivered. I said Manpower ain't gonna make all the money off me. One day I sold twenty-five boxes. Supposed to be free samples. Anybody wanted to buy it, I was up fer sellin it. We had one crazy character, he worked two or three days a week, he sold it for a dollar a case, that's twenty boxes. They payin you a lousy dol-lar-forty, you get out there and walk in all kinds a weather, cold. It wasn't costin Manpower nothin. They was makin two-somethin.

I'll tell you how crooked these cops are up here though. Right after I took over drivin I had a instance right off Foster, close to the station house. Couple off-duty cops, I guess they was off duty cause they were in their own private car, came up. They said, "It's Christmas time, how bout givin us a little somethin?" I said, "How much you want?" I give em three cases. I said, "You tell your buddies to stay off me." But they'd tell their buddies, they'd all flock on you. I got out on the Outer Drive one day. I didn't know we wasn't allowed on there till I done turned. I was fixin to come off at the nearest exit, so here comes a cop. I couldn't find my billfold, my billfold holds my license in it. He kept sayin, "Well, you know, I should lock you up, less you have twenty-five dollars' bond." All right, no sweat. He went inside, got a case, and he turned me loose, forgot it. Then I delivered some more and they got on me about playin this jingle advertisin Bold. See, I had a loudspeaker on the truck, this tape you had to play, and the police didn't particularly like that. I had to give *him* a couple cases, and then he'd say nothin else to me. It was always willin to be forgot. As long as they can get their hands on somethin they want, they don't care. Nothin out a my pocket. Job run out when the soap did.

When we got locked out a the hotel I went down and talked to JOIN. I had seen the office before, read the signs they had on the window, but I had never paid no attention to it, didn't know nothin about it. They talked to somebody and they said they was nothin they could do about it, being as it's a hotel. But it's a good organization, I'd like to see more of it. They mess around and they show the people how they bein run over, tell em what they can do, to prevent somebody with a little authority, a little money from runnin over em. Never had seen anything like it before. So far as I've seen, JOIN's pretty well certain of themselves before they act. I'm glad to see somebody proppin up, say somethin about rats and roaches. I'm goin along with what they say, checkin out these buildins, findin out violations, seein they get corrected.

Just like they said about this buildin I moved to, 4900 Kenmore. Buildin ought to be condemned. Manager's son-in-law, he said the owner won't let nothin like that happen, he'll go down to City Hall and pay off and give em a hundred or two and it'll be forgot. Just like he ought to do somethin about all this chippin paint and all. We have any heavy rains or anythin, water backs up in the basement. Sewer don't run properly. They have a nigger come down here every so often, rods it out; so far as I can see it don't do no good. Water still tends to stand down there where your garbage cans are. How's people supposed to come throw out their garbage? Manager kept the place clean, come around each week and vacuum and sweep, clean the hallways, clean the bathrooms out, but as for Goodman, Goodman didn't want to put no money into it to have repairs made.

Manager was all right, he was as nice as he could be, but his wife was the troublemaker, she's the one who come around, who got the money, never did give no receipt. Just like this old man Stone. Amanda'll tell you—she overheard the conversation. That woman come around and dunned Stone for more rent. He said, "My rent ain't due till next week, and you didn't give me a receipt from last month, and I need that receipt to show my caseworker when she comes around, show what I'm doin with the money." He kept ravin about it, she never would give him one.

Well, we got behind in the rent. Manager come over, I told him he had no right to come in the apartment. Cause I wouldn't let him in, his wife calls the cops. I'm sayin I don't have to leave. I said JOIN, Alderman O'Rourke, and the state representative all say you gotta serve notice fore you can put a person out, whether they're behind with the rent or whether they ain't. At the mention of JOIN the cops started throwin off against it. "JOIN's tryin to use poor people to support their own government. JOIN's just a bunch of creeps." I told em, I said, "JOIN keeps fellers like you and Goodman from takin away our rights." I said, "JOIN's worth more than all of you." Well, manager said somethin about putting a plug in the door and this, that, and the other. They told him where to go get the notice. Was about two, three weeks later fore he ever went after it. Then he ups and takes off. He collected one more rent yet he never did give no receipt, it was never on the books. All they was doin was gettin enough money from the tenants to cut back out to West Virginia.

AMANDA

My impression of it is, if you pay your rent, O.K., good deal. That manager has never did nobody dirt. He was as nice to me as he could be cause he knew I was a woman stranger in Chicago. He don't own the buildin, he just manages it, see. And if the tenants don't pay the rent, then he has to collect it. Now you know fifteen dollars a week, any man could keep that up if he'd just work regular. One time I owned a home, I mean I was payin for it, and I rented it out. The people got behind on their rent—they had kids. I mean I always felt real sorry for people that had kids. Well, it wasn't two or three weeks, it was four months they hadn't paid me no rent. I had kids too, I was tryin to make a livin for them. 'Nother words, my husband worked as hard as he did for his salary. I finally had to go to court, cost me five dollars for this dispossession order. I never felt so bad in my life about doin that. But in other words, just like here, the world doesn't owe you a livin. You have to get out and make it yourself.

You know when I first came here Bill said, "Why don't you go work for Jobs Unlimited?" I thought to myself, I'll never make it, you know, because I've always had a lotta pride. So he said, "Well, they'll take you to and from the job, and they's always some other girls goin." And that was the only reason that I taken it. And then he said, "Well, if you'll work say two weeks, I'll get a regular job." I'd work two weeks to reimburse him for his carfare and different things, you know. It's been two weeks. We been up here nine months this time and he's a-worked regular I'll say bout four weeks. He makes good money when he gets on that landscapin, but if he works two days a week he's really done somethin real great. He's lazy. I threatened to leave him. "I'll work, I'll work." He worked one or two days. I don't know whether I want to go back to Georgia or what. I want to bring the baby up here. I might go back, if I leave Bill, which I'm figurin very seriously on doin. I think it would really straighten im out though, let im know that I mean it.

Now I had rether, if I had a regular job, work. Two years ago I got a photographic job up here. When I first came to Chicago I was scared to get a block from my house. I even went over there, I was interviewed, I got the job and was supposed to go in the next mornin, and got lost on the way out to the job, and I said forget it. I like to never found my way back from the Loop! But now I could, and it's what I told Bill: if he could work say a week, I could quit this day-to-day, go to the employment office, they'd send me on a job just like that. What I really want to do, I'm not able to work full-time, but I'd like three days a week, or I'd like five days a week if I could work maybe four, five hours a day. I worked a full week last week. standin at a machine, but I have had varicose veins. When I work standin up, it gets real bad.

If I could ever get back to that landscapin, why hell—

Wish you'd *git* back to it!

I'm feelin all right. The weather won't cooperate. Now that the weather's cleared off, I ain't able to go. Well, that's sixteen dollars a day. I could work one week outa that, and then she could get by.

I told him the other day, I can't understand a young man with the education you've got, workin from day to day. He wouldn't say nothin. And you know he went plumb through school. He went to the best schools, private schools. He coulda went to college but he was drinkin, wild. I can't understand it. See, I went through the tenth grade and I can spell a lot better than him. That education's not doin him one bit a good. He's real slow to catch on. He's twenty-six years old and he ain't worked nine months on a regular job. I tell him he talks hisself out of a job. He likes to talk. When you go on a job you do your work and you don't do all that yackin, you know, and talkin.

You know Bill has never even supported our baby. Not one penny. I get sixty-five dollars a week from my ex-husband and I just turn it over to my mother. And then I just send her what I can afford, but as of lately I haven't been able to afford much. I sent im a snowsuit Christmas, and two dozen diapers, things like that. And then Judy, her bein a teen-ager, her clothes is a lot more expensive than the others'. That's one thing, I've always dressed my kids. But with Bill it's day to day. He feels like a big man with fifty dollars in his pocket.

Now my brother, he plans ahead, he thinks about tomorrow. He's got money, he's a boss now at the same place he's worked since he was seventeen years old, and his wife is a floor manager. He worked himself up. When he started in there he was deliverin, just deliverin. Then he got to mix the ink, and after that he kept workin himself on up, you know. You have to work to have anything. Oh, they've prospered, and they have prospered by not havin too many kids. You look at the home they've got. Carpet about *that* thick. I'm not braggin but—

Twenty-eight thousand he put out for the house alone.

Had a interior decorator to come in, match the drapes.

They gotta keep up with the Joneses.

They paid a thousand dollars for one bed. Have you ever heard of that? Big giant-size bed, I don't know what it is, but it's a purty thing. He paid six hundred for just a couch, and that's not countin now his big livin room. Every year they have it reupholstered. Their coffee table costs a hundred dollars. They got a dining-room suit they never use. Just for show.

Couldn't hire em to use it.

Fraid a coffee stain'll get on it, you know. But what's so amazin, when I had my kids, you can imagine toddlin in with six little kids, with all that wall-to-wall carpet and all them fancy whatnot things on the table, you know. I was jerkin one young un this way and one that way. I mean I've had nice homes and all, but they'd come in and track mud just as I had my floors waxed and cleaned. But my brother's kids pull their school shoes off on the front porch when they come in from school, to walk on that carpetin. He had em trained that way—well, you can't hardly blame him for that.

Now he's gonna sell his house when his son goes in the service.

He don't know what he wants.

He's gonna sell his place and buy another one.

Stupid. He don't know what he wants. He's scared somebody'll outdo him.

No, I don't think it's that, I think it's—

When somebody else buys a new somethin, he's gotta buy one to keep up with em.

Well, he can afford it.

With the money he's gettin, yeah. He could borrow for it if he sells some of them cars he ain't usin.

Lemme tell you how funny he is about his cars. He keeps ever one of em cleaned—I mean the motor, inside of it. I mean it's almost as clean as anybody's bathroom, if they keep it clean. And me and Bill was kiddin around—I said I wonder how much it costs him every year for antifreeze, to put in the cars. Six of em.

Three months later, May, in another apartment, Amanda drinking beer, Bill out somewhere.

The reason I drink, I have so much on my mind, you know. Can't sleep, worryin about the kid and worryin about this. That's a poor excuse for drinkin but then too, lotta times I drink just for the pleasure of it. If I felt like I needed help, I'd go to a charity and tell em that I was an alcoholic and I really needed help to get over it, but I don't think I'm that far along.

The baby's one year old and I said I don't want any more. I really believe I'm too run-down. Just like the baby, he was born premature, he just weighed four pounds and one ounce. I believe it's a lot of times the mother's health in carryin a baby. It's the first experience I'd had with a small baby that way. So I had a birth control put *in* me when that un was born. I couldn't hear nothin out a Bill but have it taken out. "I'll go land-scapin," that's all I'd hear. "Sixteen dollars a day. I'll make you a livin. All I want's another baby." I was stupid. I had that taken out of me and I got pregnant right off. Lost it two months ago. Now I'm three months preg-nant and this child has not got a chance. Maybe I eat one meal a day and maybe I don't eat nothin. I don't even take vitamins—why? It takes practi-cally everything I make when I do work to try to catch up with the rent or either buy some groceries. Nah! I'll probably carry about another month and lose it. But who's gonna suffer? Me. I bet he wouldn't even donate a pint a blood. I've known of times that he'd spend his last penny for a damn drink. He got his income-tax check, he spent it when we first moved in. I rented this place myself. I keep my rings out about three days at a time. Hocked em for four dollars. I get one, I lose it. I've got ten of em.

Lemme tell you how Bill does me. If I don't go in, he don't go in. I get up, lotta times I'm so sick at my stomach till I say I just don't feel like it. Well, I won't go. And he won't. We raised so much hell, I said, "Now, if you expect me to work," I said, "I cain't." Now he tries to get me to work every day, which it doesn't matter. I said, "They don't want pregnant women." The insurance company's not gonna allow it. So he says, "I'll go back to landscapin." How long's he told me that? He must've went to the beach.

As many kids as I've had, I think a man ought to really cherish a woman that's to have a baby. They put their life down for a man. What've I got? I'm gonna have to stand on my feet and work? Uh-uh. Now if I had decent clothes to wear I could work till I was probably six, eight months, and make enough to pay the hospital bill. But everything that I work for goes to pay rent, and maybe somethin to eat. I've got clothes in the cleaners I could probably wear. Are they out? Uh-uh. It's no denyin, I ain't got but one dress I can get into.

I'll have to go to a charity. I've never been to Cook County to have a baby but I went there for asthma attacks, and there's a nigger here and a white person here, and they wait on those niggers a lot faster than you, which, when I went in, they knew I was desperate. They've got interns. Let's say in the position I'm in now, if I was to go out there, well, they'd have about three interns come out and examine me, then they'd get the main doctor to come in and diagnose. After you go through a painful examination you're really ready for the bed. Where if you go to a private doctor, you got that one doctor, see, and you depend on im for the whole nine months that you're carryin your baby. You know the hospital bills'll be paid, you know you've got confidence in that doctor. Just like I'm scared of this clinic, I got an appointment but I'm afraid to go down there. They've got foreign doctors, and they can't understand what you're talkin about. These whadyoucallem, Puerto Ricans or foreign doctors, they say, "What you say? What kind of complications you havin? Are you threatenin miscarriage?" I'm gonna have mine at home.

Under the circumstances I don't have much choice. Like I told Bill, I could go back home, yes. But I still got problems when I go home. What am I gonna do—go back down there and tell my people to support this baby and send it to a private hospital, or what? When I'm legally married to a man that's supposed to do it? Uh-uh. Well, really I don't feel sorry for myself, but I could have bettered myself. And I'm a very independent person, and I'd just rather not ask my people for nothin, cause it's not their place.

Many times I've felt like comin in here and cuttin the gas on, just forget it. Yeah, I mean a person has a lot on their minds, but I'm a too much educated person to do that. I know I can make a livin for me and my kids, if I had to, which I can support them. But it's just the idea—if I don't feel like goin to work, I don't feel like it. No, it takes a ignorant person to think just like I was yesterday mornin, about just closin all these winders and just cuttin that gas on, forget it. I come in here—I've sat down a lot of times, say if he goes to workin, I'm by myself, I get a paper, I start readin it. I think, well, me and Bill ain't got no future. What's the use? He's already had one baby, he's twenty-six years old, will be soon. I'll be thirty-six. What future we got together? Oh, it's a lot of problems.

The future I want is someone to work for me and let me be a wife and a housekeeper and let the man go out and make a livin. I mean it doesn't have to be a mansion—which I ain't got nothin now, which I have had. It wouldn't make too much difference where, but I would prefer a surburb other than right in the heart of Chicago, cause I raised my kids out in the country. We raised our own garden. I've seen the time I could send one of the kids out to the garden. I'd say, "Go out there and get me a tomato or cucumber," or anything I wanted, like peach trees or pears and all that. I used to preserve em, you know, can everything. That's livin. I'm not livin now. I'm just resistin.

BILL

I'd like to get back to that landscapin, and I figure on goin back next week, if I can get this rent straightened out. I got hooked on that daily labor, I couldn't get off of it. They pay you just enough to live on. When you're gettin say ten dollars a day, they take off seventy-five cents or a dollar taxes. Nine dollars a day. Time you pay carfare, you buy somethin to eat, you pay your rent, you got nothin left. Most places you go, you have to wait at least a week or two weeks before you get paid. How you gonna do it on day labor? You can't seem to get ahead.

If I get to work I could put some money out on this car of Robert's, put some work into it. I just like to tinker with em. They help out, havin a car. The air force taught me a little somethin about mechanics and I learned a little bit on my own, watchin other people, workin on my own cars. If somebody offered a good price and Robert was willin to go along with the idea, I'd take it down and sell it. I've been offered fifty dollars up here. I think it's worth more'n that.

You know what I think about the car? I think it's keepin parkin space out there. I just don't think it's worth—

It's worth it if I could ever afford to do somethin with it. I gotta have a fuel pump and a generator on the thing. Generator runs ten bucks, fuel pump runs three.

You could work a week and fix that thing. You can take twenty-five dollars and have that car fixed, right? He doesn't care about me or the baby or our baby. You could've went to work. You could have the car runnin. Right?

Yeah, if I could get ahead on the thing. This time next week, this car'll be runnin, I believe.

All right, now what you gonna do next week?

Landscape. I'm goin out a Work for Men Tuesday so we can pay some rent. Then I'm goin landscapin, if it ain't rainin.

Am I gonna have to go?

Yeah.

Oh. Yeah.

If they'll send you out.

Yeah. You know I'm a funny person. If I have to go out, I'm gonna be a pitiful-lookin thing with that old blue dress on. Only thing I can wear.

Well if you work you can buy some clothes, but I'm not gonna be makin but a three-dollar draw each day on that landscapin. Not so easy to get ahead. We never do, we always run out of money. . . .

June. Amanda's legs were scarred, she said Bill had punched her. The next day she turned on the gas and put her head in the oven. A friend of hers had knocked on the door, got no answer, gone around to the back, seen her through the window, and got the manager to let him in. "Hadn a been for him I'd a been dead in three minutes. I didn't care." She wanted to get home now but couldn't track down her son for the money. She couldn't use Traveler's Aid because she had before, and Bill had refused to pay them back from his insurance settlement. She wanted to turn herself in to an alcoholic hospital, insisting she wasn't a real alcoholic but needed somehow to be forced to eat. Bill, she said, was collecting bottles on the beach for money, but buying only beer. He wasn't landscaping. They were evicted.

September. They had moved to another apartment where Bill was getting a five-dollar weekly rent rebate for cleaning up around the building. In addition, a friend had found him a regular job in a suburban factory. Amanda's health seemed to stabilize, Bill bought a twenty-five-dollar car in a bar one night. But the landlady hired another janitor and then suddenly socked Bill with a demand for the difference in rent, retroactive several weeks, payable at six dollars a day. Bill's check was delayed; he had to quit and return to day labor, rather than risk another eviction.

When he had paid all but $27 rent, the landlady threatened immediate eviction. For five days' grace Bill gave her the car key and the bill of sale, as security. Five days later, with the cash in hand and offered, he found the door plugged. Urban Progress Center lawyers told him the building was legally an "apartment hotel," since apartments were furnished and linens supplied; in such cases the five-day notice and its elaborate legal eviction procedure didn't apply. He called the police: they wouldn't meddle in a dispute between landlord and tenant. When the landlady refused to relinquish either clothes or car, he tried to get the State's Attorney to prosecute her for theft. Months later, when the case was finally called to a nonbinding "conference," the State's Attorney found no grounds for action.

They got a room in a fleabag hotel off Wilson, for $4.62 a night. Three days later Amanda decided she couldn't take it any longer, decided to get on welfare, thinking a warrant would be issued for Bill but hoping he would elude capture. Then she relented; Bill himself went to apply for emergency relief. The Damen office sent him to Lincoln, Lincoln back to Damen, where they tried, unsuccessfully this time, to send him back to Lincoln. They finally called his name at 4:20, explained it was too late to do anything. He checked with a neighborhood job placement office, which, sorry, knew of no opening but at Rauland's, the Zenith color-TV tube plant where many Uptown family men and women work for less than $2 an hour. "I told them I wasn't gonna work there. Ninety percent of them that works there is niggers. They've got majority rule. And I've worked there twicet and it's so damned hot in there."

But the hotel hired him as janitor. They stayed there several months. Amanda seemed calm.

December. At Cook County Hospital, Amanda gave birth to a little over two pounds of life. After 15 hours and 31 minutes it died of lung congestion.

POEM ABOUT A DEAD BABY

Say what you can about the crumpled face.
Did it resemble more a wad of tissue paper
or a funny kicked-in beach-ball
or just the face of a dead baby?

   Think. Now tell it deliberately:
   the face of a dead baby.

Report the face without hysteria:
the face had not the hint of innocence,
not anybody's innocence
and not the slackened muscles
of relief or dearly purchased comfort.

   In honest truth: the baby's face was scarred.

It's on the record: the mother said
"That baby never had a chance."
She knows she didn't get to eat enough
and got evicted in the cold too many times.

   In the cold? Can't you say it another way?
   Well no, it happened in the cold.

They shipped the body home air-freight.
For anything under three pounds
it's cheaper than one week's rent.

   That's just a simple fact.

Reveal that at the airport you observed
the face of every ribboned Air Force man
and thought how warm each mother must have felt.

> You watched each one
> but could not see his mother.

Now write this down exactly as you heard it:
maybe Hanoi was bombed today
though the Government said it was only bombing
five or six miles away, as planned.

> Write it down. Don't exaggerate.
> —Todd Gitlin

Walking the Streets: Argyle

Kids play throwing bottles at the wall. Other kids collect bottles: 2 cents apiece. An old man asks how to find Kenmore: he is a block from Kenmore. Three young guys in a car with Louisiana plates, one asleep against the window in the early morning, one reading want ads, a U-Haul trailer behind. Police tell some Puerto Ricans to get off the corner, and one answers back, "You know what happened on Division Street"—Puerto Ricans fought back there in June, 1966. In the apartment of a Mexican, over the Hour Glass Bar ("Where Time Flies"), a portrait of Christ with a bulging heart ringed by thorns, and a *Playboy* centerfold. The next apartment over is adorned with a picture of Elvis Presley. Christmas trees in both. Under the el, a day-labor office. The lady who sells newspapers used to belong to the IWW, Industrial Workers of the World. Foremost Liquors, where the head of the Summerdale Vice Squad was seen buying beer, carrying it to his unmarked police car. Wine, 50 cents a pint. The kosher butchers don't get much business. King Kastle, hamburgers 12 cents. An old man wearing a cap shuffles down the street, his key clanging around his neck. The city has planted trees in concrete bunkers along the curb. Around the corner one kid drops the softball and another yells, "Hey, winehead!" The slim West Virginian redhead in the café is looking for her husband—he left her, and tomorrow is her daughter's third birthday, "if I see him I'll kill him"—and a job. A friend mentions a factory, asks her if she knows where it is. "I don't know where nothin is cept Argyle Street." She looks twenty-five, is eighteen, and holds orgies.

Policeman: Why don't you go back home where you came from?

Lady from Kentucky: What would you know about back home? Sure I'd rather be back home, but I've got these kids and they ain't no factories for women down there. Nothin!

I got nothin to do, I *have* to watch TV.

To be honest about it, I like it better down there in Arkansas. You can't make as much money, but you've got that good clean mountain air and it doesn't take this much to live on.

I've not eaten for nine days in Chicago once. You get real faint.

The golden rule: whoever has the gold makes the rules.

This war we're in now, it seems senseless. The people that we're fightin for don't even want us over there. It's accordin to the news reports and every- thing else. I can't figure it out myself. Course there's a lot of people smarter than I am, but I don't see any point to it. There's a lot of things wrong but it's hard to say how you would improve it, unless—you'd have to almost be a politician yourself to know.

As my grandmother said in plain words, every tub must sit on its own bottom.

I come from the South
I followed the route
To Chicago a big old town

I haven't gotten any hand cream since we got married. I should go out and spend a dollar on some hand cream to make my hands beautiful so I can wash some more dishes?

You wanted that baby, you hold it.

You know they've made it a damn felony to commit suicide. It's my son- ofabitchin life and if I want to take it I'll take it.

If I told a girl I love her just to get into her drawers, I'd kill myself.

I got me hard luck
Couldn't get me a buck
All I got was the runaround

Charges $5 just to write a 'scription.

You get your ass home.

A union sells you a wet blanket and it turns out dry.

You know where the whole blame of the South lays? From the millionaires outa New York. There's your whole trouble. The Jews owns that property down there. It's not us, it's not the South, it all lays in New York. Well, you run all that there big business out of the South and put it back in New York where it belongs, and let the government take possession of that land down there. Let people have it at needs it. You'll stop seein these poor people run around here and have to beg.

If the poor people don't do it, I don't know who will.

You know what I get to live on a month? They give me the rent and then

$33.85. Welfare, disability. And outa that $33.85 I buy food stamps that're $22 worth. What the hell, I can't buy a pair of shoes, I need em bad. The precinct captain promised to give me a hand, get me a little more money so I could live decent, you know, and he wouldn't do it. So I wouldn't vote. Well, he said I was neglectin my civic duty. I says, Up your bucket, mister.

Keep on the firing line boy
Keep on the firing line

I hate the damn niggers as bad as I hate my own guts.

Only work I do is lift these beer glasses every day.

JOIN's burnt down! I'm gonna go tell my mom.

You won't get anywhere without money or City Hall behind you. I work for the Democrats in this crooked city, so I ought to know.

I'd rather steal than take that welfare.

We're gonna get
What the poor ain't got yet
Gonna keep on the firing line

It's the business people that go around saying JOIN's Communist.

We don't want their sympathy, we want our rights.

A few blocks up, a doctor has offices off the lobby of a dingy hotel. A wino had been beaten at the bowling alley when someone grabbed at the bottle sticking out of his pocket and he fought back: a wino buddy takes him to the doctor. The waiting room is always filled, all ages. The doctor is on the phone: "Yes, that's fine, come right over. Come right in." The diploma is brown and cracking, like the paintings of Jesus. In his eighties, his bent body is held together by suspenders, sympathy, a frequent but not fixed smile, no more. A thirty-second examination, then his uniform treatment, a shot of penicillin from an unsterilized needle, $1. Three times he has been charged with giving prescriptions for phenobarbital to young addicts. A woman whose two babies he delivered says he used to have a Loop suite, nurses, high fees, then decided that Christianity demanded he locate in Uptown, living off savings. His name is known all over the neighborhood.

"Now doc," says the other wino, "I know I owe you five and a half dollars, and this is five, but I haven't got it just now."

"Well, that's O.K., I trust you."

"Doc, do you think you could let me have a dollar to get a cab for him?"

"Here, take two. Good-bye, come back any time." He waves. "Next, come right in."

Outside, holding the bills, the wino says to his buddy, "Let's go get a drink and then give blood. I'll buy some gum so they won't know we've been drinkin."

Uptown News, August 28, 1966:

Commenting on the continuing problem [Commander O'Donnell of the Summerdale Police District told a local Chamber of Commerce], "We recently 'put the heat' on vagrants in the Wilson and Argyle areas, arresting 280 of them and another 110 in the following ten days. . . ."

O'Donnell praised the procedure because it usually results in jail sentences of fifteen to thirty days for these men.

We were doing pretty bad until we met up with
JOIN. Way I met up with JOIN was I noticed a
one-armed guy named Ras, he and another guy
was drunk. He had a JOIN button on. That's the
first time I ever heard of JOIN. I never did go to
meetings until a long time after that. And that's
when JOIN helped me out. When I had that fire
at 1047 West Buena I got over three hundred
dollars from the general assistance. It wasn't for
JOIN, I guess we wouldn't have it now.
                                                 —Margaret Jamison

Margaret and Joe Jamison, 26 and 35

Join found the Jamisons a place to stay, first at the Salvation Army,
then with the Dawsons, until emergency money could be wrested from the
Welfare Department. (John Dawson, hearing Joe was a veteran, called
the American Legion for help. They said the Commander was out of town,
no one else was authorized. The Red Cross was aloof.) The Jamisons were
typical of the many Uptown couples who kept join in the back of their
minds—until they needed help. When join assisted—whether snaking
through the welfare bureaucracy, providing a lawyer, prodding a landlord,
fighting an illegal eviction—they became activists, taking on the agencies
in behalf of other people in similar crises. Margaret often immersed herself
in join activity: she was as articulate as she was sharp-tongued, and relished
confrontations with power. She saw a movement of the poor as more than
the mutual extension of favors, and evangelized at times so fervently that
one friend called her a fanatic.

Margaret Jamison, a native of Chicago, is physically and otherwise the
dominant member of the family of five. She goes where she pleases, does
what she wants, and leaves the taciturn Joe to tend to the children. The
following narrative is hers unless otherwise stated.

I was six weeks old, my mother threw me out of the house and home. Put
me in Illinois Children's Home and Aid Society, where they put me down
for adoption. I went from one house to another until I finally met up with

some people named Peters. I had it pretty good except for one thing. They'd take me and beat me every day for no reason at all. And they wouldn't teach me nothing. But they'd feed me and clothe me and give me a place to sleep and send me off to school. That's all they would do. I ran away from home cause of them. Told my foster mother, "I'm going to leave you either one way or the other and I'm going to find my mother." Now I regret it.

A caseworker from the Children's Aid Society told me that she wasn't my mother; she was my foster mother and my real mother was living. So, through her, I got my birth certificate and I found out who my mother was. And I went to the Bureau of Missing Persons and I found out where my mother was. And she kicks me away just like everything else. She told me to get out of her house and stay out. So I went to my girlfriend's house. I came to school every day but I didn't live with my foster mother for a week. She had the police on my tail and she was almost ready to put me in jail for running away. I had two sisters besides me and they could get anything in the world they wanted, but not Margaret.

Fifteen years old, I met up with a cop. Cop introduced me to a man twenty-seven years old; we started going steady. I was crazy about him; he was crazy about me. I started going steady with the man and I got pregnant by him. And my foster mother found out not too long—it took six weeks to find out that I didn't come around. She took me to the doctor, found out I was pregnant; she put me away. Got put away in an institution. It's a Catholic place for unwed mothers, the House of the Good Shepherd. They put me away for one year.

Get up at seven A.M. At seven-thirty you had to be down at the dispensary; you were there till eight and then you go back to your room, to the dorm. And you had to do your work there, clean your beds up, sweep and mop and all that you were required to do. Then you went to school at nine o'clock, stayed there till twelve o'clock. Went down to lunch and then you went back to school at one o'clock. We got out of school at three o'clock and then we had to go and sit in the recreation room till five o'clock. Do your homework if you had to and then at five o'clock you could go eat. And about five-thirty when you was through eating, dishes had to be washed. Then you were required to do your duty there—mop or sweep or whatever you were told. And from six till eight you could go to the recreation room or you could go read books in the library or something. Eight o'clock you had to hit that bed. If you didn't hit that bed at eight and the lights didn't go out by eight-thirty you would be taken down and put in the hole for one night. And they would take you out of the hole the next morning and send you off to school without anything to eat.

It was dark in the hole just like a dungeon. No lights in there. A little door with a padlock on it on the outside and the windows were at least fifty feet; you couldn't see nothing. You slept in the dark. And they had rats there. That was a terrible place to be.

You were also required to go to church every day and if you didn't go to church every day, they'd take you and put you in the corner and they'd whip you. They didn't care how you felt, they'd whip you. I ain't got nothing against religion, but they tried to transform me from a Protestant to a Catholic.

They'd punish you severely anytime they wanted to. They wouldn't have no reason, just to get mad at you—they'd punish you. And if you didn't do as they say, they'd punish you too. Just like a sittin duck in a gallery.

In fact they made me lose my baby there. They made me scrub these concrete floors, stairs, I should say, and one day I fell down a flight of stairs and hurt myself and lost the baby. And all they did was say, "Well, we're sorry." They didn't realize how much it hurt. They didn't care either.

I didn't hardly get no visitors, my foster mother came once or twice and that was it. I never got to go out. I stayed in that place for 365 days of the year. All you could do was look at walls and think about everything else. And if your parents didn't come, you'd feel like going upstairs in your room and crying cause they didn't come to see you. I know mine didn't care for me; they never came to see me. I'd think about my family, if they loved me. I'd thing about my friends in school. I'd miss everything that happened at home. I would think it wasn't nothing but a prison. In fact, I tried to escape. Got as far as the recreation room which is about twenty-five feet away from the front door and they caught me. People'd feel like escaping, and they had a big high wall of concrete. They had wire, barbed wire around it. You could try to escape but they had that barbed wire on constantly, every day and night. Get shocked to death; wouldn't make it over that damn wall.

I served probation for one year. I was sent to Wheaton, Illinois, and I worked in a nursing home. And I only got twenty dollars a week and room and board. I guess that's when my poor life started. When I got out I went down to Clark Street. That's the first place I hit cause my mother was from Clark Street. And I became an alcoholic and a prostitute. I didn't make much money prostituting and I drank all my money up for alcohol.

When I was eighteen years old I was on Wilson and Kenmore. I got me a boy friend up here at 928 W. Wilson who used to come up here all the time. He was a soldier boy from Fort Leonard Wood, Missouri, and one day he got me drunk, knocked me up and gave me a baby. I went back to Clark Street cause he chased me down there. Cause he told me I was a tramp and no good, I was chased down to Clark Street and begin my life over again.

I didn't care what happened to me. I lived in these old dumps on Clark Street and that's where I met my husband. I married my husband two weeks after I met him. I didn't even have much clothes on my back but at that time he was working and he would buy me what he could afford. Two months later after I met him I—I bore a baby. He put it in his name and he raised it for seven months.

JOE

I grew up pretty hard. My father was sick off and on all his life. He had ulcers for seventeen years, then they turned into cancer and killed him. One time my father got sick and mother was pickin cotton for fifty cents a day and feedin eight of us in the family. There was me and her and my sister and my brother and my aunt and uncle and his and her two kids all livin on fifty cents a day. That was back in the first years of Roosevelt. My father was sick and went to the hospital and Mom had to run my aunt and uncle off. Times got so hard we got down to one piece of corn-bread in the house, and it watersoaked when my sister puddled it.

Right after my father died I had to quit school when I was ten years old and start washing dishes. But during the time my father was living I attended school and always had lunch, such as it was. Sometimes they consisted of nothing more than cold fried potatoes or cold gravy on a cold biscuit. I never had decent clothes like no other kids. Course I don't blame my father for that cause he was sick off and on all his life.

And then people say times was so good under Roosevelt. I've had better times all my life under a Republican than I ever did under a Democrat. A Democrat ain't done nothin but go out of his way to give me a hard time. I've been kicked around from post to pillar. They even sent me overseas and like to got me killed.

I volunteered three times in World War II and was drafted three times, rejected six times. I thought I never would make the army and then I got myself a good job and when I didn't want to go in, then they took me, sent me to Korea. Then after I was in the army seventeen months they said I wasn't suitable for the army. It took em a hell of a long time to find out, didn't it? They said I couldn't follow orders or nothin. Why did they send me overseas then? Why did they send me overseas and let my hands get frostbitten and get shell-shocked and all a that?

They promised us guys the world when we went over there but come back today and try to borrow a dollar from one of them. Here is the discharge I got. It's general under honorable conditions. That means I can never enter the army no more, which don't make me unhappy either. If I live to see one of my boys volunteer for the army I'm going to kick his hind end till his nose bleeds.

I lost the best friend I ever had; he died right in my arms. We'd been holed up in a foxhole about three weeks and we got orders to move out. He'd always wear his helmet setting on the back of his head instead of pulling it down like he should. He'd been told about that a number of times. He said it was too heavy the other way, give him a headache. We was right at the foot of Marilyn Monroe Hill and been holed in a foxhole. Been rainin for about two weeks, which we had water almost up to our waist. And we daren't to move on account of the enemy was as close to us as you are now. Well, orders come through the line that we was going to move out and when he heard that we was going to move out he jumped up to the top of the foxhole and let out a big hooray. And when he did, boy, they give it to him; the old Chinks give it to him right through the head with a burp gun. And he fell backwards and I jumped out of the foxhole and grabbed at him. I said, "I'll take you to the medics."

And he said, "No, there aint no use," he said, "save yourself."

I said, "The hell with me," I said, "I'll take you to the medics." And I had met a redhead when I was with him, my first wife.

And he said to me, he said, "If you care anything about that redhead you'll save your own self and forget about me." He said, "I'm done for." He said, "I want you to do me one last favor."

And I said, "What's that?"

He said, "I want you to write and tell my mother."

I wrote her a letter and it took me three days to write that letter. I couldn't eat or couldn't sleep or nothin. Lost the best friend I ever had; he died right in my arms. I thought as much or more of that guy than I did of my brother. I could go get his last dime or he could get my last dime, right out of my pocket. I even went AWOL with him. I got thirty-five days and he got seventeen and a half days. I got fined $315 and he got fined $175.

So I took the discharge and I went home, married my first wife. Well, we lived together about two years and two days I think it was. Different places, Cape Girardeau, Kansas City, St. Louis. And I finally got sick and couldn't work, so we had to go on welfare. I didn't know at the time my heart was botherin me.

But she said she wouldn't live with no man who had to go on welfare so she left me and went home. Gave me every promise in the world she'd be back if I could get a job. So I got me a job and went to work. Well, two weeks passed and she wasn't back so I went down there. And she told me when I got down there that she wasn't gonna live with me no more. So I said, "That's all right with me."

So I went back home and she come back up there. And she started runnin around with every Tom, Dick and Harry she could find, even including my brother. And then the doctor told me I was having trouble with a hernia. It was my heart all the time but he told me it was a hernia. Well, I was went and operated on for a hernia and he told me my chance was less than fifty-fifty of pulling through out of the operation. So she told me the night before I went in the hospital, she said, "I'm taking your kids and going to Chicago tomorrow where you will never see the kids no more."

So I figured if I'd never see my kids no more, I didn't have nothin to live for. So I jumped up and grabbed a rifle we had there in the house to kill mice and things with. I was going to kill myself and my brother had the only shell there and he wouldn't give it to me. So my wife jumped on the phone and called the police and told me, she said, "Get out here as fast as you can." Said, "This damn fool I'm married to is going to shoot hisself." So, boy, I bet they wasn't five minutes getting there and they asked me why I was going to do it so I told them. I said, "I got nothin to live for." I said, "Doctor done told me I might die on the operating table," I said, "She is going to take my kids away." I said, "What have I got to live for?" Anyway they talked me out of killing myself and I went on and had the operation.

I just got out of the hospital and she called from up here and told me to come up here. Give me a week to get up here and she'd have me put in jail. So I went to a lawyer friend of mine down home and I asked him what I should do. And he said, "Well, she can't have you put in jail; she's just telling you a lot of baloney there." He said, "If I was you and I thought I could get a job up there I'd go."

So I left home with seven cents in my pocket hitchhikin up here and when I got up here I still had that seven cents. I got me a job and worked a week as a dishwasher out here in Cicero. And I got paid and went over to her house with her. And a bunch of her people got me drunk, slipped me a micky, jackrolled me and I like to died. Still a week from my operation, see.

I was sent in front of her lawyer and the judge downtown. The judge asked me what I was making, what I was bringing home and I said, "About eighty, between eighty and ninety dollars a week." I was working at a place where they make plate metal. My job was dippin the metal down in hot ashes and it had rust and stuff on it, and bringin it out a silver looking color, see. Puttin it on racks. Anyway, judge told me I had to pay twenty a week for these kids. I wasn't tried in court or nothin and I found out now I didn't have to pay nothin, but like a fool I paid the twenty dollars.

Anyway, I went over there one week to give her the forty dollars. Well, she made up her mind she wanted fifty dollars for that week. Well, I told her I didn't have it; I didn't own that much. I had to eat myself and, you know, I had expenses myself. I didn't have it. Well, she said, "I don't want forty dollars. I want fifty or nothing." So I said, "Well then, I guess you're going to get nothin."

So I give it to my daughter, Vicky. She took it out of Vicky Lynn's hands, two twenty-dollar bills, and tore em up, throwed em down on the floor and stomped em. And I drew back to hit her; I drove my fist back and I said, "God damn you!" And she said, "Go ahead, I deserve it." And I happened to think, no, it wouldn't be worth it, the trouble I'd get into. So I walked out the door.

And it wasn't long after that time that I met my present wife, I got now. And me and this one was divorced, I think it was July 7th, 1958, and we got married on August the 7th, 1958.

But as far as her sayin I wouldn't work, it was not true cause you can ask my present wife. Up until I had this heart attack I worked for five long years, brought home anywhere from eighty-five to ninety dollars a week. We had anything we wanted. This heart attack hit me July the 29th, 1962, and I was laid off my job. We haven't had nothing since— been on welfare.

MARGARET

Joe knew what I was; Joe knew I was carryin a baby. He didn't care. He took me in, married me and raised the girl as much as he could. On the seventh month he fell down and hurt his back on his job and he got fired.

Then I had to go to work making twenty dollars a week in a queer joint on Halstead. I paid seventeen dollars for room rent and had three dollars left for food and milk. Well, this went on for about three weeks. On the third week a man come to my house. He said, "I heard from the landlady that you have a child up here and you're only making twenty dollars a week and paying seventeen for room rent. If your husband can't get a job within a week, then we will take the baby away from you."

Well, one week went by and he was laid flat on his back. Couldn't do nothin; took all his energy to watch the baby. Couldn't find a job. So a week from that day that man came back in with a policeman, a lawyer and a so-called welfare worker. They told him to meet them on the corner; bring the baby, which he did. They took the baby away from him and me and I never saw her again. I had to sign adoption papers over to them.

Well, then we went to Missouri. I couldn't stop thinking about her. It didn't work out in Missouri cause he couldn't get no job so we come back to Chicago about two months later. He got a job working for a dollar and a half an hour and things were going pretty good. Then I got pregnant with Junior. Junior come along. For about two months everything was O.K. And all of a sudden things hit rock bottom. Joe was fired from that job; he had to go hunt another job.

This kept on, on and off, on and off, on and off until July 29th, 1962, when he had a heart attack in church on Sunday. Well, we had a doctor there and we had the Salvation Army there and everything wasn't going too good. That next day I got up and I went to the welfare office with a statement from the doctor. Well, we got on welfare and I went three days later to get emergency money. From then on we lived on between a hundred and twenty-five and a hundred dollars a month. We had to move from here to there. It was kind a hard; we didn't have nearly enough. All we ate was beans and potatoes. Kids didn't have half enough clothes. Every time we got on our feet somebody had to kick us down underneath; it was either the caseworker or our friends. So I got to the point where I didn't want to have no friends. I just tell em to jump in the river and that was it.

I didn't have clothes to put on my back. I'd call the welfare and tell em and they'd say, "Well, if we don't give you enough, we can knock off your check." This kept on, it's been going on for the last three years. We have caseworker after caseworker bother one of us to go to work. They said Joe was able to do light work but he's not able to do light work; he just blacks out. He blacks out every once in a while and when he comes to he can't speak for half an hour. You can't understand him. He looks like a wild man for about five minutes after he comes to. He don't know nothing that's going on.

I think a man deserves a pension that way. And the VA hospital, they refused to take him in cause they claim he ain't got no heart trouble. And yet he's had an EKG in Denver, Colorado, that proves without a shadow of any doubt that he *did* have heart trouble, and bad nerves. That's the reason the government doesn't want to pay him. If they can get away with murder they're going to get away with murder.

Oftentimes my husband'll turn white as a ghost, like he ain't got no blood in his body. He'll hold on to his heart to keep him from falling; and when he did fall he wouldn't know what he did. Before he'd fall he'd remember where he was before he fell but after he fell he wouldn't know nothin. Just blacked out. He would come to and I would have to use sign language to him or try to talk with my hands in some way to make him understand me for half an hour. Then when he did start to talk, that was it; he was okay. But his heart was still poundin faster than it's supposed to be.

JOE

I found then that they wouldn't let my wife work because the kids are not safe to be left with me cause I'm subject to black out any minute. The caseworker told me that I can't watch the kids because it's dangerous to leave the kids with me and welfare refused to hire a baby sitter so she can go to work.

MARGARET

They mentioned something about a job and I asked her, the caseworker, if she would get a baby sitter, you know to watch my husband and my kids, and pay her until I got paid. And she said no.

This kept on a long time until I got sick and tired of it and I wrote to Governor Kerner. All Governor Kerner did was to say, "Well, your caseworker's acting in your behalf." Wouldn't get no answer, no help from him—referred to somebody else. Up to this day we've had it pretty hard. We only get a small amount—food, clothes and all that. And what we have left we have to put out for milk. People say the welfare gives you enough to live on; I don't see that. For me its only one, two dresses; for my kids about two or three changes each. And the welfare gives you enough to live on? I don't see it's right.

I have to buy at least forty dollars a month for groceries, and that's not enough for those kids to live on. Well, we live on it. I don't know how.

Whole life consists of canned goods, potatoes. My milk bills runs me twenty-five dollars a month, or thirty dollars a month, it depends on how much milk they drink. My rent runs me 95 dollars a month and I gotta get clothes; I gotta dry-clean clothes for the kids to go to school. They gotta look halfway decent. I gotta get em a new pair of shoes every month if possible; just can't make it. Wash clothes—it costs you about five dollars a week there. And by the time you get through you have about five or ten dollars left—and what for? For more food during the month like bread and butter you need, stuff like that. They don't give you enough. Then they give other people more than us. That ain't fair.

If you sell blood, and get caught, you go to jail. If you go to work and you're not supposed to go to work, you go to jail. And if you get money from other places and if you don't report it and they find out, they cut you off. So whatcha supposed to do? Starve? Just ain't right.

Then if you spend a little money on records or shoes that you don't need or something like that that you don't need, well they raise the roof off the house. "Well, you shouldn't have done this and you shouldn't have done that," and all that baloney. And then they keep an eye on you from now on.

Well, they catch somebody in your house when they come: "Oh, they're living here. Oh, they're eating your food up." You know you're not supposed to have anybody to dinner; you're not supposed to have anybody stay here. Did you know that? Or if you've got a television, "Where did you get that television? How much did you pay for it? Who did you buy it from?" Same thing with the phonograph. You tell em, "A friend of mine gave it to me." Oh, she'll say, "You're a liar. Your welfare's cut off." Some of em say, "Well, O.K.," and they write it down. Some of em say, "Well, I'm sorry but we'll have to investigate further." They go down through your whole life history from top to bottom. Just like in a prison on welfare too.

And then they want to know if your family can take care of you. Half the time they know doggone well a mother ain't going to take care of her child after she's twenty-one. It's up to you; it's not up to the mother. But yet they try to force the parents to take care of the child. They think you're a tramp if you're on welfare. I think I should get about fifty dollars more and maybe tide me over for medicine. And take the kids out to the park sometime on Sunday morning. And take em to Riverview* or go to a show with em or something like that. I think that people should have a good time regardless of if they're on welfare or not. I think they should live it up; they shouldn't sit around act like a bunch of sourpusses. And

*Amusement park, since sold to a company that razed it for an industrial park.

when you can't do it, it's kind of boring. You got to stay home and look at four walls and something like that. I'd like to go to a show once in a while. I'd like to go out on the town sometime and have dinner out. Have enough money for a baby sitter, go out for four or five hours a night every week and do what I want to do. Like go to movies, go to shows, go to anywhere I want to go. Take my kids to the park, gotta have money for transportation there. Just can't do it. You gotta stay in the house all day long; they become nothin but a bunch of wild Indians. Can't put em on these streets because these stupid people, half of em don't even know how to drive a car and they'll run over a kid and kill im if you're not watching him. Or the kids in the neighborhood take your boy and beat him up till he's black and blue; send him home with a bloody nose. And there you are—you got a doctor bill on your hands. And then you can't get no vitamins or no iron pills from the doctor, or the pharmacy, to build you up, build your kids up. You can't afford to get nothin like that. People can go down and down and down but it's hard to get up.

A woman's forced to do somethin she don't want to be, she's put in jail. Man's forced to be a bank robber; he's forced to be put in jail. Eight times out of nine you're lucky if you get by. The poor people's gotta be forced to do something they don't want to do. Like the time I wanted to go out and knock somebody over the head who think they got plenty of money. I'd like to take it and put it in my pocket. Then you kill a person. Poor people will think like that when they come to tragedy. Then walk in front of a judge, "Well, so and so, you did this, didn't you? You did that. So many months in jail or so many years in jail." I don't see how people live from day to day with all these problems they got. It just ain't fair. I think us people should run welfare, welfare shouldn't run us.

JOE

I believe, just between you and me, I believe Barry Goldwater was the man this country needed and the people just didn't have sense enough to realize it. I think he would have worked up some kind of plan whereby a poor man could go to work and we wouldn't have to have no welfare. That's my understanding of it. Had to open up the WPA again. And I don't think we would be fighting Vietnam if Goldwater had been in there. I don't think it's any of our business. I think we should keep our nose out of it. This thing with Korea was none of our business either. Johnson's bloodthirsty but I've never seen a Democrat that wasn't. I've seen three wars in my lifetime and three Democrat presidents. One hundred percent of anything is all of it, right? How come a Democrat will tell you a war has got to be, but how come there has never been one under a Republican president?

MARGARET

I worked as precinct captain under O'Rourke. We would kind a take polls, take census or something from when he'd go out and ask people if they were going to vote and why and all that. I was supposed to show up at the votin place on votin day and I didn't show up because I was sick in bed. I spent hours goin out for Goldwater, distributing pamphlets and all that—all that work for the Republican Party. I voted that day, votin day, but I didn't go to my precinct.

I didn't ask them for much. Night before votin when I was sick and I was down with the flu I went down and asked them for five dollars. See, I was supposed to get twenty dollars for precinct captain. Now I went and asked em for five dollars out of my twenty dollars so I could get some medicine; I was sick. And they told me they couldn't do it. And I think that's why I couldn't show up because I couldn't get the medicine. I didn't get a penny for workin for em.

But I think he could have done something for this country. I don't think we would be in the mess we're in right now if Goldwater was in. He was a conservative; he believed in progress. He didn't believe in war. He would've seen that people wouldn't go hungry. He's the one who brought that Social Security Act up. A lot of people don't think that, but according to the pamphlet, he's the one who changed the ages from sixty-five to sixty-two. And he believed if people was sick and on welfare or wasn't able to work, to cut em off welfare and put em on social security. Put em on the government payroll and knock out this welfare department.

I'd like to be President for one day. I'd make an amendment that these people in the United States that need help would write me and I would put an order through or have the government help em out. I wouldn't let them go hungry. I'd think of my country first and then Europe and Korea and South Vietnam can come later; let us be first. After all, we are the United States; we don't have to be pushed around. And I would sure the hell keep out of war. Let them come to us; we have plenty of fighting men in this here United States of America. Young boys go to college, boys over twenty-one that's single, even married, would be willing, I imagine, to fight the wars that they have to *over here* instead of going overseas and getting their head shot off. If my boys get shot overseas, I'm gonna investigate why.

Although Margaret distrusts the political process, she has developed a certain loyalty to certain politicians, and doesn't hesitate to call on them for help and guidance. She characteristically believes—wants to believe—that her request is acted upon individually.

She wrote the following letter to her favorite, Senator Dirksen. (She had decided Senator Percy, well known as a millionaire in the Chicago area, was as bad as the Democrats.) She wanted to be able to prove to her friends in JOIN that the Republican Dirksen shared her opposition to the war.

Dear Mr. Dirkson,

I might be putting my nose into the problems of the world, but I guess, and I hope I am not doing wrong. I, like many others, are worried what is going on in Viet Nam. People are killing themselves because of this war. I admit I have no boys in Viet Nam but people are worried like me. Questions cross our minds, and sometimes it brings us to question why we are fighting.

Oh, yes, I admit we should think of America which I truly love and believe in. You see, I am no Communist. I don't believe in Communism. I despise Communism. I was born an American, and hope, and in fact I will die an American.

I also believe we have a right to know what is going on. Sure, sometimes we need to fight other nations if they plot against us or raise a hand to hurt us. It's just like someone was to come up to me and take a club and beat me; I would have a right to get back at him. I was in the right then, but if I beat him for no reason I would be in the wrong and have the right to be punished.

Don't get me wrong. I am not questioning no one's reason for what they do. Why? This is supposed to be the United States. Is it? The laws are stupid and funny. We are supposed to have life, liberty, and the pursuit of happiness. If we do, where? We are supposed to have the right to vote, to our opinions, to our religion, and many other rights which we don't have at times.

If you go vote you are criticized for being a democrat or republican. If we say we disagree on certain things, we are locked up. Why? Is this the way we Americans have to live? I don't believe this is right. Why do we have the Constitution of the United States?

We stick our nose in other nations' problems. Why? To change them to our way? Let them live their lives and be happy. You can't teach old dogs new tricks. Also you can lead a horse to water but you can't make him drink. The Bible says, "Do good to those who hate you," also "Do unto others as you would like them to do unto you," also, "return Good for Evil."

What led to the War in Viet Nam? Did they come over here? Why are we over there? Did they abuse us? If they did I still believe in the saying, "sticks and stones may break my bones but words will never harm me." If they were over here, and started on my family, I'd protect them as far as dying for them.

I hope I haven't bored you with my questions and I'd appreciate it very much if you could explain everything. If you are unable to, please turn it over to someone who can.

Sincerely yours,

Margaret Jamison

Dirksen responded with a mimeographed summary of his version of the history of American involvement in Vietnam. Margaret assumed that the history had been compiled solely for her benefit. Later, though, she was to read up on Vietnamese history and write her own articles—defying Dirksen's version.

Just like Hitler times when Hitler was in. What Hitler said to do you had to do. If you didn't do it you would be punished. In other words, they're trying to run America like they were running Europe and all that. That ain't right. When Roosevelt was in I was a kid and I heard what my mom told me. My mom said she knew a friend out in the country had a hog farm; had two hogs. Government man came around, "How many hogs you got?" "Two." "Well, we gotta have one." You had to split your expenses with Roosevelt. Times were hard then, my mom said. She said she worked for fifty cents a day at the Lake Grand Hotel on Clark Street to feed me and my brother. That was no good. Can't feed a kid on fifty cents a day. At that time you could, though, because milk was cheap, bread was cheap, eggs were cheap, potatoes were cheap. But you can't live on that now. What would a dollar buy? A loaf of bread, pound of baloney, and you have a few cents left over. That's all a dollar'll buy.

Then they're raising these taxes. I don't think it's fair. I think we should have a say-so in these taxes raised or increased. Johnson promised to increase the taxes—he's increased them. Way I look at it, Johnson's a friend of Bobby Baker, he's a friend of Walter Jenkins, he's a friend of Billie Sol Estes, and they're all crooks. And he thinks he's better than anybody else. He don't consider the rich people and the people overseas that's fightin us; he don't consider nobody else. His main concern is overseas. Let the rich people get richer and the poor people get poorer. He ain't concerned with the poor people, won't let em become richer.

JOE

Everything that he's got today he stole from the poor working people.

MARGARET

There's colored people right here on Leland and Winthrop. In fact they are coming all over from the South. They are coming up here North and moving in with the white people. And at least half of them are hillbillies and the hillbillies don't go for it. And I don't blame them in a way. They lived up to their tradition for years, a hundred years they have lived up to it, maybe two hundred years, maybe three hundred years, but they've lived up to it. They'd say hello to a Negro, yeah, but if a Negro outstepped himself the white would outstep himself too.

A lot of people will object, saying, well, I'm a what-would-you-call-it?—prejudiced or something. I'm not. I'm not prejudiced against the colored, only the way they do. They've overstepped their power. I'll tell you, I'll feed a Negro; I'll be happy, if I'm poor, if they are poor and they ain't got no place to stay, I'll feed them. I'll give them clothes off my back. I'll give them a bed to sleep on, but I ain't going to sleep on the same bed as them. That's what Johnson's trying to put down our throats. My husband's got a saying, "If a Negro's a friend to your face, he's an enemy behind your back. He'll talk about you." Some will, some won't. Three-quarters of them will; the majority will say, "I got her right in the palm of my hand. If I tell her to jump, she'll jump. If she don't jump, I'll take care of that white trash." Exact words. What if we went around and called them niggers all the time? They wouldn't like it. That's where they are overstepping. They can call us white trash but, yet, we got to stand up and call them Negro or Mister and I don't believe in it. If they call me white trash, I'm going to turn around and call them nigger. They are just equal.

I ain't against the colored person. If they can make it in this world I'm glad; if they can't make it, I feel sorry for them. Civil rights movement, I believe in it. They have a right to do anything they want to do as a white man but they shouldn't overstep their power. The Negro that's in the Cabinet right now took a white man's job. That was overstepping, wasn't it? Just so he could prove he's got a Negro in the Cabinet. Well, the state of Illinois got six thousand Negroes down in Kerner's office. Do you think they'll put a white man in there? No. Daley got fifteen Negro whatcha-callit—guards—there, Daley has. Think they'll put a white man in there? No.

I'll give you an example of something. Negro at North and Clybourn, he's got a woman he ain't married to. He's got eight kids by her and she's on welfare and he's got a big Cadillac and he makes over two hundred dollars a week and gives it to her. And you don't think they got the right now? They got more rights than the white people got. I go out and make two hundred dollars a week, I'd get caught. They go to colleges now. They go to school with the whites; they take the white man's job. I think they have enough. They have better housing than the white people have, on North and Clybourn in all those projects.

Well, it's different if they are poor—poor people got a right to squawk. But let's take the Negroes, they shouldn't try to contest and say the white people are doing it to them, they're not treating them fair. Cause three-quarters of your jobs are Negroes. You ought to look in your population—three-quarters Negroes, one-quarter white. Negroes are taking the white people's place right now. Why are they squawking? Poor people, I admit if they are on welfare, I sympathize. But I don't sympathize with these people, Negroes, that are working every day and making eighty to a hundred dollars a week clear. I don't sympathize with the rich people, let's say.

I don't know what's to be done. They want you to bend down and give respect to them for being. They think they're Hitler. It's not America; it's a Communist way of doing things. People talking about Communism, that's where your Communism is actually starting—people overstepping their power. That's why I feel strongly. Martin Luther King's a rich man, he owns a couple of buildings in slum areas. He's rich. They can afford to take care of their own people. There should be a law that they be forced to take care of their own people. Us white people, we take care of ours. Why can't they?

What if us white people went out in the streets and started kicking them around like dogs? We're overstepping our business, right? We haven't kicked them around. Oh, in the South, sure, they were kicked around in a way, but in a way they weren't. When they butted in, when they started making their baloney in the South, then they started the trouble, but the whites were leaving them alone. They had their jobs too, the Negroes on one side, the whites on the other. It was mutual then, till Martin Luther King and Dick Gregory decided to do something and started a riot and disturbance.

In Missouri, now, they got a Negro section and a white section. And they automatically, the Negroes stick with the Negroes, the white with the whites—it's been for years. They haven't been no trouble between the Negroes and the whites. Negroes have their own privileges, everything they want, but in their own area. They got a specific area they stay in. If they bypass that area before this bill of rights came out, the white people had a legal right to knock the holy Cain out of them. I think it should be all over that way, cause that way that would keep you from fighting among each other.

The Southern Negroes at least will murder for a reason; the Northern Negroes, all you have to do is say "Hi" and they will stick a knife in your back. I seen it happen. That's why I don't have too many Negro friends. I ain't got but three, three in JOIN, I don't associate with anybody else.

Cause they take advantage of you in a way, some of them. I think if I had my choice between a Negro and a Puerto Rican, I think I would have to take the Puerto Rican first. At least they are half white. Puerto Rico is part of the United States, Africa is not. Negroes descended from Africa and that's not part of the United States and Puerto Rico is part of the United States, it became the forty-ninth or fiftieth state of the Union. At least they are in our race, that's the way I look at it. Some people might say, well, I'm prejudiced or I'm a Communist, but I ain't.

When Big and Little Dovie came out of jail after being arrested in a welfare sit-in, Margaret embraced them: "From one jailbird to another!" Later she nominated Little Dovie as chairman of JOIN. And a few months later she watched the film Troublemakers, about SDS-initiated organizing in the black ghetto of Newark, and exclaimed: "They've got the same problems we've got!" Here one of the most racist members of JOIN had to bend before the promise of alliance—first, directly, with the Dovies, then, at some remove, with black groups. She could persist in believing that most black people were still rich and pushy, but the myth was to recede and finally melt over time to the extent that JOIN and the prospects for change bulked large in her thinking.

I got a so-called buddy accomplice to me, writin a letter to the President when I was drunk. I went over to his house one night to eat supper, took Junior with me. He had a fifth of whiskey settin in there and I was drinkin pretty heavy. What aggravated it on was Junior got hold of a bottle and threw it downstairs and missed somebody by a foot, just missed him by an inch I should say, missed his foot by an inch. And the guy hollered at me and told me to keep my damn kid from doin that. And I told him to go jump in the river but I didn't use them kind of words. So he blah-blah-blah-blah, started talking and raising hell. So I went down and cleaned it up. So then that's when I got the idea. When I'm drinking I get *good* ideas—very *stupid* ideas. Most people do. That's when I got the idea I was going to play the revenge game. I wasn't going to let him get away with it, saying things like he said about my son, even though he is a little dumb.

So I sat down with this old man and his wife, and I got to kidding, wrote a letter to the President. I called him everything but a white man and a human being and I threatened to kill him. Knowing darn well that if the President of the United States investigated me, a person on welfare cannot get a gun and can't afford to go to Washington and shoot him down like

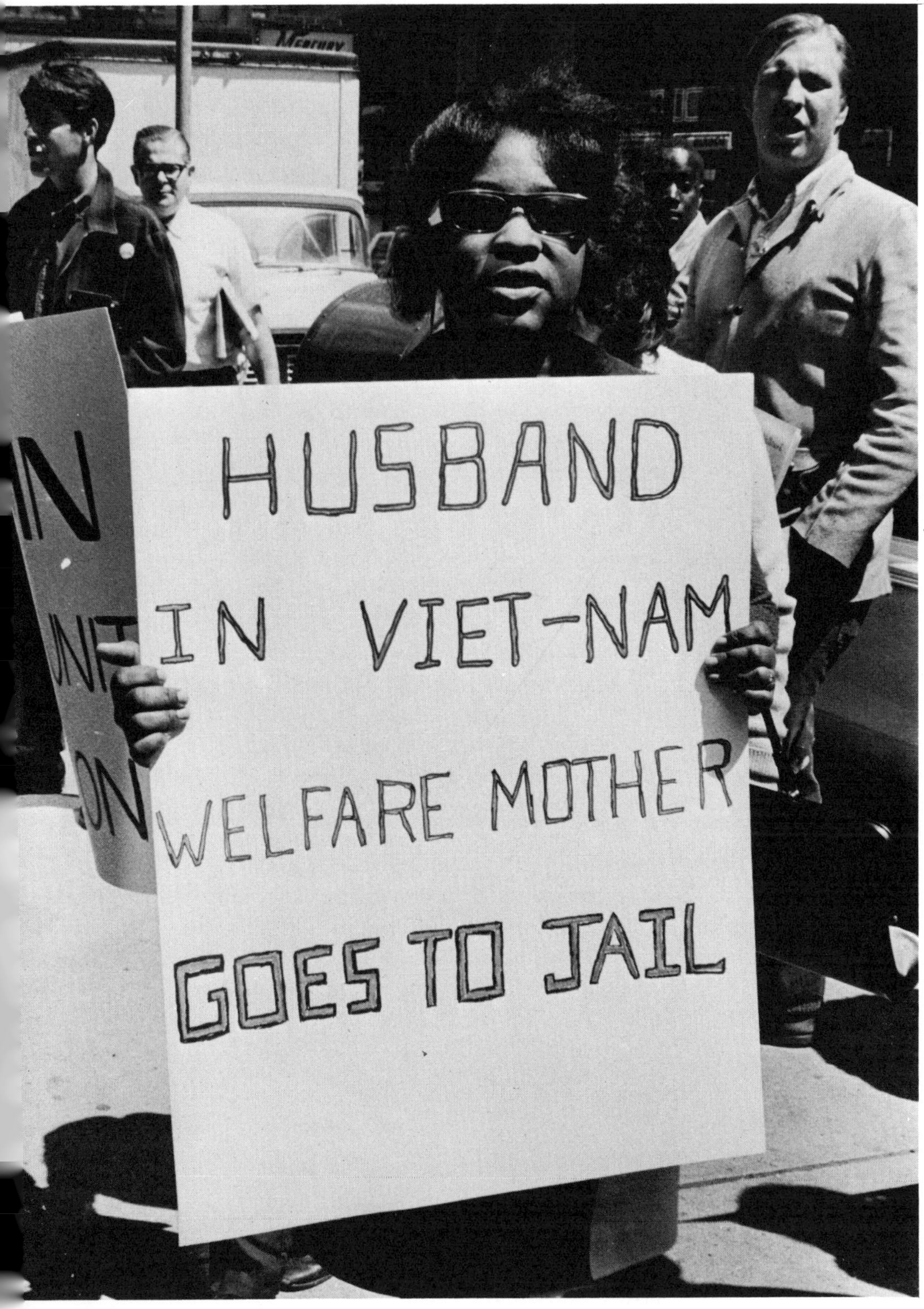
HUSBAND
IN VIET-NAM
WELFARE MOTHER
GOES TO JAIL

a dog. I signed this man's name, downstairs, to it, that was raising all the roof off the house over a little bottle bein broke. And I sent it off.

Four days later the FBI came to my house and the only way they could have found out was through my accomplice who told em, which I found out later he did. Well, they had me handwrite my name. They went all the way around and said it was a car stolen, had a check cashed, stupid things like that. And finally my husband says, "That's not it; what is it?" Then they said there was a letter written to the President of the United States. They said if I would admit that I wrote it, cause the handwriting matched, that I would get off. They would leave me alone and wouldn't bother me no more. And when I did say, "Well, maybe I did write it," they took me off and put me in lock-up.

Well, they took me 'fore a judge. The judge gave me a thousand-dollar bond. And I was supposed to go to court on a certain day and they didn't notify me. I left town about two months later and all of a sudden I heard my name on the radio and I knew something was wrong. So I took my oldest kid to my sister-in-law, my husband's sister. I had left because my mother-in-law was sick. I went down to Missouri and my sister-in-law was in Missouri at that time, and she is the one who told me my name was put all over the newscast in Cape Girardeau, Missouri. They said I was wanted for questioning by the FBI. So I gave my sister-in-law my oldest kid and we hitchhiked home with the two kids, two babies. When we got back we lived on Clark Street for one night. We had to pay a dollar a head that night—four dollars. We didn't have much, that's all we had on us. We got back on a Sunday, on Monday I call welfare up and told them I was back. And they told me to go try to go get the apartment back where I lived at, 4640 North Kenmore. And I got it back. And that night I forgot to lock the door and the next morning they come walking in at about 8 o'clock and me without a thing on. And they threw their badge at me and my husband asked em what the door was for. They said, "To knock." And he said, "Why didn't you knock?" He said, "It's too late now, you seen everything you wanted to see."

So I got dressed and they took me downtown. They told me that same day that I came back I was supposed to be in court. I didn't know. So they put me in jail that day.

The judge asked, "Why did you go down there?"

I said, "My mother-in-law was sick."

"Why didn't you notify us?"

I said, "Well, I didn't know I was supposed to notify you." So then they put me under a five-thousand-dollar bond. This time my lawyer, which they appointed, had to pay five hundred dollars pure cash to get me out on bond.

Then I went to court five times, the case was continued. I was sick and tired, I was the only one going to court. My accomplice wasn't. So I got mad. I didn't know what to do and I asked my husband what I was supposed to do. And he said, "Well, why don't you write to Dirksen?"

I wrote to Dirksen. Sat down and he dictated a letter—it was a nice letter. I said to him, "Why should I suffer for something that I wasn't the only one involved?" And I told him Bob Wood was as guilty as I was. I wrote the letter; it was proven there it was my handwriting. But *he* dictated it, he mailed it; he was just as guilty as I was.

Well, about a month later they had another trial on me and this time they put a warrant against Bob Wood's arrest and picked him up and put him in jail. Well, he pleaded not guilty and they postponed again. This kept on about one more time and then Judge Barnard M. Decker said, "Well, I'm sick of this case. I want it to be brought before trial." So they put me on the witness stand and they put him on the witness stand. Then he started lying that he had nothing to do with it. He didn't know nothing about the letter. If I wrote the letter in his house he didn't see it and I probably wrote it out in the park or something. And I probably went to a bar and got drunk. And he said he was a Christian; he went to church and he didn't smoke; he didn't drink, you know, and all that; he belonged to the Salvation Army and all that; and they started believing him.

Then my husband got up on the stand and told how I left sober, where I went and who I took with me, my oldest boy, and went to the Wood's house to eat. And the judge was listening very careful to my husband's testimony and then this Bob Wood's attorney got up and tried to scramble things around and he couldn't do it with Joe. And he got through with him and the judge asked both of them to come rise and all that stuff, you know how they do in regular court. And then the judge called me up before him and he told me the whole case was pitiful. And he said, "I'm going to do this," he said, "I'm going to give you three years and a ten-thousand-dollar fine. But on second thought," he said, "since you testified for the prosecuting attorney, I'm going to give you three years' probation." And he said, "Bob Wood, I'm going to give you probation, but there is only one catch to it. You serve two months in jail." Well, his wife started crying and he said, "And a year's probation after you get out. You are not supposed to go near her and she is not supposed to go near you."

Well, ever since then, he's been bothering me. He's been causin trouble for me everywhere I move. He said he'd never leave me alone. He'd pester me to the day I die. He'd do anything he could to hurt me. He said he'd see that I served my three years in the state penitentiary cause he served his two months in jail.

Kept pestering me more and more, wouldn't leave me alone. Sent guys over to the house telling them that I'd went to bed with them. I thought he couldn't find me in this neighborhood, but he found me. He's causin trouble for me again. Where he called the Board of Health on my building where I live now, gave them my name and Joe's name. He brought the police over to my house; he tried to start some trouble. He said he had a warrant. I found out later he did not have a warrant for me at all. He couldn't have me arrested for prostitution. Then, about three weeks ago, I found out that he was going around and he went to the welfare against me. That's why I had to go down there today. Every time he gets mad, he goes call the welfare and tell them I sold blood.

I got a letter, it said something about going to court the 24th at ten o'clock pending the case against you.

March 17, 1966
Dear Mrs. Jamison:

It is necessary that you appear at this office on Thursday, March 24, 1966— 10 a. m. in order that you may have an opportunity to discuss the claim Cook County has pending against you.

If you are unable to keep this appointment, arrangements may be made for a time to suit your convenience by calling Mr. James B. Lynn, 25 S. Damen Ave., 3rd floor at CH-3-4600.

Very truly yours,
James B. Lynn
Auditor of Excess Assistance,
Bureau of Dependency and Support

Well, I called my probation officer up. I asked her what to do about it and she said, "Well, I don't know what the charges are." So I told her I'd call back and I hung up and I asked him what it was about. And all I got from Mr. Lynn was either I had too much money or there was fraud. And I told him he was nothing but a fraud man anyway, he handled fraud cases.

So I called my probation officer back and told her it was either fraud or too much money, and she said the federal government I was under them and they would protect me every way they can. Cause I'm under their custody for two more years and if anything happens they are supposed to report it to her, not to any of them.

I went down there this morning, down to welfare office, and they wouldn't let me in at first, to Mr. Lynn just to talk things over. Just Mr. Birnbaum.* And then after he talked to him for about fifteen minutes they called me up and told me to go up there. So I went up there and they were talking. And he said that my husband's debts were going to be put along with mine for fraud cause I knew what he was doing. And any extra money, if he worked for Manpower, I was supposed to call in an report it. Then they started talking about the excess money for the emergency. My lawyer said that they made the mistake; I didn't do it. That they were O.K.'d by the case worker and supervisor and assistant supervisor at Lincoln Avenue.

Almost all welfare recipients get money on the side from some source— friends, odd jobs, selling household goods, selling blood. Welfare budgets are never sufficient to begin with and checks are often delayed by holidays or administrative carelessness. Perhaps the Jamison's "fraud" was discovered in a spot check; perhaps Bob Wood did have something to do with it. In any case, the welfare department was demanding that the $185 Margaret and Joe had collected in blood donations over a three-year period be paid back to the department. The fraud involved a little over $5 a month in "unreported income."

The department also claimed that an IBM error had awarded the Jamisons too much emergency money. They had received a check for $73.32 instead of $13.32. The caseworker at the hearing told Margaret she should not have cashed the incorrect check even though it had her name on it—and she was never told how much she was supposed to receive. Margaret could only respond, "Oh, Lord, I've got one foot in the grave and one on a banana peel."

Lynn explained to my lawyer that I did admit to selling blood. I *did* sell blood. Had to get some money to eat on. I don't know how much I've sold blood. But I did it for my kids, cause either my checks were delayed or they didn't send enough money.

So he asked me why I brought a lawyer with me, and my lawyer said, "Well, they said something about somebody coming to the house and said they were from Lincoln Avenue." And that the money had to be paid back

*Irv Birnbaum, the Chicago attorney who has given a great deal of time to represent JOIN members without fee.

in sixty days or I had to go to jail. And they checked up and found out that no one was sent from there to my house. See, a man named Summers come to my house Sunday night and he had everything on record: how much blood I sold and how much my husband sold and all the information he wanted. I don't know who he is; Mr. Lynn said he's going to investigate and see what's going on. But I have to pay my blood money back, plus my husband's.

I told Mr. Lynn who's doing all the dirty work. I told him where he lived, his name, and his probation officer's name. He said he was going to get in touch with Mr. Wood and get in touch with his probation officer.

But he said there was something else very serious that he couldn't talk about right now. Oh, I have an idea what it might be—Bob Wood saying I'm a prostitute. That I've been going out on my husband since I been married. If I was a prostitute, I'd have money! Probably paying someone to say it. Everywhere we move he goes to tell the landlady what I was and all that. He don't tell that he was my pimp nine years ago over on Clark Street. He used to go around and get me dates and the dates would pay him and then the dates would pay me and I would turn around and pay the police off. They came every night and took the money off of me.

I named Junior after my husband. I named Jesse after Jesse James cause Jesse James—according to history his mother was shot and he stood up for his mother cause she was a good mother and he was a good son. He went wrong, sure, and he committed murder and all that but the railroad was the fault of it cause the railroad *killed* his mother. He had to fight fire with fire and it affected his mind automatically for to rob banks.

Man from a railroad comes in, they want to buy the property. They came in to see if Jesse and Frank James were home. They weren't home; neither were home. Only his mother. And they got mad and they threw a bomb in her house.

JOE

Wasn't nobody there but the old lady and she was sick in bed. I don't call that an outlaw. I hope my sons would do the same thing for me.

I just hope, I hope when he grows up, he's got half the nerve and courage as Jesse James. I don't see Jesse James as an outlaw, myself. Anybody came huntin me and I'm not there and they been told I'm not there, gonna throw a bomb at my house and kill my mother, boy this world won't hold me and them both, I'm tellin you. People see the story of Jesse James, I don't know how they can call him an outlaw. I don't think he was wrong in robbing from the rich and giving to the poor either. I think JOIN *should start doing some of that.*

MARGARET

I don't think he meant to kill people. There's a story about he got on a train once and there was a poor old lady there. She had about five dollars and she gave the five dollars to him. And he turned around and said, "M'am, is that all you have?" And she said, "Yes, that's all I have." He says, "Well, here," and handed her a hundred more. He said, "Bill it to the railroad." And when he was shot—I think that was terrible. Right in the back—his own friend.

Now you take my oldest boy, now. He's the hardest one to get along with cause he don't want to understand people; he don't want to go to school; he don't want to learn. He'd rather play around and get into trouble than to learn something and behave himself. Gotta use a strap on him constantly. And the little one is getting to the mean point where he'll do to me like Junior. And Jesse's getting to be just like him, because he's taking example off his older brother.

The Jamisons' three sons are hydrocephalic (mentally retarded), undernourished, thin and spindly-legged with big bellies. With nowhere to go, they run back and forth through the three-room apartment, converting anything from a belt to a stray piece of wood into a plaything. Indoors, they usually wear nothing but underpants: cleaning and laundry bills must be kept down. The enforced instability of their parents' lives must weigh heavily on them: even the oldest at six is not toilet-trained and cannot speak in full sentences.

Margaret made some feeble attempts to put the oldest into a special school for the mentally handicapped, but welfare's first thought was that parental neglect was the cause of the problem; Margaret quickly dropped the subject in fear that all three children would be taken from her. The welfare department knows that one of the few rights left to recipients is the right to their children; it is a common threat to tell the parents that the children will be "placed" in a foster home if they can't or won't take care of them. Margaret remembers her youth too vividly—she recalls it on the edge of tears—to risk the same for her children.

The oldest, Junior, is enrolled in the kindergarten at Stewart School. Margaret walks him the two blocks and picks him up every day. He came home one day with the traditional note pinned to his shirt: his teacher asked his mother to come early the next day. Afraid of what would ensue, Margaret asked one of us* to accompany her to school.

The teacher was about twenty-two, pretty, fresh from college, eager and seemingly sensitive to the children. But all she knew of the neighborhood was the children. She had never been in their homes, had met few of their parents, didn't know the depth of their poverty. (She did know to bring old clothes for those who came without shoes or shirts: short of involvement in the neighborhood, a tender teacher's only recourse is charity.) She did realize that Junior needed special attention, but told us regretfully that "the number-one problem in Uptown is not enough EMH (Emotionally and Mentally Handicapped) classes and not one single social-adjustment class."

Margaret's first thought was that Junior had started a fight with the other children; she began to defend him, saying that he often came home beaten up because the other children made fun of him and took advantage of his lack of coordination. The teacher said she tried to prevent fights and, in fact, found Junior a very likable and friendly child. "Let me give you an example of Junior's behavior," she said. "Yesterday Junior

*N. H.

was walking on the desks and I said, 'Junior, do you walk on the furniture at home?' and he said he did." Margaret answered as she felt she was expected to: "I beat him with a strap when I catch him at it."

What the teacher didn't know is that the furniture in the Jamisons' succession of cheaply furnished apartments is so wretched it hardly matters and, of course, Junior and Jessie and Billy all walk on it.

What the teacher also didn't know is that Margaret does use a strap all too frequently, to keep her children out of trouble, or off her nerves, in a vain attempt to give some order to their world bounded by four cracked and dirty walls. She long ago gave up trying to make her children understand what she wants; she has trouble enough understanding what they want; she can only make them "mind."

I don't like this place, but I tell you, I don't like this doggone moving around all the time. I moved sixteen times in the last three years and you think I'm gonna move again?

JOE

But this here ain't no different than Buena. Here they got rats and roaches, broken windows, broken walls up on the third floor where we did live. The walls are all caved in up there. And we spent twenty dollars of our own money for paint which the landlord refused to buy. So about six of one, a half dozen of the other, no matter where you live in Chicago. The landlords only want one thing and that's your money.

Last night we had no lights from four to six-thirty because he was too tired to call a electrician. When the manager come in he fixed it hisself. He cut the light off in the kitchen and give us lights everyplace. That old man told me, "I might fix it Saturday if I want to, if I take a notion. If I don't, I won't." And I told him what he needed was a maintenance man around here. He said, "Now, don't start telling me what I need or you can find another place to live."

Ninety percent of these landlords up here in Chicago want this In-God-We-Trust. To hell with you. You live with mice, rats, and roaches and even snakes. We had an apartment one time where they even found some snakes in there. Landlords don't ever do a damn thing. It don't matter where you live, here is the same way. We got a light in the kitchen right now that could set this house on fire. And assuming my kids did set that house on fire over there on Buena, I don't know whether they did *or not, but assuming they did, I'm scared to lay down at night. I'm scared they might try it here too.**

MARGARET

Hell of a world. Three-fourths the world ain't doing their best, the other fourth is trying. Three-fourths is true to themselves, the other fourth is trying to be for the other people. But the majority is hitting the minority and that's it.

Take, for instance, an organization like JOIN. JOIN's trying their best to do things for people but people that don't want anything done for the people—big shots—they push you. And they're making it hard for the people that're trying to help the other people. They're just like a tug of war. One side is gaining, the other side's trying to gain and it's hard. They don't know which way it's gonna end up. Something's gotta be done.

How could we better the government? Very easy. I'd say we could replace everybody. We have to rechange the whole system of the United States. If the people weren't so afraid of the big shots in this country—I, myself, I'd be willing to stand in front of Daley. I wouldn't accuse him of being a thief or nothin but I'd come right out and say we need a whole new government. Oh, I'd be insulting the government and they'd call me Communist and try to get me for treason. How the hell can I be a Communist and been in the United States twenty-six years and I don't associate with no Communists? If I knew any big shots, by God, I would try to do it. But it's hard for a little person like me or you or anybody else to do it. Another thing—they would all be in favor of the system right now as we got it. They won't listen to the poor person's views of point. What they do, they'll hurt you instead of help you. Knock out your voting rights; knock out your right to even walk down the street. And that's not right.

And yet the Constitution says we got a legal right to our opinion; got a legal right to vote. We got a legal right to our own religion but yet we ain't got a right to say it if it's right. We are going to have to be like animals in the woods—fight, fight. We are going to have to fight for our own survival.

*Joe was too quick to take responsibility for the calamity. The Urban Progress Center people JOIN brought to check that apartment were sure the fire had started in the wiring, behind the walls.

Urban Renewal Means Poor People Removal

July 26, 1967

A lady in a blue suit and a white pillbox hat chairs the first meeting of the Uptown Conservation Council, appointed by Mayor Daley to approve a plan for renewal. She says conservation is a "giant step forward." Anticipating objections from an unexpected audience of JOIN members —"you are our guests here and I hope you will behave as proper guests do"—she points out: "I as chairman have only objective views on the future of the community."

JOIN says she owns an ad agency which counts the Uptown National Bank as a customer. The other members: A man who misses this meeting because he's in Europe; owner of a gas station and a $30,000 house; an executive of Kemper Insurance (finally excluded: he has moved from his $145-a-month, one-bedroom Marine Drive apartment); Japanese-American son of the owners of a $120,000 Uptown building; secretary to the Director of the McCormick Boys Club, pet charity of Combined Insurance President W. Clement Stone; a housewife from a $23,000 Dover Street house; a doctor who lives on an auxiliary moat off Marine Drive; the (liberal) chairman of the figurehead Montrose Urban Progress Center Advisory Council; a bourgeois (of course) Negro who has lived in Uptown forty years; a priest from St. Thomas Church. At least half the board must be property owners, by statute.

Doug Youngblood of JOIN gets up: "You say you're really interested in the area. Why don't about five of you get off the board and let some people on who know what's going on? We're not statistics, we're people, and we're not gonna be moved around like a bunch of pawns."

The chairman: "How long have you lived in Uptown?"

"About a year and half."

"I've lived in Uptown twenty-one years," triumphant, putting an end to the discussion.

A woman in the audience, not a JOIN member, has lived on Sunnyside two years. She'd moved from Hyde Park, where "conservation"—town houses, higher rents—had driven ten thousand people out of the neighborhood now made safe for the University. "We're not discussing urban renewal," says the doctor on the Council. "We're discussing conservation." Urban Renewal Commissioner Hill intones, "There must be participation and responsibility on everyone's part. We're not going to solve our problems by making generalized criticisms. We must have mutual respect and understanding between groups." But the chairman must satisfy herself she is a free agent, and she says she will ask the Mayor if he can appoint new members of the Council, from "members of the lower socioeconomic classes"—the word "poor" would stick in her throat, but the point comes lumbering across. Commissioner Hill leaps into the breach: "When you say other socioeconomic classes, I don't know what you mean"; anyway the Mayor has already made his choices.

Someone who does know what she means is an old JOIN member, whose voice commands attention even in the bitterly contested room:

"I'm not being represented. You do not represent me. I have never seen actual representation by actual people who have earned their living by the sweat of their brow. It has always been the property owners." She shakes with emotion. "For your own sakes, make room at that table for people who do not have what you have—not for the sake of the poor or

anyone else but for your own sakes!" The meeting adjourns. Police are outside snapping pictures of JOIN members. "Let's show em what they done in De-troit last night!" shouts a drunken John Dawson.

The Firing Line, February 8, 1968.

LUM ARE PROFITABLE

by "a lady who has been pushed
around by slumlords"

My family and I moved from Windsor Street to the Bobo building last spring. We had lived there about three and a half weeks when the city took it over and closed it down as it was unfit for people to live in. When we asked Bobo for heat, he would say, "Turn your oven on." After the city took it over we got an eviction order.

We then moved across the street to Ruby Brenner's building at 1133 Sunnyside. Then's when Billy, our son, fell down the stairs. He was in the hospital for two weeks. We sued the landlord, and so about a week after Billy got out of the hospital they made us move.

From there we came over here—848 Eastwood, which was infested with mice—but we didn't know that till after we moved in. When I moved in I asked the landlord whether the building would be torn down because of the Urban Renewal thing, and he said no, not for about two years. So I went ahead and painted my five rooms, and spent $50 to get the exterminator to come because of the mice.

We have lived here for about five weeks now. Two weeks ago we got an eviction notice—THEY ARE GOING TO TEAR THE BUILDING DOWN!

I told the manager of the building that we can't move until Sunday morning because my husband works nights. They said if we're not out by Friday they're going to turn off the lights and heat. This is against the law, but slumlords don't go by the laws.

The Council began to consider sites for a junior college in Uptown. There are hardly any local, state, or federal funds for low-cost housing, even if the Council were to decide that the fate of the neighborhood ought to be determined by the people who live in it. An anonymous Urban Renewal Agency official once said, "If we had to go to a referendum for all the programs, we might as well shut up shop tomorrow."

In the summer of 1969 the Poor People's Coalition of Uptown, which included many former JOIN members—John Dawson, the Dovies, the Goodfellows (now Young Patriots), and others—halted plans for the junior college. For a while, at least, the neighborhood would remain intact.

Mother Courage and Her Children

Juanita Simpson and her four sons—David, Carl, Michael, and Joe—are some of Uptown's many Indians. Actually she is half American Indian: her father was East Indian—"they are the original Indians, you know; old Indians"—and she tries to fuse her two Indian backgrounds in a single identity. Because she fails, she finds herself not so much an Indian as simply a resident of Clifton Avenue. Though dark skin brings her and her sons some dark looks, they are as much at home in race-spotted Uptown as they would be anywhere. "How are you?" you ask. "Oh, just here."

Her husband was killed in a hunting accident five years ago; she is on welfare. Michael is mentally retarded—at age twelve he is still in the third grade of the public school. Carl is a junior in high school. He paints surrealist visions. He and Private First Class David share an intellectuality and an interest in science usually attributed only to the children of the middle classes.

Mrs. Simpson—no one ever uses her first name—is illiterate in English. She is very religious, something of a mystic, though her thoughts are on this world, not the next. Harking apocalyptically to Masonry, ESP, and yoga, she remains a realist.

She will do what is right for her children at any cost; she is Mother Courage.

MRS. SIMPSON

It is no honor to have to be on relief or aid to dependent children. It's no disgrace but it's not no honor. It does something to you, something that I can't explain very deep. It makes you feel like you've lost all your rights. You have no right to vote, you feel that way. You feel that you have nothing to look forward to. You are walking around dead in mind, you can't even think straight. The category they put you in, you don't feel human any more. After they get through talking to you you feel just so low like you're just smaller than a little animal. There just isn't any foundation in it. You're not getting anywheres. You're going farther back instead of ahead. And sometimes it just seems impossible to buy food and pay rent, buy clothes. And to look decent and to *live* decent and to *be* decent you have a pretty rough time in this world. Course it pays off in the long run because you want to be decent, but *because* you want to be decent and respectable the big guy thinks you are a fool. They think you have no right to try to go forward because you are on some kind of relief or aid to dependent children. It keeps the kids in a bad frame of mind when they aren't living under nice conditions. They don't allow you to have a television. If you got a television you got to sell it. If you got a new radio or anything in the house new, maybe it doesn't cost over ten or fifteen dollars, they want to know how did you buy it.

So you have to live as poor as you can, what else can you do? You don't have the money to do nothing with. Half your time we don't have enough chairs in the house. Now, as it is, to sit on, we got, I think, three chairs in the kitchen because we got burned out and lost everything we had. We got a table in there that the welfare gave us: the legs is broke on it, they need fixing. That's the way they give it to us. Supposed to be one hundred thirty dollars' worth of furniture and it's nothing but junk. Got a bed in there, it's about to fall apart. And I mean, well, living under those conditions, it's just hard for me to explain to you—I'm trying the best I can. When you leave home you hate to come back. It's just that depressing.

And many times you know people you would like to invite to your house but you don't want to invite them because you figure, well, our house doesn't look as good as theirs, or probably the social service might come in and want to know, "Well, who are these people visiting you?" If they sit down at your table and you give them a cup of coffee and the caseworker comes by, they want to know, "Is this person contributing any finance toward your family? And where does this person live and where does this person work?" And you just don't have no rights as a citizen when you get on this here assistance that they give you. It's very nerve-racking. It keeps you under a mental strain. You go to bed nervous, you get up nervous. You want to do better, but you don't have anything to go upon to do better.

Then they'll offer you some kind of a little job that doesn't pay no more than maybe seventy-five cents an hour, working probably five days a week.

And if you have a family of four children or five children you cannot support those children on that type of money, and pay rent and buy food and clothes for em and send em to school looking as decent as any other children that are decent-looking going to school. Well, if you don't accept that type of job that they give you, many times they cut your help off, which is your assistance. Or they hold your check up and I mean you just aren't making any progress. You're just at a standstill.

They take away all your decency. If you have a grandmother that's dead, they will ask you all of the details on her background. And she can't do you no good because she's dead and buried. And your grandfather's dead—they will ask you about him. He can't do you no good, he's dead and buried. They ask you your whole life's history. They almost ask you why were you born.

My oldest boy, he went in the service. When we got burned out he was very much disturbed. We was sleeping on floors at some friends of ours. He got hisself together one day and he made up his mind on the spur of the moment. He said, I want you to sign these papers. I'm going into the army. I'm sick of being on this here kind of thing they call aid. It's embarrassing to be on this. When I go to seek employment, when they find out how old I am, they say I'm not old enough for full-time work. I have to do part-time work after school. If I get a job and work, he says, part-time, it isn't enough to do any good. And the minute the social service finds out you are working part-time they will deduct that off of your check." So my son, who is seventeen years old, says, "I'm going in the service, I'm going in the army. They can take their little help and keep it."

Now, those are the words he told me: "I'll be able to finish my education in there and I'll get a wonderful training. I'll at least know what I'll be eating at least three meals a day. I don't know what kind of meals they'll be but they'll at least be meals."

Now that he is in the service, this caseworker thinks that he should send his allotment home to me. And he doesn't get that much money. When he gets out of the service he's planning on getting married. Now this caseworker wants him to give me his allotment so that they can deduct that off my budget. Which I wouldn't be able to live off of that small amount that he would send me home.

So then I informed the caseworker when he first went in, that he was in the service. Well now, Mrs. Morelli, she's a very fine caseworker, she didn't take him off of the check. So just before Christmas another caseworker comes out to the house, a new one, a young lad. He says to me, "Mrs. Simpson," he says, "we forgot to take your son off of your budget.

Now I will have to deduct seventy-four dollars off of your check in the month of January. So what you do, your son was allowed thirty-two dollars," he says. "So you take the thirty-two dollars, since your son is not here anyhow, and," he says, "save it till the month of January. And you won't be so short when we take this big lump off of your check."

I says, "Well, can't you take part of it now and part another time?"

He says, "No, the record's made out already and sent in." You know he knows, he's a caseworker. He is supposed to know. Sure he knows. I says O.K.

How can you save? What can you save and how can you save? Well, it's fair for them to take him off the budget. He's not living here with me to receive that money. But I reported it to the first social worker. If you be decent with em, you see what happens, huh?

So I mean it's very disgusting really when you think of it all. And there's no future, I mean it does something to the youngster's mind. And the majority of the youngsters it makes almost criminals out of em because the conditions they are living under. Most of the majority of people that are on relief, aid to dependent children, their children, they don't have the privileges that other people's children have because most of the time they don't have necessary food and without necessary food, without eating proper, children cannot sit in the classroom in the school and study properly. They can't think as clear as other children that have those things.

Some families they have mother and father. The father works and he makes a good salary and he is able to buy the necessary foods that they require for children to give the necessary vitamins and calcium. People on relief, they eat a lot of starches. They'll eat rice maybe two, three days in succession, probably cereals, oatmeal, and a lot of potatoes. Well, to be frank with you they really need meat every day, not once or twice a week. So if they don't get those necessary things they become weak. The majority of children, that's why they get polio, and I think cancer also, because they don't have the proper foods, and not enough vitamins like meat, vegetables. A family that has four children they have to live off of a dollar a day, approximately thirty cents for each meal. That isn't sufficient for children, children need milk every day. But you're lucky if they get one glass of milk a day, and this is very true. Like now, my son came in from school and he asked me in the kitchen, "Ma, do we have any milk in the refrigerator?" I had very little in there. He would not drink it. He said, "Leave it for the little ones because it's not enough to go around for all of em."

They're very much worried and concerned about those other people that are hungry and starving over in other countries and many of the people right here in this country are eating out of garbage cans. I have saw this with my own two eyes. I don't see too much about where they're trying to solve the problem here.

They are worried about sending soldiers over there in this Vietnam to keep it free here. If they would just mind their business and not try to get everything. It's like they took everything away from the Indian people in the beginning, they fooled em with some jewelry and beads, took the country away from em. They still want everything. A lot of those countries over there, they've never bothered us, but they know we want everything, we want to grab everything, we want to claim everything. You know why we're there? Hell, in plain English, the rich man wants everything. The world is in a heck of a predicament. If this is supposed to be a free country we are supposed to live as good as anybody else. We are supposed to live as good as Rockyfeller. And if you ain't darn careful—you talk about sending soldiers over there to keep us free—you gonna have war but in a different way. The poor people right here, because a whole lot of people they don't have work, they got children, they haven't got food. What else is it but a war? Right here you gonna have it. You don't have to be a great religious man or a minister to look in your Bible and you'll see. And your Bible isn't anything but a history: it's a history book. It tells you all about this war.

"CAN YOU COOK?"

Don Smith, Director of the Montrose Urban Progress Center, was invited in February, 1966, to speak to a JOIN meeting. He was already having trouble holding his own with an audience that saw his poverty war from the receiving end, but his real difficulty came when Mrs. Simpson, straining all during the meeting for a chance to talk, was finally called on. She walked unhesitatingly to the front of the room and spoke directly in Smith's face of her experience with a highly touted program of the Center. Though she wagged her finger and squared her bulk before him, her manner held no menace, only sincerity. But Smith, unaccustomed to such close approaches, unaccustomed perhaps to being addressed as a person and by a person so visibly unabashed, backed hard against a table, where he leaned throughout her humble harangue. At first he was power arrogant; then power surprised by the good humor and practiced patience of his powerless adversary; and finally foot-shuffling power without a word to say, confident of nothing but that when the meeting ended the authority would still be his. The italicized questions are Smith's.

I'm going to their classes every Thursday. I'm trying to learn how to stretch this money that I have—very little—and you're supposed to make a meal for twenty-two cents. So I'm trying to learn to stretch this money and get a few extra meals in there, you know, through this home economic program.*

Is it working?

No, it ain't working so hot, I'll tell you.

Does it work at all?

No, really not.

You losing money? Well, I don't see where I'm gainin too much. *You losing money? You losing money?* Listen—no, but I'm not accomplishing too much.

Well, you know it takes more than a day. Wait one second now! Well, I'm going now, I think I have to go approximately eleven or twelve weeks.

Thursday I goes there, the Jane that's supposed to learn us how to cook she's not even there. This home economics class opens up at one o'clock— one to three. So we started I guess approximately somewheres around two o'clock. So here she is, this here one, she was a substitute; she wasn't the regular teacher.

She said, "Now, you take two potatoes." She says, "I boiled them already." They was hard as a rock! She takes them and she says, "Now, you take them and cut em up." I cuts em up. She says, "Put em in the casserole dish here." I puts em in there. She says, "Now you pour this sauce on there." And she says, "You puts this yuke-tons over it," which means dry toast all chopped up into pieces, you know, it's a fancy name—old leftover bread, you know. And we put that in the oven with this sauce made out of powdered milk and a little cheese. Of course if you don't have the money to get the cheese you still have to substitute it and use your imagination, you know. So she says, "Now stick it in the oven." She lets it cook and she's watching her wrist watch there, you know. So when she pulls it out, she puts it on the table. She says, "Now, then, we're going to sample it." Why the doggone potatoes was hard as a rock! This is the truth.

If President Johnson—God bless you, wherever you're at, I hope you live forever to help us in this country—believe me, if he's paying those kind of people to teach that program, somebody needs to send him a telegram and tell him to stop. I'm not a fancy cook. *Can you cook?* Can I cook? You come to my house, be my guest, hear. Name the day. I cook old-fashioned,

*She had been told by her caseworker that she was required to attend the classes; she went from fear of losing her checks.

hear, but it'll be done, it won't be raw. And it'll be clean, believe me. That woman's wasting my time in getting me to stop and come there. I'm a little bit stupid on knowing everything that's happening, because I don't have a college degree. But I have common sense.

How many times have you been there, once or twice?

I been there several times when it first started. I've attended classes before I got burnt out. See, I'm a fire victim.

A WORD FROM THE WISE:

COOK COUNTY
FOOD STAMP PROGRAM

SANDWICHES TO SIZE

Match your bread slices for a neat sandwich.

Cut sandwiches into small sections for younger children.

We're poor people but we are human beings; we are not pigs; we are not dogs; we are not cats. We are intelligent; we can use our intelligence at all times if we so desire. We know what it is to suffer from being hungry. We know what is to suffer from being outdoors and having our children not dressed properly when we don't have enough money to buy clothes with.

Some of those people that have those good fancy jobs, that sit down behind the desks looking all sweet and pretty and smelling down with this here Number 5 cologne and all this elaborate perfume, these guys sitting around smoking cigars off of this war-on-poverty money, wearing these white-collared broadcloth shirts what they're buying with some of that money, they don't know what it is to suffer because they aren't poor. They've never had to suffer.

A lot of those people that's holding those big jobs with those big seats, they're only doing them because they want to get next to this Mr. Jones because, oh, he's a big shot and he's got plenty money, he's well known, he goes all over the country, he travels everywhere, he goes to Europe and different places, he goes to the White House, you know. He's worth so many million dollars. "Well, how will I get next to him, just because he's got it?" That don't mean that *she's* gonna get any of it, you know what I mean. That's his money. If anything he's gonna just use her and make a fool out of her. Well, she'll let him use her in order to keep that job working there for Mr. Jones. She isn't going to do anything for these poor people. I'm telling you like it is. When I didn't have no food, three cans of pudding was donated to me from the war-on-poverty program; four cans of onion soup and four cans of beans. It's true. Is that where all that war-on-poverty money's goin?

You there: I hope that with God's help that you will make a better place to help the poor people and join with other organizations that's for the right thing, that want to help. One of your ladies told me, "Stay away from JOIN, they're no good." That was a terrible statement to make. These same people here, these JOIN people, gave me clothes, gave me sheets to put on my bed, which I had no sheets, and brought me food. It doesn't make sense.

And I'm an American Indian. This is my damn country. Course everybody took this country away from me, but this is still my country. This is my humanity. I got a son in the service fighting to keep the freedom for the rich big shots.

She was for months a regular at JOIN meetings, delivering long but perfectly timed speeches that made her a favorite. When newcomers came around, she delivered inspiration: "It's a small organization but we have to crawl before we walk." She soon warmed to JOIN's momentum, the we're-all-in-here-together spirit of the meetings, as if she were back in her evangelical congregation. Once she brought sandwiches and sodas for the entire Organizing Committee—she had earned a little extra money, sew-

ing. But the community of the outcast was not enough; she had more practical motives. She would humbly ask JOIN to make small but definite improvements in the neighborhood. "While we're all runnin our fat traps, talkin about the welfare and about the bad housing conditions, we been livin in bad housing conditions for years, and we're just runnin our traps. We aren't makin too fast a progress. We're makin a little but not fast enough." She proposed a nonprofit day-labor agency; she proposed home industry (sewing, lamp shades) for welfare mothers. Always she suggested, as deferential before JOIN as before Don Smith: "It's just an idea. . . . It's just one person's opinion. . . . Do you think we could?" JOIN couldn't.

Aware that JOIN lacked the power, still she kept coming, cautioning that "you gotta get close to the people who count." Once she proposed asking Sargent Shriver for a donation: "We want to help carry on his war on poverty here." Or, denouncing building inspectors: "Our President Johnson, if you send him complaints, I am quite sure that we would get some consideration. Our President ain't just gonna tell his staff, 'Disregard that letter that come in here from that thousand people.' He don't do business that way." (This provoked Ras Bryant to whisper: "That's what she thinks. Wouldn't give a quarter for im.")

Once she took direct action. JOIN in April was picketing a repair shop that had refused to return a member's radio, and she came to watch and to bring coffee to the picketers: with police around, she feared arrest, and who would take care of the kids? But somehow, perhaps with the invitation standing so close, she decided to picket anyway, shouting, "We don't like cheats," giggling to discover herself doing something that was for her incongruous. The picket succeeded—the radio returned, the store pledging good behavior—but when on later occasions she was asked to picket, she found herself too busy. Picketing agencies downtown was "for people what don't have kids"—she walked the two youngest home from school every afternoon—and she remained fearful. When in May the Dovies were arrested in the office of the Public Aid Director, for demanding their welfare due, she wanted to know if "it's legal to put on a sign that Hilliard [then Director, Cook County Department of Public Aid] would rather see some of the good citizens in jail than to give them rights"; she was angry but her fears were confirmed. Then in June she told us her church disapproved of JOIN, that people with problems belonged at the church. She was secular enough not to let that keep her away, but realistic enough to confine her participation to matters of direct personal advantage.

One night in September she was disturbed from her sleep, and from her back porch witnessed the shooting of Ronnie Williams by the police (see p. 394). Ronnie had thrown down his gun, she confided; the police had shot out his brains as he lay wounded on the ground; she was appalled and terrified, but she would not make a statement, would not get involved.

In November, 1966, on a delegation making collective demands on welfare—Christmas bonuses, posting of the list of special allowances to which recipients are entitled, the right to organize in the office, instructions to caseworkers not to force mothers into work programs—at a prearranged meeting with the Acting Director, she and some other welfare mothers wedged in their personal grievances at every opportunity. Her intrusions could not be so easily scorned as mere personal quirks, for her problems were urgent, the collective demands too narrow to encompass them. This in turn was not simply a failure of JOIN's solidarity, but a consequence in part of the complexity of welfare rigamarole, the machinery breaking down in hundreds of large and small ways, impaling one recipient in this way and another in that, dividing them, so that they have trouble agreeing on a common diagnosis and a common stand. The trouble would not dissolve until recipients collectively controlled the entire welfare enterprise.

"My boy needs shoes right now," Mrs. Simpson said, "but I didn't want to bother you people, because I know you have a lot of people to help." And two caseworkers had told her that welfare was paying her light bills, but her lights had been off for four months. And she wanted to go to work, she insisted, and had requested an afternoon appointment at Washington Street, so she could get the kids off to school. The appointment came down for 8:30, "and I'm not going to go." The affable Acting Director met the smallest, most personal demands—"insofar as it is in my power"—but in Mrs. Simpson's case and others he only sympathized. "The real problem is in the data processing. These are very serious administrative problems but I'm sure we can iron them out." "All we know," said JOIN's Peggy Terry, "is that we go hungry."

Mrs. Simpson muddled through. Months before, she had said, "I'm sick of this stuff. I don't care if they cut me off." Now she resolved to find a night job.

CARL SIMPSON, 15

The neighborhoods I've lived in, they've usually been semi-slum areas, not exactly slum areas—but you could call Wilson Avenue a slum. Dead Man's Alley, that's what Clifton's known as. Well, this is the type of neighborhood I've lived in all my life as long as I can remember and I'm getting tired of it. There's nothing I can do about it, nothing at all. . . .

We had just been going to all kinds of schools and my brother he just got sick and tired of it and dropped out and joined the army. And that's the only thing I have to look forward to, really—joining up. He tells me it's pretty bad in there too, but I think it's the best thing for him, cause staying around here, say ten days out of the month there's no food in the house. He used to go out with his friends and borrow hub caps, you know, and stuff like that and sell em to get some money. I did too. I admit it, it was the only way we could get any money cause, well, the check that we get it's some sort of aid for dependent children. It allows you to subsist, you don't *exist*, you *sub*sist—down, down, down. They allow say something like two meals a day with the money that they give you.

I seem like an absolute pessimist, right? I am, I am. You better believe that living around this place makes you a pessimist. There's nothing to look forward to except maybe after school, getting a job and living in the same conditions, unless I can get a pretty good job, which doesn't look so bright. And tomorrow there'll be less to look forward to, and the next day less, and less and less, so forth and so on.

From what I've seen of poverty and squalor, that's what I expect to find all over the States. A couple of blocks from here, a wonderful neighborhood. And I've seen pictures of the White House—in certain parts you can see poverty surroundings and the Capitol dome right there. That's amazing! Right there in Washington, D.C. I guess the neighborhoods went down. Originally I guess they were like status quo in front of the Capitol, but now . . . It's fantastic, a veritable land of opportunity—ha! I've heard that countless times and I just look at the person and shake my head. It's disgusting. From what I've seen of America, it's a pretty miserable place. That's beginning to be one of my favorite words to describe America—miserable. It's miserable.

Did you ever hear of Fulbright? He's a senator. A couple of months ago I didn't like him at all. He was saying, "Give up in Vietnam, get out, let em have it." Well, I was against him, but now I guess I've changed. I still don't like the guy—he's like Walter Lippmann, he's always saying, "Give up." I still don't like him. Guess I'm a bit of a patriot.

But I'll tell you what it looks like now: a lot of idiots in power running around trying to kill off everybody. That's another thing I've got to look forward to. You might say I'm a conscientious objector or something like that, but I don't want to go over there and fight in that little dismal swamp. What's the use of it? My brother will probably be over there sooner or later, and as soon as I join, as I intend to, they'll probably send me over there. So it's just a miserable world. I'd send one bomb over there, like

Goldwater, if I'd've been of voting age I'd've voted for Goldwater. Send the bomb over there and blow em all up. Not kill everybody but make it pretty radioactive. The Communists couldn't get in or out, there would be no more trouble unless it started one last war, which would end it all. Maybe a few survivors left over. Soon or later, fifty, sixty years from now, the radiation would stop. Probably be better off than it is now. And then it would all start all over again. The cave man would invent the slingshot and the bow and arrow, more weapons, more, more, more, so we'd get the bomb again and it would happen all over. What's the use?

Corrupt politicians, the gangsters, all of em, I'd send em to jail first of all. All the money that they've got away with, if it could be recovered I'd get it and split it up among the needy, socialize it. See? I'm a radical. Anything that would better the position of the people that really need it, I'd do it. But then there's not much chance of my ever doing that, is there?

That's how it started out in Fascist Italy. Well, the general condition of the population was pretty bad. And this smart guy Mussolini comes along, he tells em, "Now look, you socialize everything in Italy and I'll have everybody living off the fat of the land." Right. That's the same thing that's probably going to happen here sooner or later, only it won't work, cause the government won't let it. There's no chance of overthrowing the government. Maybe we have got the right to, as Jefferson said, but you try it now, it'll never happen. I don't know.

Lots of things like that bother me. I don't know why; just bothers me. A few of my friends at school, I guess you'd call us radicals. These guys that I eat lunch with, we talk about all this stuff. One or two of em, they believe in a God, a Heaven. And I'm sort of an agnostic atheist now and it bugs me so much, and we try to convince them, it's been impressed in your mind by your parents. They suppressed you mentally. They *made* you believe there's a God. Have you ever seen a God? They say no. They don't know why they believe in God. My mother's a religious fanatic! Ooh, that kills me, trying to make me believe in a God.

I don't know why I'm here. Probably be better off somewhere else, Venus or Mars, somewhere like that; a plant life form. Go rent an isle in the Bahamas, which doesn't seem possible. Where nobody can ever bother you, no bombs can ever drop, and you can live in peace and quiet. Sort of a utopia. Really great sound. . . . But if I had that island, I'd want someone to do the farming and the labor and all that, and soon political societies would jump up and it would all be in the same grim mess like it is now. So what's the use? No island at all. We'll just forget about the island. I don't know why I'm here.

Carl is an artist; he talks about his paintings:

We were studying the evolution of famous artists of Germany, like Hogarth the first, the second. And they started out with something like the dance of death. A skeleton leading a lot of people into Hell. And I liked it, so I started drawing stuff like that.

Well, it's symbolization. This skeleton, see, that's death, which is always hovering over us, right? You walk down the street, you might get ran over by a car, a bus; smoking cigarettes, you might catch lung cancer. What's the use? And the weapon down below, and blood dripping off the ax: I call it "Executioner." That's just to further symbolize death. He's not executing nobody in particular; it's just my way of putting it on paper, what's happening in the world.

I had my name in the neighborhood paper a couple of days ago for a gold key I was awarded for a painting I did. It was on display at Wieboldt's, a downtown store, along with a lot of other ones. There was one of a vampire standing in a doorway. I called it, "Come into my Parlor, said the Spider to the Fly." It's really gruesome.

I don't do anything like that in art class at school. Everything's so bright around there, you just feel creative and it comes out beautiful like a house in a sunset. But then once in a while I begin to feel morbid. Then I do something like that Blood Roses, Blood on the Ax, Blood All Over. It's the surroundings I live in, just living around here, I guess. It's very seldom that I see anything beautiful around this section of the city. I guess I seem morbid, right? I am.

PFC DAVID SIMPSON, 18, AFTER NINE MONTHS IN THE ARMY

I don't want any part of the army whatsoever. I hate the army. It just doesn't make sense. Every man in the United States Army is a professional killer. He is being paid to kill. The reason I say this is because maybe he has never killed a person, maybe he never will. But there's always the chance that he may go to Vietnam or wherever the war happens to be at the present time. Because there will always be wars. As long as there's man, there's going to be war because of greed. You've got a million dollars and I don't and I want your million dollars. I see a way I can get it, I'm going to take it. I mean, not me personally, cause I don't much care, but this is the way the average person thinks. The average person is very greedy. Oh, I'm greedy too, everyone is greedy, but there's an extent to which greed can go and then still maintain your sanity. And most people in the army are greedy.

Now the war in Vietnam. As far as I'm concerned it's a senseless waste of human life; it's a *senseless* waste of human life. So why are we in Vietnam? They try and brainwash you to their way of thinking, try and tell you we're there to stop Communism. It's none of our business, as far as I'm concerned. We're violating the Monroe Doctrine. I believe the Monroe Doctrine says something about we're not supposed to stick our nose in other people's business; in essence, something like this. Anyway, if those people want to be Communists, let em be Communists. Who are we to say, "No, you can't be Communists, you're going to be capitalists or you're going to be thus-and-so?" We are trying to prove something, that we are a powerful nation, we are trying to scare other nations. If we can get the point across that we can take on all comers, then we figure other nations won't bother us. We are going about it in a very bad way, trying to prove something like this. I think the United States is becoming a warmongering nation.

How many miles is Cuba from Florida? Ninety some miles, little ole miles. Now the United States is big. And as big as the United States is, do you seriously think that we care as to whether Cuba would become Communist or not? I don't think we care. The thing is, the whole bit is benefiting politicians—all politicians.

Barry Goldwater, for instance: now this is my personal opinion and may be wrong. A lot of people would think it is wrong. But if I had been twenty-one at the time when Barry Goldwater was running for President, I would have voted for him because I believe seriously that Barry Goldwater would have ended the whole mess. See, we're doing too much waiting and stumping and hemming. If we're going to have a war, let's get in there and have this war and get it over with. You have no way of going around picking the good from the bad, but human lives are going to be sacrificed no matter what. Human lives are being sacrificed today, right now in Vietnam in the undeclared war, so why not just declare war and get it over with, forget about it? Once it's done, once it's through, then we can be safe. There won't be any more people killed.

I believe Barry Goldwater would have actually bombed Cuba. Yeah, this would have meant a lot of innocent people dying and everything; but like I said, personally, I think if the Cubans want to be Communist, let the Cubans be Communist, the Vietnamese be Communist, everybody else be Communist. But the United States doesn't want to be Communist, then it shouldn't be Communist. This is the United States' privilege; this is Cuba's privilege; this is Vietnam's privilege. See what I mean? The whole thing— let everybody do what they want to do as long as they don't infringe upon other people's rights.

And I don't see how Vietnam is infringing on our rights by wanting to be Communist. I'd say safely more than half the country are Vietcong.

So I couldn't really say why we're in Vietnam. I don't know. That sounds funny; I'm a soldier in the United States Army and even I don't know why we're in Vietnam. I may have to go to Vietnam and fight for a cause that I don't even know why I'm fighting. And if you ask the majority of the United States soldiers, "Why are we fighting in Vietnam?" they'll give you some off-the-wall answer and ten-to-one they'll say, "I don't know." This is really true. And neither does anybody else know, for that matter, except the bigwigs. They might know. It's probably benefiting them very greatly.

Now, for instance, we are supposed to have a governmental system run by the people, for the people, and of the people, you know and all this kind of stuff. Well, if the President says something, well then you have to do it. There's no two ways about it. If you don't then you get thrown in the pokey.

Well, I know that if they sent me to Vietnam, I'd do this for a purpose. I'm not sadistic or anything like that but like I said, self-preservation is the first law of the land. If I was under live fire and I had to kill them, I know I have to kill them or they are going to kill me. The first one that I killed—this would be to show all the American people—I'd take a little silver bar and I'd put it on the stock of my rifle. And for everyone after that, I'd put a gold bar, and I'd try and get everyone that I could. Not because I want to, but because I'd have to for this reason: to prove my point. And then when I got back, they'd want to decorate me and all this kind of stuff. And when they got ready to put the medals on me, I'd take my rifle and I'd hand it to them and say, "Look at the stock and count all these bars." And when they counted them, whatever it happened to be, a hundred or two hundred, you know, whatever amount that I killed, I'd say, "Now, I went over there in a land where we shouldn't have been. It wasn't any of our business what those people were doing. And I killed these people for you, just to keep freedom in the United States, or so you would call it. And now, here you're going to take these medals, these three-dollar and four-dollar medals, and you're going to decorate me with these medals. Is this all my life is worth to you? Or all their life is worth? A handful of medals? For me to go and kill people I've never known? I'm going to kill human beings for you and then you're going to give me a handful of medals? You know what you can do with your medals? You can take em and stick em." I wouldn't care if they gave me a dishonorable discharge or put me in the stockade for years or whatever it'd happen to be.

Chicago *Sun-Times*, July 2, 1967.

War Spending Rises Here

Area Share Is $3.5 Billion

The prolonged Vietnam war is stimulating business for Midwest producers of conventional military supplies. Ammunition makers in Indiana, Northern Illinois and Wisconsin in 1966 more than doubled the 1965 dollar value of production, and 1967 figures show further increases. . . .

In the spring of 1967 Mrs. Simpson drifted away from JOIN, and we lost touch. Then we ran into her on the street one evening: she was on her way to work. Animated, she explained she was working overtime, six nights a week.

"Where?" we asked.

"I work for the government, at a defense factory. I make the triggers they put on these guns."

Our faces must have twisted. All we could think to say was, "How does that make you feel?"

"You know what I think about it. But, my dears, my kids gotta eat."

Carl Simpson went through the Upward Bound program and won a scholarship to an Eastern prep school.

Medic David Simpson was shipped to Korea, then to Vietnam. After some months he was entitled to Rest and Recuperation in Hong Kong, where he was reported Absent Without Leave.

Revival

I wandered so aimless
Life filled with woe

North Side Missionary Baptist Church, a storefront on Winthrop near Argyle. This is the eighth day of the "Old Fashioned Revival," leaflets have been tucked in mailboxes and under windshield wipers for blocks around, but there are only thirty people including kids. Most of the adults are family men in their twenties and thirties, dressed as if for a dutiful outing, not a long-awaited community gathering. The preacher drives up in his late-model station wagon, in suit and tie. He waits for more people to show up, not really expecting any, not really disappointed: an outsider, he rides the circuit on air suspension, he is only doing a job. His dress, his polish, his aloofness separate him from his congregation; unlike Bill Bryant and his fellow West Virginian preachers, he moves above, not through his flock.

Hard times and troubles,
No place to go

In Daisy, West Virginia, hugs and greetings merge into the first song; here the service starts suddenly, stiffly; it is an effort. The prayers here are formal, almost sedate: no jumping up and down, even for a denunciation of educated people, who think they know more than the Bible. There are few tears. The only enthusiast is a man in his seventies bouncing like Rumpelstiltskin, praying for "a colored woman and a hundred Puerto Ricans, Hallelujah! Hallelujah!" He says his friends walk him to church and leave him there, embarrassed. But the congregation doesn't join him, doesn't shout "Help him, Jesus!"; his prayer like his life is his private affair.

Then hope it came
Like a stranger in the night

The women fidget, sing two verses and trail off, more worried than West Virginia churchgoers whether they stay on key. The men are most often called upon to sing. The preacher, in normal—not Southern singsong—tones, says Jesus must be coming because knowledge is increasing—TV, radio, planes, satellites—though "people don't love each other the way they used to. I can remember when we put pallets on the floor. That was true fellowship." But these are barroom times that call for realism. "Use your telephones tomorrow, get a friend to come to chuch." His audience listens, inserting only an occasional "That's right" into his predictable speech—more a speech than a sermon.

Praise the Lord
I saw the light

A ragged Indian enters with wife and child, walks down the aisle drawing stares. Neither preacher nor deacons pay attention to them, but the old Rumpelstiltskin takes them aside, apparently convinces them, leads them toward the podium, coaxes them to kneel. Some of the saved make a perfunctory prayer; the preacher brushes past them with ostentatious hauteur; there is no such self-congratulation as we saw in West Virginia, all the gathered sharing in the collective triumph of converting a lost soul.

I saw the light
I saw the light
No more darkness
No more night

The saved men hug each other for the first and last time, quickly; in Daisy, the hugging and handshaking, a kind of square dance within the ritual, greeting and farewell both, is the main ceremony, prolonged and communal. There all the saved turned to the unsaved and pressed them hard. In the storefront most of the saved men prepare to leave, though one ardent deacon warns a disbeliever that Hell is even hotter than the steelmill fires of Gary and Hammond.

Now I'm so happy
No sorrow in sight
Praise the Lord
I saw the light

Outside there is talk of tomorrow's work. There are television, movies, parties, places to go; despair, the backbone of the Daisy church, has become malaise. A small boy passes, wearing an army helmet camouflaged by rubber jungle leaves.

Don't Read
the Papers Much: III

Gains on Slums Told by Daley

Mayor Daley issued a statistical report Saturday outlining steps being taken by the city government to eliminate slum housing by the end of 1967. The report was released for publication prior to Dr. Martin Luther King Jr.'s Sunday rally at Soldier Field and march on City Hall.

"It does no good to banish the rats, if the building itself is in terrible condition," said Abel D. Swirsky, deputy building commissioner in charge of community conservation.

**I was standin by my window
On a cold and cloudy day**

700,000 Poor Counted in Chicago

Raymond M. Hilliard, Cook County public aid director, has said that slum operators receive one-third to one-fourth of the $5,000,000 a month paid in the county in welfare rent allowances.

Four Chicago business leaders painted a picture of their city and its environs Thursday as "the richest and most efficient section of the most powerful nation in the world." The latest figures, said one speaker, indicate that after federal income taxes, the average income for Chicago households climbed to $9,478, compared with $9,128 for the New York area and lesser amounts for Los Angeles, Detroit and Philadelphia.

In "ticklish" areas, such as the beaches, the commander sends policemen adept in human relations.

**When I saw the police come rollin
For to carry my brother away**

Unemployment in Chicago is now down to "the hard core of the unemployable," the city's top business leaders were told Monday during a session with Mayor Daley.

"What this means," O'Rourke explained, "is that, with the expansion of the borders of the conservation area, we will be able to tackle some of the hard core problems that have been plaguing us. For example, we will be able to consider the revitalization of the commercial area along Broadway between Wilson and Lawrence."

Will the circle be unbroken?
By and by, Lord, by and by

Yielding nothing to his critics, School Supt. Benjamin F. Willis last week told the Uptown Chicago Commission of the hopes and problems of public education. . . . "Of my last 10 years," he said, "I would speak in terms of pride, progress, and problems." . . . Willis was driven from the meeting by W. Clement Stone, millionaire insurance executive.

One reason for improvement is men like Chicago's able superintendent O. W. Wilson, former dean of the School of Criminology at the University of California (Berkeley), who feels that "the function of the department is to maintain an orderly society, not just to enforce the law."

There's a better home a-waitin
In the sky, Lord, in the sky

Broken panes plague schools; Senn hard hit

Senn high school, 5900 N. Glenwood, was hardest hit among local schools with 17 broken panes. Goudy school, 5120 N. Winthrop, had 14 broken panes.

Chicago Living Costs Hit New Peak

The war in Vietnam costs about $100,000,000 a day

Police Ask Quiet Summer

JOIN Newsletter, November 24, 1965.

POLICE

by Raben Halsey

It's a damn shame when if a man sits on the corner, the law will run him off for no reason at all. They don't need nobody to run us off the corner. When we're ready to get off the corner, we'll go ourselves. When we get ready to go home, we know where home's at.

Police think the people in this neighborhood are scum; someone to run over so they can get a reputation. I ain't talking about the whole force, just the police at Summerdale who are looking for a big reputation.

We've got to organize to fight the police. We can't fight one another. Police brutality is outrageous.

JOIN Newsletter, February 16–28, 1967.

Public servants? ha!

(Dear Editor, Don't use my name on this. It isn't very flattering to our police force and I wouldn't want to wind up on the wrong end of a billy club.)

Chicago is known to have one of the finest police forces in the United States. Whoever said that couldn't have lived here. They've never walked down the street and had a cop threaten to beat them up for no reason. They've probably never had to ask a cop for help.

Well, I did. . . .

On October 12, 1966 at about 5:00 in the morning I had to go to the hospital to have a baby. We called a cab but nobody would come out. (We're on Welfare and unless you get an OK from your caseworker, you just can't get a cab. I guess you just have to live there and suffer until the Welfare Office opens.)

We had no choice but to call the police. Well, after about a half hour they finally came. They rang the bell and shouted, "Hurry up, lady! We haven't got all day." I guess he never had to walk down 3 flights of stairs with pains about 3½ minutes apart. Do you think those cops would offer to help? No! I had to go down the stairs and climb in the paddy wagon without any help.

When we got to the hospital I climbed out, without any help from them of course. As I was going in, one cop said, "Hey lady, next time call a cab!"

They're a great example of civil servants. Sure! They're Chicago's finest—but the question is—Chicago's finest what?

JOIN Newsletter, March 11–20, 1967.

COPS IGNORE DYING WOMAN

When Juanita Cunningham of 837 West Windsor passed away March 4, she left behind 8 children and hundreds of friends. To most, she was another mom and to others she was an exceptionally close buddy and pal.

Twelve years ago Juanita and her family came up to Chicago from Osceola, Arkansas. . . .

Juanita took very ill Friday evening and all efforts to reach medical aid was in vain. Doctors refused to come because she was a welfare recipient.

The police were summoned at 2:00 am. When paddy wagon # 6237 arrived they refused to move her. They said she wasn't a sick woman— only a sympathy case. The attitude of these officers was a disgrace. They used profane lanage to the daughter and sister who were only begging for their help.

Finally at 4:00 am the police were called again. This time the call was answered by two very nice policemen. They took Juanita to Cook County Hospital. Upon arrival there she began hemmorhaging at which time the cops rushed her right on to the doctors.

The doctors determined she had a very bad infection, and she was rushed upstairs. They told Jane (her sister) that Juanita was very sick and within minutes of death. When she explained that they had tried to get help for several hours, the doctor only hung his head and said that a few hours may have made a difference. Juanita died there late Saturday night. Could this have been prevented if she could have gotten to a doctor earlier? We will never know. . . .

The Firing Line, June 25, 1967.

POLICE ASK FOR QUIET SUMMER

BRUTALITY ???

"What about police brutality?", someone asked. Sergeant Gegner replied that the police are an imperfect organization and "the Police Department weeds them out."

Moses told the people, mount up your asses and your camels and I'll lead you to the promised land. Roosevelt told em, said sit on your asses and light up your Camels, this *is* the promised land. Now Johnson's kickin your asses and raised the price a Camels and stealin your promised land.

That's the way it goes. First your money, then your clothes.

—Buddy Tompkins

Buddy Tompkins, 27

We first met Buddy Tompkins when he threw a tomato at one of us. T.G. was acting in a JOIN skit performed at Friendship House, a Wilson Avenue pool hall and social center for young guys. The skit recreated a speech by poverty commander Sargent Shriver in Washington, and its interruption by angry warred-on poor people, including one of the leaders of the Friendship House circle. T.G. was playing a big shot on the platform, making cracks about the poor. As "Shriver" spoke, American flag hanging from his hat, the "audience" of JOIN members revolted. First they heckled, then they took over the "meeting." A tomato flew. We learned later we had encountered the cocky Buddy Tompkins, a Friendship House stalwart.

He is handsome, articulate, mercurial. His bitterness drives him to radicalism as fiercely as it drives him to drink. As he moves closer to JOIN over the months, there is still an edge to his politics, a secret, a bitter knowledge, as if an old man inside him is asking where it will ever end. But he is not prevented from trying to organize a people's movement back home, or from sharing a speakers' platform with Martin Luther King, Jr.

He is a natural actor, and during the summer of 1966, when he gave this interview, he was rehearsing a play with a war-on-poverty-sponsored program. By the end of the summer, the program had been cut off; the actors, acted upon, were picketing the Urban Progress Center.

First was God—He made land and man
Second Adam, Eve and Holy Land
Women can't figure man for love
As the sky is for the dove.

Then meeting the girl, everything calm
Meeting of Father, meeting of Mom
Given marriage papers, two months time
No use waiting for the church bell chimes.

Husband to work, leaves sweetheart behind
His poor friends can't make work on time
Jealous is husband, and mad is friend
Tickled is the wife, she can see the end.

Lives on Kenmore, three-room flat
Husband leaves town, lover comes back
Stays happy nine months of year
Little baby brings lots of fear.

Lovers see years of labor and sweat
Even his love isn't nice little pet
She begins to cry and asking why
He begins to ask if baby is nigh.

He can't get to work and loses his job
So they fight over who's the big slob
She moves to Clifton and life begins
Then ADC has a helping hand to lend.

No use going home, nothing there
So wash your face, and comb your hair
Somewhere, someplace a man is waiting
You think a bar stool is place of dating.

So find your man and back to the house
That's where sex, shit and all is quiet as a mouse.

—Buddy Tompkins (1965)

I grew up in most of my young days in the state of West Virginia. My father was a coal miner. We just lived in surrounding towns, near Beckley. About '47 or '48 the doctors made him leave the mines because he had third stage silicosis and TB in his left lung, so he went then to a small place in Virginia called Meadows of Dan and bought a farm there. There was still five of us children at home, and from '48 until 1954, well, my mother and father and myself and sisters and brothers, well, we just more or less self-supporting ourself on that farm there. I had very strict parents, they was very religious, both of em, and as all kids with real, very strict parents, you know, you always have to step out a line more so when you're in a group, to prove that you belong.

So my father couldn't really get any breath as to maybe walk a half a block, and he'd have to sit down and stop and rest, so from the time that I was about eleven years old until '54, I was sole supporter of the family. Farming. Like for instance now, they was no fuel other than wood. You had to take your crosscut and go to the woods and saw your trees down and trim them, then drag them in with a horse and saw them up. And on top of all of that I had to do all of the plowing and disking. Then when you got your crops in the ground, seeing that they was taken care of, and just regular farm work. Nineteen fifty-four, my father, we took him to the hospital and his lungs was so ate up with this silicosis, when they put him in a oxygen tent why the forcing of the air into his lungs busted both of his lungs. Well, my father's people were all in Virginia and my mother's people are all from West Virginia, so after my father died why mother up and sold the farm and moved back to West Virginia. And things were pretty hard for a while.

And when I moved back to Beckley I wanted to drop out of school to join the air force. I guess I've always been more of a broad-minded person. I know what I'm gonna do tomorra, I never wait on it to come. And so I finally connived around and got my age set up and everything. I wasn't old enough, you know.

Well, after I got in there things got to goin pretty good, they made me go ahead and finish my education. I had to go to school four hours a day until I graduated. I got the general equivalency diploma from the government, see. Well, I was sent to the 779th AC&W squadron in Montana, it's a isolated radar site, aircraft warning, and when they started to checkin me out for clearance and everything else, why they checked up and found out I really wasn't old enough when I joined. So they gave me a general discharge under honorable conditions which would reinstate itself in six months. They put me out, and I come back home to West Virginia. And I was runnin around, boozin it up, and everything else, and so I guess these boys that I used to run with fore I went in the service, well, they sorta had em a little racket as to where they was stealing cars and stripping them and everything like that. They'd take them and ride em around town and nothing'd never be done. One of them was an adopted kid of the man that owned the large drugstores and everything around, you know. One of them had some kind of franchise on the beer distributing around there. They was all pretty wealthy. And so we went to this joint there in Beckley, top of the hill, and we all went in the same car and got pretty drunk. So next morning when I woke up, well, the state police was taking me out of the car. And the keys were still in the car. So he asked me, said, "This your car?"

I told him no.

He said, "Well, whose car is it?"

I said, "I *don't* know." And he said, "Well, I know who the car belongs to." Said, "It's a stolen car."

I told him, "Well, I'm sorry." I didn't know nothin about it, see.

And he told me to get out and he started to put the handcuffs on me and then he told me, said, "Reach in there and take the keys out of that car." So I took the key out of the car.

"Put it in your pocket." I put it in my pocket. So they took me up to the jailhouse and took me in jail, told me, said, "Empty your pockets." And I emptied my pockets and he said, "What's those keys?"

I said, "Well," I said, "they're the keys to that car up 'ere, you made me take the keys out of the ignition, and put em in my pocket."

He said, "You mean those are the keys to the car that I caught you in?"

I said, "Yeah."

He said, "Well, book him for possession of stolen goods." See, they came to me, you know, they wanted me to tell who drove the car up there and everything else. And these businessmen in the area, that their sons were involved, came to me and told me said, "Now, if you don't say nothin about our sons being with you, we'll go and talk to the judge and get you a lawyer and everything and get you off on some probation and we'll see that everything's taken care of."

So when I went to court why nobody'd still shown up, you know, and judge asked me how I plead. I told him I plead guilty. So he give me one to ten years in the state penitentiary in West Virginia.

And I was up there from '57 to about '61 and made parole out of there to South Dakota, and my grandmother was on her deathbed. Mother called the institution and told the warden that she would like to have me come home, you know. And I was to be released the same morning, see. So I appealed to the parole board, asked them if they could grant me permission so that I could go to my home town, see my grandmother and then go on to Rapid City, South Dakota. They told me "No," said, "you're not allowed in the state." Said, "You're barred out of the state unless it's immediate death of the family," and then I'd have to notify the Sheriff's Department when I go into town, see. If I don't notify them, why they'd pick me up and put me in jail.

So I went on to South Dakota, and when I got to South Dakota, why my sister's mother- and father-in-law, they told me my grandmother had died see, while I was en route up there.

And I guess I took a pretty ugly disposition toward the world, you know. I figured, "Well, if I'm gonna receive this kind of treatment the rest of my life, why I'll see if I can't dish a little bit of it out." And I guess right then is where my whole life sorta changed. I used to be very happy-go-lucky, all the time. And I adjusted myself to it, but I don't know, it's really always bugged me a lot, and I can't see goin out of my way to smile at someone. And then after I came out of the institution, I always was very active in sports, and I could a played baseball for the Triple-A baseball team in Rapid City, I was good enough, but—I had a prison record. And some of the laws and regulations and rules that you have to abide by when you're on parole, like you can't make a loan, you can't buy a car, you can't leave the county, you can't leave the state, you have to go to church, they'll tell you what church to go to, you can't go fishing, you can't go hunting unless you're in a group with written permission from the state of South Dakota *and* the state of West Virginia, you can't make any debts, you can't open a bank account. Well, you could get up a the morning and go to work, come home, watch television, go to bed. See, you have a curfew law too, gotta be on. When you're on parole like that you really have a very tight rope to walk, because all it takes to violate your parole is just someone to go to your parole officer and say, "Look, I'm scared of this guy, I'm afraid that he's liable to do me physically harm or anything like at," and he has to lock me up and send me back, see. It's very tedious. There are no constitutional rights. That's like Roosevelt's fireside chats, it's in the past.

So I went to my parole officer and I said, "Sir, I request permission to get a driver's license. I need it. I made foreman on the job and I need a driver's license because I have to drive a truck." So he granted me permission. And I took the test and got my license and about a month or so later I said, "Sir, I'd like to request permission to buy me a car so they won't have to get up every morning and take me to work and come to get me and bring me back and everything else." So he comes down and tells me, said, "Go ahead and buy you a car." I said, "All right, thank you." And I was living with them, doing pretty good, and I said, "Well sir," I said, "how about me movin out, you know, gettin on my own, gettin me a place of my own?" "Go ahead. Ain't nothing wrong." So I moved and turned in my driver's license number and my car license tags and everything and gave him my change of address and everything like I was supposed to do. So right before Christmas, I'd saved quite a bit of money and I went down and told him I said, "I'd like for you to request for the state of West Virginia for me a traveler's permit so I can go home for a visit for a few days." He said O.K. So he writes me out a traveler's report, see. So when I get to West Virginia, well, I go to my mother's and I stay there about half a day and they come and arrest me, put me in jail.

On my parole revocation they had me charged with leavin the state without permission, buyin a car without permission, gettin a driver's license without permission, changin residence without a permission, not holding— what do they call it—an upstanding position in the neighborhood. Everything that they allowed me to do, well, that's what the state had me charged with, see. So I explained it the best I could; and they turned me loose, I went on back. So when I got up 'ere I told him, I said I had to sell my car. That's one of the conditions they released me on.

"Naw, you don't have to sell your car," said. "That was just a misunderstanding," said, "I'll get it all straightened out and everything." So I never did drive my car out of state no more. When I wanted to go home I just caught the bus and went on home. But they tried to send me back to the penitentiary two or three times, for something that was their own fault. I mean it was just a constant uproar, you know: coming to my job, trying to embarrass me into quitting, and messing with me constantly. Well, I just got fed up with it. I said if I'm gonna have to live like this, which I hadn't done anything to begin with, well I'll just make the best of it. If nobody wants me because I made a mistake which really wasn't my fault, I said I'll just see how damn hard I can make it on the rest of the world. And so I just started bustin mouths and stealin what I could steal and everything else. Started crackin safes and I got two years in the penitentiary up there for safe-crackin, and I had a pretty bitter outlook toward everything and it really didn't matter. The only thing that I looked forward to was gettin out, revenge and all of this crap.

See, you get in there, and after you in there for so long, well, all you've got to do is just set around and think. And you build such hatred in yourself, you know, until—well, for instance, when I got a letter from my mother it was just like Santy Claus, it'd been so long since I'd saw any of my people. Well, I couldn't hardly visualize in my mind what they looked like. Really gets to you. You got to fight and fight and fight. You don't know whether somebody is going to stick something in you or what's happening, you know. And you really build up a stiff hatred in there. Seemed like ever since my Daddy died I've had some pretty hard blows, one after the other. Every time I get on my feet I get knocked off, you know.

So when I got out of the institution up there, my brother wrote me and asked me to come to Kansas City, and I went down there and got some pretty raw deals from my relatives there, and I met a guy and went to D.C. with him, and we got a job up there in Alexandria, and we was just tourin Washington and goofin off and just runnin around. So we tired up there and cut out and went to Martinsville, Virginia, and the same thing down there. We would just go and work and save a little money and move on and find another job and work and piddle around. And I finally ended up in Bristol, Tennessee, and I got a job down 'ere, worked as a mechanic at a service station, and I worked down 'ere a while. That's where I met my wife.

And so, you know, I talked to several people, they told me that there's plenty of money to be made in Chicago and everything. So after I met my wife and we got married, well, I told her, "Well, I think we'll just go to Chicago. I believe I can get a job up there." At the time I had a '50 model Ford and so I took my wife and kid by my mother's place. My mother said they could stay with her until I got a job, a place for em to stay. So I left my wife in West Virginia with my mother, came up here to look for a job. When I left West Virginia I think I had about nine dollars in my pocket. But as everybody else comes to this town, when I come up here I really didn't have any idea of the city bein this large and the directions, how the streets and everything was laid out. So I finally got me a job, one of these Zenith places out here, and I worked out there for a while.

I had the back bumper off my car and the front bumper both, and the traffic cop on the corner run out in the middle of the road, flagged me down one day. Told me, said, "You're gonna have to take that car off the road." Said, "Don't bring it through here no more." Said, "If I ever catch you," said, "I'll give more tickets than you can pull offn that thing." So I had to take my car off the road and I didn't have no way backwards and forth to work, you know, so I had to start lookin for another job. And I found a job at Rauland's. I worked out there until they found out that me and my brother both was workin there, and they didn't like to hire relatives at the time. Factories hate to hire relatives or husband and wife and buddies because most generally when one gets mad and quits the other one'll quit and go with him. So I told my brother, "Well, I'll just quit." I didn't care. Hell, I was lookin for a job when I got that one.

And I used to hang out on the corner of Leland down here, Leland and Sheridan Road, and I was just more or less waitin to find some way to go get a job or somethin. Well, one of the boys down there asked me if I would be interested in teachin weightliftin at one of the places up the street, after work. I was in pretty good shape then, and I've lifted weights and boxed and had a quite a bit of sports activity and training. I told em, well, I had to find a job. So they told me, said, "Well, he can help you find a job." And I told him yeah, I'd go up there. And I used to go up to Friendship House to start off with, the evenings, and I had four or five different classes up there. And out a that, well, the Reverend asked me if I would consider workin in the community under him. Explained the job and told what we had to offer the people and how many great wonders we could do for them and everything like that. So I told him why sure, I'll take the job. So I was an ex-con and I couldn't be hired under the federal government, see. So he had to go somehow through Deton Brooks* and a bunch of em down there. From what I gathered, is that the federal government donates so much money to the city of Chicago each year to do something more or less to attract the public's eye and show them what's happening in this and that. So this fund had accumulated over the years, and so the Reverend finally got with them at the Urban Center and Brooks and the rest of em and they agreed to pay my salary out of that, see, to let me work out of Friendship House.

So I started working out of there, more or less planning events for the community on the advertisements and more or less publicity stunts, and touring the churches in the suburbs and givin speeches to the old ladies and all of this shit. I started the Reverend's ex-convict program, I made all the personal contacts and introduced him later. See, after you're in the neighborhood for a while and you get a reputation of bein a square guy, one who doesn't snitch or talk, guys'll come to you and ask you, you know, "How much do you think this is worth?" or, "Do you think I should keep this kind of merchandise or get rid of it?" Just over the weeks and months, in bars and everything else, well, I just got to meet the guys and got along with em, and I'd go home with em, meet their families and everything like that. Then after I made a good solid contact with em, why then I'd come out and tell em the kind of work I was doing, and they'd be interested in going up to the center and meetin the Reverend and stuff like that. I finally convinced the guys he was pretty square and they could go up and talk to him and I was more or less his sort of handyman.

So after all of this came about, well, my contract was coming up to be renewed. So they asked the Reverend for a blow-by-blow description as to what time I used to sign in, what time I used to go home, how many contacts I made a week, a day, what I done with my time, and I mean it was just impossible to get, but they told him that this would have to be done. So at the end of the year, well, he sort of round-about complained and said he couldn't do it but he'd try to do it and I told him that I was gonna go

*Director of the Chicago Committee on Urban Opportunity.

'head and leave and find me another job. See, he wanted to keep me on and pay me out of his own pocket till he got it straightened out, see, which was puttin him in a pretty bad spot. And he done it for a couple weeks there till I caught him, and when I caught him I told him, "Well, that's it. No more money out a your pocket." And so he told me it wasn't comin out of his pocket and tried to get me to stay, and so I just told him I quit, rather than put him in a spot. And so he wanted me to apply for a smaller business loan down at the Urban Center. And I went down there, applied for the loan. I was going to have a small moving service in the Uptown area, instead of having to rent a U-Haul. And I had to get recommendations, I got em from the Uptown Chicago Commission and I got em from Glenmary Sisters, Friendship House, Hull House, Council of Southern Mountains, JOIN—I had them from all the preachers around the community and suburbs and people on the Outer Drive and just everybody. I mean I had enough recommendations, I'd probably could've run for Congressman if I'd've wanted to, you know. Which it really wasn't hurtin themselves.

The loan didn't come through, so I sat around as long as I could, and I had my wife and kids up here you know, and I just took my wife and kids back down to Tennessee where her parents live. And the guy I used to work for before I came up here gave me my old job back, and we stayed with her mother and father a couple days till we could find someplace to live. We was gonna try to find a furnished apartment—couldn't find one. So we went down and bought thirteen hundred dollars' worth of furniture and rented us a house and everything, and doing good. So one day my mother-in-law called me at work, said, "Buddy, you better come home." I figured something's pretty drastically wrong, because her being so countrified and everything she'd never call me. So I got off from work and went home and my wife and kids was gone, and I went over at my mother-in-law's and they wasn't there, and I asked, I said, "Where's Carol and the babies?"

She said, "Well, they're not here."

I said, "Well, where'd they go?"

She said, "Well, I'm not gonna tell ye." Said, "I'm gonna have to wait for my husband to tell ye." She knows when I get mad I get pretty violent.

And so that evening my father-in-law came over to the house. He told me, "Buddy," he said, "you been done wrong."

I said, "Well, I gathered that by now."

He said, "If I'd a known anything about it, knowed it was happenin," he said, "I'd a stopped it."

"But," I said, "what's wrong?"

He said, "Well," he said, "you know Carol was married before, didn't you?"

I said, "No, I didn't know she was married before. Nobody never told me nothing about it."

He said, "Well, her husband came over to the house today while you was at work and told her that if she didn't go back to him, which she's still married to him, that he was goin downtown, swear out a court order and take her baby." See, the second baby's mine, but she had one baby that belongs to him. The baby isn't really his but the adoption came about when they were married, see. But the thing that got me is that I didn't know that she'd been married before, see. And he said, "What you gonna do?"

I told him, "Well, I really don't know what to do." And I asked him, I said, "Is there any way I could get to em and talk to em? Will you tell me where they at?"

And he kinda figured I'd get messed up, so he said just to go on forget about it, let it ride a couple months and he'd try and straighten things out for me. That I could come back and we could see what we could do.

And I told him before I left, I said, "Well, they's one thing I can do." I said, "I want my baby regardless how things come out, and I don't want nothin to do with her. That's out." So I was just so mad and worked up and everything and I was settin around drinkin and I figured, well, I'll just go back to Chicago. I don't know whatever possessed me to do it: I just went out and went down to my neighbor's and borried me an ax, just went back in the house and chopped all the furniture up, just wrecked everything that was there. Packed my clothes, went out, got in my car and left, come back to Chicago.

WILSON AVE.

Imagine people with a strong belief
    Without a home or job and no relief
Think of a street seven blocks long
    And of countless people who just drink and roam.

And of children out in the cold
    With no one caring and no one told;
Of mothers who hustle men every day
    So their children's head at night may lay.

And of parents who aren't working hard
    Branding their children as criminals-at-large
Or those parents who are working nights
    Whose children give beer parties with delight.

Meeting up with people without education
    Dedicated talk but no dedication
Kids are walking Wilson, can't read or write
    But just interested in drinks and fights.

Building standing dirty, filthy and old
    With broken windows and stinking toilet bowls
High price rent, without gas and lights
    But eviction, if tenants buck and fight.

No place to go—haven't any family ties
    Just seven starving kids and their cries
Can't get them on the ADC
    Haven't been here a year, you see.

But Daddy does drink and takes pills
    Then everyone wonders, why he kills
It wasn't that he meant to, was just to be
    Why Dad's in jail, we can't see.

For the slogan stands on Wilson Street
    Every man fights to stay on his feet
So Daddy doesn't get it in the end
    Just his little Mommy and the other ten.

Didn't come to this town to stay long
    Just came for hoping to prolong
With starving kids and no possessions
    Here we stand—in another depression.

                —Buddy Tompkins

I guess about the first poetry I ever tried to write was when I was in about the fifth or sixth grade. I was settin in the classroom, you know, and it was a real bright sunny afternoon, I was just drowsin and sleepy and everything, and I had my notebook open and I was just sittin there and started writing about how I wish, you know, that I could be by the river, or how I wish I could be under the shade tree with my feet in the river, something like that. And she caught me, you know, and took my poem and everything else. And I never did think anything seriously about it. I wrote poetry all the time I was in the penitentiary and they wouldn't let me keep it when I left. Some people liked what I wrote but to me it's like the poem about Wilson Avenue. I guess it took me five minutes to write it. It seems childish. Oh, it has a good clear meaning and everything, but after you work with them people and you know the circumstances, you know the neighborhood, you know what can be accomplished and what it is and how the people act and why they act that way, and just set it down and write you a line and then pick you two words that rhyme and get you a meaning out of the thing, it's not hard. I never did find it hard.

I like to watch people, study their ways, thoughts, more or less try to out-guess them, read their mind, what they gonna say and how they gonna act and stuff like that. Now I understand these people. I've growed up with em, gone to Holy Roller church with em, I've spoken tongues with em, I've handled snakes with em. They're a very religious people and they will shut you out unless you are one of them. Now here's my own conception. I don't know, I may be wrong, but just like the Reverend—now the Reverend is makin a livin by usin the poor low-down white people, see. He's financin his office and everything he does. I've been with him and listened to his speeches and everything, and the people in the surrounding neighborhoods and such who doesn't know the people, they go to the church and they set down and they talk about sob stories: "Now these are the poor white Southerners that can't help themselves, they haven't any education"— but these poor white people they talkin about founded this damn United States almost. They made it up, kept alive, kept namesakes goin, built homes and places, and lived under circumstances that these people couldn't even *dream* about. But they want to keep this image of these poor hill-billies staggerin out of Virginia, Tennessee, West Virginia and Kentucky and Alabama and down in there, comin up the road in an old damn beat-up car with a chaw of tobacker in his mouth and no shoes on and a pair of bib overalls. And they want to keep this image and keep the poor white people down and talk about em like a damn dog instead a droppin the image and really gettin to the basic thing and lifting the pressure off of them so that they'll feel like human beings and start attending churches— which 95 percent of them are very religious people. And they want to know why they don't attend the churches, they want to know why they feel shitty when their children go to school and the kids come home and they explain the real live situation and the circumstances that they have to go to school under, and the mothers and fathers of these children understand, see. Just like a Nigro doesn't want to be shoved into an all-white classroom, he feels like an oddball, a shiteater or something. But they want to keep this image stuck down on the hillbilly's head, and everytime you see it in the paper, well, that's the image that you get, see. But they don't want to start workin on some kind of aid or emergency assistance to help these people and for to build a community instead of a damn working clique or a clock or something. These people are used to workin eight hours and goin home and talkin to their neighbors and eating and getting out and going to a show or something. They don't want to understand that these poor people that they're talkin about are so damn tickled to death just to be livin, eatin, and payin their rent, that they don't know what to do. They don't have enough education to really get a good job and they're no damn moneybags, but they understand how they're held down and really can't get out and work and strive and accomplish a lot of things that a person could on the same job with a higher education than he has. But it's always "that poor hillbilly." Do you know the money that's being sucked out of people that's drivin on sad sick stories of poor hillbillies?

And the Urban Progress Center doesn't and won't give a damn about nobody if they can get your name and address and names of your children and such as that. They're interested in the contracts and the annually report so they can say, "Well, I have processed maybe one thousand to fifteen hundred people through the Urban Progress Center this month." See, that looks good on paper. They don't give a damn what the community looks like or nothin else.

Why, hell, anybody can walk around Chicago, the Uptown area here, and go into a few beaten, battered and dirty filthy apartments, they're easy to find, and find a lot of kids sick, and a lot of people who need the rent paid or need a little groceries or some carfare or something like that. It seems to me as if they're just digging and digging and digging up enough shit from the neighborhood around here to keep it goin long enough to keep all of these people—I don't know whether they want to call themselves organizers, whether they're striving for a higher-paying job, or whether they want self-recognition, I really don't know what they want. But I do know one thing, they're not doin the Uptown area a damn bit of good, not a bit. I have been here when they started and I'm here now and I still see them and they haven't accomplished a damn thing except beg money out of the churches, and they're not helping nobody. Maybe every now and then someone'll get a little good out of it, you know. Maybe they'll get a basket of food, or maybe they will get a week's rent paid, maybe they'll get taken to the hospital or something like that, but if I get my damn leg broke and you taken me to the hospital and I don't have a nickel in my pocket, when a man puts a cast on my leg, kicks my ass out on the street, you still haven't helped me, so to speak. But they really think they have accomplished somethin, and they're not doin shit.

Now somewhere, somehow along the line, I really been sold on JOIN and this direct action. But out of all of this picketing and all of this singing and all of this swinging I never seen JOIN accomplish anything. I been singing and shouting and making a damn fool of myself with the rest of em, but they talk about money, we got no money; they talk about power, we got no power. Why hasn't nothing been done? I believe that JOIN has a little higher goal, but all self-recognition, every bit of it. To be downright honest, JOIN doesn't a bit more give a damn about the poor white people than I care about the poor Eskimos. They're using them to more or less accomplish goals for the SDS. If they accomplish getting a welfare check or getting someone on welfare or something like that, why don't they dig in a little deeper and find out now—"I look here at Buddy Tompkins' records and I see where he's had one, two, three, four jobs in Chicago since he's been here. Now I wonder why he quit that first one. I sent him out there." Why didn't he ask me whether I liked it or not? Why didn't he find out if I was sick or had a family problem? Why didn't he ask me what kind a work I wanted? They knowed I was desperate. Why shove me into something that they knew that eventually I would quit because I didn't like it? Why not dig down and get a problem instead a just riding on top of it and lettin the poor guy just set there and squirm under the pressure and the heat? I've watched em, you know, and I've listened to them. And I try to understand what they're talkin about and gather all I can and sort of work it up myself, and sometimes I'll go off and write it down and sorta outline the whole thing and I'll try to figure around it. I could be wrong, but if I'm wrong I apologize. I really don't know em that well.

I don't know what to think. I'm so damn confused. I guess that's why I stay with my face tore up all the time. They's so many things that I can't understand, I just don't have a clear understanding of them, to satisfy my own mind. Now religion really doesn't bug me because I know definitely I can't understand it. I can't accept the Bible as a whole, and the Bible says that if you can't accept it as a whole you can't split it. So I can't accept it all, so I guess I'm against it. I know approximately how many times the Bible has been rewrote, how many different translations.

I kinda like to think my God moves like electricity. I know he's there and if I really wanted to sincerely meditate and really think about it I can feel it, if I want to. Maybe it's an emotional God or something, subconscious God. Maybe God is a subconscious mind, maybe it's a feeling. I really don't know. But how in the hell can he accept the world as it is today, and the people as they are doin?

FAITH AND LOVE

I was told in my childhood
Wonders would never be understood
Like when the people spoke of God
Never questioned just agreed and nod.

Even the years of my teenage life
The words would cut like a knife
Everyone tries explaining his actions
And no one could bring them to fractions.

All these believe in some one else
But few could believe even them selves
Knowing of God and showing all mistakes
Never receiving nothing but heart aches.

How could we survive, or try it alone
When not one can understand his own
Still every one will tell you for FREE
That there's a GOD, just believe me.

—Buddy Tompkins

UNTITLED

A large place may be bare
And one picture with long hair
Down on his knee's in the dust
Casting eye's towards heaven as a must

Loose clothing and hands on a rock
As if his heart was on a for-got
Nothing but dark clouds all above
Still praying that people will still love

His words not forgotten but neat
Hoping people will hear and repeat
And by believing that people are good
Believing it or not—alone he stood.

—Buddy Tomkins (1965)

I think about everything. I can't understand myself. I really can't figure out what makes me tick. I can't understand my impulses, my reflexes, because actually a lot of things, and a lot of times, many many things I do are habit-forming, they're reflexes, and I know they're wrong but I have such a hateful temper that I just got to let em ride. Sometimes I go on a rampage every now and then. I just go and drink, and then eventually maybe I'll come up on something and I stop. Just like poetry. Now I can't write poetry unless I'm drunk, I can think so much faster and clearer and keep so many more thoughts in my head, and I really can't express myself to other people unless I really get worked up or mad or something like 'at, and I can't understand why I let my reflexes and emotions do me this way, see. I really don't know.

Now, I got a couple of good goals I've set for myself, you know, and I'm going to see if I can't go for em. I'm gonna go ahead and save my money, try to go to college and begin writin. I don't know how far I'm

gonna go but I'm gonna give it all I got, I mean I'm almost certain I know I can write. I've just never tried hard enough. I have an imagination, hell of a imagination. They's incidents—I could write a play on what I done to get in the penitentiary and the lousy sloppy experiences I've saw, incidents I saw happen, everything else.

I understand that pretty soon you gonna have to have a college education before you can get married, fore you hit that bed. And I feel that if I can stay out of trouble, I've done pretty good.

We want a whole lot of leavin alone.

—An Uptown resident on the
march against police
brutality

Peacemakers, Goodfellows, and the Police: Summer 1966

Buddy Tompkins at twenty-seven was older brother to a grouping of younger guys too loose to be called a network, but more definite than a statistical population. Their history is the history of JOIN's first whole-hearted engagement with the under-twenty-five energy of Uptown.

They began as the Peacemakers Club. Clayton, a brash eighteen-year-old member from the coal country of western Kentucky, described that phase:

I started bummin around on Leland Avenue. That's where the fun begun. That's where I learned the life of Chicago. That restaurant there on the corner of Leland and Sheridan, they used to call the Hut, Dixie Hut—it's gone now—that's where we used to hang out, a bunch a boys there, all from the South. Mostly you'd meet em through girls. You'd talk to a girl or somethin, she'd invite you over, you'd meet guys, mess around with em. Usually when you'd first meet a bunch you gotta fight about half of em. I guess about twenty-five of us went around together for about eight, ten months. Then we decided we was gonna organize, gonna name the bunch. We had fun, we had parties and stuff like 'at. Wore our jackets like we were a gang. We were tryin to fight everybody. We just had our one place, we didn't want nobody else comin in and messin it up. . . .

We had the whole area, from Montrose to Lawrence, anywheres in between there, between Clark and the Lake. Nobody, north, south, east or west, came in within it, startin trouble. . . . There's two things that you don't mess with in this neighborhood: that's a guy's woman or his car. Some don't care for anything else but them two. . . .

And that's where I learned about dope and fightin. Wish I'd left em alone. You know what a benny is? That's mostly what it was. And we used to really get hopped up on it. And lot of the guys took em to stay awake, cause we was up four or five, six days at a time without goin to bed, drinkin, runnin around. And I was workin, and then runnin around every night and stayin out all night and then goin to work the next mornin, I had to have somethin to keep me awake. . . .

We got in trouble with the cops, and they told us if we didn't bust up, we was all goin to jail. They were always comin around, searchin us, bustin up eight or ten guys. One mornin real early, about twelve, the cops come to the restaurant. There was two girls they wanted to see. Anyway, one of em said somethin, she said somethin back, he pushed her up against the wall and started chokin her. So this friend of mine, he didn't like it, so he told the cop to get his hands off of her. The cop wouldn't, so he smacked the cop, and they got him outside and about beat him to death. I still got the picture of it, it was in the paper. He got a year, in County, "resistin arrest." It's gonna be a lot wilder in about another week, when he gets outa jail. He's from Kentucky too, from up in the hills, the eastern part, Harlan County.

This friend, Charles Otis, had a fierce reputation and his return was awaited with a mixture of enthusiasm and fear. He would bring back good times, but the police would surely have it in for him: two of the arresting police had been heard threatening to kill him when he got out. In the meantime, most of the Peacemakers had gone straight, the name a memory, the jackets hung in closets. Gene, also eighteen and an ex-Peacemaker from Tennessee, said:

After we'd get through drinkin we might fuck a broad or either go out, get in a fight, shit like that, and we did like that for I guess six, seven months, just fuckin, fightin, screwin around. Then the cops got Charles Otis and guys stopped comin around a lot then. Cops had got us all afraid. Then some of em started gettin serious over the girls, girls they'd fucked with. And they'd take her and leave, or either get married, shit like that. They weren't actually tired, they just had other things to do. Maybe problems, you know, in their family and stuff. But some don't never come out of it, Charles Otis, for instance.

"I just quit runnin around," Clayton said for himself. "Started stayin home, workin, stayin home. George was my help."

George was the Reverend. He recruited not only Clayton and Tompkins, but Marvin Jackson and Gerald Akers, past president and vice-president of the Peacemakers, and put them to work as Tompkins described, running a pool hall and social club on Wilson Avenue. For the hard core of Tompkins, Jackson, and Akers, the Reverend was a mighty deliverer. Akers said he'd been popping pills, smoking marijuana, and contemplating suicide the day the Reverend had walked into the Dixie Hut. A few months later Akers and Tompkins had taken a public-speaking course, Akers was answering the phone with assurance, conducting the daily business of the club, and drawing a respectable salary from the Urban Progress Center.

Akers, from a coal-mining family of fourteen, was also studying the dictionary, hoping, by his own account, to be known all over Chicago as an up-and-coming hillbilly. Some of his former friends came to see him as "high-eaved," highfalutin, and he moved into that uncomfortable no man's land reserved for the poor who climb alone and too fast: somewhat detached from their old peers but for a long time, maybe forever, faintly subsidiary in their new-chosen circles. Such people, pinched by their upwardly mobile guilt, become vulnerable to radical appeals to their undisposable pasts and identities—especially when couched in new and erudite accents. So it is with the black bourgeoisie, so it was with Gerald Akers, but Gerald took his newfound radicalism seriously, took care to maintain his old roots at the same time. He was reached first by a young non-Southern neighborhood man, a veteran of civil rights work in Mississippi who had returned from college to his own roots; and then by a JOIN organizer. Still studying the dictionary, Akers decided in April, 1966, to travel to the Citizens' Crusade Against Poverty conference in Washington, where organizers and poor people had been invited to talk about the war on poverty. The liberal financiers got more than they bargained for. War-on-poverty employees booed Sargent Shriver off the platform. Akers was among them, and as the only white he became something of a special hero to the radical student organizers.

He came back to Chicago fired up, confirmed in his new loyalties. He agreed promptly to speak to a student rally against the draft, where he revised his already fervent text with remarks like this: "They say people who're against the war, who demonstrate and agitate, are Commonists. Well, who ever heard of a hillbilly Commonist?" "My first fight is here," he said, "and the fight I'm fighting is the war-on-poverty fight. We been dyin for the rich all our lives. Why should we defend them? The people we're fightin over there, they're poor and starvin too." After denouncing the student draft deferment and the Urban Progress Center, and reading Buddy Tompkins' "Wilson Avenue," he departed from his text once more: "What I've said today is what I feel. I ain't been brainwashed and I'm nobody's tool. I say what comes out of me, what I feel."

His old buddies had their doubts. When the soft-spoken uncitified Tennessean Marvin Jackson ribbed Akers one day, "You'd protest a piss-ant crawlin across the floor," after Akers defended some student antiwar sit-ins and Marvin thought they were "stupid," it was tempting for some organizers to assume that Marvin was the unenlightened one. But other organizers, with a finer feel for the neighborhood's texture, were spending more time with Marvin, Gene, and other ex-Peacemakers. At the same time, the Reverend closed Friendship House, deciding to work with elders but leaving the young guys no place of their own, and no more interesting hangout than JOIN. Then, in June, the Urban Progress Center fired Akers for "falsifying his time sheet," an administrative abbreviation for having hooted Sargent Shriver.

Though his supervisor, the Reverend, had in fact permitted Akers to go to Washington, and lobbied in his behalf, the ruling was final. The young guys got jumpier. Older loyalties revived in defense of Akers. Marvin said he was ready to sit in against the OEO director. No direct action beyond a picket was ever taken, Akers and the Reverend trying (without success) to arrange a quiet settlement, but Marvin and some others recoiled in further disgust from any middle-class intrusions into their neighborhood—war on poverty, ministers, radical ex-students, all of them.

As summer opened there were long, slow, sweet evenings on the beach, young guys and JOIN organizers—those relaxed and informal occasions in which lasting organizing linkages are always forged. Marvin, in a "sad lonesome mood," having just split up with his wife, would sing country-western songs about men in bars, men in prison, men on the road, and once in a while something gently chiding the organizers' college-folk tastes, like "Red is the color of my true love's eyes, in the morning." And this one he wrote:

IS IT ALL BECAUSE OF YOU?

> I walk the streets at night
>   With my head bowed low
> I don't remember
>   Who I see or where I go
> I walk alone and cry
>   Because I feel so blue
> And I wonder
>   Is it all because of you?

Chorus
Is it all because of you
   I'm feeling lonely
Is it all because of you
   I'm feeling blue
This old ache in my heart
   Is oh so painful
And I wonder
   Is it all because of you?

I go to movies
   And I think that I'll feel better
I set down alone
   The way I always do
Then she kisses him,
   I start to feeling lonely
And I wonder
   Is it all because of you?

I try to sleep at night
   But all I do is toss and turn
And recall the things
   You used to say and do
Then my eyes break down
   And cry until the morning comes
And I wonder
   Is it all because of you?

Marvin and some others came to JOIN meetings, listening, playing their minds over the JOIN rhetoric of community power, trying to puzzle it out. It sounded good, but then why did the ex-students dominate? Friendship with a few organizers left them no less estranged from the organization, with its highfalutin talk, its preoccupation with older people, its unfamiliar leadership. "Hell, man," Junior told a friend, "you don't wanna go to a students' party. We do the watusi and the frug, they do the sophisticated watusi and the sophisticated frug." They waited in the wings: until an occasion arose for their participation, they would continue to watch, to razz from the sidelines.

Then Uptown made the occasion the organizers couldn't. It began with a ratbite. The enraged father of the injured baby had seen the rent-strike picket of another building in the spring, remembered JOIN, met one of the Friendship House ex-cons, then chairman of the JOIN housing committee, and persuaded him to check out the building. It was appalling even by the standards of the neighborhood. In the words of the baby's mother: "Our bathroom ceiling is falling down, the insulation is peeling off the wiring. The windows—we've got our own private air-conditioning system because there's no putty in the windows. The linoleum's peeling off the floor, with dead bedbugs underneath. There isn't a faucet in our apartment that doesn't leak. No screens, paint's chipping, we asked for three days to get a toilet seat. He turned off our lights the day before our rent was due. The baby's milk is spoiling in the refrigerator and I don't know what we're going to do tonight, because the lights usually keep the rats away and if we don't have any light we're going to have fun. The landlord won't admit that there's any rats or roaches or bedbugs in the building. A hundred dollars a month, with our own furniture! He says, 'Well, I know welfare rent schedules and I can get a hundred dollars for this apartment.' He knows exactly what he can get, the highest he can charge in order to have welfare recipients in the building, so he takes advantage of it. He puts on a real smooth bit with the caseworker, you know, really soft-soaps em." The disgusted manager volunteered her apartment for a tenants' meeting to discuss a rent strike. Half the tenants were there. They divided, but as if to clinch the matter the landlord burst in and fired the manager on the spot, replacing her a few days later with an upwardly mobile hustler who had made opportunistic feints toward JOIN and counseled a waiting-game. The tenants remained split, just the situation in which the weight of an organizer may throw the balance toward collective action.

The next meeting of JOIN's housing committee was unusually well attended. The ex-con asked backing for a rent strike. There was a long debate: Were the tenants ready? Since the landlord had gotten some tenants to threaten violence, was the risk too great? Should the new manager be alienated from JOIN? Most skeptical were two of the dominant ex-students, who hoped the new manager, representative of a more stable type in the neighborhood, would prove a more durable ally than the tenants. But the vote went six to five for proceeding: three ex-students and three community people for, five ex-students against. The two skeptical ex-students promptly called the decision "stupid." Since their work would count heavily in the next week's organizing, their opposition amounted to a veto.

Word spread to the young guys that the ex-con had been humiliated. The merits of the issue were beside the point; they cared little about the building. They saw only that a "community person" had been affronted by two ex-students; the power of the ex-students, always obvious, became illegitimate; it was no longer a mere nuisance, but a threat to their integrity. They had to intervene, probably would have intervened on some other ground had the building not become an issue. At the prompting of a friend-organizer, Bob, they called an emergency meeting for the next night, July 8. Everyone sensed impending crisis, maybe doom.

Marvin came late; rumor had it he was so angry he had talked of bringing a gun. But Tompkins, Akers, and the rest easily made the meeting theirs. Akers blasted the ex-students with their own rhetorical weapons. Who could believe the ex-students were committed to the community, when they could always slink back into middle-class comfort? Then why should they hold power in a poor people's organization? And if the poor could not rule there, where else could they? Some ex-students tried to defend themselves, almost pleading, but the insurgents had already seized the moral initiative. But now what did they want? Whatever it was, they had JOIN's permission, even JOIN's blessing, but they couldn't work in the shadow of the old history. The rent strike was not their affair. It was the inspiration of one organizer, Bob, to pull them away for a few minutes, and when they returned they had determined to have their own form,

with their own issue, the issue that belonged distinctively to them: the police. Everyone felt vindicated; JOIN having attracted new energy and let it find its channels, the young guys having discovered their strength. Redemption and new beginnings, here as always, had required crisis.

The young guys met again the next night, alone, and decided their first task would be to find jobs for their friends. "You feel different walkin down the street if you have a job," said Gene. "You know the cops won't bother you." They prevailed upon Marvin to lead them, though his personal life was a shambles. Having come this far he could not turn back.

But Bob quickly convinced Marvin that many young guys with jobs still didn't feel protected. The way to reach them was to attack police brutality, frontally. They decided to collect affidavits on police brutality from their friends, for publicity and legal action; and to call a larger meeting. Needing a name to reserve a meeting room at the Urban Progress Center—for they would have to be clearly different from JOIN—they became the Uptown Goodfellows.

Bob suggested to Marvin a community patrol, patterned on one devised in Watts: Goodfellows would drive around the neighborhood, unarmed but for notebooks and cameras, to put the police on notice. The first night of Uptown's patrol, the police got the point: they would not submit to observation. Bob and Marvin spotted policemen beating a Mexican-American kid on Wilson Avenue; writing down badge numbers, Bob was rammed into the wall and arrested for disorderly conduct and assault. A few days later Marvin wrote this "Ballad to Michael":

> It was late one night, the cops were riding round
> Looking for someone to stomp into the ground
> When just as they passed
> A little boy threw a glass
> They stopped but they didn't hear a sound.
>
> They remembered Michael from some time ago.
> He was fast asleep and so he didn't know.
> Two policemen came inside
> And turned on all the lights.
> They grabbed him and then they said Let's go.
>
> As they opened the door that led into the street
> They shoved him and he fell to his feet.
> And when he turned around
> They knocked him to the ground.
> They hit him till his head began to bleed.
>
> By this time another policeman joined the fun.
> He tried to get up but he was nearly done.
> I could tell he was in pain
> But they kicked him just the same.
> Michael pleaded but they kept on with their fun.

Still they beat him with their clubs and fists and feet.
Michael was helpless as he lay there on the street.
Plenty people were on hand
But no one would give a hand
As poor Michael just lay there in the street.

I wonder what this world's becoming to.
You can't even trust the men in the blue.
I'm sure the man above
Didn't mean this to be love.
If he did then it's not right for me and you.

For Marvin, whose third song was to be a hymn, this was a considerable blasphemy.

The first big Goodfellows meeting drew more than twenty guys; the next, fifty. They were riotous and disorderly affairs, but the guys were beginning to come together again, a few signing up for patrols, some agreeing to collect affidavits. (By the end of the third meeting, more than fifty had been signed.) But the next step, whatever it was to be, needed the authority and energy of Charles Otis and his following. Charles had just been released from jail, but before Marvin could get very far with him he had been arrested again. He had been coming home from a party with a friend. The friend had gotten into a fight with a Puerto Rican. Later that night the police arrested Charles on a warrant sworn by the Puerto Rican, claiming he had stolen his wallet and sunglasses. Charles was charged with strong-arm robbery and locked up on $5,000 bond. Marvin investigated and found an eyewitness, a young Catholic priest who said Charles had done nothing. In fact the sunglasses had fallen on the street during the fight: the priest had them himself. He was prevailed upon to write a letter, cosigned by the Reverend and other respectables, asking the State's Attorney to drop charges, or at least to let Charles out on his own recognizance. A week later the appeal was refused. A JOIN organizer raised the bail money.

On the way to pick him up at the jail, Marvin told one of us* he was planning a white lie for the good of the Goodfellows. He had warned the organizers before not to broach the delicate question of race with Charles; Charles had once had his arm sliced by a black; "he's the meanest guy in Uptown" (half in admiration, half cautioning) "and he **hates** niggers";

*N. H.

there's a time for everything. But Marvin himself had been infected with the JOIN spirit, had learned "that Negroes are poor and we're poor, that the cops belt us around like they do to Negroes, especially that if we're ever gonna stop bein poor, it's gonna take Negroes and whites together to do it." Driving back from the jail, Marvin turned to Charles: "Charles, this might break your heart, but some colored guys gave us the money to get you out. They're fightin the police too, and they really had to scrape to get this money, because their guys are in trouble too."

Charles was very cool. "I don't care, man," he said. "Those niggers are in it too, man. You know I used to run with some niggers, didn't I, Marvin? Good guys, too."

Charles Otis brought with him the untamed wing of the old Peacemakers, those who had never felt comfortable at Friendship House. When the Dixie Hut was demolished they had removed to Eva's, a nearby restaurant, where they made innocuous headquarters. They still affected Charles's peculiar swagger, a grinding motion of the shoulders and hanging of the arms that made them seem to lumber forward rather than walk. One of them, Jerry Smith, from Alabama, joined the nightly patrol, where he learned that the organizer Bob had marched through Mississippi in June in the wake of James Meredith. "Shit," said Jerry, "if the word ever gets back to Alabama that I've been goin around with a freedom rider, I'm through!" When Bob suggested they go over to the JOIN office to sing, Jerry said he'd sing anything but "We Shall Overcome." The baiting was friendly, the ordinarily volatile race issue succumbing to the larger, more proximate fact of organizing momentum. Jerry would confront organizers, announce that in Alabama "we don't serve niggers in restaurants," insist on getting an argument in rebuttal, and then brag, "Well, you know, Eva's serves niggers too."

Charles and Marvin wanted action, wanted to weld the young guys into a force against police abuses, rather than leave them by their separate devices exposed to the massed power of the law. Although the organizer, Bob, argued against them, they pushed through a proposal to march on the police station, demanding civilian review, an end to brutality, and the dismissal of one particular plainclothesman, Sam Joseph. Joseph was Charles's nemesis—it was he Charles had found mistreating the girls at the Dixie Hut—and without doubt the most feared cop in Uptown. One Goodfellow told Marvin, "If you ain't scared of him you're either a fool or crazy." "Well, I ain't scared," said Marvin, "so I must be a fool or crazy," but his bravado was showing. Joseph was also Chicago's most decorated policeman; he seemed to court trouble as well as heroism, and he had important defenders. A year before he had made the mistake of beating a middle-class boy, who brought charges through the Police Department's Internal Investigation Division (IID). The case for brutality was so strong that the IID had recommended a thirty-day suspension, whereupon several aldermen had called for an investigation of the IID. "This is a foul day for Chicago," said one. "Officer Joseph has been a credit to the police department and a guardian of the peaceful elements of the community," said another. The Mayor asked Superintendent Wilson to take a "personal interest" in the case. Wilson did; he dismissed the charges. Joseph stayed in Uptown.

The march was set for August 11, ten days away. Buttons appeared:

PEOPLE

MUST

CONTROL

THEIR

POLICE

Leaflets:

ARE THEY PROTECTING YOU?

Goodfellows divided up the blocks and spread the word. The impending march moved to the center of the neighborhood grapevine.

And the police got the message too. Petty harassments became daily, and not so petty. A policeman asked Marvin one day, "How much education do you have?"

"Fifth grade."

"Then how are you going to control me?"

"See, you're doing what you always do, putting me down because of my education."

"You're never gonna control me."

A nearby camera kept his face jovial, but there was menace enough in his tone. Another time Sam Joseph told Bob, "We're gonna march all over your heads." Leafleteers were stopped, threatened with littering charges and dark appointments in an alley.

A few days before the march, one of the old JOIN corner guys unexpectedly said he would come along. Although at most times he saw himself as a member of a small, distinct grouping—this corner, that block—the march was an event that promised to overcome the most provincial impulses. I* found him on the corner on the eve of the march. No, he

*T. G.

couldn't go. (Not "don't want to," but "can't.") Some months before, he had been arrested for disorderly conduct (for standing on the corner); the arresting plainclothesman had withheld the warrant on him on the promise of $10 a week for ten weeks. The bribe was almost fully paid off, but the warrant was still outstanding. And moments before I arrived, the plainclothesman had appeared to say that if he was seen on the line of march, the warrant would be issued. The young guy, of course, had paid in cash; he would have no proof, either of blackmail or of betrayal. He didn't march.*

The police's main weapon was intimidating force; a close second was the support of Uptown's older, more settled people, who wanted a buffer between themselves and the unruly young. But in the heat of their rage, the police confused their weapons, and the Sunday before the march they treated the respectable citizens of a busy block to a full-dress verification of the worst horror story the Goodfellows could have told.

One witness to that Sunday's beating was Amelia Jenkins, a sharp-witted I've-seen-everything building manager. Chicago-born but married to a Southerner, she was a community leader in the strict sense—someone whose choices carry weight for definite others. She had befriended a JOIN organizer—he said from curiosity, she said from pity—but remained anchored to her private life, to the wry hope of getting by. In fact, on the subject of the August 11 march she would shed her usual playfulness for a diatribe against Charles Otis and his friends, whom she blamed for disturbing the peace of Leland Avenue: why did the otherwise quaint and even admirable JOIN have to sully itself with such hoodlums? "We have read your letters on police brutality," she and six others wrote to the News-letter. "Most of us all said to ourselves, O.K. now, JOIN must be stretching it just a little. But after witnessing this incident last night, it has made a believer out of us." Let her speak at length for what she reveals of the teller—the flow of her respectability as it crashed against the police reality—as well as the tale:

Well, this man was givin em a struggle at first. I'll give him credit for that. He wasn't gonna go. . . . Everybody standin around said they had already started beatin im in the apartment, fore they took im out a the apartment. Now I didn't see that, I wouldn't say that they done it. But I

*Three weeks later, he was picked up on the corner, thrown in a paddy wagon, taken into the alley, and beaten with billy clubs, and his wallet was stolen. After running the maze of police depositories he subsequently retrieved the wallet. The cash was gone.

seen em when they got im down in the hall and he set down—whether they threw im down or not I don't know—but he was sittin up against the glass door and that's when another squad car come up then. And finally three more of em come up. And when they come out, they hit im, one, two, three, all three of em, boom, boom, boom, as soon as they got im outside in front. And that's what really started the rest of the crowd then. After that I never seen the man throw any more punches. I seen im one time when they pushed him, he kicked his leg, but now whether he was aimin at one a the police or not, I don't know. You can't hardly blame im for halfway tryin to defend himself, not gettin that kind a treatment. And he wasn't even treated like a white man. Treated more like a dog.

Now they said he was drunk, but he didn't act that drunk to me. Cause he was talkin too sensible to be drunk. And he was speaking with intelligence. He was saying, "Well now, I want you to get a good look at what's happening." He said, "Get an idea of how your police force acts." In fact the first thing I thought of was, maybe he was one of JOIN's members, you know, the way he was goin against the police brutality. But evidently he's a man that's probably just been pushed around so many times that he figured, Well, I'm gonna get whipped when I get down there so I may as well take it out here. . . .

When they come out, I turned away because I didn't wanna watch what was goin on. But I went across the street, they had throwed him down, they hit him with their billy clubs and they was jabbin im in the stomach. They got im down and had his face turned and pushed up against the curb. And then one cop took his knee and put it in the side of his head to hold him down. Three of em stood on his legs, just stood there. . . . He was already handcuffed when they come outa the building, but when they got him down, they handcuffed his feet together. And he kept screamin, you know, "This is injustice, I didn't do anything." Well, then they kept callin more and more and more cops. So finally they had eight squad cars there and eleven cops. And all those people they was screamin, "Turn him loose! What'd he do?" And there was this one cop stood right out in the middle of the street and he just dared em. Minute anybody screamed, he said, "Come on out here and you get a little bit of it! If you don't like what's goin on, you come out and get a little bit of it!" And showed em his fist or his billy club. So I happened to say, "Why don't they let the man up?" So the cop heard me, the one that was standin on his head, and he turned over and looked at me, said, "You don't like it, lady? Why don't you come over here and you help him up?" So I told him, I said, "I know who you are, you're the one that wouldn't come up after that Indian that was drunk up in our apartment." And he's the one that refused to get a drunken Indian out of my building. But he was brave when he had the other twelve behind him. They just kept it up. Every time he acted like he was just gonna move a little bit, to get a little air, they'd either kick him or poke him or hit him. Now when they'd ask what he'd done, they just kept sayin, "You all holler you want help, now this is our job, we're doin what we have to do." And the man he started beggin. He said, "If you let me up I'll get in, I won't give you no more trouble." They said they was gonna hold him until the paddy wagon come. And finally they got tired of standin on his leg and they just got down and kneeled on his leg. But he couldn't possibly move.

Now, just like I said, I'd read about it, and I know they do it when they get you to the station, but I never dreamt they'd do it out there, with that many witnesses watchin em. Cause that street was full. Oh my God, there were about a hundred people around, at least. Everybody was screamin. They were all yellin to the cops, "Turn im loose! Let im up! What'd he do?" And the rougher the people got, the smarter the cops got, and they kept takin it out on that man. They just kept kickin im. And the one cop said, "Get these kids away from here! Get these kids away from here!" That man yelled, he said, "No, let your children watch." He said, "Let em know what this is called justice, let them see what the police officers are supposed to serve and protect and do." And every time he'd open his mouth why they'd ram that knee right down in that head. Well, they had the side of his face bleedin from pushin it so hard. . . .

Now one man asked them, asked em all—he had a piece of paper and a pen. He said, "I want your badge numbers." Young fella in a checkered shirt.* Well, the one cop, he said, "You want badge numbers? Here, here's mine." Oh, he was proud to give im his un. But when he tried to get the sergeant's badge number, the sergeant said, "You're not gettin my badge number. If you want it you come down to the station and get it."

And there was one woman, now I don't know who she was, but she was really readin em a verse. Oooh! Now she called them every name in the book, and she told em just what she thought. And he told her to shut up and go away before he put her in the paddy wagon too. And I believe if she'd a kept on they would have put her in, cause she was really callin em down in front a all them other people out there. And he said, "You wanna join him?" And that man turned around, "Yes, they wanna join me, yes, they want to." He was tryin to encourage everybody, you know, to get a little mob goin there but nobody did. Lot of em said afterward they wished they had. . . .

*Bill Carter. He and Amanda, who had just happened along, verified this account.

Some a the cops didn't go over there, I'll say that. Some of em just got out a the squad cars and watched. They didn't join in on it. But those that was doin the beatin was pretty proud that they was doin it. And the kids all standin around—that's nothin for children to see. And my daughter walked over and I led her away, I wouldn't let her look at it, because let's face it, we do try to teach the kids that the law is here to help us. And then they'll get a good view of that, and they'll say, "Well, why should I try to do the right thing if I'm gonna get this if I—" Oh no. Uh-uh. I didn't want her to see it, I just got her and made her go on away. . . .

Well, when the paddy wagon got there, they picked him up by his feet and by his hands and they threw him in the paddy wagon. Well, when they did, his legs was hangin out. And they just took the door and they just slammed it on him, full force. And it sprung back open again, they just took it, about three of em, and pushed it back again. Then the sergeant come back around and told that one guy that had been yellin, "Hero," said, "You too, buddy." Said, "Bigmouth, you come with us." So they took him then, put him in the paddy wagon. . . .

When it was all over there was thirteen cops there, cause I stood there and counted em.

People wanna do somethin, and yet they don't wanna do anything where they'll be publicized. They might sign a petition or somethin like that but there's too many people, just like when they work in a factory—they're willin to sit around and gripe about it in their apartment but they're not willin to go out and do anything about it. . . .

"Will you march with us?" we asked.

Yeah. I know there's gonna be one, two, three, four, five, six people in this building to go, and maybe seven, depending if the guy has to work nights. Cause I've done went and talked to everybody in the buildin, and most of em all said, "Well, not too crazy about goin, but if you and your old man go, we'll go right along with you."

Her husband added, "I've never seen anything like that, and I've been around this city a long time. A thing like that has to be stopped. Whether it's JOIN or O. W. Wilson, somebody's gotta stop it."*

*"In recent weeks there has been especially strict law enforcement in Uptown because of excesses in public drunkenness, damage to property, and threats to people in the area. Whether this strict enforcement of the law resulted in police brutality or not, I do not know. I personally have not been advised of any brutality by the police." Alderman O'Rourke, *Uptown News*, August 16, 1966.

August 11 the Carters marched, the Jenkinses didn't: political inclinations shrink before the mingled pressures of overtime work, children, fear. But there were 250 marchers over the 1½-mile distance, half of them young Southerners. Passing by the black blocks, Jerry Smith, tickled by his new tolerance, smiled and said, "Let's march through Niggertown." "Yeah, let's do that," said an Arkansas friend, "cause all we need is to get one. You know how they are bout followin a sign." Fears of police violence dissolved in that spirit. Through Uptown the marchers, now integrated, were watched in apprehensive silence, but at the police station a mile away—in an adjoining working-class area of two-family homes, where many police live—several hundred jeerers gathered to appreciate their protectors. With them were members of an Uptown gang whom the police had promised free run of the beach for drag-racing in return for their appearance. (The police later reneged, and the gang turned toward the Goodfellows.) Bob, Marvin, Charles, another Goodfellow, and the young Catholic priest met with the Commander, who glanced at the dozens of affidavits presented to him, modestly disclaimed the power to discipline his police, and taped the meeting "for Superintendent Wilson." "He says

he knows nothin about brutality," Charles said later. "He's gotta know, he's the boss here." The Commander in turn tried to discredit the march by waving a mug shot of Charles and displaying his arrest record. An officer told Charles as he was leaving the meeting, "We'll get you, Otis. We'll kill you." The press considered this hearsay.

News media were caught off guard by this unprecedented demonstration, the first in anyone's memory by whites against brutal police, and they moved to assimilate the new fact in their old stereotypes. Utterly apart from JOIN and Uptown, but in the same weeks, Martin Luther King had been leading open-housing marches into white enclaves in Chicago. On August 14, the liberal Sun-Times jammed the two facts together and libelously misquoted Marvin Jackson to produce a story that made sense to them, about a march "to the Summerdale station to protest police handling of 'counter-demonstrators' at open housing marches. . . . Jackson said that most of them had taken part in the abuse of the rights marchers." They need not have intended to slur, so fierce is the liberal prejudice against poor Southern whites, so bullheaded the need of the white moderate to occupy the moral center, manufacturing extremists careless of side. The reporters would not have understood the rage of Jerry Smith, who spurred us to arrange a meeting with the city editor. "There was niggers on our march! Mexcans and everything!" said Jerry, insisting no one he knew had attacked civil rights marchers. The editor apologized for the unexplained, "unfortunate" error. No retraction was published.

Retribution follows the just faster than justice. Marvin was abruptly fired by the suburban factory where he worked, with no explanation. Charles and his friends were stopped and frisked nightly, and Charles told Bob not to be surprised if some of the Goodfellows passed him without so much as a hello: "Police been tellin us if we're seen with you they'll bust us." Another Goodfellow backed him up: "Guys were told they would be busted and beaten if they had anything to do with JOIN." Even a wino said that when he had shown his JOIN card to the police as identification, they had taken him to the station and beaten him.

Pacification, in Uptown as in Vietnam, finally depends on the overwhelming might of the occupiers. The night of September 1, the JOIN office was raided by local police and state narcotics agents. About twenty laughing policemen tore down a wall, scattered files, broke chairs, smashed a mimeograph machine, opened a locked box containing membership cards and dues—"a reasonable search," they said. Two organizers who happened to be present were arrested for possession of marijuana and amphetamines and—if that was not enough—hypodermic needles. The police arrested the untouchable Reverend in a simultaneous raid on his office, and also took Marvin Jackson to the station, but released him there, perhaps to cast aspersions on his loyalty. (An organizer was later told by a newspaper reporter that his paper had received an anonymous tip that Marvin had informed on JOIN. If the police thought they could split the organization so clumsily, they were wrong.) "The light's shinin brighter on Wilson Avenue," said Marvin the next morning. "A lot more people are gonna come to JOIN because of this." Another Goodfellow thought JOIN would close up; when the office opened the next morning, he was impressed. But the raid cost JOIN a good deal of support, from people like Amelia Jenkins; the stakes of protest had climbed. The *American's* Page One headline read:

Nab Uptown Protesters in Dope Raid
Pro-Viet Cong Literature Found

And the screaming innuendo taking the entire first page of the neighborhood paper was not rectified by their report on September 13 that 25 North Side clergymen had issued this statement:

Clergymen protest police narcotics raids

That the manner in which the searches were carried out in no wise allays the suspicion that the entire action was taken to discredit individuals and groups whose presence and work in the Uptown area had brought them into conflict with existing conditions and interests which had reasons to oppose their continued unhampered operation.

Nor was it mitigated by JOIN marches downtown, organized in large part by an energized Buddy Tompkins. Over months of court proceedings, the police testimony turned out to be so self-contradictory, the charges so embarrassingly absurd, they were ultimately dismissed, but the damage had been done. And that wasn't all.

Two nights after the raid, Ronnie Williams, brother of Goodfellow Kenny, was shot and killed by Task Force police on Wilson Avenue. Accounts varied. All agreed that Ronnie had quarreled with Kenny and shot him through the shoulder, that he had started to run through the parking lot under the el tracks when police arrived. Police said they ordered him to halt; he turned and shot at them; they returned his fire and found him dead. The medical examination had revealed two wounds.

A half-dozen witnesses with whom we spoke said Ronnie had never fired at the cops, indeed had dropped his gun; panicked, he kept running; the police kept shooting, scooping up Ronnie's gun as they ran by; hit, he fell against a parked car; from closer range, they fired again, spinning him off the car and onto the ground, where an officer put a bullet in his head point-blank. Another witness rushed up, asked the officer what had happened. "Just another dead hillbilly," was the reply.

The undertaker told one of us* that he saw four bullet holes: two in the back, one in the head, one in the arm. Would he testify to that effect? No, the city would take away his license. The body was buried back home in Kentucky.

The six old men of the coroner's jury two weeks later returned a verdict of "justifiable homicide," though they never discredited the testimony of the witnesses, nor did they produce a civilian witness to corroborate the police story.

The mother of Ronnie and Kenny stopped by the JOIN office a few days later. "I told my husband I'd be gone for twenty minutes, but I've been walkin around for hours. I'm not satisfied at home, I'm not satisfied out here on the streets, I'm not satisfied nowhere." She said Ronnie's widow "got stopped by the cops yesterday, and they saw her JOIN button. You know I got her to JOIN. And they said, 'Why're you wearin that button?' And she said, 'To stop this goddamn police brutality!' They didn't like that! Boy, I was never so proud of her—I never did hear her cuss before. . . .

"I never thought the cops was good but I didn't used to feel the way I feel now. You wouldn't know how I feel 'less you lost one yourself. I just don't want to talk to em. Smitty, the colored cop, he used to walk on Wilson Avenue here, he's up on Argyle now. He'd always give everybody a break, and he was good to me. He'd say to me, 'You know the white Southerners and the Negroes is alone in the city, we got to stick together.' Smitty's good, he's real good, but now I see him on the street and I just can't talk to him."

*N. H.

Her neighbors and Ronnie's friends—he had many friends—were edgy but the young guys were unorganized. The march now seemed a failure: it had brought nothing but a dope raid and a murder. "Won't they learn," asked Kenny, "before somebody in their own families gets killed?" But the Goodfellows' leadership, always fragile, now lacked the cementing force of a timetable, the patrols ceased as young guys lost interest and crumbled. Bob went back to finish college.*

Marvin Jackson returned to his wife, who feared for him and insisted he work regularly and live in a better part of town. Not long afterward they separated again, but even after the Commander reportedly admitted that dozens of police (not including Sam Joseph) had been transferred as a result of the march, his resolve was shattered. Opposed to the war as he was, he joined the U.S. Army. He had been overorganized, coaxed too far too fast to catch his breath. But he was no "loss." Wounded in Vietnam, he began distributing an antiwar GI newspaper on his return to the States.

Buddy Tompkins, a good spokesman but never a Goodfellow organizer, realized he was a radical and decided his mission was to organize his countrymen back home in West Virginia. He left this poem behind him:

> We hear the stories of the wisest men
> But it's always the ones with money who wins
> We know Black and White aren't strong enough to fight
> And everyone judges these people with delight
> Even those who knows what it means to vote
> They also have the same hands around their throat
> And a fool fighting for his citizen rights
> So he can get them right this same night
> There still stands this great mass of men
> Who will have to fight to the end
> For our words of small, or of a group
> We are or should all become fighting troops
> For no one knows this story so true
> As the people who are fighting to see this through.

---

*Finish he did, and then he returned to the Midwest, working in the National Organizing Committee with poor and working-class young whites in Cincinnati and other cities.

The general bitterness had been framed by Charles in an interview with
The Movement, a San Francisco paper:

I been here eleven years. When I first came out here the police would stop you and say, "OK, kids, get off the street." They was always nice about it. And every year it was a little bit worse. First they started pickin you up for nothin. Then they started to whuppin you. Now they framin you. Like I said, it's gettin worse. Now they kill you if they get a chance, and ain't gonna say nothin about it.

I tell you, people are gonna get fed up with it. And they'll start pickin em off one by one. That's my opinion.

But Charles himself was lying low while his trial for strong-arm robbery was still pending. The witness-priest had cooled his affection for the young guys. (Another clergyman said the priest had yielded to pressure from the archdiocese.) One morning a drunken Charles rammed his car into another car, and, expecting doubled reprisals, he fled the city.

"Charles Otis was the leader," said one of the disenchanted Goodfellows. "Everyone would follow him. Now there's no leader. There are lots of groups and each is separate." They had never been involved fully in planning the march, discussing what would constitute success and what failure. The principle of joint action had been asserted, true, but too many had expected to end police brutality with a march, if they expected anything at all. Now they would suffer reprisals for action, and saw no counterbalancing prospects. Groups returned to their separate street corners. Beaten, some muttered of Molotov cocktails.

New leaders would have to work more slowly, less flamboyantly, talking to young guys one by one, hanging out with them in bars and pool halls, plucking guitars with them, folding them into a more democratic structure. Whether there was time or not, time had to be taken. This was Gene's assessment. Made radical in that way himself in the course of the summer, Gene now came on the JOIN (later National Community Union) staff full-time, where he has worked two years at this writing. Late in September he brought in an old friend, Bobby Joe Wright. Gene and Bobby Joe began the steady work of rebuilding the Goodfellows, this time from the bottom up.

I finally found somethin that someone don't
own or control.
What's that?
The rain.

—Bobby Joe Wright

Bobby Joe Wright, 18

Sideburns, a rough-edged street look, but a gentle tone of voice that just grazed the listener. A voice from the Chicago streets but for traces of a soft Southern accent: he had lived his first three years in a small town in northwest Georgia. His grandfather had owned "four or five gin mills," "he had more money than Carter's had Liver Pills," but he had favored other children and left Bobby's father to work in a sawmill. But life for Bobby began in Chicago, and the accent took over his voice only when he was tired, or putting it on.

When we met he was eighteen and roaming for ideas. During the first interviews, just after Gene brought him to JOIN, *he would break off to ask about Don Duncan, whose pamphlet on Vietnam was lying nearby, about LSD, about Bob Dylan.*

This is where I grew up, around Wilson Avenue. I used to get in trouble a lot over there. See, I'd go around breakin into things, robbin, stealin—just generally gettin in trouble. I was about twelve years old the time I started gettin in trouble. I wasn't robbin things for the money, see. I was just doin it to have sonething to do. Didn't have nowhere to go and play or anything, so we went out breakin into things, me and a couple friends a mine.

When I was about ten years old I was thinkin about goin to bed with girls. I'd heard things about it when I was younger—you know, you hear stories and that's about it. One day your friend says, "Come on, we'll go over here and we'll try to go to bed with this little girl, or that little girl," things like that. So it happened down in a basement. Too much, man. Really. We were all down in the basement playin. This little girl was down there. We were settin there playin, the next thing you know we're kissin on each other, the next thing you know you got your pants down and everything. You don't really know what you're doin, but it felt good and you want to do it again. We went off in a corner, listened for people. After that it was always somebody different, some other little girl around the neighborhood. Then when I started growin up, I started to be with girls older and older. Like from fifteen up till now I never went out or made it with a girl under twenty-one. Man, like when I was fifteen I was goin to bed with women.

When I was twelve years old I used to carry a pistol and used to have all kinds a money on me. Found an easy way to make money. I was very young, didn't even have any peach fuzz on my face, but I was almost six foot tall, jet-black hair, and the beginning of my trouble was with a friend a mine, Tex, down on Clark and Diversey. He told me that some man was lookin at me and if I would go to bed with this man he would give me some money. So I was kinda curious—I didn't want the man to do anything weird to me so I asked him, you know, "What's he gonna do?" And he said, "He won't do nothin to you, he'll eat you. You know," he said, "suck your dick." And it sounded good. So we got on the bus and we went down past Division Street up into this really shabby-lookin hotel. It's just this horrible scene, you walk into the room and there's a little cot threw up against the wall and no sheet on the bed. Like the dude told me to take my clothes off and I took my clothes off and he done this thing and it was fun, got a nut, and it was a way to make money, was what it was after that. I mean like the dude didn't even show me directions how to get outa the buildin. He took off right after that, because I was a minor, see, and you can really get your ass in trouble. He left me my money and he left me an extra quarter to get on the bus where I wouldn't have to break my five-dollar bill. And I stumbled out and got on the bus and came back. And I gave the money to Tex. Very very young. Not realizing the value of money at all. I said "Here, Tex," and I gave im the five dollars, and I said, "Let's go over to the restaurant, I wanna have a sundae." I order this big fuckin dollar sundae, Hollywood Special, and like I never bothered to ask him for no change or anything. And I did this for quite a while. He would set me up with people and like I'd give him the money. He never asked me for the money, I just gave it to im. And after this went on for a while it finally come to me that I was givin him my money and I didn't have any, and so I just started keepin it to myself, which was O.K. because he didn't mind. I just started hustlin all by myself. He's one a the guys responsible for teachin me how to shoot pool. He would take me down and beat me outa my money, after I started keepin my own. He wasn't no big shark or anything but he knew how to play and I didn't. And that's how I got to know the pool game.

One time I was offered money to go up and make a movie. This guy was a sailor and he said, "I know this guy who's got a camera, would you like to come up and make a movie with me?" And they named it "Tom Sawyer" or somethin. And he took me up to this house and first scene was a big bubbly bath and I took off my clothes and I got in the bathtub and I stood up and washed and he took pictures of my prick and stuff. Then I get outa the bathtub and I come into the livin room and there's a white sheet stretched out on the floor and all these spotlights and there's this movie camera. It's freakin me out, man! All the cat wants me to do is just lay there. And so I lay down and I can't get bothered, I can't get a hard-on, because all these fuckin lights! And like the cat got down and he did his thing, he sucked my dick, my dick got hard—a lotta queers' whole thing is just the size of a man's prick. If you got a big prick, you got it made. And I'm not braggin but I'm doin pretty good, and they dug it. I think I received ten dollars for the whole movie. But no more films for me. . . .

My mother asked me one night, like what did I do at night and where did I get all this money that I brought in, because I would always give her money or buy her stuff. So I told her I was out goin to bed with queers and she asked me did they do anythin to hurt me, and I said no, that they just sucked my dick and that was it. I mean how else do you explain to your mother that you go to bed with a man without just comin out and sayin it? She just kinda grinned, O.K., and walked away. She was always open to me and the night life of hustling, bringin home chicks or bringin home men. I didn't make it a habit to bring home men but I made it a habit to bring home chicks, and she never say anything about it. She always let me do what I want. I would introduce her to whoever I might bring into my house—Daddy would always tell me to go out and get a job. "You shouldn't be out at night, you should go out and get a job and become somethin in the world." But me and mother always talked about stuff and she was never closed to anything I had to say.

See, I got fed up with school. It seemed like in school that you couldn't talk. I mean even outside at recess time you couldn't talk. I mean they were the leaders and we were the followers, see, and anything they wanted, they got it, see. I had to hit a couple of teachers cause they pulled my little brother's hair. See, my little brother'd be talking or somethin and the teachers, they wouldn't say, "Please be quiet." "Shut up!" you know, things like that. And my brother hollered at one of em and he grabbed him by the hair and drug him out the door. About that time I was comin down the hallway and I saw him. So I hit him with a chair. I got suspended. I was about ten then.

So we was runnin around one night, me and a few fellas I know, and we didn't have nothin to do so we decided to go inside the school. See, after school was closed. So we got in there and we started thinkin about how sarcastic some of the teachers are, so we tore up Stewart School.

And then we went over to Goudy and did the same thing. See, they was both closed for about two weeks. Tore up all the records and busted up everything. And that's when the case began, that's when the law was after me.

They saw us comin out of the school. We was carryin hi-fis and movie projectors, we left our fingerprints all over the place. We had ink all over us and glue from bustin bottles against the blackboard. We sold the record players and the projectors for three dollars apiece—see, we wasn't out for the money, we was just out to be doin somethin.

I was on the run for about a year and a half. I couldn't go home cause I knew if I went home my father would turn me in, so I stayed away from home for about a year and a half, travelin to various cities, hustlin pool. I went to Minneapolis, Detroit, little places like that. I went to the South for a while, down in Georgia. It's the same thing as that movie.* You walk into this strange place, you don't know nobody, and when you go to a strange place you don't carry your pool stick in there till you get to know the people. You go in there and you're lookin around, you act dense, see— you act like, well, I don't know nothin about pool. And some guy'll come up and say, "Well, come on, I'll play you." So you play a few friendly games of pool with him and you let him beat you. And the next thing you know he wants to raise—"Well, how about let's shoot one game for a dollar?" "Well, O.K., I'll shoot you a game for a dollar." And you let him beat you. You let him beat you about five times like that. And then maybe you win one or two. Then you start winnin three and four. And then he wants to raise the bet, see. It goes up a hundred, two hundred dollars a game.

And a different girl every night. Nothin serious, you know. One-night stands. You run into little things like people can't be satisfied by their husbands and boyfriends. I never thought any of that was true till I experienced it. That was good, man really, cause I marked it down as experience.

But I got sick of hustlin after a while, cause you make a lot a enemies that way. I was on my way to Florida and I decided I was gonna come back to Chicago. I was fed up with runnin. There's not another place in the world like Chicago. Well, there's probably better cities than Chicago but in Chicago you know everybody. See, you go to a strange town you don't know nobody, you gotta start makin friends and everythin.

*The Hustler.

So I came back, went home, lay down and went to sleep. I thought maybe my father'd let me slip by, but he didn't. He called the police when I was asleep and had me arrested. They would a never caught me. I'm not braggin or nothin but I was just too slick for em—they were one place, I was another. I had people tell me where they were at and everything. So they never could pin me down, you know, cage me. So my father, he didn't like what I was doin, so he sent me up. I guess it was better for me that they caught me then instead of lettin me keep on doin it. I'd probably turn out to be a murderer or somethin. I think I was fourteen then.

I went to the Audy Home* for four months; from there I went to IYC.† Turned out to be an all-right place, that place. In there they know you're not gonna be there for a long time, so in the daytime you don't go to school or nothin. You just sit and play games, watch television, do anything you want inside the building. You get to watch television till ten o'clock at night, then you go to your room and everybody's locked in separate rooms. And there you stay for two or three months, just doin that all day. When you first go in there they take a razor and shave your head, take your mug shot before they cut your hair. Then you go see the dentist. He gives you a tooth- brush and then you get enrolled in which dorm you go to. But it's pretty nice out there, they let you go to gym once a week and you get to box in gym, wrestle, play basketball, use the medicine balls and the weights and stuff. Everything they got out there is to build your muscles, it doesn't build your mind any. They don't have anthing out there to build your mind. And if you're in Dorm One, every time at mealtime, see, you get to walk over to the kitchen, which is about half a mile away, because they don't serve meals in Dorm One, cause they don't have a kitchen there, and it's a pretty nice walk. At least you get out. And out there if you're caught talkin they don't beat you or anything, they lock you up in your room. That's where I tore the beds up. They locked me in my room, wouldn't let me have my cigarette one day, so I tore the bed right up out of the ground. I threw it up again the door—them big thick doors made of steel, you can't break em. So I took my sheet and stuck it down the toilet and flooded the room. I had to stay in there with all that crappy stuff. Two days away was my court, and they look over your record and see how you been doin. I went up in front of em and I was sent away to St. Charles.‡

First time was hell. I didn't know nothin about the place. Had to do a lot of fightin. Like the big colored guys, they seemed like they wanted to rule

*Chicago detention center for juveniles awaiting trial.
†Illinois Youth Commission.
‡St. Charles School for Boys.

the grounds, see, because there was a lot more of them than white guys out there, and we'd have to fight em all the time. They get mad, see, and they pull a bunch a weird stuff. See, they ain't no females in there except for the schoolteachers. They's talkin about they wanna have sex with you and everything, and you got to protect yourself from em, see. I never seen a white guy do that, come up to another guy and say, "Well, I want you." You know, just think they're doin somethin big, but they're not.

The big guys was the guys that could hit harder than other people. The one who could kick the most ass was the leader. I never was on the bottom, I never was on the top either, but I got my way pretty good, you know. After you fight the guys once or twice they don't want to fight you no more cause they know you'll stick up for yourself. But those who won't fight will always stay on the bottom. Just like out here—you gotta fight for what you get, or you'll always be on the bottom.

And that school there, they don't teach you nothin. You set there and argue with the teachers or you fight the boys there. It was like goin to a gymnasium, see, you had to fight your way out. So come twelve o'clock we'd have to go home for lunch and we got a big gymnasium clear across the campus—from the school house to the gymnasium was a good two blocks, and they have guards patrollin the two blocks, and you're not supposed to talk. And you're supposed to stay in pairs. But a bunch of us'd get up and gang together and talk about cars and play nasty tricks on people. Some of the guards would let you go at it see, they'd let you talk, cause they know how it is, you know, and some of em won't, and the ones that won't, they'd catch you talkin and they'll take your head and they'll butt your heads together, practically crack your skull; or they hit you in the mouth or somethin. Miserable bunch a people. We'd go swimmin once a week, and down there at the swimmin pool, this guy he's got a little chain, see. And you know in any pool in the world, you're not supposed to run, cause you could slip and bust your head or somethin and kill yourself. And we'd go swimmin in the nude out there, and if he catches you runnin, he'll stand you up on the edge of that pool and he'll take that little chain he's got—and you're naked, see—and he'll just start hittin you with that chain. He gives you a chance but that damn thing—I seen kids they got scars on their back today from that thing. Just work em across the back.

And in the summertime we'd go out and play ball and things like that, see. And we was playin ball one day and the superintendent's dog got hit by a car and they sent the ambulance after that dog. And about that time this boy was tryin to steal home and went to slide and the guy who was up at bat took that bat and hit him across the leg with it and just broke his leg, see. But they sent the ambulance after that dog. And they just come and got him in a bus. Picked him up—didn't put him on a stretcher or nothin, just picked him up and threw him in that bus, you know, like that dog was better than he was. He had to stay in there six months for that busted leg.

Sunday we'd get to go to church, which was boring as hell. It was really a blast though, you know, when they give you the little wine and the bread. Everybody used to go up there, not to confess or not to get what-do-you-call-it, they didn't go up there for that reason, they went up to get the wine, you know. That was one of the first things I heard: "Hey, you get wine on Sunday if you go up and kneel down and let the preacher touch your head or somethin, you get some wine." Really, it's a fact.

We used to smoke aspirins out there, that was how we got high. You crunch em up real fine and put em in your cigarette, really fine. We used to sniff kerosene, that'll get you stoned out a your mind.

You get beat up in there by the guards and things get bad in there but the guys take it out on each other. A lot of the guys realize it too. They get in fights with each other, cause if they hit the guard they know they're gonna either go to solitary, which is hell, or go get more time put on you. They can't get to the guard so they take it out on each other, and they only go to work detail, which is cleanin up the barn, shovelin cow manure, and shovelin coal, things like that. Out there to punish the bad guys that get in fights and everythin we had a stack of coal here, about thirty-two foot high, and about fifteen foot away from it there'd be nothin. We'd take that stack of coal and move it over there. Next day we'd take that same stack of coal and move it back. And you talk about somethin that's hard to do is take a shovel-load full of coal and make you walk clear around that pile. So you got about a forty-foot walk and then you dump it. And then you do the same thing all day.

It's just like living on the outside, cept the big people, the guys that got more power than you, they let you know it a little bit more than they do out here, see.

They're just regular people that's gettin paid a salary to do somethin.

Their job is to keep us in line, no matter how they do it.

I finally got fed up with people tellin me what to do—and I spent a week in solitary. See, you only get four cigarettes a day. All right now. One mornin I was talkin, so the man was gonna take my cigarette. We'd call him the man cause he's the head of the house. And I said, "Well, I'm sick of you people takin my cigarettes and you tellin me what to do." He said, "Well, what can you do about it?"

I said, "Well, I could stand right here without movin."

He said, "Well, I'll send you down to see the man"—that's work detail. See, they send you out in the fields and make you work.

I said, "No you won't, cause I'm not movin from this place."

"So, well, I'll send you down to the box"—which is solitary.

I told him he wasn't gonna do that either cause I wasn't goin to move, and three or four of em come in there and drug me out and drug me down to the box and put me in there.

And it's miserable in there. It's smaller than a bathroom. Just big enough for a bed and you. In the wintertime they leave the heat off, see, and in the summertime they turn it on, and there's no way to get no air in that little room. You gotta stay in there with all that sweat in solitary.

Once a day you take a shower, at the end of the day. Right. You take off all your clothes, which is just a pair of pants, that's all you got on, you take off your pants and you walk out of your room, you walk about three steps and they got the shower, see. You jump in your shower, you take your shower and they hand you a towel, and then you're standin there dryin off and they take a big bucket of cold water and they throw it on you. So your towel's soakin wet, see, and you ain't got no way to dry off. So the idea of this throwin a bucket of water on you, you got to get down on your knees and scrub the floor with your towel, then you gotta drip dry. And in the wintertime kids'd come down with pneumonia and everythin else in there. They give you your regular three meals a day, if you wanna call it that. There's no salt in the food and no sugar in the food and what I really think it is is leftovers but they say it comes straight from the kitchen. I don't know. And no milk, nothin. You get a old wooden spoon to eat it with. No cigarettes. And it's dark, no lights. You just set in there and think and go crazy.

I was in St. Charles for nineteen months. When I got out my mother said, "Well, now you're gonna be a *good* boy, see, you're growed up, you learned some manners in there." But really it made me worse. I come out and I had the reputation of bein in jail, and that's all people would look at you for. "You been in jail, ain't you?" And I'd say yeah. I wasn't ashamed of it but then I got the reputation of being in jail. So they sent me to Montefiore, that's a school for bad boys. I mean you come home every night but the teachers are brutal and they're these big guys that look like football players, and if you smart off to them they're gonna crack you in the head with a stick. They got a kick outa beatin people down there. They did. It was a mixed school on the South Side and down there it seemed like the colored kids were gonna try and run over you, see, like they'd want your lunch or somethin. And you get in a fight down there and the teachers would jump in and they'd beat you half to death. And they don't teach you nothin down there. That's what really made me drop out of school, was that.

So I had a choice. I could work or I could just bum around. I decided to bum around. I figured, well, I'm young. Why not? It was my choice and I took it.

Me and my brother were drinkin one day, and I was in the back of the car and I was drunk. I had a quart of beer in my hand. And my brother was out breakin into cars, see. He wasn't tryin to steal anything, he was just busting his fist through cars, cause he was drunk. And the cop come up to him and he pulled him over towards the car where I was. There was about three cops, four cops, and my brother's rowdy when he gets drunk, and the cop pushed him up against the car. And about that time my brother turned around and he smacked the cop right in the eye. So the cop jumped my brother and I jumped the cop and then the cop jumped me and another cop jumped me and another cop jumped my brother and they beat the hell out of us from here to the station and then they beat us in the station, and they let me go, they couldn't get me for nothin. They just beat me cause I was tryin to protect my brother. Dirty cocksuckers. You know a whole police station'll stand there and watch a cop beat a guy, and they won't raise a hand to stop him.

So I ended up back in St. Charles. See, when you're on state parole, if you break curfew you go back. See, you're not allowed on the streets after a certain hour. They think you're a gangster now, after you've been out there once. So I was out two months. I got busted for curfew and went back for nine.

I remember the second time I was there the cottage was overcrowded. There was like about seventy guys, and they didn't have enough room for em to sleep in the dormitory, so I got to sleep out in the hallway, where there was no guard or nothin. I had a ball out there—by myself, you know. It was just the idea that everybody's in there and I'm out here. It's a lotta fun. I ran the linen room and I had it made down there. This time I was just tryin to be good to get out. Bein good in my own little way. I'd do stuff that I wouldn't get caught at. I stoled a pack of cigarettes one day and they never did catch who did it. Said, "All right, if the guy don't show up with the cigarettes, nobody smokes." So I was back there in the linen room smokin while everybody else didn't have any. Next day everybody got theirs and I still had nineteen or twenty left in the pack I had stole, so I kept em. And whenever he passed out cigarettes I got them and kept them and I'd have cigarettes when nobody else would have em. I was on the drum and bugle corps; I got to go out into the city with a bunch of other kids to play in marches and stuff, drum and bugle. So we'd get to smoke out there when the rest of the kids didn't, and we'd get all the pop we'd want and look at the women and shit like that.

Course you get lonely for women, and to be outside, have your freedom back. I'd think about gettin me a car when I get out. And I remember one time they let me go home for two weeks, but I had to be back and I hated like hell to go back there. Boy, did I hate that. Only reason I went back, I knew I'd be gettin out in two weeks.

I remember I got my plans, plans furlough—while you're in school they're meetin', once every two months, see, and they give you an ace or a deuce or plans or plans furlough. An ace is a month, a deuce is two months, and plans means that you're O.K. to go home, in about two or three weeks you'll be going home, soon as your plans go through. And I remember I got my plans, I think it was on a Friday and I was scheduled to go home Saturday. And the linen room boy that was helpin me, I didn't like him for some reason, and I was hungry that night, so I made him give me his meat loaf, see. I told him if he didn't give me his meat loaf I'd kick his ass when we got back down in the linen room. So he gave me his meat loaf and I ate it. And he went and told the damn old man, and the old man pulled me in the goddamn shoe room, said, "You take his meat loaf?" I admitted it. I know he had me caught as soon as he said it. Says, "All right then, I'm going to put you on work detail tomorrow," and that was the day I was scheduled to go home. If I'd a went on work detail I might have stayed there two or three more months. So I went up there and talked to the cottage mother and said, "Look, I been a nice guy since I been here and tomorrow I'm scheduled to go home but Mr. S. wants to put me on work detail." I knew her real well then and she was real nice. So come the next mornin, he called out the work detail and I was waitin for my name to pop up. It didn't pop up though. I was happy as hell.

It's about a mile from my cottage to the front gate and on my last trip out I looked at everything, said I remember it, I'll never be back. Then I started thinkin, well all these poor kids that's in here and never get out. Every now and then I look at a clock and I say, well if I was in there I'd be eatin dinner now or I'd be settin down, I wonder what the guys are doin. I mean it's not easy to get to know somebody six or eight months and then never see em again. We'd always talk about—well, I guess we'll run into each other on the outside. We used to give each other our addresses but we'd lose em or tear em up or somethin'.

I went up to see my parole officer, who made the arrangements for me to go to Nettlehorst School down on Broadway. And he told me that I was the first St. Charles guy that would be in the school and that I would really have to act good. So when I first went into the school, the kids they just looked at me for a while to figure out what I was, and I was the biggest one in the classroom. I weighed damn near a hundred and eighty pounds and I made the teacher look small. We all looked at each other in the classroom and then we went out to recess and then all the kids started comin up to me and askin me about St. Charles and stuff and how was it. I think I was braggin about it—it's a big thing to be from jail. I mean like it's sorta like power over people who hasn't, because they never experienced it, and they'll try to be your friend just to find out what it was like. Before I graduated I had complete control of the school. I went to school when I felt like it, I taught gym—a lotta the teachers didn't want me in the class-room so the gym teacher, who's a groovy friend a mine, would let me come up and teach class. Then when I graduated eighth grade all the teachers were tellin me how nice I'd look in a suit. . . .

They sent me to Lakeview High School, home of unwed mothers. I walked in and I was still the biggest kid, and I just felt I couldn't fit with em. They just seemed to be kids. So I walked in, walked around for two or three hours, then walked out. I never bothered to go back there. I was just too big. And besides I would get a lot more out of bein out on the street from two in the evening till eight the next morning, out hustling, than I would settin behind the desk and listenin to all this bullshit. They teach you small things, they teach you so much history, they won't go ahead and get a qualified history teacher for pupils. They'd give you a book that you're supposed a go through in six months, which is a history book, which tells what they wanna tell. You have four pages on maybe the Indians, three pages on the explorers, and 395 pages on America and how great America is and how they keep people in other countries alive. You know they never said anything really about anybody havin to starve or anything. They didn't do none a that. They never told me that people were pushed up from the South lookin for jobs, although I did know that, cause my mother was pushed up on that scene. They never told me about welfare systems. They never told me police do hit you. They Walk You Across The Street, was what I was told. That's crazy. Poor high school kid gets out of school and a cop beat him to death, he'd think he's a madman or somethin. "Hey—you're not supposed to do this, it wasn't in the textbook!" I'd change it all. I wouldn't let the teachers shout at the kids—I'd have 'em say things more politely to the kids—and I'd make smokin legal in my school, and at gym, instead of doin exercises I'd let em box, wrestle, somethin like that. Gettin up there doing exercises ain't teachin you nothin. What are you goin to do if you get in a fight out here, start doin calisthenics? Start showin a guy how to do a push-up when he hits you in the mouth? I'd have the teachin methods the same but I'd trust the students a little bit more. I wouldn't let the teachers go down in the lunch room and smoke, not unless the kids could.

The school system's fucked up. They say it's fer our benefit but I doubt it. They got the power over you, and I think if you give some people that authority, they take it in the wrong way, see, they're gonna run over people.

You know its nice to have a high school education, don't get me wrong, but I've learnt more since I dropped out of school than I have durin my whole school years. I think you learn more from experience than you can from a book. It's nice to have a high school education and everything. I go look for a job, I put down high school education, and I do these jobs that require high school education. Say I get me a job in a factory, I was supposed to workin on the assembly line or somethin. All right now, durin lunch break or when the assembly line slowed down, I'd go over to a machinist, see, and I'd ask him to teach me, and they would. That's how I got the experience. Only way people learn is if they want to. And they say only way people get ahead is if they want to. People say, "Give yourself a chance." You give yourself a chance, you go out, you try to do good, but people won't accept you unless you've been ninety years in college. But still I could take a boy that's been through college and he still can't run half the machines I can run. I'll still have to set him down and show him how to run them machines.

When I left school my brother Charlie was workin at Bankers and Merchants, where they make rubber stamps, and he said that he could get me on there, so I jumped at the chance to get a job, because you need money. And I went in, and I was workin on an Addressograph machine. I would take out these file plates that were filed alphabetically and put em in this machine and run off invoices. And I wore my white shirt and tie and walked around the factory and felt important at makin a dollar-twenty-five an hour.

It was really a drag workin in the office. We would come to work and we would bullshit about little dinky personal things and nothin that meant anything. Somethin to me that would've meant somethin was maybe gettin a union in that office. I mean that. I mean this isn't somethin that came about because I'm in the Movement. Like when I was workin at the factory, I took my own time and went into the factory, I found out that part a the factory had a union. The office part didn't. And I was wishin that somebody would bring up the fact that there's no union in that office.

Everybody was bitchin about the wages and about the boss, but they would never try to come up with anything to do about it, because they were all hung up in the—"If I don't get paid, what happens?" And after a year I got a dime raise, I was makin $1.35 an hour, and I guess one night I was feelin depressed and I went back to my old hustling corner and I really made a lotta money that night, so I didn't bother to go back to the factory.

I was down on the corner nightly, regularly, doin my hustlin. It was a full-time thing. I was livin with a friend named Bill. We shared an apartment and we'd go down to the corner and hustle up our money and we ate on it, and we paid our rent, bought our clothes with it. And then I got into an affair with a chick, very beautiful girl, and me bein young and everything I was fallin in love with every girl that gave me a wink. And we got to know each other pretty good, we started seein each other regularly. Like her parents were into a big thing cause her mother was goin out with other men while the father was working. And right then I shoulda realized that she would eventually do the same thing. Which she was doin. After I caught on to it we split up.

Things got really bad and I stopped eatin and I stopped hustlin, so my brother Charlie, who was livin out in Riverside* with his future wife-to-be, he said I could come out there and live with him. So I went out to Riverside and stayed a couple a weeks before I got a job at a cardboard manufacturing company. I mean it was really a bad company. Like my job was the clean-up job because I had less seniority. I would push around this big buggy and throw paper in it and stuff. The guy who ran the printin press, he was an O.K. guy but he had one bad habit: like he would report to the manager each night who didn't work, or was caught sittin down or somethin. Eventually I got fired, because me and him had a couple of little run-ins together. I heard that his policy was to tell on people and I approached him with it and asked him and he said, "Yeah, I don't like to see people settin around and not workin." I said, "Well, you don't have to tell the boss about it." And he got all upset and was gonna hit me with a hammer, steel hammer. Two other guys jumped in and I got fired. I took it to the steward cat because I was there exactly thirty days the day I got fired and I was gonna try and see if I could push it on into bein a union member and stayin. But that never happened. They wouldn't accept me. So I decided it's time for me to rest, so I gave up work. And so I bummed around Riverside, but to tell you the God's own truth them people are so snotty and stuck up out there, I couldn't live with em. Nobody talks to you. I mean

*A suburb of Chicago.

they think they're higher than you, they don't want to have nothin to do with you, see. Even my brother, cause when he was fourteen he went to this Positive Thinking school, cause he was in Kemper Insurance Company doin a little flunky old job and they paid him to go to school at this Positive Thinking thing. I'm not like that. I don't care how much money I got, I still want to be with people. When I bought my brand new car, I come around here and I drove my friends and my friend's mother anywhere they wanted to go. And I had six or seven hundred dollars in the bank, a brand new car. I didn't care: it still didn't make me better than the other person. I still hung around on corners at night and bummed cigarettes. I had all that money and a new car. Didn't bother me.

Anyway I came back to Chicago and Pat, the girl that I'd known a long time because she used to go out with my brothers, had just recently had a baby. We saw each other a couple times after she had the baby and I got used is what happened. Because the chick was a lot older than I was. And like we saw each other a couple a times and she didn't have sex for a year, you know, havin the baby and then havin to wait seven weeks afterwards, so she asked me to go to bed with her, because we knew each other for a long time, I guess, or somethin. So I went to bed with her and fell in love with her, a supposed love affair where we was gonna get married. And I would come over in the daytime and I could bum around her house and make out with her and take her to bed at night, and then she got into the scene where she liked nice things. And my father was gonna sign for me a new Chevy, air-conditioned, beautiful, and I would pay for it with his help. The first deal was half-and-half and then he couldn't hold up his share and I took it over. I was makin pretty good. Back then hustlin was good but hustlin ain't shit now, you can't make nothin, night life in Chicago now is dead compared to what it was five years ago. But this chick was tickled pink over the car. For a while I was supposed to marry her.

Then I'd call her up and she wouldn't see me. One a them scenes, you know. She would bullshit and never give me a straight answer. So I drove up to her house one night and I just waited. I turned off my car lights, I set in the car and I waited. And this Pontiac pulls up in front of me and there's this guy in it, and that's all I see, and he's settin out there in front a me for quite a long time and I said, Wow, that poor sucker must be in the same shape I am, he's waitin for somebody to come home. Next thing I know, up comes this head outa the seat and it's my chick, that I'm supposed to marry. And he walks her to the house, kisses her good night. So I crank up my car and go over to the gas station and I call her. And she says she doesn't wanna see me no more. Which was O.K. with me.

After I broke up with her I went back and started more time on the corner. I got to meet some chicks on the corner and I was fuckin them, and fuckin around and not really takin care a myself, drivin them all over town, and I cracked up my car on the expressway. And I really got gypped because the company that gave us the car, you know, when you buy a car and you ask em to put insurance on it they usually put financial responsibility, and like I found out later I didn't have any financial responsibility after this guy'd hit me and pushed me into another car. So I had to give it up because I wasn't workin.

And I was hangin around on the corner, and the whole crowd I run with was gay because I made my money off of em. And like I met Bob, who's an artist, and I went to bed with him once, and we just started becomin close friends after that and talkin about people, talkin about the television programs, books, just anything that we felt like talkin about.

He's the kind of guy that's wrapped up in music and art and that's his own little world. Like he pays attention to politics and things like that, but he doesn't feel that he could do anything about em, so he just paints and listens to his music. He loves Simon and Garfunkel. Even today, I still go over to him and we talk about the war, we talk about black people, how they're havin their problems, and he teases me about the "Communist organization" that he didn't believe in. But he kinda sees what they're doing because he sees black people being pushed around, he sees what people do that have more money or own the building. I mean like he janitors the building, and he sees all this and he's very smart, he's read a lot, and he knows a lot. He was talkin different stuff. He was talkin stuff I never heard, that I wanted to hear because it was something that I'd been thinking about. You know, I'd never discussed it with anybody. He was tellin me about things that the government of the United States had done. He talked to me about the bombin on Hiroshima and he said they didn't have to drop that bomb directly on that city, they could have dropped it out in the ocean and scared the hell out of em. Instead they dropped it right on the city, destroying a bunch of people, injurin em for life and killin em. He was tellin me how they didn't have to do that. I mean he said it in a way, he explained *why* they didn't have to do it. And I believed him—just the way he put it. He explained to me that the bombing of Pearl Harbor didn't have to take place, because it was supposed to have been some soldier or somethin that had told some people that Pearl Harbor was gonna be bombed and they didn't do nothing about it. So this stayed in the back of my head. I still had it in my mind, but I wasn't ready to talk to nobody about it. I wanted to listen more and find out more about the world, and through the years I've heard people mention how the government really fucks over the people—it says that the people are supposed to have the right to decide for themselves, which they don't have that right at all, there's always somebody to decide for them and that's how I got to run into JOIN and everything. I found out I was a radical about four weeks ago, as soon as I found out what the word meant! Then I discovered that I'd been a radical for about five months.

A lotta queers are radicals, really, and they know a lot. When two of em get together they lead a very interestin conversation, you can learn a lot from em. They're sociable, they're really nice people. Man, I ain't got nothin against em. People say they're sick. I don't think they're sick either. They're not sick, man. It's just their own little way of gettin their satisfaction. Like some people get their satisfaction out of makin records like the "Eve of Destruction." That's his own little way, and people think he's crazy for making a record like that. I wanna learn that song, the "Eve of Destruction." Too much, man.

Don't you think we're on the eve of destruction? Now see there's this one guy, let's take Daley for instance, man. Like he's a big guy, you know, he's up there, and like there's people always tryin to get up there, right? Everybody's fightin for the top. And I think that everybody fightin for this top, that when they get up there, like there's too many people that want the top, you understand what I mean? Now like there's only one guy that can be the greatest guy in the world or the richest. Now a bunch of people are tryin to get to this goal. When they all get up there, it's all gonna end, you know? I mean they'll be killin each other to get what they want. They will, man. They'll actually be killin each other to get what they want. I mean it's happenin now, like some particular person didn't like Kennedy, so he killed him. Why? Because Kennedy was doing something right.

He got shot the same reason Lincoln did, they were both tryin to help the colored people. Seems like all the good guys get shot, don't it? Lincoln was tryin to make it where all people were equal and he got shot. Kennedy was tryin to help the colored folks get what they wanted, or move anywhere they wanted or something like that. So somebody didn't like what he was doin, cause with him up there they couldn't get there. Like I figure somebody paid Oswald to knock him off. I'm sure of it, cause somebody else wanted his seat, man. Like every day they're killing somebody, man, to get higher.

And I really think we're on the eve of destruction, man, with all this shit about the wars and everything. People are gonna get fed up with wars and just to satisfy their own mind they'll start killing people.

See, "if the button's pushed, there's no running away. Take a look around you, boy, it's bound to scare you," and if you really look at this damn world today, it will, it'll scare the hell out of you! It drives people nuts and right away they want to either kill theirselves or somebody. Is there any explanation why Speck killed them nurses, man? He could have been all twisted up in his mind about the world today. It just drove him stark ravin mad, and the first person he got his hands on he killed.

They take these guys in the army and they tell em, "Well, you're fightin for the good, you know, you're fighting to help the U.S.A." When this guy gets out he finds out that all he did, he went over there and he killed a bunch a people to help the people over here to get more money and more power, that drives him, it eats him, man.

That's like them bombers that refused to drop that napalm, man. Somehow the word got to em that they were doin wrong, and it'd eat em, man, and you watch: after this shit with Vietnam is finished and the kids come out of this army, and they find out that they were over there killin innocent people for nothing, it's going to get to em, man, they're going to go stark ravin mad and they're going to end up killing a bunch of innocent people.

When the Vietnam war started, I didn't pay much attention to it. I was just livin my own little world, you know. I didn't think of nothin, man. I just thought of what was gonna happen to me.

I'd either bum around the house or go play pool, or walk, watch television, but really never think about anything. Now when I lay down at night maybe somethin would pop in my head what they said about the war. That's how I really got started on this kick. Things that people told me stayed in the back of my head, and when I did have a free minute or two it would come out. I think it's sort of like fate that does this to you, man. You know, you keep these things in the back of your head, and you don't know when you're really free, but somethin knows when you're really free, and it brings it out, it shoves it up front where you think about it, and you lay there two or three hours thinkin about it. It only happens every now and then, but it does happen.

Then I started hearin that our guys are winnin, our guys are winnin, and I started hearin more and more people complaining about the war in Vietnam, then I decided to look into it. And I started thinkin about it three or four months ago and readin about it. Then I decided that we don't have no damn business over there, which we don't. It's North and South fightin, right? Just like the Civil War. Now what in sam hill have we got to do over there? All these children and people over there gettin killed, our young boys are gettin killed. And you know who's the first one they grab to go over there? It's the hillbilly, the guy from the South.

Now what I think they should do is take every asshole that had any say-so about this war, stick *them* over there in a uniform, not as a general, not as a major or somethin—as a PFC, man, like they're the first ones to hit the beach; and let them hit the beach, and let them dive bullets. Then they'll really see what they started. All they see now is—well, here's a war and we can make money off of it.

And then when I started in JOIN I heard about these poor people here wanting better things that JOIN was gonna try to help em get it. I ran into my old friend Gene one day and he told me about the place, said it was to help the poor people. I figured, Well, I'm poor, I'll help myself. So Mike* asked me to go out with him one day to pass out these leaflets, so I did. I started talkin to people and lookin at people on Wilson Avenue—somethin causes em to be there—and I just spent all my time there.

I always knew I was a hillbilly, I was Southern, but before JOIN I used to avoid Wilson Avenue. There was a lotta drunk people there and I just couldn't face that street. I couldn't understand the fact that all the people driven up from the South did not get placed in a good job or they couldn't get a job and got on welfare. I just thought that they were all just lazy bums because that's what my fuckin father preached to me. His own brother is a wino and he calls im a fuckin hillbilly, fuckin bum. "He drinks and he won't get off his ass and go to work." That's all I heard. I was a proud hillbilly, I guess you'd call it.

My father used to be a drunkard himself, drunk all the time, but one day he got hit with a iron bar in back of the head, caused epileptic to set in, and him and mother stopped drinkin after that. So they come to their senses and· they figured, Well, the best way now to get started is to get on welfare. I remember when we were on welfare I didn't know where my next meal was comin from or nothin. And they were happy together. They were tryin to get somethin, get ahead. Pretty soon they got down to business, like they didn't miss work for four, five years straight, they would do without to put money in the bank where they could move into a better apartment. Daddy's a bartender and Mother works and they still go to work and put money in the bank, and now that they got ahead they're always arguin and shit like that, they're miserable. They got what they want now but they're still not satisfied, they want more.

I think it's normal that they do that, man. I think if the people in Up-town get what they want, if JOIN and the people of Uptown get together and get these people better housing and stuff, they won't be satisfied, they'll want more. See, when you get somethin, when you get to be middle-

*Mike James, a JOIN organizer.

class, and you get so much money, it changes you. You can't be bothered with the rest of the people. That's why the middle-class people, they can't be bothered with the poor people, cause they got what they want and in a way they get their money from the poor people and as long as poor people's gonna give em this money they're gonna keep em down there, keep em poor. And when say these poor people get up to middle-class they're gonna forget what it was like to be poor and they're gonna be makin their money off the poor people. When you get power it does somethin to you. Like if we get power over the police, if we get our way with em, it'll do somethin to us. We don't know what yet, but it'll do somethin. I'm hoping it's for the best. I'm hopin that when we do conquer somethin, like urban renewal or the better housin and stuff, if we get *our* way about it and JOIN runs into some money, I hope, I hope, I really hope that JOIN'll stay the same, the people will stay the same, still tryin to fight for the poor.

I dig talkin about not likin police. I never did go for police officers too much, but I never thought I would come to see somebody else actually approach me and say the same thing. But now that I tried to talk to a few people I'm really discouraged. Nothing's getting done. Nothing. I get the impression that the people don't care, they're happy, they got what they want right now. Look at me, man, I was happy before I found out about the government and the war in Vietnam. I was really happy just leadin my own little life. I wasn't rich or nothin, I didn't have a great deal a money, but I was happy in my own little way. Now that I heard about all this war in Vietnam and how the government's runnin over people and the people with money are runnin over the people, I'm twisted around, I'm not happy. The only time I'm happy now is when I'm on that pot. That's the only time I'm happy. Cause I got this carefree attitude like I did before I found out about all these things.

When you're high, you're yourself, but when you're not, you're playin a role, a big stage performance. Just like the world—take Chicago. It's one big stage, man. Everybody's got their own different roles that you gotta play. Like you play the man that gets up and goes to work for twenty years or thirty years of your life, same old dull routine each day, but when you're high, you're really yourself, cause you're settin there and you're thinkin, you don't care, you're there to have fun and there's nothin else in your mind. You think about what's goin on and you want to get out and do things about it.

When people aren't high they live their daily routine, their part in the play. And maybe their part is that they never get no fun out a life, they never have nothin really to laugh about. Then when they get up high, they never had anything to laugh about, so right away they start laughin. They don't know what in sam hill they're laughing for, but they're laughin, and they're really laughin and enjoyin it. They're themselves—they wanta laugh, but their script says that you're not supposed to laugh, you're supposed to go to work. Play the part, man. You got the name, play the game. You know, they put a name on you; that's what you go to do. And I used to have a name on me but I took that off, man: the name was work. You know, the regular first-class asshole that gets up in the mornin, goes to work, comes home, gets up, goes to work, does this for five or six days. Then he gets this little bit of money which he has to pay out to somebody else, then he does the same routine over and over again. Like people are really lost on the weekends, you know that? Like they don't know what they're gonna do, so what do they do? They sit around the house, diggin in their ass.

Have you ever noticed Chicago, man? Like nobody has time. Like what do these people do? They get up seven o'clock in the mornin, they get on the bus, ignorin everything, they listen to the news and read the papers —and ninety percent of the time they're just tellin a bunch of shit. All right, they go to work and sit in that office all day or they slave in a factory. They come home so exhausted and just set back and watch television, go to bed, and this is their routine till they die. And if you ask them, "Why don't we go out, look around, see what's happenin, you know" —"No, I ain't got time." Like yesterday I was downtown, and I needed a match for my cigarette. We was in this big department store. And here come this guy rushin by, and I asked him did he have a match and he said, "Yeah, I got a match," but he kept walkin and I had to walk with him to keep up with him to get the match. So I grabbed him, I said, "Hey, why don't you slow down?" He looked at me like I was some kind of nut. Like that man was movin too fast. He was constantly runnin, like he's a machine or somethin, man. You push a button, he's gotta do this for eight or ten hours. Then you turn him off. That's what it is out here these days.

In the schools it starts, man. It really does. It starts when you're five years old, when you first go into school. Before you reach the age of five you sleep, you play, you run around carefree. But once you get to the age of five you got this obligation to go to school, so it's the routine, there's your routine, it's startin now. You go to school, you come home, no time for playin now—you got homework to do, you got to go back to school tomorrow mornin so you gotta get in bed early. And when you get in upper grade school, it seems like they start tellin you, "Well, you gotta get a education to work." Now right away they start poundin in your head that you gotta be obligated to get this education where you could go out and do the daily routine of goin-to-work, comin-home, go-to-bed, go-to-work. They teach you how to run—how to run for a buck, how to run for the rich, how to run from the cops.

Now I've only got one obligation and that's to JOIN. I feel obligated now to get things to change. Like I have to get up in the mornin now and run out and organize, and I gotta have this on my mind constantly, what I've got to do the next day, or when am I supposed to see this person or that person. Now I'm doin this on my own free will, you know. There's nobody makin me do this. It makes it a lot different.

Everybody needs money in the bank, nice place to live, and a steady job. Yeah, I'm proud to say I'm workin when I *am* workin, but I'm not ashamed to say I'm not workin, cause I've worked. Right now I don't need no money, I don't have no bills, all I got's myself to look after. I'm not doin too bad at that. Now I got something to occupy my time, workin and hangin around with the fellers, talkin to em, gettin drunk or somethin. And what aggravates the hell out of the cops is cause they can't bust me on anything. There's nothing they could get me for, cause I haven't done anything. But one a these days they'll bust me for something. And they're gonna really lay it to me. They'll get me for something, even if it's a phony charge, like yesterday.

We stood on that corner about ten minutes, and this one guy he was over there throwin firecrackers. And the police officer was watchin him, but yet they busted us all, and they were gonna get us for loiterin, see, cause we didn't have no firecrackers on us. That's why Curtis started talkin about constitutional rights. Said, "You ain't gonna search me" when they took and threw him up against that car. If they wasn't too many people around then Curtis would a got his head beat in, cause that cop grabbed Curtis and pushed him, you could hear the thud when he went up against that car. They was about nineteen, twenty people watchin us, that's why he couldn't hit him. Now what goddamn law says you can't stand on the corner for fifteen minutes in this free world today? Free world—huh! They've always got somebody there to tell you what to do.

If you belong to JOIN and you tell a cop, you're going to get your head busted. Cause the cops don't want to see this place improved. If these places improved, half the cops either lose their job or be sent to another district. People won't be payin off the cops cause they'll know that they've got a decent home, they're workin, and when a cop don't get paid off he's mad as hell cause he's not makin no money.

People's gonna get sick and tired of it pretty soon. Then they're gonna

start doin somethin about it, and it ain't gonna be nice, either. I mean they're gonna be more and more cops end up gettin killed, and they're gonna be more and more people end up getting killed. In other words we're gonna have a little old war of our own. The cops against the citizens, that's all it's gonna be. Cause you can look at a cop now, he'll arrest you or he'll shake you down and, if he can't find nothin on you that man'll call you every name in the book. They called me every name in the book yesterday except a white man. They called me a nigger and a Puerto Rican, every damn thing, cause they didn't have nothing to get me. They had a look in their eye like, "Boy, I'll get you one of these days." And that's what it's gonna end up bein if they don't cool off a little bit, cause a lot of people are gettin sick of em pushin em around and everything.

I haven't figured out an alternative yet cause I don't think there is one. Daley or these people that own these factories, they don't have what they want, and them are the kind of people that want everything. And as long as they can, they're gonna keep the poor people down there. I feel like this: I look at Chicago as a big machine and the wheels are rollin all the time, and they're rollin faster and faster, you know what I mean? Now eventually on every machine the wheels get hot and bust. Now that's what's gonna happen here. Things are gonna get goin so fast its just gonna bust, and everything's just gonna quit—the people, they're gonna quit, they're just gonna stop, man, they're not gonna care. They'll have their own little world of their own to go to.

Without breaking rhythm he had begun humming The Sounds of Silence. *"I really like it, cause it tells the truth about the world today. Everything they say in that song is true." So we played the record and Bobby talked, song and comment blurring into some form more than the sum of the parts:*

THE SOUNDS OF SILENCE*

Hello darkness my old friend
I've come to talk with you again
Because a vision softly creeping
Left its seeds while I was sleeping
And the vision that was planted
 in my brain
Still remains
Within the sounds of silence.

That's what's gonna happen when the big wheels stop rollin: everythin's gonna be violent and darkness, and the seed's gonna be planted in their head that they're gettin out of it, that they stop what they're doin and they start thinkin about the future. That's what I think. Listen to it.

In restless dreams I walked alone
Down the streets of cobblestone
Neath the halo of a street lamp
I turned my collar to the cold
 and damp
When my eyes were stabbed by the
 flash of a neon light
That split the night
And touched the sounds of silence.

Now everybody gets out and walk by theirself, through the streets of cobblestone. When they get bugged about something, they'll turn away from it. They'll turn away from it. And the flash of the neon light, man, is like a big bar, drags everybody in to get a drink. You understand?

And in the naked light I saw
Ten thousand people maybe more
People talking without speaking
People hearing without listening

Now listen—nobody's listenin but they hear it, I don't see how. Like

People writing songs that voices
   never shared
No one dared
Disturb the sounds of silence.

"Fools!" said I, "you do not know
Silence like a cancer grows
Hear my words that I might teach you
Take my arms that I might reach you"
But my words like silent raindrops fell
And echoed
In the wells of silence.

And the people bowed and prayed
To the neon god they made
And sign flashed out its warning
In the words that it was forming
And the sign said the words of the
   prophets are written on the
   subway walls
And tenement halls
And whispered in the sounds of
   silence.

*"The Sounds of Silence," by Paul
Simon © 1964 Charing Cross Music.
Used with permission of the publisher.

Johnson'd be up there talkin: they
don't hear Johnson—they hear what
they're sayin to themselves, that's
what they hear. They don't hear
what he's sayin cause they don't care
no more. Great, man. Really.

They bow and they pray to the bar
which they're goin to—when they
get in trouble, when they don't know
where to go, where to turn, they go
to this bottle to drink, which is like
their God, you know. It's not the
way I want it to be; that's the way
it is now. Right now you have to
care what people think of you by
what you say, you understand?

Like if you say too much they're gonna think you're a Communist, man.
People like police officers, see, people that are mixed up in politics, you
gotta watch what you say in front of em or right away they're gonna think,
"Well, he's a Communist." Which is really not true, you're not a Communist, you just want things to change, you want to see things different.
You raise a kid in the world today and they're too ashamed or they're too
scared to tell anybody what they think, cause other people'll think, "Well,
they're a Communist," or, "They're a kook," so right away they go write
on the walls. That's what I think it means. They don't want to come out
and say, "Well, here's what I think." Instead they'll go down to that
subway wall and they'll write it, like "Screw you," "Down with so-and-so,"
"Up with so-and-so." That's the profits, man. That's what you get for
bringin up a kid. That's the profit of it all, right there, on them walls, man.
It's truth what they're sayin. Sure, you know, I wrote on em a lotta times.

Now, if I ever got high on pot or anything and listened to that record, I'd go completely out of my mind, man. I would. Cause it tells the truth, and when you hear the truth, you want to get out and do somethin about it, you want things to change. Any way you can get em changed, you want em changed. You don't care if you have to go out and beat somebody to death to get it changed, you want it changed.

Bobby became one of JOIN's *mainstays, on salary when* JOIN *had the money, working here and there when money ran out. With Gene, the Dovies, and others, he studied at a* JOIN *school taught by ex-students—set up at the request of the community people now needing to know, because they had become organizers, the structure of the city, taxes, politics, class, union history, the press, urban renewal, the war. Bobby and Gene revived the Goodfellows, opening a Ping-pong hall, organizing a band, slowly drawing in other young guys to form the kernel of a future movement. Each venture survived for a time and then succumbed to the young guys' trampling quest for novelty, but the two organizers secured an overriding life style, a way of letting a phase work its way out, then moving past it. With his new access to middle-class delights, Bobby developed a taste for literacy, wrote poems and articles for the* JOIN *newsletter, started a play, read his first books (*In Dubious Battle, One Flew Over the Cuckoo's Nest*). He told his draft board he was a conscientious objector. He, Gene, Tompkins, and a few others founded a National Communion Union (NCU) school to train radical students as organizers of the white poor. Later he was to work with the Young Patriots, an Uptown group allied with the Black Panther Party, with its own breakfast-for-children and other community programs.*

Eighteen months after the first interview, he measured the distance he'd come:

I useda not wanna go around niggers. I useda never go around black people, except when I was into my hustlin scene. I knew some colored boys and they became friends and stuff, but I guess you would call em exceptional.

I remember down on the West Side, we lived there even before black people moved to the West Side, and the neighborhood started to change. It was a lot of white, as I remember it, and then colored people started comin in. There was a lot of fights underneath the train viaduct, and I remember a man who'd been down at the lagoon fishing and he come back and somebody had whipped him with his fishing rod and he said a buncha the nigger boys done it. And a lotta times I would be chased home from school, because the school started turnin into a black one. We'd fight before I got to know em, and then most of my friends were black. But all the white families just started movin out and after so long our family had to move out. It was sorta like a run-out: we was gettin rocks through the window. But before we left, Daddy had an accident where he thinks and we all think that a colored man caught im in an alley and hit im in the head with an iron pipe. That's what caused the epileptic fits, like I mean he couldn't walk or talk or remember anything. He never did like colored people, but I don't recall before him ever sayin anything about niggers—except he told me stories about settin on his porch and shootin a nigger man in the arm, who used to work for Daddy on the farm back in Georgia. I don't know why, but he just never like em. I guess that's because back in the South, where he was brought up, that was the rough times on the colored folks: like they really got the shit kicked out of em for no reason, just for bein black. But after we moved from the West Side towards Wilson Avenue, Daddy hated em even more. He won't talk to one. He'll avoid em. I doubt if he'd let a Negro insurance man come in the house, that's how his hate is for em. I think he would pay im from the door.

When he was workin in a bar down on Madison two colored people came in and one of em pulled a gun, they were gonna rob the place, and Daddy pulled his gun and shot one and the other un ran and like he chased him two or three blocks, which is entirely illegal, because a man's robbin your store, you got a right to shoot im in the store, but you ain't got the right to shoot im outside the store. And Daddy chased im down and shot im. He really got in a lotta trouble over it. And I remember the night he came in and talked about it and he specified "nigger." "Two nigger men." He won't say Negro and he won't say colored, he'll call em niggers. I got up tight when Martin Luther King was killed and the West Side was havin a lot of action, a lotta riots, a lotta lootin and stuff because my father worked right down there. Like I was really afraid that if someone did come in that store and start somethin he would right away shoot somebody, and probably end up gettin killed himself, because he's very stubborn.

So for a long time I didn't dig colored people. I think that's an inheritance thing. When it really started changin was when I got into JOIN. I got into JOIN and there was Dovie, and Dovie was a big influence over me changin. Both the Dovies, and the colored boys down at the hot-dog stand.*

*Encountered when one of them was beaten, he said, by an off-duty policeman, and JOIN offered legal help.

They just seemed like they wanted to get along. I was open, I wanted to get along, I mean I didn't close em right off, but I don't think I made any attempts to talk to em, except when I started hangin around there. And somehow we just got to talk to each other. She was part of JOIN, which I was part of, and I had to talk to her. And I started findin out all these things about black people bein really fucked over for so many years, you know, and I also started findin out about my own people bein fucked over as much as they was, and like it changed my whole view about things.

Like when I started talkin to Dovie and them, I started goin and seein other black organizations, and like I really got tore apart there for a while from Dovie and all the guys on the corner cause I went down to WSO* and met these colored people who, me bein white, I felt white. They pushed it on me that I was white. And they would talk about killin all white men, and fuck the white man. And that really got me up tight. I got part a that racial thing back. Like I didn't talk to Dovie for a long time because of the WSO thing and I was really down on niggers because of a few fuckups. But black people have their own things to do, and they're gonna do it. They're together. Right now, my feelin toward the colored people is, they're O.K. I don't hate em. Matter of fact I've met quite a few colored people that I really dig, and we've got to work together.

I just see organizin as just talkin and becomin friends with people. In my past year and a half of runnin around, talkin to people about building organizations which would have control, people controlling politicians and factories and police and stuff, a lot of it was frightening. I mean meetin a lotta new people, talkin a lotta stuff that I knew a little about, a lot of times I would get caught on things. Things would back up on me, because I couldn't run it off like a book. Because it's not like a book. Because when you're talkin to people you can't talk to em too hard or they'll agree with you to get you away from em. "O.K., I agree, good-bye," and you'll never hear from em again.

It's nice to walk down the street, walk down Clifton up to Wilson, and there on the corner are five people standing that you know, and they know you from JOIN. And you can go up to talk to em, or you're in a hurry and you can just rattle off, "I'll see you later," and go on about your business and catch up with em later. It's nice when you don't have to stand there and talk with em for a half an hour, that you can go away and they'll be there when you get back. Or if they won't be there they'll say, Well I'll drop over later. See, like it used to be you'd walk from Clifton to Wilson

*The West Side Organization.

and somebody said, "Oh, there's one a those JOIN Communist people." It's not like that any more. People know JOIN's there. And if they have any problem they try to get in touch with JOIN. I'm known as JOIN in the neighborhood. It's nice to walk down the street and know that I'm known as JOIN and people are not callin you Communist.

I feel more dedicated than when I started cause things are startin to happen and I was partly responsible for buildin things that happened. I had somethin to do with organizing people to march on City Hall, I had things to do with that NCU school. It all causes things to happen, it causes people to get together. People know it's urban renewal tearin down the neighborhood and they know they're gonna be kicked out and that's a good feelin when they start organizin to do somethin about it. You get a great feelin when you see a group a people standin around demanding stuff that is rightfully theirs. I mean it's theirs and they never had it before and they want it now. It makes me feel good that after a year and a half the neighborhood has changed like that. And it seems to be throbbin with excitement of people wantin to do stuff, about the stuff we've been talkin about for a year and a half, and the things they've been listenin to and checkin up on. They wanna do it now, a lotta people around there.

So I can't drop out now, cause for one I don't want to. Things are in such a state where you have to fight em through and maybe eventually come up with an organization of people who control the community. It's gettin a lot tougher to be known as a political organizer. Police are a lot tougher—they know you now.

Now we gotta start findin out how to get like people elected on the urban renewal board, get community police—I mean we just gotta start gettin this stuff. I would like to some day see a square block elect a police officer to patrol that area. You don't need two or three police officers patrollin that one area, especially if the police officer who does that area is elected by the people of that area. I wouldn't want some guy livin in Oak Park come over and patrol that street at night. And once it's a person in the area that the people in the community get to know, I just don't think that much crime would be happenin, because nobody knows the police officers now. You just know em by Sir or whatever their little badge number says. I just feel that somethin like that is a goal that I wanna see, that people would have control. I developed that idea out of JOIN: we'd talk about what kind of police we wanted.

I would like to see, in the welfare department, community caseworkers. And people who set on boards, like the draft board center, is completely away—maybe the Uptown draft center should be in Uptown. The only thing you get to know about your draft board is when they say, "Come on, you gotta go fight." And aldermen should live in the ward, not the fancy part of the ward but in the heart of it. If it's a slum he should live in the slum, cause he's the one that's got power to do somethin about it. It would be nice if you could see im walkin down the street and you could say, "That's the alderman," you don't have to go shake his hand and smile at im. That's just the alderman. We elected him. He listens to us.

If we did get people in Uptown ready to move, there always has to be somebody on top. There always has to be a leader. And I'm just thinkin about how really fucked up the world is, and back when I started in JOIN I was thinkin: say we did get control. What was puttin me kinda up tight then was, How are these people gonna be when we build the organization, who supposably are the leaders? Are they gonna be using the people that they're supposably leading into justice? It seems that people has always lived off other people. JOIN talks about people control, which is O.K., but even if you have a board a people as a decision-making body, from elections in the community, this board a people are gonna be maybe paid so much more than anybody in a factory would be gettin. The only way that I could see of really gettin any kind of control would be to have it where politicians just made a dollar-twenty-five an hour, or the standard wage, or maybe a guaranteed annual income for everybody, and whoever wanted to be a politician would run and be elected by the people. That's when people starts gettin big heads, is when that extra twenty thousand a year comes in, and they start gettin proud.

Some day we might be able to get a little control. If demands get hard and people really get down to demandin stuff, they'll give it to em to keep em from demandin. They'll give to em to keep em off their back. But from the way things look right now, bein paranoid, after this summer I just don't know. There might not be nobody after this summer. Given the war, given the Korea crisis, given Red China and all these crises the United States is havin with other countries, plus all the goddamn crises the United States is having with its own goddamn country, the United States is just gettin cornered, the government of the United States is gettin into a bind. They're gonna have to do somethin, I don't know what. They could panic and destroy us all or they could just seddown and try to work with us, everybody try to work together instead of working over one another and steppin on somebody. And somehow the government and the people should get together, don't they be the government and we be the people. Let's be the people, let's all be the people.

I don't like to hear about community people versus "students." We shouldn't have to use that word, we're all community people. The people who're working in the Movement to create change, the people who don't dress in the white shirt and tie, who don't have nice pants, who have to wear corduroys and have to wear their shirts for four days and they don't get to eat regularly, they don't get paid. A lot of em who're tryin to get into the deep part of the Movement are a lot of kids who feel guilty for bein rich. They feel guilty and they wanna try to go out and they feel like missionaries who's goin out and help bring the Indians to reservations, they're gonna be our guidance, we're gonna follow em—a lot of em do receive checks from their parents and stuff like that. But a lotta kids who are really into the Movement don't. They live off what they can get. Like me, when I first met JOIN, I didn't go back down to the corner that much, I didn't go hustling, I dropped out a that to start gettin into this. Like I lost all my contacts for money, I lost all my contacts for stolen merchandise. I never used to be broke. I never used to have to wear the same pants three weeks, which I've had these damn pants on three weeks. If I'd've played my cards right I could've been a tool-and-die maker, which makes a hell of a lot of money, I could be married, have money in the bank, and a car, and not worry about all this fuckin shit that I have to put up with. I gave up all the things that I could have been to become what I am, which is a radical.

But now, knowin all the stuff that I do know, I don't think I could drop back into the society which I came from. I can't go into a factory and work eight hours a day for twenty years, not unless I know that I'm buildin for somethin in that factory, somethin that's not just gonna better me. I'm not lookin for better me, I'm lookin for better everybody. Like makin it these days means you're gonna make it even if you have to step on a hundred thousand people. Even if I did decide to get married, I'd work for an organization like JOIN, and I'd have to ask em to pay me where I could survive. If they couldn't pay me, me and my wife would have to just get along the best way we could. I mean that's what a girl would have to put up with to marry me.

Now bein in the Movement I've found out all this stuff about the government, about wars, about the past wars, about maybe the future wars, about the atomic age in which we live, how a baby's placed in the world before he's born. The school teaches him what they want to, and after you're twenty-one you're still bein brought up, you're bein brought up by society. You're a pawn in their game. You have to do it. If they want you to go to the army, you have to go or you're a Communist or somethin. See I can't see havin kids now, because I don't wanna bring my kids up in a society like this. It's a fuckin mixed-up society. Like you come into this world and you're placed, you're either gonna make it or you're gonna die an old man with nothin. I just wanna see a man sixty-five, retired, healthy, and not have to live in a two-fifty-a-day room. I don't wanna see dirty sloppy houses, I don't wanna see dirty sloppy streets, I don't wanna see police every way I turn. I don't wanna see that, that's not the way a society's supposed to be run. You know, it's a mean world, and like to me, when my father says I have to go out and make it, when he was preachin that to me, I didn't wanna do that, that's not what I wanted, because I've been in the factories and I've done the nine-to-five thing and I've seen that's not what I want. And what I'm doin now is, I'm makin it, I'm doin what I want to do, I'm makin what I want, and this is what I see as makin it. *I'm doing what I want to,* and they ain't nobody sayin that I have to do it. It's me, it's sort of a freedom thing. I've heard people say I would like to do this but I can't because of this. I'm doin this because I want to. And I'm makin it. I mean, this is my scene. I'm makin it. It's not easy at all but I can't see me stoppin the work I'm doin.

THE STORM

As they looked down from their mighty throne
Out onto the land that they ruled
All they saw were people
People fighting
People dying
And the people were crying
We are not going to stay down here any more.
As they scream the sky grew dark and the rain began to fall,
And the people began to push from the back, people from all
Places and they spread over the throne and over the land.
And then the sun came out behind the clouds and then you
Saw the water so calm and so clear and an inch higher.

—Bobby Joe Wright

Walking the Streets: Clifton

One way. At the southern end, two long courtyarded buildings have been rehabilitated by the Kate Maremont Foundation. Some blacks live here (federal money was involved) and some night gangs of eleven- and twelve-year-olds throw rocks at their windows, shouting "nigger." In the winter, coal—if it is delivered—covers the street. Three teen-agers walk down the sidewalk, kicking wine bottles. One says, "You two are always gettin ahead of me, I'm gonna have to whup you." Two stores sell used stoves and refrigerators. A car is stalled, passers-by help push it. At the corner of Sunnyside, a concrete courtyard strewn with rubbish, burned furniture left from a fire, children.

Fires are frequent up the block, and the city finally demolished one building. A block club organized by JOIN petitioned the Park Department, held rallies and an election (seven hundred voted Yes, with not one No) in the summer of 1967, demanding a playground in the vacant lot. A playground was promised. In the interim months, a truck hit a boy in the adjacent alley, two fires broke out in the next building. The lot filled with stripped-down cars, a couch, a sprung-out chair, a sign: "No Dumping." A bare-soil playground it became, by occupation. A new sign reads: "This property has been purchased by the City of Chicago as a playground. Richard J. Daley, Mayor."

Rent-strike picket line. A child asks her mother what is written on the picket sign she is carrying. "No Rent For Rats," the mother reads.

"What's a rat?"

"You know Freddy who lives in the wall? He's a rat."

You don't know who your enemy is now.

I want to move so far from this neighborhood it'll cost a dollar to send me a nickel postcard.

You're poor, you'll steal because you're hungry. But if you're rich you'll be always worryin about your business or what if there's a fire in the two buildins you own. If you're poor all you got to worry about is your family. And when the depression comes, if you're poor you won't have that much to lose. But if you're rich you end up jumpin off the tops of the buildings, like they did in the thirties.

Hell, if I had a small tractor and ten acres, I'd never want for somethin to eat. Just a small truck farm—garden a vegetables, tomatoes and cucumbers and sech, and a couple hogs for meat.

Mommy, I saved a nickel for you today.

**I can't get no
satisfaction
I can't get no
satisfaction**

I burnt my thumb when the stove exploded, two kitchen windows blowed out. Gas man said it wasn't safe but the landlord, he said it was O.K.

I've lived in this community for thirty years. I work for Jobs Unlimited and make a dollar-fifty an hour and then they take out six bits a day. Now is that a livin wage?

I've been on ADC three months, I've had three caseworkers. I never know who to ask for and when I get him he doesn't know anything.

Hey, have you ever smoked OPBs? Other people's butts? When you're hard up for a smoke, buddy, it's somethin funny.

I used to believe in God before I come to Chicago, but I seen there's no hope up here.

I'd love to have a little place to stay, to say grace over, to have in my possessions till I die. Well, that's the way they feel down there on South Side. This hyar big money men is got em a-squeezed. You know how come the colored man to kill all them car salesmans? Cause he's hard-pressed. You go to hard-pressin a man and he's gonna do somethin. And he paid for that car and double-paid for that car, and they kept on a-chargin him. I don't care if he's black, white, yaller or whatnot, I don't believe in bein a dog over a few dollars.

**Cause I try
and I try
and I try
and I try**

Told my caseworker I worked one day cleanin. Had to tell em, cause the people where I live at are so nosy, someone might have called em. So they held up my check till I can verify that I'm not workin steady. Worked one day, five dollars. That ain't much, is it?

Some of these houses in Uptown are so run down that they'd have to be fixed up before they could be condemned.

JOIN means people gettin together and righting a wrong, whatever that wrong may be.

I can't get no
I can't get no

I told the landlord, "You cain't scare me, cause I don't scare no more."

The reason that the colored people have gotten more than the poor white people is because they put up a bigger complaint about it. Maybe if the poor white people would put up the same thing that the colored people had to do, maybe we'd get someplace too. My family is very prejudiced against the colored. Even say anything about the colored and my father'll have a heart attack. I believe it was back in 1943, the big race riot, my uncle sat up on the railroad tracks at Fifty-third and Halsted, with a shotgun, killin people. Every time a black head'd pop up, he'd go *pow*. But they've got a common problem that's the same thing we do. And why should we fight separately over a common thing when we can get twice as much done when you fight together? It all boils down to a struggle between the poor and the rich.

The Sunnyside corner is the closest Uptown has to a plaza. Crowds gather in seconds. In July, 1967, as one of many fires blazed in the corner building, children were playing—as always—on the unattended fire truck. When the flames had been extinguished, one fireman discovered his hat missing. Within minutes, ten police cars and a paddy wagon drove up, and police, guns in hands, began searching the crowd and nearby buildings. Amazement, at the force deemed necessary to apprehend a ten-year-old prankster, boiled to anger. Meanwhile, firemen strapped a bicycle to the back of their truck, saying it belonged to the thief, they would keep it in retribution. A JOIN woman (N.H.) and a Goodfellow organizer told the firemen they had no right to the bicycle; one fireman called the JOIN woman a bitch. The Goodfellow stepped toward him, asked him to repeat himself. A nearby policeman grabbed "the punk," locked him inside the paddy wagon. The crowd surrounded the wagon, families and young guys both chanting, "Let him go! Let him go!" A hundred people "Let him go!" The police hesitated. "Let him go!" They ordered the return of the commandeered bike, and let him go.

Mrs. Dovie Coleman lives on Clifton, her apartment a continual meeting. Big Dovie, raised in Shaw, Mississippi, sent to St. Louis at nineteen by her mother when she threatned to beat up an imperious employer, part black, part Indian, ex-maid, ex-hairdresser, organizes welfare recipients in Uptown. Most are white. They include a Chicago woman who a few months earlier thought "the niggers are taking over the government," a Kentucky woman who had screamed at a Cook County Hospital doctor, "No nigger is gonna deliver my baby—don't you touch me!" She and her niece, Little Dovie, were the first black people in JOIN. Early in 1967, she reviewed two years of organizing:

"The problem is that we've been fightin each other, and never got to see the real cause. The real cause has been that the poor white thinks he's better than the nigger, while the big shot guy is sittin up there laughin at both of em. As long as we fight, we ain't got time to look at what he's doin. In JOIN we make a joke out of it, we neutralize it, call each other 'nigger,' 'hillbilly'— we're makin play out of it. We're takin all the poisons and all of the meanings out of the word, where it used to be very touchy. I can remember what JOIN was like when I first came to a meeting. Somebody whispered, 'What's that nigger doin here?' and everybody said, 'Hush up, you're not supposed to say that.' It was a touchy word. Nobody gets mad now. Me and Little Dovie made a big difference because we had immediate contact with the white people and we found out about each other and found out we had the same problems. It wouldn't have happened if we hadn't been around. They would have been more prejudiced than ever—it would have been an all-white organization, somethin else to brag about.

"It's a long drawn-out fight but it's worth every bit. You can't quit, you can't stop, you've got to go on. In the long run we're gonna accomplish the goal we set out to, which is to have major change. Like in welfare, get rid of caseworkers, or higher budgets, or have a guaranteed income. That would help us, but we would have to have guidelines to watch it, like the war on poverty. We could accept it on certain grounds and it would make a lot of difference.

"We haven't accomplished any real thing, but we've planted the seed. It's a beautiful thing: that seed is planted, it's not gonna die. And we've given a little hope in the lives of people that a little change is possible. It's like somebody caught a germ of cancer ten years ago: it's gonna kill him sooner or later.

"We're tryin to change the whole damn society, but we have to work on little things. Have you ever watched a sunflower in the early morning? It opens up gradually from a little bud. That' how JOIN is growin, slowly but surely."

Epilogue: Demands

We alert you to our anguish, an anguish we might have tried to conceal in trappings of anthropological or sociological or political analysis, but choose instead to lay before you. The price of this book guarantees that all but a few of you are no more than spectators to the way of life and politics in these pages: this is given, it explains our familiarity with you, since the price and the fact that you are reading a book at all already tell a great deal about you. Then, you should know that most of the individuals who consented to speak to you through these pages did so for one of two reasons: "I don't care who knows" or "It might do some good." Displaying their lives, they demand something in return.

Sympathy, understanding—good, but these are the luxuries of the middle classes; we need not waste many words telling you they are cheap forms of engagement, really of disengagement. If we have disrupted your stereotype of poor white trash, Li'l Abner, the iggerant Wallacite farm boy fixed immutably and exclusively in race hatred, surrogate for your own guilt—better. And if somehow, against all odds and headlines, you still believed that America works, or needs only a few fine tunings, that it rewards integrity and hard work, and that poverty is the fault of the poor, and if we have helped you see the political and economic structures of this country from the bottom and freshly—still better. Perhaps you see now that the viciousness of Chicago police during the Democratic Convention was no more than a televised summary of their daily practice. Perhaps you may also understand now that poverty is not a consequence of neglect but of exploitation, that men and women like the ones in this book have been worked out like coal mines in order that you may have the freedom to read about them: in order that private profit might be made, some of which is invested in universities to keep the profits coming and your hands clean.

And perhaps, like the radicals who organized JOIN, you will conclude that you ought to be alongside these people, because their struggle is yours and because they sway in the balance between the George Wallaces and the yet unnamed redeemers of their populist past. For you we would sound a reveille: you should take this chronicle as testimony to the hope beneath the despair of radical organizing. You must help restore a tradition, and this is long and arduous work, with JOIN no more—but no less, either—than an ambiguous model.

So long have poor whites been "only a pawn in their game," the politicians preaching, "You got more than the blacks, don't complain," the populist heritage deflected into bitter racism and anti-Communism, the energy of the young drained into migration and cars (where class feeling is worked out privately every day, passing a Cadillac on the expressway) and the flight toward a receding but recurring mirage of security—so long that the tradition of resistance and struggle must be rebuilt with the most excruciating patience. JOIN *as a neighborhood organization*—like many organizations of the New Left—has crumbled, winning victories too small or too easily claimed by the authorities: and tomorrow for many, especially the elders, does not look fearful enough to risk today. But as much as any radical project of the mid-1960's JOIN did train a band of leaders who will not be easily stopped, who work on the other side of hope and despair, because they've been, as they say, "turned around," because they have no choice, faced with a system organized to disgrace, suffocate, starve and even kill them. JOIN's Peggy Terry ran for Vice-President in several states on the Peace and Freedom ticket with Eldridge Cleaver in 1968; several of the former Goodfellows formed the National Organizing Committee, to seed new white working-class projects and expound the justice of the poor-white cause; others organized the Young Patriots, who, as part of the Poor People's Coalition, halted the plans for the junior college proposed for Uptown, and who are trying to bring free breakfasts and a health clinic to the neighborhood. A few of the ex-students and Goodfellows created *Rising Up Angry*, a newspaper bringing revolutionary ideas to young whites of the high schools and streets. The other ex-students moved on to other radical projects, partly because the Uptown natives wanted to stand by themselves, partly because it was time for other kinds of organizing work, as America began to fall apart at the seams. JOIN therefore stands as both failure and success, episode and premonition: radicals will learn from it or not, and thereby make the final judgment, for this is no time for vicarious history, appreciation, or scorn delivered from the armchair.

The people so incompletely present in this book are "beautiful," certainly, but only because they learned how to suffer their condition. Their condition is *caused*, by capitalism, a system that values property above life, the few above the many. This country has the wealth to make everyone beautiful not because he suffers but because he doesn't. The best tribute to these people, therefore, would be to take America back, place by place, institution by institution, from the corporations which fatten from misery, the warmakers who murder the patriots of the world, the media and schools which flatten all our minds and teach us to buy what we don't need, from the government which greases the wheels and the law which enshrines injustice and the police who exact by force what the rest cannot by authority. Too many people have waited too long in line with their grievances. They ought not to be asked why they can't wait, but only why they have waited so long. There is no peace, no order, no justice, no solution, short of a new American Revolution that keeps power and wealth at their source, with the people.

70 71 72 73 10 9 8 7 6 5 4 3 2 1